Psychological Treatment of Older Adults

An Introductory Text

The Plenum Series in Adult Development and Aging

SERIES EDITOR:
Jack Demick, *Suffolk University, Boston, Massachusetts*

ADULT DEVELOPMENT, THERAPY, AND CULTURE
A Postmodern Synthesis
Gerald D. Young

THE AMERICAN FATHER
Biocultural and Developmental Aspects
Wade C. Mackey

PSYCHOLOGICAL TREATMENT OF OLDER ADULTS
An Introductory Text
Edited by Michel Hersen and Vincent B. Van Hasselt

Psychological Treatment of Older Adults

An Introductory Text

Edited by

Michel Hersen

and

Vincent B. Van Hasselt

Nova Southeastern University
Fort Lauderdale, Florida

Plenum Press • New York and London

Library of Congress Cataloging-in-Publication Data

On file

ISBN 0-306-45234-0

© 1996 Plenum Press, New York
A Division of Plenum Publishing Corporation
233 Spring Street, New York, N. Y. 10013

10 9 8 7 6 5 4 3 2 1

Printed in the United States of America

Contributors

RON ACIERNO, Department of Psychiatry and Behavioral Sciences, Medical University of South Carolina, Charleston, South Carolina 29425-0742

STEPHEN J. BARTELS, Departments of Psychiatry and Community and Family Medicine, Dartmouth Medical School, Concord, New Hampshire 03301

GARY R. BIRCHLER, Psychology Service, Veterans Affairs Medical Center, and Department of Psychiatry, University of California, San Diego, California 92161

LOUIS D. BURGIO, Center for Aging, Division of Gerontology and Geriatric Medicine, and Department of Psychology, University of Alabama at Birmingham, Birmingham, Alabama 35294

ELLEN M. COTTER, Center for Aging, Division of Gerontology and Geriatric Medicine, and Department of Psychology, University of Alabama at Birmingham, Birmingham, Alabama 35294

LEAH P. DICK, Geriatric Research, Education, and Clinical Center, Veterans Affairs Medical Center, Palo Alto, California 94304, and Stanford University School of Medicine, Stanford, California 94305

BRAD DONOHUE, Center for Psychological Studies, Nova Southeastern University, Fort Lauderdale, Florida 33314

LARRY W. DUPREE, Department of Aging and Mental Health, Florida Mental Health Institute, University of South Florida, Tampa, Florida 33612

BARRY EDELSTEIN, Department of Psychology, West Virginia University, Morgantown, West Virginia 26506-6040

WILLIAM FALS-STEWART, Harvard Families and Addiction Program, Harvard Medical School, and Department of Psychiatry, Veterans Affairs Medical Center, Brockton, Massachusetts 02401

DOLORES GALLAGHER-THOMPSON, Geriatric Research, Education, and Clinical Center, Veterans Affairs Medical Center, Palo Alto, California 94304, and Stanford University School of Medicine, Stanford, California 94305

SHIRLEY M. GLYNN, West Los Angeles Veterans Affairs Medical Center and Department of Psychiatry, University of California at Los Angeles, Los Angeles, California 90073

BENJAMIN GRABER, Graber Psychiatric Associates, 12711 Davenport Plaza, Omaha, Nebraska 68154

C. V. HALDIPUR, Department of Psychiatry, State University of New York Health Science Center, Syracuse, New York 13210

MICHEL HERSEN, Center for Psychological Studies, Nova Southeastern University, Fort Lauderdale, Florida 33314

KIMBERLY D. KALISH, Department of Psychology, West Virginia University, Morgantown, West Virginia 26506-6040

LINDA A. LEBLANC, Department of Psychology, Louisiana State University, Baton Rouge, Louisiana 70803

JOHNNY L. MATSON, Department of Psychology, Louisiana State University, Baton Rouge, Louisiana 70803

WILEY MITTENBERG, Center for Psychological Studies, Nova Southeastern University, Fort Lauderdale, Florida 33314

KIM T. MUESER, Departments of Psychiatry and Community and Family Medicine, Dartmouth Medical School, Concord, New Hampshire 03301

BENOIT H. MULSANT, Division of Geriatrics and Neuropsychiatry, Western Psychiatric Institute and Clinic, Department of Psychiatry, University of Pittsburgh School of Medicine, Pittsburgh, Pennsylvania 15213

LYNN EMER NORTHROP, Department of Psychology, West Virginia University, Morgantown, West Virginia 26506-6040

WILLIAM T. O'DONOHUE, Department of Psychology, University of Nevada Reno, Reno, Nevada 89557

ROGER L. PATTERSON, Mental Hygiene Clinic, Veterans Affairs Outpatient Clinic, Daytona Beach, Florida 32117

WILLIAM HARRY PETTIBON, Center for Psychological Studies, Nova Southeastern University, Fort Lauderdale, Florida 33314

LAWRENCE SCHONFELD, Department of Aging and Mental Health, Florida Mental Health Institute, University of South Florida, Tampa, Florida 33612

NATALIE STAATS, Department of Psychology, West Virginia University, Morgantown, West Virginia 26506-6040

ALAN B. STEVENS, Center for Aging, Division of Gerontology and Geriatric Medicine, and Department of Psychology, University of Alabama at Birmingham, Birmingham, Alabama 35294

LINDA TERI, Department of Psychiatry and Behavioral Sciences, University of Washington School of Medicine, Seattle, Washington 98195

GEOFFREY TREMONT, Department of Psychiatry and Behavioral Sciences, University of Oklahoma Health Sciences Center, Oklahoma City, Oklahoma 73142

VINCENT B. VAN HASSELT, Center for Psychological Studies, Nova Southeastern University, Fort Lauderdale, Florida 33314

MARILYN S. WARD, Department of Psychiatry, State University of New York Health Science Center, Syracuse, New York 13210

BRUCE A. WRIGHT, Division of Geriatrics and Neuropsychiatry, Western Psychiatric Institute and Clinic, Department of Psychiatry, University of Pittsburgh School of Medicine, Pittsburgh, Pennsylvania 15213

Preface

This multiauthored introductory textbook could not have been conceived or brought to fruition 10 or 15 years ago. Indeed, at that time relatively little attention was accorded to the psychological needs of older adults. The general tenor of the field then was that older adults would not benefit from psychological intervention. As we now know, this was a faulty assumption that has been discredited with empirical data. Indeed, clinical research data adduced, primarily in the last decade, clearly documents that older adults do benefit from specific psychotherapies that are tailored to their unique presentation of symptoms.

Given the explosion of interest in this area (as evinced by increased investigatory activity, national funding, and media attention) and the increased number of masters- and doctoral-level courses devoted to this topic, we felt that the time was right for a textbook in the area. Such flurry of activity also has been fueled by statistics showing how our population by the year 2030 will consist of 30% who are senior citizens. Moreover, since 12% of older adults in the community are estimated to have diagnosable psychiatric disorders and 40% to 50% of older adult medical inpatients have a concomitant psychiatric disorder, the task for clinicians in the next century will be overwhelming.

Psychological Treatment of Older Adults: An Introductory Text consists of 16 chapters, with 7 chapters in Part I (General Issues) and 9 chapters in Part II (Specific Disorders and Problems). Chapters in Part I examine historical perspectives in clinical geropsychology, social adaptation in older adults, assessment of older adults, clinical neuropsychology of older adults, medical assessment, competence and other legal issues, and treatment in residential settings. Chapters in Part II cover topics such as anxiety-based disorders, late-life depression, depression in Alzheimer's disease, schizophrenia, mental retardation, organic disorders, substance abuse, sexual dysfunction, and marital discord. Chapters in Part II have sections on the description of the disorder or problem, case identification and presenting complaints, history, selection of psychological treatment, concurrent medical treatment, course of treatment, follow-up, overall evaluation, and summary.

Many individuals have contributed to the final published product. First of all, we thank our eminent contributors for sharing their thinking with us.

Second, we thank Burt G. Bolton, Christine Apple, and Christine Ryan for their technical expertise. And third, but most important, we once again thank our friend and editor at Plenum Press, Eliot Werner, who makes it all happen.

MICHEL HERSEN
VINCENT B. VAN HASSELT

Fort Lauderdale, Florida

Contents

PART I

GENERAL ISSUES

CHAPTER 1

Historical Perspectives in Clinical Geropsychology

Brad Donohue, Michel Hersen, and Vincent B. Van Hasselt

CHAPTER OUTLINE

Introduction
History of Geropsychology
  Prescientific Myths
  Early Gerontologists
  Early Gerontological Publications
  Interdisciplinary Study of Gerontology

The Impact of World War II
Behavioral Research with Older Adults
  New Developments in Gerontology
Summary
References

INTRODUCTION

Throughout much of history, it was rare for persons to reach the age of 55 because of inadequate medical treatment, starvation, neglect, disease, and poor hygiene. Indeed, as recently as the 17th century the average human being could expect to live only about 35 years. Presently, however, the average life-span is approximately 75 years, largely as a result of advancements in medicine and health care. The human life-span continues to expand and will inevitably contribute to a number of problems, including the role and adjustment of senior citizens in society. Indeed, the world's population for persons over 60 years of age is expected to burgeon beyond 1 billion within 35 years (Shuman, 1987), and

---

Brad Donohue, Michel Hersen, and Vincent B. Van Hasselt • Center for Psychological Studies, Nova Southeastern University, Fort Lauderdale, Florida 33314.
Psychological Treatment of Older Adults: An Introductory Text, edited by Michel Hersen and Vincent B. Van Hasselt. Plenum Press, New York, 1996.

approximately 30% of the general population will consist of senior citizens by the year 2030 (U.S. Department of Health and Human Services, 1987–1988). The increased proportion of elderly citizens has already brought about new social problems that have yet to be addressed. For example, there is a serious shortage of mental health professionals with adequate geriatric training. There are few training programs in university and medical settings for geropsychology (clinical psychology of older adults), and those extant are relatively underfunded. This is particularly distressing given that at least 12% of older adults in the community are estimated to have a diagnosed mental disorder (Regier et al., 1988). Further, it has been estimated that 40% to 50% of older adult medical inpatients have a concurrent psychiatric disorder (Rapp, Parisi, & Walsh, 1988). As the number of older adults increases, however, so too will the impact of this population. In fact, over 22 million Gray Panthers, representing the advancement of retired persons, already have enhanced political, social, and economic clout for this age group and have voiced their needs to the general public and the government. Although there has been a growing (albeit gradual) societal awareness of concerns of the elderly, geropsychology as a field of study is a recent phenomenon that was largely nonexistent prior to the latter half of the 20th century. This chapter will review some of the significant factors that led to the establishment of geropsychology. (In this chapter the terms *geropsychology* and *gerontology* are used interchangeably.)

HISTORY OF GEROPSYCHOLOGY

Prescientific Myths

In prescientific theorizing, myths were advanced to explain the aging process. Since few persons lived beyond 30 years of age during ancient times, religious leaders formulated myths to explain the rare occurrence of older adults in society. According to the Greek Hyperborean myth, healthy individuals who lived for a long time were thought to be favored by the gods. Many persons preferred not to adhere to the contention that their destiny was completely determined by gods. Consequently, new myths were devised to obtain longevity as being at least partly under human control. For example, according to the "rejuvenation" myth, humans could extend longevity through sexual behavior or by ingesting special herbs and waters. The rejuvenation myth instilled hope and was particularly appealing to prosperous adults, who were better able to obtain such resources.

Although empirical research has led to a clearer and more accurate understanding of the underlying determinants of aging for contemporary society, vestiges of the rejuvenation myth remain. Humans still attempt to gain greater health, vitality, and an extended life-span from vitamins, spas, and rigorous exercise. Extreme examples include being injected with lamb fetus cells at Dr. Niehan's clinic in Switzerland or being injected with genetic material from fetal cells at the Peter Stephen Private Clinic in London (Woodruff-Pak, 1988).

Early Gerontologists

The rigid acceptance of early myths, fostered by theologians and members of clergy, hindered the development of geropsychology as an area of scientific study. In fact, the first applications of empirical methodology to geriatric issues did not appear until the late 1600s, a time when life expectancy was still relatively short. Like their predecessors, pioneering gerontologists were primarily interested in discovering ways to increase the human life-span. However, these early scientists denounced the widely accepted myths. As a result they were often publicly ridiculed and sometimes executed for religious heresy (Woodruff-Pak, 1988).

Francis Bacon was one of first scientists to study older adults. Through careful observation of this population he concluded that poor hygiene had the most deleterious effect on the aging process. He postulated, therefore, that improvements in hygiene would reduce germs and disease and increase life-span. His ideas contradicted earlier beliefs that life-span was determined solely by the gods, and he was publicly scorned by religious leaders.

Bacon's work paved the way for 18th-century scientists, such as Benjamin Franklin, to conduct empirical investigations of the elderly. Franklin was internationally renowned for his belief that human life-span could be prolonged only through conscientious scientific study. He also hypothesized that rejuvenation of deceased humans could occur if the stimulating properties of electricity could be harnessed. He tested his hypothesis with deceased animals, but after repeated failures abandoned this project.

Quetelet carried out pioneering studies to discover the natural laws of human development and aging and is considered to be the first gerontologist (Birren, 1961). Although he contributed much to science, he is perhaps best known for his tome entitled, *On the Nature of Man and the Development of His Facilities*, published in 1835. This book stressed the importance of systematic evaluation when measuring human abilities (e.g., hand strength). He also examined the productivity of playwrights as a function of age and included some of the earliest published data on the psychology of aging.

Francis Galton succeeded Quetelet as the next major contributor to gerontology (Woodruff-Pak, 1988). At the 1884 International Health Exhibition in London, he performed the first prominent study employing standardized instruments to measure developmental abilities across the life-span. He measured many attributes, including grip strength, vision, hearing, and reaction time in over 9,000 persons ranging in age from 5 to 80 years. Moreover, Galton was the first scientist to empirically demonstrate that the majority of human capacities atrophy with old age.

The first experimental attempt to change the constitution of the human body in order to increase life-span occurred when a 73-year-old named Charles Brown-Séquard injected himself with monkey testicle extracts (Woodruff-Pak, 1988). After he announced his experimental practices in a public lecture in 1889, he was accused of being senile and was publicly mocked. Although he claimed that he felt rejuvenated, he died 5 years after the injections were performed.

Early Gerontological Publications

Prominent publications in the early 1900s helped to stimulate gerontological interest among the scientific community. In 1908, Minot published *The Problems of Age, Growth and Death*, and that same year Metchnikoff published *The Prolongation of Life*. Metchnikoff believed that yogurt cleansed the gastrointestinal tract of age-accumulating bacteria and therefore enabled yogurt eaters to live longer. *The Prolongation of Life* popularized his theory with a diverse international audience. Hereditary etiologies of aging were also considered during these times, as demonstrated in Pearl's (1922) *Biology of Death*. Interestingly, Pearl ignored environmental influences entirely and believed that aging was caused by heredity alone. These early 20th-century books represented initial attempts to describe and understand the processes of aging. The authors erroneously attempted to explain aging as a unitary process with a single cause and thus were lacking an effective integration of biological, social, psychological, and hereditary influences (Woodruff-Pak, 1988). Nevertheless, these volumes reflected the unidimensional thinking of the times.

G. Stanley Hall's *Senescence, the Second Half of Life*, published in 1922, was an attempt to better understand the nature and functioning of old age. Hall reviewed a wide variety of gerontological issues pertinent to the biological and social sciences. His fascination with death led him to perform the first empirical investigation of death and dying, and one of his experimental contributions to gerontology was his finding that age and religiosity were not necessarily correlated (Woodruff-Pak, 1988).

Interdisciplinary Study of Gerontology

During the late 1930s, scientists began to study living systems in their entirety, and the aging process began to be examined in an interdisciplinary context. For the first time, agencies such as the Josiah Macy Jr. Foundation began to sponsor research programs and conferences for the elderly on a large scale. The Josiah Macy Jr. Foundation and the National Institutes of Health funded "later maturity" conferences in the early 1940s. These conferences were attended by professionals from a wide range of disciplines who presented information pertinent to psychological, intellectual, and economic functioning and concerns of older adults.

In addition to multidisciplinary conferences, writers of books and monographs began to integrate the ideas of other disciplines. For example, Cowdry's (1939) *Problems of Aging* comprehensively reviewed the basic principles of aging utilizing plants, protozoa, invertebrates, and insects to provide a foundation from which to address human psychological issues of aging.

By the early 1940s, conferences and interdisciplinary volumes helped to create a growing acceptance of genetic and environmental factors as pertinent to the psychology of aging. Most importantly, however, interdisciplinary collaboration made it possible to advance the field of gerontology in a broader context.

The Impact of World War II

As gerontology was beginning to establish itself as a discipline, World War II interrupted research on older adults. Furthermore, this conflict curtailed public recognition for gerontologists who were making significant achievements. Nevertheless, important contributions to the field of gerontology were made during this period, particularly in the area of intellectual and behavioral performance. Since most young adults were involved in the military, studies were conducted in most modern nations to increase functioning and productivity of older adults working in factories. James Birren studied American servicemen and found that their performance was significantly affected by age. In 1940, Surgeon General Thomas Parran appointed a National Advisory Committee to assist in the formation of a gerontology unit within the National Institutes of Health. This unit later became known as the National Institute on Aging and assisted other organizations with establishment of laboratories and research programs to study the aged after World War II. In addition, the Gerontological Society of America was founded in 1945 to encourage professional interdisciplinary discussion of older adult research. A year later the first International Congress of Gerontology was held in Liege, Belgium. Also established during the mid-1940s were the Gerontology Research Center of the National Institutes of Health, the Nuffield Unit of Research into Problems of Aging at the University of Cambridge, as well as the American Psychological Association's division of Maturity and Old Age and the American Geriatrics Society. These efforts have led to exponential growth in the number of publications (Riegel, 1977) and completed doctoral dissertations (Woodruff-Pak, 1988) that are specific to geropsychology.

Paralleling the growth of gerontological research centers in the United States has been the establishment of scientific journals in the field of gerontology. Initially focusing on physiological research with older adults, the *Journal of Gerontology, Experimental Aging Research*, and *Experimental Gerontology* have become more psychologically oriented over time. The *International Journal of Dying and Human Development* examines social gerontological issues, whereas the *Journal of Geriatric Psychiatry* is psychoanalytically oriented. A broad-based psychological perspective is espoused by the *Gerontologist, Psychology and Aging*, and, more recently, the *Journal of Clinical Geropsychology*. These publications consider relevant assessment and treatment issues pertinent to older adults and heuristic dissemination outlets for practicing psychotherapists and researchers working in gerontology.

Behavioral Research with Older Adults

The first applications of the behavioral model to problems of the elderly occurred during the mid-1960s. However, little behavioral research was carried out with the elderly until the early 1970s (see discussion by Wisocki & Mosher, 1982). Even today, relative to other clinical populations, behavioral research with older adult populations is largely neglected. In fact, from 1963 to 1984 the number of gerontological articles of behavioral orientation published in established journals averaged less than a dozen per year (see reviews by Burgio, 1985; Wisocki & Mosher, 1982). Lebowitz and Niederehe (1992) point out several reasons to account for such lack of interest in behavioral research with older adults. First, many researchers believe that older adults suffer from biological degeneration that cannot be ameliorated with behavioral techniques. Others believe that research findings with younger populations can simply be extended upward to the problems of the older spectrum of the population. In addition, many mental health professionals regard older adults as uninteresting and less compliant than younger individuals. Further, confounds common to elderly populations (e.g., use of medication, physical atrophy) make research difficult, particularly for clinicians who are not experienced in this area. In attempts to remedy this situation, federal agencies such as the National Institute of Aging, the National Institutes of Mental Health, and the Administration on Aging recently have provided research and training grants to professionals and programs that address the issues and problems of older adults.

New Developments in Gerontology

In 1982, the United Nations General Assembly sponsored the World Assembly on Aging in Vienna. This convention addressed global social and economic trends and was the first international assembly of its kind. Soon after this assembly, the American Psychological Association originated *Psychology and Aging*, a new research journal specifically designed to address relevant topics in gerontology. More recently, behavioral gerontology special interest groups have been established within psychological organizations such as the Association for Advancement of Behavior Therapy and the Association for Behavioral Analysis. In 1990, the National Agenda for Research on Aging was formed under the auspices of the National Academy of Sciences/Institute of Medicine. The principal aim of this project is to investigate and carry out research in clinical geriatrics, social and behavioral investigations, health delivery services, and biological aging processes. Recognizing the need for geriatric education, the American Board of Internal Medicine, the American Academy of Family Practice, and the American Board of Psychiatry and Neurology have all established examinations for geriatric competence. To meet these demands, over 20 medical schools have organized specialized geriatric programs; all of these will emphasize the scientist-practitioner model.

SUMMARY

Although it was rare for humans to reach the age of 55 years during early history, ever increasing life-spans have led to a greater proportion of older adults in contemporary society. Recognizing the needs of this population, professionals have dramatically increased their clinical and investigative efforts in the field of gerontology over the past several decades. Historically, the latter half of this century witnessed an exponential increase in research. Unfortunately, older adults are still a seriously underserved population. Yet, per capita, older adults are more likely to have a mental illness than any other age group, although they account for only 2% of general outpatient psychology clinic referrals. Despite the upward trend of gerontological research and community service in recent years, there is a marked shortage of adequately trained professionals in this area. This is not surprising given that academic training facilities specific to gerontology in medical and university settings are scarce, and geropsychology course work is noticeably absent in most curricula of professional schools of psychology and psychiatry. Obviously, the development of such programs and course work is warranted.

The present book, then, is specifically directed to filling a gap in the literature with respect to the psychological treatment of older adults. Given the increased investigative activity in the area and greater national funding for such projects, many papers have appeared on this topic since the 1980s. However, the clinical and empirical data that have been adduced have been presented in many disparate sources, and we of course feel the need for a more concise and systematic exposition of all of the assessment and treatment issues.

The book is organized into two parts: I, General Issues; II, Specific Disorders and Problems. In Part I the reader is presented with seven chapters in addition to our historical perspectives. Included are issues of social adaptation, behavioral assessment, neuropharmacological assessment, medical assessment, legal status and competency, intergenerational issues in families, and residential treatment. In Part II, the treatment of nine specific disorders and problems is presented in a case history format, with the following interchapter outline:

1. Description of the Disorder or Problem
2. Case Identification and Presenting Complaints
3. History
4. Selection of Psychological Treatment
5. Concurrent Medical Treatment
6. Course of Treatment
7. Follow-up
8. Overall Evaluation
9. Summary

Disorders and problems covered are anxiety, depression, depression in Alzheimer's disease, mental retardation, organic disorders, alcoholism and drug addiction, sexual dysfunction, and marital discord.

REFERENCES

Birren, J. E. (1961). A brief history of the psychology of aging. *Gerontologist, 1,* 67–77.
Burgio, L. (1985). *Behavior analysis and intervention in geriatric long-term care.* Paper presented at the Florida Association for Behavior Analysis, Tampa, FL.
Cowdry, E. V. (Ed.) (1939). *Problems of aging.* New York: Macmillan.
Hall, G. S. (1922). *Senescence, the second half of life.* New York: Appleton.
Lebowitz, B. D., & Niederehe G. (1992). Concepts and Issues in Mental Health and Aging. In J. E.

Birren, R. B. Sloane, & G. D. Cohen (Eds.), *Handbook of mental health and aging* (2nd ed.). New York: Academic Press.

Metchinkoff, E. (1908). *The prolongation of life*. New York: Putnam.

Minot, C. (1908). *The problems of age, growth, and death*. New York: Putnam.

Pearl, R. (1922). *The biology of death*. Philadelphia: J. P. Lippincott.

Rapp, S. R., Parisi, S. A., & Walsh, D. A. (1988). Psychological dysfunction and physical health among elderly medical inpatients. *Journal of Consulting and Clinical Psychology, 56*, 851–855.

Regier, D. A., Boyd, J. H., Burke, J. D., et al. (1988). One month prevention of mental disorders in the United States. *Archives of General Psychiatry, 45*, 977–986.

Riegel, K. F. (1977). History of psychological gerontology. In J. E. Birren & K. W. Schaie (Eds.), *Handbook of the psychology of aging* (pp. 70–102). New York: Van Nostrand Reinhold.

Shuman, T. M. (1987). World Assembly on Aging. In G. Maddox (Ed.), *The encyclopedia of aging*. New York: Springer.

U. S. Department of Health and Human Services (1987–1988). *U. S. Senate Special Committee on Aging: Aging American—trends and projections*. Washington DC: Author.

Wisocki, P. A., & Mosher, P. (1982). The elderly: An understudied population in behavioral research. *International Journal of Behavioral Geriatrics, 13*, 89–102.

Woodruff-Pak, D. (1988). *Psychology and aging*. Englewood Cliffs, NJ: Prentice-Hall.

CHAPTER 2

Social Adaptation in Older Adults

WILLIAM HARRY PETTIBON, VINCENT B. VAN HASSELT, AND MICHEL HERSEN

INTRODUCTION

The phenomenon of aging has long been of interest to observers of human behavior. The systematic and empirical study of the process and behavioral effects of aging, however, has burgeoned dramatically over the past quarter of a century. A primary reason for such increased interest in our older population is that substantially more people are living longer. Indeed, in the early 1900s, the average male life-span was 45 years; today, it exceeds 72 years. Further, persons 65 years and older comprise almost 13% of the population; based on current population trends and continuing medical advances, the U.S. Department of Health, Education, and Welfare (1976) predicts that 50% of the population could be middle aged or older by the year 2100 (see also U.S. Bureau of Census, 1993).

WILLIAM HARRY PETTIBON, VINCENT B. VAN HASSELT, AND MICHEL HERSEN • Center for Psychological Studies, Nova Southeastern University, Fort Lauderdale, Florida 33314.

Psychological Treatment of Older Adults: An Introductory Text, edited by Michel Hersen and Vincent B. Van Hasselt. Plenum Press, New York, 1996.

Also, by the year 2010, the number of Americans over age 85 is projected to double (White House Domestic Policy Council, 1993). Aside from increased longevity, today's older adults are healthier, wealthier, better educated, and more politically active than at any previous point in history (Neugarten, 1974).

Aging requires changes in thinking and behavior across the life-span. Indeed, we react to physical, psychological, and social demands in order to survive. Yet, old age (65 years or older) is a difficult period for many individuals. Stressors common in old age (physical illness and disability, bereavement, reduced income, loss of occupational and social status) are unprecedented and intense, and they require extensive modification in thinking and behavior (Bennett, 1980; Butler & Gleason, 1985; Bytheway et al., 1989). Although such changes are inevitable and universal, it is evident that older adults are as heterogeneous as any other group in our society. Therefore, generalizations about how people adapt to the demands of aging are difficult to make. Further, the effects of aging are as different as the coping styles evinced by older adults. As we age, individual differences continue to influence the manner in which we react to the demands of daily living. And how well a person adapts determines the quality of life he or she will lead in old age.

The purpose of this chapter is to examine the process of social adaptation in older adults. First, we identify and examine social adjustment problems common to the elderly. Next we discuss the process of social adaptation in general and among older adults in particular. Sections on assessment and treatment of social dysfunction and associated psychological and behavioral difficulties in the elderly follow. Finally, we offer suggestions for future research and clinical practice in this area.

PROBLEMS OF AGING

Human beings adapt over the course of the life-span. Most older adults develop and maintain social interests and attachments throughout their lives and adapt to changing demands. In spite of individual differences and other problems inherent in the study of adaptation, determination of an older adult's ability to react to personal and environmental stresses and demands is central to an understanding of how the quality of life will be shaped subsequently. To examine more precisely the unique features of the adaptation process in older persons, it is useful to take a chronological, developmental perspective. How, then, is the process of adaptation to social demands different for older persons than it is for younger individuals?

Older adults generally experience changes in social roles, status, and support networks. As we age, losses of spouses, family members, and friends are more common (Stevens-Long, 1979). These losses, and their significant and negative emotional sequelae, often necessitate changes in family and community relations (Bahr & Peterson, 1989; Kimmel, 1980). Also, most older persons retire from their professions (voluntarily or otherwise). This factor affects the frequency and quality of relationships with others. Loss and reduction of income (and the resultant increased financial pressure) are common among the elderly, and such factors limit opportunities for social interaction (Atchley, 1977). Additionally, our culture tends to value youth and devalue old age. Thus, interpersonal behavior is influenced by social dynamics in which there is stereotyping and discrimination of older adults. Here again, the result may be diminished social interaction (Kimmel, 1988).

The experience of personal loss is a shared experience for most older persons. Too often, however, it is assumed that the elderly have the capacity to accept losses of family and friends, health, income, vocation, and material goods. Exposure over a lifetime has presumably "conditioned" them to accepting change and loss. Unfortunately, it appears more likely that material, personal, and social status losses, combined with diminished cognitive abilities, frequently contribute to emotional and behavioral difficulties. Indeed, it has been estimated that at least 25% of older adults exhibit social and emotional adjustment problems (Goodstein, 1985). For example, depression and anxiety are common among the elderly (Hersen & Van Hasselt, 1992; Hersen, Van Hasselt, & Goreczny, 1993). In fact, depression is the most commonly diagnosed disorder in older adults (Blazer, 1982). And the suicide rate at age 65 is approximately 50% higher than for younger populations nationwide (McIntosh, 1989). Moreover, white males over 65 are at greatest risk for suicide in the United States (Busse, 1992).

In addition, illness and injury are more frequent in older adults (Busse & Maddox, 1985). Related difficulties include decreased physical strength, stamina, and flexibility. Indeed, nearly 45% of the elderly are considered to suffer from physical disabilities (Goodstein, 1985). And beyond limiting potential for social interaction, physical health problems exacerbate burgeoning financial pressures.

Cognitive abilities generally decline in old age and are frequently related to physical health problems. Sensory and motor processes diminish progressively. Memory impairment is relatively common among older adults, as is slowing or deterioration of reasoning processes. Dementia, a global reduction of mental functioning, is also more prevalent in older adults. Indeed, nearly 3.5 million elderly persons suffer from some form of dementia, with an estimated 1 million or more considered to be seriously demented (Sulzman, 1989). Thus, older individuals may have a diminished cognitive capacity, which further impedes their ability to react effectively to the increased demands of aging (Busse & Pfeiffer, 1973).

Overall, then, older adults generally are required to redefine their social roles and to reshape their patterns of interaction with others to reflect changes and limitations in life-style and vocation imposed by aging. Consequently, adaptation to changes in life caused by aging can be exceedingly challenging, if not problematic or seemingly insurmountable.

SOCIAL ADAPTATION

How can we conceptualize the phenomenon of social adaptation in order to better examine and understand this process in older adults? Kahle and Timmer (1983) describe adaptation as a process of "fitting a person to the environment

and fitting the environment to the person" (p. 49). This perspective is reminis-
cent of Piaget's (1952) view of the goal of adaptation: "when the organism is
transformed by the environment and when this variation results in an increase in
the interchanges between the environment and itself which are favorable to
preservation" (p. 56). Thus, adaptation is an ongoing process in which an
individual and/or the environment reciprocally adjusts to create a positive
equilibrium. Social adaptation occurs when this equilibration occurs in a social
context.

As a dynamic and continuous process, social adaptation is a complex
phenomenon involving the interaction of a variety of abilities and activities. The
following discussion highlights some of the variables instrumental to the process of social adaptation (see Figure 2-1).

Social Perception

Social perception refers to the manner through which an individual collects
and processes information about interpersonal interactions and behaviors in
social contexts. Successful adaptation to social demands depends largely on an
individual's ability to perceive, interpret, and understand the social context and
cues within which he or she functions (Bellack, Hersen, & Himmelhoch, 1996;
Morrison & Bellack, 1981). To function as adaptive organisms, we must be able to

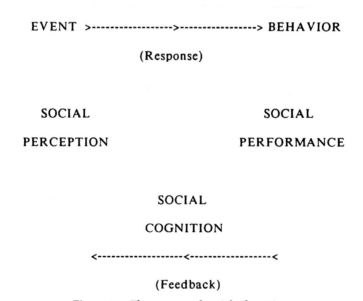

EVENT >------------------>-----------------> BEHAVIOR

(Response)

SOCIAL   SOCIAL

PERCEPTION   PERFORMANCE

SOCIAL

COGNITION

<-------------------<------------------<

(Feedback)

Figure 2-1. The process of social adaptation.

make sense of our social environments. A person's level of sensitivity to the environment is a critical component of social perception skill. Such sensitivity includes the ability to accurately observe and appreciate not only the actions of others, but also their personal characteristics, feelings, and possible motives (Rothenberg, 1970; Tagiuri, 1969).

Social Cognition

Social cognition is the mechanism by which we seek to interpret and understand the social environment. In general, cognition refers to mental processes in which perceived information is transformed, reduced, stored, recovered, and utilized (Neisser, 1967). Social cognition involves formulation of hypotheses, beliefs, attitudes, and norms pertaining to social interactions. These are utilized to structure our understanding of the social environment and then to make informed choices about how to respond to interpersonal demands. Once a situation is perceived, interpreted, and understood, and an active response is deemed necessary, choices about social performance are made. These usually take the form of interpersonal behaviors expected to elicit a reinforcing outcome for the individual. Strategies for generating and initiating these favorable alternatives are sometimes referred to as social problem-solving skills (Goldfried & D'Zurilla, 1968).

Selection of specific social behaviors is based on a number of influences. In addition to the above-mentioned perceptual and cognitive abilities, behavior is determined by an interaction of motivational factors, environmental constraints, and the interpersonal skills repertoire of the individual. Figure 2-2 shows this relationship.

For example, an employee may be listening to his or her employer giving orders to implement something (behavior) and decide that the boss is providing the wrong instructions (perception). Whether or not the employee decides to correct the employer would be influenced by his or her view of its importance (motivation), the possible impact of giving critical feedback (consequences), and an estimate of his or her ability to offer feedback to the employer in a socially

PERCEIVED   BEHAVIORAL

SOCIAL DEMANDS -----> SOCIAL   -----> CHOICE

ADAPTATION

- Motivation   - Social skills

- Environmental limits

Figure 2-2. Influences on socially adaptive behavior.

acceptable manner (social performance skills). To the extent that the employee's decision results in a favorable outcome, it can be considered as socially adaptive.

Behavioral consequences serve as motivational factors that shape both cognition and behavior. Developmentally, most individuals learn to anticipate and seek potential rewards and to fear and avoid possible punishment. Positively reinforcing social behaviors are therefore more likely to be emitted than alternatives responses. Situational or environmental conditions (i.e., behavioral antecedents) also act to inhibit or facilitate various social behaviors by limiting behavioral choices or contributing to reinforcing contingencies. For example, living in a nursing home obviously provides different social limits and opportunities for older adults than living independently.

Social Competency

Social competency, based on an individual's repertoire of verbal and nonverbal interpersonal skills, is another important factor in social adaptation. Identification of social skill deficits and attempts to remediate these deficiencies have been the focus of considerable clinical and investigative attention for several years. Bellack and Hersen (1979), Lewinsohn et al. (1984), and others have documented the relationships among inadequate social skills, social isolation, and various forms of psychological dysfunction (e.g., anxiety, depression).

Specifically, social skills may be viewed as learned interpersonal behaviors that allow persons to (1) communicate effectively with each other (Trower & Argyle, 1978) and (2) obtain social reinforcement from other people. Social skills include both verbal (e.g., voice volume, intonation, response latency) and nonverbal (e.g., eye contact, affect, physical gestures) response categories that have been indicated in previous research as requisite to interpersonal effectiveness. Clearly, an individual deficient in such abilities would find it difficult to function adequately in social encounters. However, since requisite skills vary across situations, a standardized taxonomy of social skills and their behavioral referents has not been established (Sprafkin, 1984). As we will discuss later, however, categories and types of skills specific to disparate populations and settings have been developed.

SOCIAL ADAPTATION IN OLDER ADULTS

Older adults appear to be slower to make adaptive responses to stressful changes than younger persons (Lawton et al., 1976). For example, older adults may find it difficult to initiate and maintain new self-care behaviors such as unfamiliar, but necessary, medical procedures. Such reluctance or inability to adapt may be compounded by a lack of social pressure or support to do so. Moreover, it has been widely asserted that older adults tend to withdraw from social activity as they age (Levy, 1981; Tunstall, 1966). The "disengagement" theory of aging proposed by Cummings and Henry (1961) explains this apparent tendency as a "universal and predetermined" feature of aging. This theory, however, has been criticized as deceptively simplistic; many older persons are *forced* to withdraw from social activity. Furthermore, such withdrawal may not be their preference. And although social disengagement may be common in older populations, it is far from ubiquitous (Butler & Lewis, 1977; Tallmer, 1973).

An alternative view of successful aging, the "social reconstruction model" proposed by Kuypers and Bengston (1973), contends that older adults are capable of a surprisingly high level of adjustment that can be enhanced by programs that promote competence in social interaction. Still, the observation that older persons generally withdraw from social demands (rather than adapt to them) has been documented empirically, as has the observation that social withdrawal and isolation can lead to a variety of problems in daily living (Busse & Pfeiffer, 1977).

Level of social adaptation later in life is best predicted by degree of adjustment and adaptation in younger years (Palmore, 1969). Coping styles that were effective earlier in life appear to provide adaptive attitudes and skills in the aged (Pfeiffer, 1970). Further, enduring characteristics, such as internal locus of control, have been associated with more active social involvement and better emotional adjustment in the elderly (Wolk & Kurtz, 1975). For example, inpatients on geriatric units who were assertive and took more initiative in self-care had better hospital prognoses; those who were socially isolated had significantly longer hospital stays (Ross & Kedward, 1978). In a survey of psychological problems in older people, Abrahams and Patterson (1979) found that loss of familiar social roles and constricted interpersonal interactions produced significant negative psychological sequelae. By contrast, the ability to take social initiatives, organize patterns of varied daily activity, and maintain social relationships outside the home resulted in far fewer complaints of personal (and interpersonal) problems.

It has been suggested that for some older individuals, limited social contact is a familiar personal style and not necessarily antithetical to adaptation (Cumming, 1964). For many older adults, however, social isolation has deleterious effects. Cognitive processes in general, and social cognition in particular, have been found to deteriorate as a function of physical, emotional, and social isolation (Dolen & Bearison, 1982; Ernst et al., 1978). In a review of previous research in this area, Bennett (1973) concluded that social isolation negatively affects older individuals by reducing social skills and attitude independence and by contributing to the development of affective disorders and diminished cognitive functioning. This conclusion is supported by a longitudinal study of an inner-city elderly population which found that persons with adequate social networks had fewer psychological symptoms and greater ability to adapt to social demands (Cohen et al., 1985).

An investigation of elderly residents of retirement hotels and apartments in Florida revealed that individuals who were socially active and who provided support to others were the least likely to report physical and psychosocial problems (Stein et al., 1982). Further, a study of older adults receiving treatment for marital problems, depression, and adjustment difficulties indicated that short-term counseling was most often effective when it focused on strengthening absent or deteriorated interpersonal skills (Kosberg & Garcia, 1988). In a study of

69 community-dwelling older adults, assertiveness and social support were found to correlate with reduced depression, suggesting that older adults who are more isolated and less assertive are at greater risk for depression (Kogan, Van Hasselt, Hersen, & Kabacoff, 1995). Overall, it appears that for most older adults, ongoing social interaction and a repertoire of adequate social skills increases the ability to respond adaptively to social demands.

In a study by Hersen et al. (1995b), the relationship of assertiveness, depression, and social support was examined in a sample of 100 visually impaired older adults receiving rehabilitative services at a lighthouse for the blind. Resulting data indicated that irrespective of the sex, type of impairment, age of impairment, and duration of impairment, there were significant correlations between social support and depression ($r = -.48$), assertiveness and depression ($r = -.29$), and social support and assertiveness ($r = .39$). These data suggest that in the absence of social support and assertive responding, the older visually impaired adult is likely to become increasingly dependent, socially isolated, demonstrate a low degree of self-confidence, and consequently suffer from depression (ranging from mild to clinical proportions).

In a subsequent study by this team of researchers (Hersen et al., 1995a), 199 visually impaired older adults were administered the Wolpe-Lazarus Assertiveness Scale (WLAS), the Geriatric Depression Scale (GDS), and the Interpersonal Support Evaluation List (ISEL). A factor analysis of the WLAS yielded a three-factor solution accounting for 25.2% of the variance. Factor II of the WLAS (general inhibition) yielded a moderate positive correlation with depression ($r = .39$) and a moderate negative correlation ($r = -.31$) with social support. Again, as in their previous work with older individuals with visual impairment, high depression scores were associated with low assertiveness, and low assertiveness was associated with inadequate social support.

ASSESSMENT

Accurate assessment of social adaptation in older persons is essential to the development of treatment goals where significant deficits are observed. Through clinical interviews and the use of self-report measures, we can obtain valuable information about social adaptation in an individual. Comprehensive functional evaluation strategies for older adults have been developed through efforts conducted at the Older Americans Resources and Services (OARS) Program at the Duke University Center for the Study of Aging and Human Development (see George & Fillenbaum, 1985). Also, omnibus personality measures, such as the Minnesota Multiphasic Personality Inventory (MMPI-II), have norms suitable for use with older persons and provide useful data about affect and personal styles (Butcher, 1990). Further, the Quality of Life Inventory is a heuristic general indicator of success or failure in social adaptation and is based on ratings of life satisfaction and quality of life (Frisch, 1988a).

Since social adaptation is an ongoing, interactive process involving a variety of influences and abilities, it is often more clinically useful to measure level of functioning at different points in the adaptation process. For example, we can examine intrapersonal variables in relation to disparate aspects of social perception, cognition, and performance. Also, interpersonal skills involved in specific social behaviors can and should be evaluated.

Social Perception

With older adults it is especially important to assess and rule out organic brain dysfunction as a cause of difficulties in social interaction or perception. Disturbances in perceptual skills due to organic causes can be identified and quantified using brief mental status examinations, neuropsychological batteries (e.g., the Halstead-Reitan Neuropsychological Test Battery), or more specific measures such as the Bender-Gestalt or Holland's Communication Activities of Daily Living (Lezak, 1983). Once brain dysfunction has been ruled out, impressions regarding apparent social dysfunction can be obtained via behavioral observations, analog tasks (e.g., role-play test), and/or by using available rating scales of social perception (see Wixted, Morrison, & Bellack, 1988).

Social Cognition and Problem-Solving

As with perceptual processes, cognitive styles, skills, and limitations can be measured through observation and testing. Cognitive variables of interest include overall intellectual abilities, particularly any apparent decline in functioning over time. Special emphasis is to be placed on an assessment of cognitive capabilities, such as memory and reasoning. These processes influence adaptive abilities and can be affected by medical problems associated with aging, as well as by affective disorders that are prevalent among older adults.

Other factors influencing social cognition are frequency, severity, and duration of personal and interpersonal problems, deficient coping skills, and unavailability or underutilization of social support. A variety of assessment devices has been developed to provide information about these areas, though few have been specifically constructed or adapted for use with the elderly. Beliefs about self-efficacy are also influential in shaping social cognition and can be evaluated through the use of self-efficacy scales (Bandura, 1982). Level of understanding, beliefs about, and competence in abilities related to social problem solving can also be observed and rated. Skills under this rubric might include identification and definition of interpersonal problems, generation of possible solutions, decision making, and implementation and monitoring of solutions (D'Zurilla, 1986; D'Zurilla & Sheedy, 1992).

In addition, affective status of the individual shapes cognitive style and ability. Instruments such as the Geriatric Depression Scale have been developed specifically for use in assessment of mood in older individuals (Yesavage, Brink, & Rose, 1983). Also, existing measures such as the Beck Depression Inventory have been utilized with older adults (Kogan, Kabacoff, Hersen, & Van Hasselt, 1994; Olin, Schneider, Eaton, Zemansky, & Pollock, 1992).

Social Performance and Social Skills

For many years, investigative attention has been directed to the relationship between social skill deficits and interpersonal problems (Zigler & Phillips, 1960, 1961). As will be discussed shortly, precise identification and quantification of social skills deficits leads to the development and application of interventions intended to remediate areas of deficiency. And evaluation and treatment of impaired interpersonal skills can have immediate and dramatic effects on improving social adaptation. Assessment strategies for evaluating social skills with older adults include use of structured interviews, ratings by significant others, self-reports, self-monitoring, and direct behavioral observation (see Hersen, Van Hasselt, & Segal, 1995).

Bellack (1994) argues that measurable social skills can be divided into three broad categories: (1) general or global skills, (2) abilities associated with content of verbal interactions, and (3) nonverbal and paralinguistic capabilities. Global skills might include assertiveness, problem-solving ability, appropriateness of affect to interpersonal situations, and ability to cope with social anxiety. All of these capabilities can affect the general character of social interactions. Components of verbal communication are more specific and can involve fluent articulation of thoughts, acceptable expression of positive and negative feelings, constructive questioning, willingness to compromise and to negotiate demands and commands, and ability to express agreement and disagreement.

Nonverbal or paralinguistic abilities are also important to social interaction since much of communication is accomplished without language. Examples of paralinguistic behaviors are facial expression, personal appearance, gestures, gaze or eye contact, posture, proximity, touch, latency of responses in conversation, speech duration and word count, and speech dysfluencies. Categories of observable social skills are presented in Table 2-1 (Bellack, 1994; Wilkinson & Canter, 1983).

Most of these behaviors are readily observed and quantifiable for purposes of evaluation. Ideally, such observations would be carried out in naturalistic settings. This type of in vivo observation, however, is generally impractical. Consequently, most behavioral observations are conducted via analog tasks (i.e., clinic or laboratory simulations of real-world interpersonal encounters). One example of such a procedure is a role-play test in which the individual is asked to respond to prearranged social scenarios. Responses are typically video- or audiotaped and retrospectively rated on the aforementioned verbal and nonverbal behaviors. Role-play tests devised for use with other populations can be adapted to assess performance in situations more relevant to older adults (Hersen, Bellack, & Turner, 1978).

TREATMENT

Several therapeutic strategies have been implemented to (1) (re)shape the social-cognitive processes and perspectives of older individuals and/or (2) teach

Table 2-1. Categories of Measurable Social Skills

Global behaviors

Assertiveness
   Standing up for one's rights
   Making requests of others
   Coping with refusal
   Showing appreciation
   Refusing a request
   Making apologies
Problem-solving ability
Affect appropriate to interpersonal situations
Ability to cope with social anxiety

Verbal behaviors

Conversational language skills (listening/speaking)
   Fluent articulation of thoughts
   Acceptable expression of positive and negative feelings
   Constructive questioning
   Willingness to negotiate/compromise
   Ability to express agreement/disagreement

Nonverbal behaviors

   Facial expression
   Posture and gait
   Proximity
   Personal appearance
   Conversational length sequencing and pacing
   Speech dysfluencies
   Gaze/eye contact
   Gesture
   Touch
   Identifying vocal cues

them new, more functional interpersonal skills. These approaches are described in the sections below.

Cognitive Behavior Therapy

Cognitive behavioral interventions, including Personal Construct Therapy and Rational Emotive Therapy, have been used with older persons in efforts to improve their psychosocial adaptation. For example, Florsheim et al. (1991) adapted the Ellis (1962) "A-B-C" model of emotion to successfully treat a 68-year-old, depressed woman. Therapy involving restructuring of personal constructs, the system of beliefs by which people make sense of the world (Kelly, 1955), was successful in the case of a 75-year-old woman, who following her husband's death had become severely depressed and excessively dependent on her neighbor (Viney, Benjamin, & Preston, 1990). As she "reconstructed" her view of the world (in 10 sessions of instructions and coaching), she reported that depression abated and that she was again able to achieve personal independence.

Social Skills Training

Social skills training has been used increasingly to improve social functioning in older adults. Skills interventions typically involve modification of a variety of verbal and nonverbal response components that have been identified in previous research as important for effective social performance (Donohue, Acierno, Van Hasselt, & Hersen, 1995).

Social skill interventions have generally consisted of a combination of direct instruction, performance feedback, role playing, positive reinforcement, behavioral rehearsal, modeling, and homework assignments. Several areas under the rubric of social skills have been targeted for change in older adults, including positive and negative assertion, friendship-making, and conversational skills. Further, social skills training for older adults has been conducted in both institutional and community settings.

Institutional Programs

Much of the social skills training with the elderly has been conducted in institutional contexts. These endeavors have yielded varied results. For example, Berger and Rose (1977) designed a behavioral program to train 25 elderly nursing home patients in interpersonal skills. This intervention incorporated coaching, modeling, behavior rehearsal, feedback, and a "step-by-step," sequential development of skills. Results indicate that residents who received skills training, relative to nontrained controls, displayed increased rates of social behaviors in situations for which responses had been explicitly taught. Results of role-play assessments, however, revealed that newly acquired skills did not appear to generalize to novel situations. Unfortunately, however, gains were not maintained at a 2-month follow-up (Berger, 1979).

In a social skills training effort with 66 psychogeriatric patients, Lopez (1980) combined precounseling with different levels of "overlearning." Overlearning involved repeated behavioral rehearsal for more trials than needed to produce desired changes in behavior. Moderate overlearning enhanced skill training in the treatment setting. But here again, the newly trained behavior ("expression appreciation") failed to generalize to residential settings.

Ballesteros, Izal, Diaz, Gonzalez, and Souto (1988) developed a conversational skills training for nonpsychiatric residents of a residential care home that yielded significant increases in communication skills, such as receiving information, speaking up, and giving information, in members of the treatment group relative to controls. The 18-session program consisted of behavior rehearsal, feedback, modeling, discriminative and verbal reinforcement, verbal instructions, and homework. Treated residents also demonstrated a significant decrease in scores on the Zung Self-Rating Scale of Depression and a significant increase in self-reported assertion. These changes were maintained at a 3-month follow-up probe.

Vaccaro (1990) exposed six institutionalized aggressive elderly patients (three men and three women) to social skills training that involved instructions, modeling, role playing, and feedback. Observational ratings conducted by staff indicated that all participants displayed reduced rates of aggressive behavior in the training setting, which subsequently generalized to interactions on the ward and in other social situations. Further, these improvements were still evident 5 months following formal termination of initial treatment.

Fisher and Carstensen (1990) conducted another study documenting generalization effects. Three female nursing home residents were trained in conversational skills using instructions, modeling, coaching, role playing, feedback, and contingency management strategies. Direct observations of positive, negative, and neutral social interactions with staff members, nursing home visitors, and other residents revealed improved quality of interchanges outside of training and in more naturalistic settings.

Community-Based Programs

Enhancement of social functioning in community-based elderly persons has received only a modicum of attention, although these endeavors have met with some success. In one of these efforts, Toseland and Rose (1978) evaluated the relative efficacy of (1) behavioral rehearsal, (2) training in problem-solving skills training, and (3) group work for teaching social skills in 53 volunteers age 55 or older recruited from a Wisconsin community. A 3-month follow-up role play and self-report assessment showed an improvement in subjects' ability to deal with difficult interpersonal situations that required assertive behavior. However, there were no significant differences found among three interventions.

In another study, a 6-week assertiveness training course based on identification of specific problem situations, role play, and utilization of behavioral homework assignments improved interpersonal power relationships and self-concept of 42 participants, age 65 or older (Franzke, 1987). Findings were based on change scores on the Assertiveness Inventory and the Burger Scale for Expressed Acceptance of Self.

Six moderately depressed, isolated older women were trained, using a brief, structured social skills approach that invoked role play, homework, and individually selected target behaviors, such as beginning conversations, paying compliments, and dealing with difficult people (Engels & Poser, 1987). Results were evaluated using audiotaped behavioral role plays; self-report measures of assertion, self-esteem, and symptomology; and individualized goal attainment scales. A 3-month follow-up indicated that all subjects evinced gains in interpersonal performance.

A 23-session group program for older Hispanic clients focused on development of personal skills (communication of feelings, differences in communication styles, and body language), interpersonal skills (assertion training and effective listening), and group skills (goal setting and problem setting) (Edinberg, 1986). Changes in the seven females and one male were assessed informally in the group context during final sessions. Participants were better able to verbalize feelings and use specific communication and interpersonal skills in their daily lives as a function of treatment.

In a series of case studies, Engels (1991) reported positive outcome with brief intervention among community-based older adults. Social skills training included behavioral role play, goal setting, and cognitive restructuring. Engels argues that the most effective programs incorporate a concrete rationale and goal setting, high levels of structure and predictability, and stepwise, sequential learning.

Using a multiple baseline design, Donohue et al. (1995) carefully assessed the effects of social skills training (SST) with a 65-year-old woman suffering from major depression (Geriatric Depression Scale Score of 22) and severe macular degeneration. During baseline assessment, this client's Wolpe-Lazarus Assertiveness Scale scores were 15 and 14, reflecting marked unassertiveness. During the course of the initial assessment (which included administration of the Structured Clinical Interview for DSM-III-R; Spitzer, Williams, Gibbon, & First, 1992), the client reviewed her difficulties adjusting to macular degeneration, including confrontations with others in the environment, markedly diminished social activity, and failure to perform daily living skills. Over the 2 years since the visual diagnosis was made, the client had become progressively more socially isolated to the point that she was uneasy when requesting assistance and social support from friends. Prior to her visual impairment, the client had enjoyed a healthy and productive social life.

Role-played scenarios germane to the client's situation, requiring negative assertion, requests for assistance, and social involvement, were developed and videotaped during baseline, treatment, and the 7-month follow-up period. A skills approach, involving instructions, role playing, modeling, feedback, and positive reinforcement, was applied subsequently for negative assertion, requests for assistance, and social involvement in multiple baseline fashion in both clinic and home settings until preset criteria were met. Specific targeted skills (negative assertion, requests for assistance, and social involvement) improved considerably. More importantly, there were dramatic decreases in depressive symptomatology to a nonclinical level and concomitant increases in the client's ratings of happiness. That is, as assertiveness for a variety of categories improved, the client's depression dropped (Geriatric Depression Scale score of 7 at the end of initial treatment). Gains in social skill generally were maintained during the 7-month follow-up period, with exception of the 6-month probe, when booster treatment was required to bring about renewed improvement. Particularly striking was the client's improved mood after social involvement was targeted. At that juncture, she was able to increase frequency of social requests with success.

The social skill treatment protocol that was used in the aforementioned case has been expanded to a full-length treatment manual by Donohue, Acierno, Hersen, and Van Hasselt (1995b). The manual describes the social skills training approach in an initial 12-session format for the treatment of older depressed, visually impaired adults. The social skills training strategy focuses on increasing frequency and level of effectiveness with which visually impaired older adults interact with others across three interpersonal spheres (e.g., negative assertion, requesting assistance, and requesting social involvement). As previously documented in Donohue et al. (1995), the thrust of the social skill intervention is to maximize social integration and forestall social isolation. In addition to specified treatment strategies, our empirically derived program employs standardized assessment measures (e.g., role-played vignettes, questionnaires) to evaluate therapeutic progress on a repeated basis. During the subsequent 6-month maintenance phase, four booster sessions are carried out to reinforce and consolidate efforts to apply social skills in the environment and to reestablish any skills where there may be some decrements. Emphasis during maintenance is on reviewing effective utilization of social skills and problem-solving difficulties that have been encountered in the postinitial treatment period.

Over the past decade, Lewinsohn's Coping With Depression (CWD) course, which focuses on increasing frequency and quality of rewarding social interactions, has been adapted for use with older clients (Lewinsohn, Hoberman, & Clarke, 1989; Lewinsohn, Munoz, Youngren, & Zeiss, 1986; Zeiss & Lewinsohn, 1986). Participants in CWD are taught to monitor their moods, improve their sense of well-being through relaxation training, and increase frequency of pleasant events while decreasing negative events related to mood changes. The structured, specific, and concrete nature of this approach makes it particularly suitable to the older adult population (Teri, 1983). Indeed, a psychoeducational approach incorporating CWD to train 68 community-dwelling older adults in coping skills (including social interaction to counteract depression) yielded promising results (Thompson & Gallagher, 1983). That is, participants in a 6-week course reported significant improvement in level of life satisfaction and social activity and a concurrent diminution in negative cognitions on a variety of self-report measures.

Table 2-2 summarizes research findings in the area of social skills training with both institutionalized and community-dwelling older adults.

SUMMARY

Adaptation to stressors and challenges encountered in old age is a complex and often problematic process for human beings. New and often undesired social roles; personal, material, and social status losses; and reduced physical and mental abilities result in affective, cognitive, and behavioral problems for many older individuals.

Despite the recent heightened interest in the psychological aspects of aging, the process of social adaptation in older adults has received relatively little

Table 2-2. Social Skills Training with Older Adults

Reference	No. and type of subjects	Type and length of treatment	Method of assessment	Outcome
Institutionalized				
Ballesteros et al. (1988)	16 care home residents; 11 women, 5 men; age range, 78–81 years; mean age, 79 years	Social skills training; behavioral rehearsal, feedback, modeling, discriminative reinforcement, verbal instructions, homework. Two 90-minute sessions for 9 weeks (18 total)	Structured social skills interview; Zung Self-Rating Depression Scale. Rathus Assertiveness Scale, Conflictive Situations in Institutions For the Elderly Inventory	Treatment group scored lowest on Zung Scale, increased conversational skills and assertive behavior, decreased aggressive and inhibited responses
Berger (1979) Berger & Rose (1977)	25 nursing home patients; 14 women, 11 men; age range, 47–97 years; mean age, 77 years	Interpersonal skills training; coaching, modeling, rehearsal feedback. Three 45-minute to 1-hour sessions on 8 social situations	Role play of situations presented in training rated by trained judges	Skills Training subjects increased social skills over controls; unable to maintain advantage at 2-month follow-up
Fisher & Carstensen (1990)	3 female nursing home residents; age range, 79–89 years	Direct training for specific skills; problem presentation, coaching, behavioral principles training, modeling. role playing, feedback, discussion. Training to mastery of skills criteria over 14 weeks	Behavior Role Play Test modified from Berger; observer ratings of nursing home behavior	Increased frequency and quality of interactions in natural settings
Hoyer et al. (1982)	49 inpatients of state psychiatric hospital; 33 women, 16 men; mean age, 66.8 years	Structured Learning Therapy (SLT); modeling, role playing, performance feedback and transfer therapy for selected skills (Goldstein et al., 1976). Twelve groups met 5 times over 2 weeks for 40 minutes	Direct Test: response to audiotaped vignettes; Minimal Transfer Test: response to novel vignettes; Role Play Test: all tests evaluated by trainers	Subject acquired selected skills: "expressing a complaint"

Study	Sample	Treatment	Measures	Results
Lopez (1980)	66 inpatients of state psychiatric hospital; maean age, 65.5 years	Half of subjects received precounseling prior to training; training was Structured Learning Therapy: modeling, role playing, social reinforcement, transfer training Overlearning stressed	Direct Test; Minimal Transfer Test; Role Play Test	All treatment groups acquired targeted skill; medium overlearning enhanced skill transfer, high overlearning decreased skill acquisition and transfer, precounseling had no effect
Vaccaro (1990)	6 verbally aggressive elderly; 3 women, 3 men; age range, 62–71 years; mean range, 66 years	Instructions, modeling, role play, and feedback One 60-minute session weekly for 18 weeks	Observation and rating by staff members	Decreased aggressive behavior generalized to social situations; improvement maintained at 5-month follow-up
Community-dwelling				
Donohue et al. (1995)	65-year-old depressed female with visual impairment	Social skills training; fifteen 1-hour sessions during initial treatment; 4 booster sessions during 7-month follow-up	Role-Played Performance Test; Requests for Assistance; Social Involvement Requests; Wolpe-Lazurus Assertiveness Test; Geriatric Depression Scale; Weekly Happiness Ratings	Improvement on all measures, including behavioral and self-report at conclusion of initial treatment and maintained during booster treatment
Edinberg (1986)	8 Hispanic elderly; 7 women and 1 male; mean age, 71.3 years	23, 30-minute therapy groups focused on personal skills, interpersonal skills, and group skills	Observation, informal rating by group leaders	Increased in ability to verbalize feelings and use communication skills
Engels (1991)	3 women; age range, 63–70 years	Social skills training; screening, behavioral role play, homework, goal setting, cognitive assessment and restructuring; 10 weekly sessions, 60 to 90 minutes	Individual case study	Improvements in target behaviors; enhanced subjective well-being

(continued)

Table 2-2. *(Continued)*

Reference	No. and type of subjects	Type and length of treatment	Method of assessment	Outcome
Community-dwelling (cont.)				
Engels & Poser (1987)	6 women; age range, 62–70 years	Structured social skills training; identification of target behavior role play, homework; 9 initial group sessions over 5 weeks; 3 booster sessions over 3 months	Audiotaped behavioral role plays of target behaviors; depression, anxiety, and interpersonal sensitivity scales of the Symptom Checklist Goal Attainment Scaling	At 3 months all subjects improved targeted behaviors
Franzke (1987)	42 AARP, Nutrition Center members over 65: 26 women and 16 men	Assertiveness training; identification of problem situations, role play, behavioral homework; 6 different groups for weekly sessions	Expressed Acceptance of Self Scale; Assertiveness Inventory	Self-reported improved self-concept and effectiveness in interpersonal power relationships
Thompson-Gallagher (1983)	68 Community-dwelling elders; 95% white female, 2% white male, 3% nonwhite female; mean age, 68.4 years; age range, 60–82 years	Lewinsohn's Coping with Depression Course: psychoeducational program of mood monitoring everyday, monitoring everyday pleasant activities and unpleasant events, goal setting, self-reward techniques; 6 weekly 2-hour classes	Beck Depression Inventory (BDI), Life Satisfaction Index (LSI-Z), Automatic Thoughts Questionnaire (ATQ). Older Persons Pleasant Events Schedule, Older Persons Unpleasant Events Schedule	Decline in depression at 2 months follow-up; decrease in negative cognitions; increase in life satisfaction and activity level
Toseland & Rose (1978)	53 Wisconsin community residents; 75% women, 25% men; age range, 55–85 years, mean age, 69.2 years	Behavioral role play; problem solving; social group work	Audiotaped role play test rated by trainers; Gambrill-Ritchey Assertion Inventory, Group Evaluation Inventory	Increased ability to handle difficult interpersonal situations

investigative attention. From our review, however, it is apparent that older adults are not homogeneous and that their difficulties adapting to life are, in fact, quite significant and varied.

At present, type of residential setting is often used to distinguish among groups of older persons for purposes of assessing social functioning and treating related problems. Thus, community-dwelling elders are differentiated from residents of nursing and retirement homes, as well as from persons in psychogeriatric settings. While these distinctions are to some extent understandable and useful, they neglect more relevant disparities among older adults. Assessment strategies and interventions based on more relevant diversity factors, such as gender, socioeconomic status, education level, cultural and ethnic background, cognitive functioning, and/or affective status, need to be developed and refined. Criteria that acknowledge the heterogeneity of the older population are needed to evaluate more precisely the experiences, abilities, and needs specific to such older adults. Level of social adaptation could prove to be one such useful criterion.

Beyond the issue of diversity, older individuals often encounter more varied problems than their younger counterparts. Therefore, the importance of developing specific techniques for evaluation of social adaptation in older adults is evident. Increased consensus on specific behaviors associated with quality of life (indicative of successful social adaptation) would make such assessments more precise.

Care must be taken to assess and treat older adults on an individual basis. Appropriate evaluation and treatment for one 80-year-old person might not be suited to another person the same age. For elderly persons with more intact perceptual and cognitive capacities, verbal therapy with or without skills training may be adequate. For those with organic brain dysfunction or the chronically mentally ill, however, structured behavioral treatment regimens (e.g., contingency management, and/or repeated skills training and behavioral rehearsal) are requisites.

Social skills training has been the focus of recent efforts to improve the quantity and quality of social interactions in older adults who may have difficulty adapting to their environments. These remedial activities are based on early findings showing that increased social interaction has a positive influence on the quality of life for both younger and older persons. Further, both institutionalized and more functional, community-dwelling elders have been treated using different psychoeducational techniques, with mixed, though encouraging, results.

REFERENCES

Abrahams, R., & Patterson, R. (1979). Psychological distress among the community elderly: Prevalence, characteristics, and implications for service. *International Journal of Aging and Human Development, 1,* 1–18.
Atchley, R. C. (1977). *The social forces in later life: An introduction to social gerontology.* Belmont, CA: Wadsworth.

Bahr, S. J., & Peterson, E. T. (1989). *Aging and the family.* Lexington, MA: Lexington Books.

Ballesteros, R. F., Izal, M., Diaz, P., Gonzalez, J. L., & Souto, E. (1988). Training of conversational skills with institutionalized elderly: A preliminary study. *Perceptual and Motor Skills, 66,* 923–926.

Bandura, A. (1982). Self-efficacy mechanism in human agency. *American Psychologist, 37,* 122–147.

Bellack, A. S. (1994). Treatment of chronically mentally ill patients. Workshop presented at Nova Southeastern University, Ft. Lauderdale, FL.

Bellack, A. S., Hersen, M. (Eds.). (1979). *Research and practice in social skills training.* New York: Plenum Press.

Bellack, A. S., & Hersen, M., & Himmelhoch, J. M. (1996). Social skills training for depression: A treatment manual. In V. B. Van Hasselt & M. Hersen (Eds.), *Sourcebook of psychological treatment manuals for adult disorders.* New York: Plenum Press.

Bennett, R. (1973). Living conditions and everyday needs of the elderly with particular reference to social isolation. *International Journal of Aging and Human Development, 4,* 179–198.

Bennett, R. (1980). *Aging, isolation, and resocialization.* New York: Van Nostrand Reinhold.

Berger, R. M. (1979). Training the institutionalized elderly in interpersonal skills. *Social Work, 24,* 420–423.

Berger, R. M., & Rose, S. D. (1977). Interpersonal skill training with institutionalized elderly patients. *Journal of Gerontology, 32,* 346–352.

Blazer, D. (1982). *Depression in late life.* St. Louis: C. V. Mosby.

Busse, E.W. (1992). Quality of life: Affect and mood in late life. In M. Bergener, K. Hasegawa, S. Finkel, & T. Nishimura (Eds.), *Aging and mental disorders: International perspectives* (pp. 38–55). New York: Springer.

Busse, E.W., & Maddox, E. L. (1985). *The Duke longitudinal studies of normal aging: Overview of history, design, and findings.* New York: Springer.

Busse, E.W., & Pfeiffer, E. (1973). *Mental illness in later life.* Washington, DC: American Psychiatric Association.

Busse, E.W., & Pfeiffer, E. (1977). Functional psychiatric disorders in old age. In E.W. Busse & E. Pfeiffer (Eds.) *Behavior and adaptation in late life* (2nd ed.). Boston: Little, Brown.

Butcher, J. N. (1990). *The MMPI-2 in psychological treatment.* New York: Oxford University Press.

Butler, R. N., & Gleason, H. P. (1985). *Productive aging.* New York: Springer.

Butler, R. N., & Lewis, M. I. (1977). *Aging and mental health: Positive psychosocial approaches.* St. Louis: C. V. Mosby.

Bytheway, B., Keil, T., Allatt, P., & Bryman, A. (1989). *Becoming and being old: sociological approaches to later life.* Newbury Park, CA: Sage.

Cohen, C. J., Teresi, J., & Holmes, D. (1985). Social networks, stress, adaptation, and health. *Research on Aging, 7,* 409–431.

Cumming, E. (1964). New thoughts on the theory of disengagement. In R. J. Kastenbaum (Ed.), *New thoughts on old age.* New York: Springer.

Cumming, E., & Henry, W. E. (1961). *Growing old: The process of disengagement.* New York: Basic Books.

Dolen, L. S., & Bearison, D. J. (1982). Social interaction and social cognition in aging: A contextual analysis. *Human Development, 25,* 430–442.

Donohue, B., Acierno, R., Hersen, M., & Van Hasselt, V. B. (1995a). Social skills training for depressed, visually impaired older adults: A treatment manual. *Behavior Modification, 19,* 379–424.

Donohue, B., Acierno, R., Van Hasselt, V. B., & Hersen, M. (1995b). Social skills training in a depressed, visually impaired older adult. *Journal of Behavior Therapy and Experimental Psychiatry, 26,* 65–75.

D'Zurilla, T. J. (1986). *Problem solving therapy: A social competence approach to clinical intervention.* New York: Springer.

D'Zurilla, T. J., & Sheedy, C. F. (1992). The relation between social problem-solving ability and subsequent level of academic competence in college students. *Cognitive Therapy and Research, 16,* 589–599.

Edinberg, M. A. (1986). Social competency training with hispanic elderly. *Clinical Gerontologist, 4,* 56–58.

Ellis, A. (1962). *Reason and emotion in psychotherapy.* New York: Lyle Stuart.

Engels, M. (1991). The promotion of positive social interaction through social skills training. In P. A. Wisocki (Ed.), *Handbook of clinical behavior therapy with the elderly client.* (pp. 185–202). New York: Plenum Press.

Engels, M., & Poser, E. (1987). Social skills training with older women. *Clinical Gerontologist, 6,* 70–73.

Ernst, P., Beran, B., Safford, F., & Kleinhauz, M. (1978). Isolation and the symptoms of chronic brain syndrome. *The Gerontologist, 18,* 468–474.

Fisher, J. E., & Carstensen, L. L. (1990). Generalized effects of skills training among older adults. *Clinical Gerontologist, 9,* 91–107.

Florsheim, M. J., Leavesley, G., Hanley-Peterson, P., & Gallagher-Thompson, D. (1991). An expansion of the A-B-C approach to cognitive/behavioral therapy. *Clinical Gerontologist, 10,* 65–69.

Franzke, A.W. (1987). The effects of assertiveness training on older adults. *The Gerontologist, 27,* 13–16.

Frisch, M. B. (1988a). *Quality of life inventory.* Waco, TX: Baylor University, Psychology Department.

George, L. K., & Fillenbaum, G. G. (1985). OARS methodology: SA decade of experience in geriatric assessment. *Journal of the American Geriatrics Society, 33,* 607–615.

Goldfried, M. R., & D'Zurilla, T. J. (1969). A behavioral-analytic model for assessing competence. In C. D. Spielberger (Ed.), *Current topics in clinical and community psychology* (Vol. 1, pp. 151–196). New York: Academic Press.

Goldstein, A. P., Sprafkin, R. P., & Gershaw, N. J. (1976). *Skill training for community living: Applied structured learning therapy.* New York: Pergamon Press.

Goodstein, R. K. (1985). Common clinical problems in the elderly: Camouflaged by ageism and atypical presentation. *Psychiatric Annals, 43,* 99–312.

Hersen, M., Bellack, A., & Turner, S. (1978). Assessment of assertiveness in female psychiatric patients: Motor and autonomic measures. *Journal of Behavior Therapy and Experimental Psychiatry, 9,* 11–16.

Hersen, M., Kabacoff, R. I., Ryan, C. F., Null, J. A., Melton, M. A., Pagan, V., Segal, D. L., & Van Hasselt, V. B. (1995a). Psychometric properties of the Wolpe-Lazarus Assertiveness Scale for older visually impaired adults. *International Journal of Rehabilitation and Health, 1,* 179–187.

Hersen, M., Kabacoff, R. I., Van Hasselt, V. B., Null, J. A., Ryan, C. F., Melton, M., & Segal, D. (1995b). Assertiveness, depression, and social support in older visually impaired adults. *Journal of Visual Impairment and Blindness, 89,* 524–530.

Hersen, M., & Van Hasselt, V. B. (1992). Behavioral assessment and treatment of anxiety in the elderly. *Clinical Psychology Review, 12,* 619–640.

Hersen, M., Van Hasselt, V. B., & Goreczny, A. J. (1993). Behavioral assessment of anxiety in older adults: Some comments. *Behavior Modification, 17,* 99–112.

Hersen, M., & Van Hasselt, V., & Segal, D. (1995). Social adaptation in older visually impaired adults: Some comments. *International Journal of Rehabilitation and Health, 1,* 49–60.

Hoyer, W. J., Lopez, M. A., & Goldstein, A. P. (1982). Predicting social skill acquisition and transfer by psychogeriatric patients. *International Journal of Behavioral Geriatrics, 1,* 43–46.

Kahle, L. R., & Timmer, S. G. (1983). A theory and method for studying values. In L. R. Kahle (Ed.), *Social values and social change: Adaptation to life in America.* New York: Praeger.

Kelly, G. A. (1955). *The psychology of personal constructs* (Vols. 1 & 2). New York: Norton.

Kimmel, D. C. (1980). *Adulthood and aging: An interdisciplinary, developmental view.* New York: Wiley.

Kimmel, D. C. (1988). Ageism, psychology, and public, policy. *American Psychologist, 43,* 175–178.

Kogan, E. S., Kabacoff, R. I., Hersen, M. & Van Hasselt, V. B. (1994). Clinical cutoffs for the Beck Depression Inventory and the Geriatric Depression Scale with older adult psychiatric outpatients. *Journal of Psychopathology and Behavioral Assessment, 16,* 233–242.

Kogan, E. S., Van Hasselt, V. B., Hersen, M., & Kabacoff, R. I. (1995). Relationship of depression, assertiveness, and social support in community-dwelling older adults. *Journal of Clinical Geropsychology, 1,* 157–163.

Kosberg, J. I., & Garcia, J. L. (1988). The problems of older clients seen at a family service agency: Treatment and program implications. *Journal of Gerontological Social Work, 11,* 141–153.

Kuypers, J., & Bengston, V. (1973). Competence and social breakdown. A social-psychological view of aging. *Human Development, 16,* 37–49.

Lawton, M. P., Patniak, B., & Kleban, M. H. (1976). The ecology of adaptation to a new environment. *International Journal of Aging and Human Development, 7,* 15–26.

Levy, S. (1981). The aging woman: Developmental issues and mental health needs. *Professional Psychology, 12,* 92–102.

Lewinsohn, P. M., Antonuccio, D. O., Steinmetz, J. L., & Teri, L. (1984). *The coping with depression course.* Eugene, OR: Castalia.

Lewinsohn, P. M., Hoberman, H. M., & Clarke, G. N. (1989). Coping with depression course: Review and future directions. *Canadian Journal of Behavioral Science, 21,* 470–493.

Lewinsohn, P. M., Munoz, R. F., Youngren, M. A., & Zeiss, A. M. (1986). *Control your depression.* Revised and Updated. Englewood Cliffs, NJ: Prentice-Hall.

Lezak, M. D. (1983). *Neuropsychological assessment* (2nd Ed.). New York: Oxford University Press.

Lopez, M. A. (1980). Social skills training with institutionalized elderly: Effects of precounseling structuring and overlearning on skill acquisition and transfer. *Journal of Counseling Psychology, 27,* 286–293.

McIntosh, J. (1989). Official U.S. elderly suicide data base: Levels, availability, omissions. *Omega: Journal of Death and Dying, 19,* 337–350.

Morrison, R. L., & Bellack, A. S. (1981). The role of social perception in social skill. *Behavioral Therapy, 12,* 69–79.

Neisser, U. (1967). *Cognitive psychology.* New York: Appleton-Century-Crofts.

Neugarten, B. L. (1974). Age groups in American society and the rise of the young old. *Annals of American Academy of Science, September,* 187–198.

Olin, J. T., Schneider, L. S., Eaton, E. M., Zemansky, M. F., & Pollock, V. E. (1992). The Geriatric Depression Scale and the Beck Depression Inventory as screening instruments in an older adult outpatient population. *Psychological Assessment, 4,* 190–192.

Palmore, E. (1969). Predicting longevity. *Gerontologist, 9,* 247.

Pfeiffer, E. (1970). Survival in old age: Physical, psychological, and social correlates of longevity. *Journal of the American Geriatrics Society, 18,* 273–289.

Piaget, J. (1952). *The origins of intelligence in children.* New York: International Universities Press.

Ross, H., & Kedward, H. (1978). Social functioning and self-care in hospitalized psychogeriatric patients. *Journal of Nervous and Mental Disease, 166,* 25–33.

Rothenberg, B. B. (1970). Children's social sensitivity and the relationship to interpersonal competence, interpersonal comfort, and intellectual level. *Developmental Psychology, 2,* 335–350.

Spitzer, R. L., Williams, J. B., Gibbon, M., & First, M. B. (1992). The Structured Clinical Interview for DSM-III-R (SCID). *Archives of General Psychiatry, 49,* 624–629.

Sprafkin, R. P. (1984). Social skills training. In R. J. Corsini (Ed.), *Encyclopedia of psychology.* New York: Wiley.

Stein, S., Linn, M.W., & Stein, E. (1982). The relationship of self-help networks to physical and psychosocial functioning. *Journal of the American Geriatrics Society, 30,* 764–768.

Stevens-Long, J. (1979). *Adult life: Developmental processes.* Palo Alto, CA: Mayfield.

Sulzman, C. (1989). Treatment of the agitated demented elderly patient. *Hospital and Community Psychiatry, 39,* 1143–1144.

Tagiuri, R. (1969). Person perception. In G. Lindzey & E. Aronson (Eds.), *The handbook of social psychology* (Vol. 3). Reading, MA: Addison-Wesley.

Tallmer, M. (1973). A current issue in social gerontology. *Journal of Geriatric Psychiatry, 6,* 99–108.

Teri, L. (1983). The role of age in the treatment of depression: Unanswered questions. *Psychotherapy in Private Practice, 1,* 29–31.

Thompson, L.W., & Gallagher, D. (1983). A psychoeducational approach for treatment of depression in elders. *Psychotherapy in Private Practice, 1,* 25–28.

Toseland, R., & Rose, S. D. (1978). Evaluating social skills training for older adults in groups. *Social Work Research & Abstracts, 14,* 25–33.

Trower, P. E., & Argyle, M. (1978). *Social skills and mental health.* London: Methuen.

Tunstall, J. (1966). *Old and alone.* London: Routledge Kegan Paul.

U.S. Bureau of Census. (1993). *Population profile of the United States: 1993.* Washington, DC: U.S. Government Printing Office.

U.S. Department of Health, Education, and Welfare. (1976). *Facts about older Americans.* Washington, DC: U.S. Government Printing Office.

Vacarro, F. J. (1990). Application of social skills training in a group of institutionalized aggressive elderly subjects. *Psychology and Aging, 5,* 369–378.

Viney, L. L., Benjamin, Y. N., & Preston, C. (1990). Personal construct therapy for the elderly. *Journal of Cognitive Psychotherapy, 4,* 211–224.

White House Domestic Policy Council. (1993). *Health security preliminary plan summary.* Washington, DC: U.S. Government Printing Office.

Wilkinson, J., & Canter, S. (1983). *Social Skills Training Manual: Assessment, program design, and management of training.* New York: Wiley.

Wixted, J. T., Morrison, R. L., & Bellack, A. S. (1988). Social skills training in the treatment of negative symptoms. *International Journal of Mental Health, 17,* 3–21.

Wolk, S., & Kurtz, J. (1975). Positive adjustment and involvement during aging and expectancy for internal control. *Journal of Consulting and Clinical Psychology, 43,* 173–178.

Yesavage, J. A., Brink, T. L., & Rose, T. L. (1983). Development and validation of a geriatric depression screening scale: A preliminary report. *Journal of Psychiatric Research, 17,* 37–49.

Zeiss, A. M., & Lewinsohn, P. M. (1986). Adapting behavioral treatment of depression to meet the needs of the elderly. *The Clinical Psychologist, Fall,* 98–100.

Zigler, E., & Phillips, L. (1960). Social effectiveness and symptomatic behaviors. *Journal of Abnormal and Social Psychology, 62,* 231–238.

Zigler, E., & Phillips, L. (1961). Social competence and outcome in mental disorder. *Journal of Abnormal Psychology, 63,* 264–271.

CHAPTER 3

Assessment of Older Adults

Barry Edelstein, Natalie Staats, Kimberly D. Kalish, and Lynn Emer Northrop

---

INTRODUCTION

The psychological assessment of older adults poses challenges for the clinician comparable to those faced by such eminent sleuths as Hercule Poirot, Jessica Fletcher, and even Sherlock Holmes. Indeed, anyone drawn to murder mysteries would find the assessment of older adults an equally challenging, intriguing, and

---

Barry Edelstein, Natalie Staats, Kimberly D. Kalish, and Lynn Emer Northrop • Department of Psychology, West Virginia University, Morgantown, West Virginia 26506-6040.

Psychological Treatment of Older Adults: An Introductory Text, edited by Michel Hersen and Vincent B. Van Hasselt. Plenum Press, New York, 1996.

provocative undertaking. The thorough assessment of an older adult has many of the characteristics of a murder investigation, requiring consideration of the intimate interplay of physical, psychological, and environmental variables. Any investigator or clinician worthy of his or her salt would, for example, question everyone familiar with the behavior of the individual of interest (never trusting one source), directly inspect the environment in which behaviors of interest occurred, employ the most accurate, reliable, and valid measurement instruments, gather clues resulting from the interactions of the target individual with the environment, obtain descriptions or directly observe the interaction of the target individual with significant others, determine who gained and who suffered as a consequence of the individual's behavior, assemble clues (assessment results) from multiple sources to establish convergent validity for hypotheses, and systematically test hypotheses until a satisfactory and empirically defensible conclusion could be reached. Though the assessment of older adults and the investigation of a murder share principles and procedures, they part company with the consideration of their functions, notwithstanding the analogous relationship between a murderer and a disease or disorder. A host of assessment functions could be articulated, as older adults are assessed for a variety of reasons. The most common reasons for assessment are to determine (1) whether an individual is cognitively impaired, (2) what constitutes the best placement for an individual, (3) the extent and nature of functional capacity, (4) the capacity to make decisions, (5) whether an individual is appropriate for nursing home placement (e.g., PASARR evaluations), (6) diagnosis, (7) a plan for appropriate interventions or care, and (8) the effects of interventions and/or care.

In the following sections we will discuss many of the factors one should consider when assessing an older adult. An exhaustive discussion of such factors is beyond the scope of this chapter. However, we will address what we believe are the most salient issues in older adult assessment. We will begin with a presentation of various factors that could influence assessment results and follow this with discussions of psychometric considerations, factors to consider when selecting an assessment method, and multidimensional assessment. We will end with a brief discussion of the psychometric properties of the assessment instruments frequently used with older adults.

CONSIDERATIONS IN ASSESSING
OLDER ADULTS

Biases

Before one looks to the environment for factors influencing the assessment process, one must first consider one's own potential biases and their possible influence on the assessment process. Clinicians are not immune to holding negative, prejudicial beliefs about older adults, termed *ageism* by Butler (1969). Lack of knowledge about older adults can produce a set of false beliefs that can influence behavior toward them (Rodeheaver, 1990). Among the false beliefs are the following: "(1) aging brings an end to productivity; (2) the aged naturally desire to disengage from society; (3) older people are inflexible, set in their ways; (4) senility is a normal part of aging; and (5) the aged are (or should be) serene and accepting of these changes" (pp. 1–2). Such beliefs can affect many aspects of assessment and treatment planning (Dupree & Patterson, 1985). For example, interviewers working with older adults have been found to dominate the interview, be less respectful, less patient, and less engaged than with younger adults (Greene, Adelman, Charon, & Hoffman, 1986). Gatz and Pearson (1988) argued that generalized age biases may affect individual older clients, offering the example of depression, which may be overlooked, misdiagnosed, or treated differently or less effectively than it would be in younger adults. In light of the foregoing, it behooves the clinician to consider his or her general knowledge of older adults and notions about age-specific deficits and excesses before proceeding with assessment of an older adult.

Psychological Considerations

Some older adults experience attention deficits, cautiousness, low performance expectations, and related performance anxiety (cf. Eisdorfer, 1968), motivation difficulties (time and energy expenditure), and a variety of fears associated with aging, each of which can influence the results of assessment and may, in some cases, be the foci of assessment. Though older adults may experience many of the same psychiatric disorders as younger adults, the form taken in older adults can be quite different. For example, the objects of older adult fears may differ from those of younger adults. Older adults are more likely to fear mental and physical decline (see Fry, 1986, for a discussion). Older adults may fear loss of sensory processes, falling, decline of cognitive capacities, loneliness, physical, illness, physical disability, strangers, separation from significant others, pain, and loss of control of bodily functions.

Psychopathology in older adults can lead to performance decrements that might not be expected from younger adults. For example, Kennelly, Hayslip, and Richardson (1985) found that older adults who are more depressed and/or who experience response-independent feedback demonstrate greater degrees of impaired performance on measures of verbal-auditory short-term memory than do younger adults. Similarly, Hayslip, Kennelly, and Maloy (1990) demonstrated that older depressed individuals, as compared to older nondepressed individuals, had greater impairment on tasks requiring effortful processing and were more prone to report fatigue.

Physiological Considerations

The physiological changes to be discussed in this section occur to a variable extent with older adults and should not be viewed as inevitable consequences of aging.

Sensory Systems

Sensory deficits can have both direct and indirect effects on the physical and psychological integrity of the older adult, requiring the clinician's attention to factors that are often of less importance or relevance for the assessment of healthy younger adults. Such deficits can influence information processing, mobility, independence, social behavior, and even self-concept. We will attempt to touch on a few selected sensory deficits that deserve the assessor's attention. The interested reader is referred to Whitbourne and Powers (1996) for more detailed discussions of physiological changes accompanying the normal aging process.

Visual System

Changes in the visual system can lead to numerous changes in behavior or test performance that are of importance to a clinician. Decreased pupil size (miosis), pigmentation (opacification) and thickening of the lens, and loss of elasticity in the lens capsule can result in decreased visual acuity (usually presbyopia), with loss of lens elasticity accounting for approximately 90% of the loss in accommodation (Winograd, 1984). Increased lens thickness leads to reduced contrasts at the retina, causing increased light absorption and light scattering within the lens. This results in increased susceptibility to glare and problems resulting from abruptly changing light intensity (Marmor, 1992). As the aqueous humor becomes pigmented over time, the amount of light reaching the retina is reduced and shorter wavelengths of light are absorbed. This results in changes in color perception. The increased lens opacity and the decrease in pupil size that accompanies aging reduces the amount of light reaching the retina by as much as 66% between the ages of 20 and 65. The reduced pupil size combined with decreased retinal metabolism is associated with decreased adaptation to darkness and light (Winograd, 1984). Decreased depth perception occurs with age, with age differences being greatest at short distances where accommodation and convergence are most important. Various diseases (e.g., diabetes mellitus, cataracts, glaucoma, senile macular degeneration, myotonic dystrophy, hypoparathyroidism, Wilson's disease) and medications (phenothiazines, corticosteroids, antibiotics, antimalarials) can also compromise the integrity of the visual system (Hunt & Lindley, 1989; Winograd, 1984).

The foregoing visual deficits could result in diminished performance on tests requiring adequate vision, changes in social behavior resulting from a failure to recognize friends and acquaintances, reluctance to participate in any activity requiring reasonable visual acuity, falls resulting from poor visual acuity, and automobile accidents resulting from glare and rapid changes in light intensity.

When assessing a visually impaired individual, one might consider the following recommendations:

1. Do not assume the examinee's preferred means of communication. Ask the examinee how he or she prefers to communicate. Determine whether the examinee prefers braille, large print, or other means.

2. Ask the examinee to describe any idiosyncrasies involving color, contrast, or field deficits (Shindell, 1989).
3. Ask the examinee to describe any problems with lighting in the assessment room, such as glare or insufficient lighting.
4. Limit nonverbal directions; rely more heavily upon verbal or kinesthetic cueing (Shindell, 1989), and use multimodal (say and do) directions when possible.
5. Be careful when interpreting the behavior of severely visually impaired examinees. For example, the examinee may arrive early for an assessment session or may have rigid scheduling requirements that may be more a function of available transportation than resistance (Shindell, 1989).
6. Avoid using high-gloss paper for self-report inventories, visual aids, and for figure drawing tasks.

Auditory System

Hearing becomes impaired beginning around the age of 25 (Zarit & Zarit, 1987). Pitch discrimination declines steadily until approximately age 55. More dramatic losses occur in the higher frequencies after this age. One in three individuals over the age of 60 suffers from significant hearing impairment (Zarit & Zarit, 1987).

Hearing loss can also result from drugs (e.g., certain antibiotics, aspirin, quinine, alcohol, tobacco, carbon monoxide, certain diuretics), circulatory disorders, noise, and certain organic disorders (e.g., acoustic neuromas, syphilis, multiple sclerosis, cardiovascular accidents, Paget's disease) (Vernon, 1989).

Hearing loss has been associated with social withdrawal, suspiciousness, hostility, depression, and paranoia among older adults. Hearing loss can result in speech perception difficulty in general and significant impairment in the ability to understand broken or rapid speech, and/or in the ability to accurately hear speech in the presence of background noise. Hearing loss can result in a reduction in the number of leisure options (e.g., religious services, television, social gatherings) and can reduce one's ability to recognize emergency situations).

Vernon (1989, p. 155) offered the following recommendations for maximizing the likelihood that an examinee will understand oral communication:

1. Do psychological testing in a quiet setting. Background noises are the worst blocks to the hard-of-hearing person's understanding of speech.
2. Be sure there is good lighting on your (the speaker's) face. The worst situation is a window behind you or any shadow on your face.
3. Face the client and speak slowly and distinctly. Do not overexaggerate your mouth movements.
4. When it is necessary to repeat, try to rephrase the concept being expressed.
5. Position yourself close to the patient.
6. If possible, provide the test questions in writing as well as orally. For example, in administering the Wechsler Adult Intelligence Scale-

Revised (WAIS-R) to hard-of-hearing patients, it is helpful to have the questions and directions typed on individual index cards.

7. If communication breaks down, feel free to write out key words or sentences.
8. Assistive devices such as audio books, FM listening aids, amplifiers, and so on should be used if available and desired by the patient.
9. Be patient. If the client does not understand, help him or her by writing, speaking slower, and so on. Do not show anger or frustration; the client cannot help being hard of hearing.
10. Take frequent breaks. It is a stressful, demanding task for an older hearing-impaired person to lipread a psychologist for an entire psychological evaluation.

Other suggestions include the following:

1. Do not necessarily rely upon the results of audiograms obtained in quiet environments if one is really interested in an examinee's ability to comprehend the examiner's speech. A hearing (speech perception) check should ideally be performed under the conditions of assessment and perhaps in public settings if hearing is suspected of contributing to psychosocial problems.
2. Do not overarticulate, which can distort speech and facial gestures.
3. Be vigilant for selective (i.e., functional) hearing impairment characterized by hearing losses associated with task demands, poor motivation, and perhaps fear of performance failure.
4. Failure to answer a question could result from, among other things, failure to hear or inability to understand (comprehend) the question. In contrast to Vernon's (1989) suggestion, when repeating a question, one might consider phrasing it exactly as it was initially phrased. If the individual doesn't respond, the question can be worded more simply (Zeiss, 1992).
5. Ask only one question at a time.

Somesthetic System

Somesthetic senses also do not escape the aging process, although the effects are less clear-cut than those of other sensory modalities. These senses include information about touch, pressure, pain, and ambient temperature. Aging affects sensations of body orientation and movement (Laidlaw & Hamilton, 1937; Whitbourne, 1985), which must be considered when assessing presenting problems and formulating treatment programs that involve movement and coordination. Though one expects to hear more reports of aches and pains from older adults, evidence about changes in pain thresholds is inconclusive (Whitbourne, 1985). It is difficult to sort out changes in absolute sensitivity to pain from changes in thresholds for reporting pain. Nevertheless, reports of pain must be considered by the clinician. Pain arising from acute and chronic diseases can control patient behavior and easily result in underestimations of performance capabilities.

Musculoskeletal System

When considering movement of older adults, one must not only consider muscle strength and coordination but also the strength and resiliency of the bones and the conditions of the joints involved in the movements (Whitbourne, 1985). This is particularly important when considering the general performance capabilities of an individual and adaptive functioning. From approximately the age of 70 on, considerable loss in muscle strength occurs (30% to 40%), with greater loss occurring in the legs than in the hands and arms (Shephard, 1981, as cited in Whitbourne, 1985). Cartilage and ligaments can become calcified with aging. Degeneration of joint cartilage can cause pain with movement. Again, reports of pain must be considered in light of the effects of pain on an individual's general motor performance, as well as psychological test performance.

Some of the more prevalent motor problems that might influence the assessment process and overall case conceptualization include parkinsonism, essential familial or senile tremor, senile chorea, apraxia, peripheral neuropathies, muscle weakness (myopathy), and the side effects of various medications (e.g., neuroleptics) (Schlenoff, 1989).

Medications

Older adults are more likely to take medications and also more likely to take multiple medications than younger adults (Montamat, Cusack, & Vestal, 1989). Slowed absorption, increased distribution of fat-soluble drugs, and slowed metabolism and excretion of some medications can increase the likelihood of drug toxicity and unwanted side effects (Bressler, 1987; Martin, 1990). Older adults are more sensitive to some drugs and less sensitive to others than younger adults. All of the foregoing factors must be considered when beginning an assessment of an older adult because of the likelihood that some or all of the behaviors of concern may be due to drug toxicity, the interaction of multiple drugs, and/or the side effects of the drugs. Failure to do so can incorrectly result in the attribution of behaviors to acute or chronic diseases or psychiatric disorders.

PSYCHOMETRIC CONSIDERATIONS

Psychological measures are not designed to address the needs of all individuals (Yesavage, 1986). Consideration of the psychometric properties of assessment instruments and methods is of paramount importance when selecting a method or instrument for an older adult. Failure to do so can lead to inaccurate assessment results and their attendant problems (e.g., misdiagnosis, inaccurate research findings, inappropriate treatment choices). Older adults may differ from other age groups in their psychological symptomatology (Himmelfarb & Murrell, 1983), physiological health (Hertzog & Schear, 1989), cognitive abilities (Gallagher, Thompson, & Levy, 1980), and response sets, as previously mentioned in this chapter. All of these factors may contribute to inaccurate assessment outcomes. One must be particularly vigilant with regard to psychometric issues when assessing older adults, since so few instruments have been developed with the older adult in mind. In the remainder of this section we will consider the psychometric properties we believe are most important when considering assessment instruments and methods for older adults.

Norms

Norms refer to the available test result data from individuals in a circumscribed group or specific populations (American Psychological Association, 1985). The availability of normative data for older adults is essential when using norm-based instruments. Comparing assessment results of very capable older adults with those of younger adults, for example, may result in inappropriately lower test scores for older persons (Yesavage, 1986). Though these lower scores may result from physiological changes that occur with age (e.g., slower reaction time and processing speed), they will not cause an older adult to appear less capable than a younger adult when appropriate age-related norms are available. Thus, assessment instruments that have been normed with older adults allow one to interpret performance independent of age-related differences.

Demographic characteristics are also important normative considerations. Older adults vary on such characteristics as occupation, location of residence, educational background, ethnic background, diagnostic group, and socioeconomic status, to name a few (Hertzog & Schear, 1989). The demographics of the sample used to establish norms for the test under consideration should be representative of and generalizable to the individual to be assessed. Moreover, discretion must be used in reporting assessment results in light of any significant differences between the normative population and the individual being assessed. If an assessment measure has not been appropriately normed for an individual, reports of assessment results should explicitly state that interpretation is subject to error as a result of insufficient data on the assessment method (American Psychological Association, 1985). For example, if an older adult with learning disabilities is assessed with an appropriately age-normed measure, but the measure is not normed for individuals with learning disabilities, the lack of diagnostically appropriate norms should be noted when the results are reported and interpreted.

Reliability

Reliability is the "degree to which test scores are free from errors of measurement" (American Psychological Association, 1985). That is, reliability is an index of how well the assessment instrument produces consistent results from the same individual when changes in the individual's performance are accounted for. The most important psychometric properties for standard assessment instruments are internal consistency, interrater reliability, and test–retest reliability. Another reliability consideration that may be of greater importance for interviews is accuracy (White & Edelstein, 1991).

Internal consistency is an estimate of how well each item within a test correlates with the other items and measures the same construct (Kaszniak, 1990). As language and meanings change from generation to generation, one must be particularly conscious of the appropriateness of semantics and their potential effects on responding (Kaszniak, 1990). Age differences in social desirability may also affect the internal consistency of a measure. For example, older adults often respond with less candor to questions regarding sexuality than do younger adults (Yesavage, 1986). Therefore, such questions may be of less value in an instrument when used with older adults (Yesavage, 1986). In addition, certain age-specific illnesses may increase fatigue and reduce reliability, as previously noted. In light of the foregoing, one might need to assess reliability within specific diagnostic groups rather than just age groups. For example, clinicians and researchers must use caution when assessing older adults in the later stages of progressive dementia using assessment measures or techniques reliable only for older adults without cognitive impairment (Kaszniak, 1990). Lastly, as older adults may require shorter tests due to fatigue or a limited attention span, some degree of reliability may be lost with lengthier tests. One must weigh the losses incurred with shorter tests (e.g., decreased stability and generalizability) with those associated with the physical condition of the individual being assessed.

Interrater reliability refers to the consistency of scoring, direct observation, and administration among assessment administrators or raters (Graziano & Raulin, 1989b). Potential variance in scoring, rating, or test administration may lead to significant errors in assessment results (American Psychological Association, 1985). The types of variables being compared between administrators will vary according to the assessment method or device employed. As many assessment measures require a degree of subjectivity in their scoring, the degree of agreement between administrators should be reported with assessment results. Interrater reliability can easily be affected, for example, by instances of ageism wherein ratings are negatively biased by a clinician's preconceptions of older adults. In contrast, clinicians with positive biases toward the elderly may inflate or exaggerate positive results, perhaps in a seemingly innocuous attempt to "help" the individual. If the degree of agreement between raters is not reported, the extent of subjectivity involved in scoring the device should be considered and noted.

To reduce measurement errors, clinicians should be appropriately trained for test administration regardless of the population. With older adults, one should be particularly conscious of interviewer age biases that may confound results and influence interrater reliability. Furthermore, research suggests that more questions are answered by older adults when rapport is established with the test administrator (Freitag & Barry, 1974).

Test—retest reliability (temporal stability) refers to response consistency across time, that is, the ability of a test to produce the same results on separate occasions (Graziano & Raulin, 1989a). Stability can be affected by disorders common to the elderly such as dementia and delirium, resulting in inconsistent performance due to fatigue, attention span deficits, or even changes in mental status over the course of a day. In addition, diagnosis-specific reliability for the old-old and very-old populations is extremely limited, making it difficult to find measures with established test–retest reliability for these age groups (Kaszniak, 1990).

Validity

Validity is the most important factor to consider in selecting an assessment measure and refers to the "appropriateness, meaningfulness, and usefulness of the specific inferences made from test scores" (American Psychological Association, 1985). When assessing older adults, the validity issues of particular concern include face, content, construct, and external validity (Kaszniak, 1990).

Face validity refers to the individual's perception of the test. Older adults tend to be sensitive to seemingly patronizing, childishly worded test questions (Kaszniak, 1990). Soliciting the opinions of older adult pilot-subjects about the face validity of items may be effective in avoiding poorly worded questions.

Content validity refers to the extent to which the variables measured in the assessment instrument are an appropriate and thorough sample of the variables required to answer the question asked by the instrument (American Psychological Association, 1985). For example, when testing older persons, questions should be age appropriate in terms of symptom specificity (Kaszniak, 1990). Depression, for example, is often mistaken for cognitive impairment in the elderly (Yesavage, 1986; Hayes, Lohse, & Bernstein, 1991; Cavanaugh, 1993). Older adults tend to report primarily somatic and cognitive symptoms of depression such as slowed reaction time, loss of interest in activities, and fatigue. Failure to appreciate these characteristics in some older adults can result in two problems. First, as many of these symptoms are often associated with "aging," depressed older adults may be considered psychologically "normal" because a clinician has assumed that symptoms of depression are merely symptoms of physiological deterioration due to age. Thus, the depression goes untreated. Second, because such symptoms are characteristic of depression in younger adults, an older adult may be treated for depression that does not exist.

Construct validity refers to the ability of an assessment device to measure appropriate symptoms or behaviors based on a model of the area of interest. Constructs that apply for other age groups may not appropriately characterize older adults. Factor structures of assessment instruments may vary among age and diagnostic groups, making it difficult to develop hypotheses for older adults using tests developed with and for younger adults (Kaszniak, 1990). In addition, physiological changes that often accompany the aging process (as discussed earlier) may interfere with measurement of a construct (Kaszniak, 1990). "Caution is therefore necessary in the interpretation of what hypothetical psychologic process or construct a given task is actually measuring" (Kaszniak, 1990, p. 434). As a result, constructs must be developed from a conceptual framework based on the current literature on older adults and should be continuously reevaluated for their appropriateness (American Psychological Association, 1985).

External validity is the extent to which the results of a test can be generalized to other individuals, conditions, and places (Graziano & Raulin, 1989b). One must be cautious when generalizing results from samples of older adults, as validated models and constructs are somewhat limited for this population. In addition, it is a common misconception to regard older adults as one circumscribed group. The label *older adults*, however, represents a heterogeneous group encompassing individuals varying in age as much as 30 years or more and with a wide variety of characteristics and proclivities. Many older adults live independently within the community while others are institutionalized. For these and the foregoing reasons, it is difficult to characterize older adults as one homogeneous group without making inaccurate generalizations (Kaszniak, 1990).

The number and variety of assessment devices designed specifically for older adults is limited, often making it difficult to find age-appropriate measures for the variables of interest. The literature suggests, however, that the differences between older adults and other age groups are significant enough to require the use of tests that have been normed or validated with older persons when testing them. If no age-appropriate measures are available, then results of available tests should include a statement about the possibility of measurement and interpretation errors. Additionally, a multidimensional approach to assessing older adults may reduce inappropriate conclusions from the use of inappropriate assessment measures.

SELECTING APPROPRIATE
ASSESSMENT METHODS

This section will discuss different assessment methods and their respective advantages and limitations when used with older adults. The following information is not all inclusive and is to serve as a rough guide for selecting particular assessment tools. However, as with younger individuals, the ultimate selection of methods of assessment should reflect both the questions asked and the idiosyncrasies of the subject. Ideally, the coordinated use of multiple assessment methodologies will enable the clinician to piece together a synthesized pattern of useful information.

Self-Report

Self-report measures are typically pen-and-paper questionnaires on which subjects respond to statements about thoughts, feelings, and behaviors. Under favorable conditions, self-report instruments are easy to administer and score, cost-effective, and can provide valuable information on a broad range of phenomena. There are several caveats for using self-report instruments with older adults. To begin with, some instruments may be inappropriate for use with this population. Inventories and scales are often developed for younger adults. Consequently, measures may lack norms for older adults and/or fail to take into account the different etiological factors accounting for symptomatology in the elderly (Hersen & Van Hasselt, 1992), as noted in the previous section. Instruments may also surpass the reading and comprehension level of some older adults (Gallagher, Thompson, & Levy, 1980), particularly if dementia is present. Instructions and layout of the questionnaires themselves may be difficult and confusing for some older adults. Finally, versions of self-report instruments for visually impaired individuals may not be available.

Another caveat concerns response sets and test-taking behaviors characteristic of some older adults. For example, scores may be influenced by a tendency toward greater cautiousness, anxiety about receiving negative feedback, and risk-avoiding behavior when confronted with a situation of evaluation (Poon et al., 1986). Accuracy of self-reporting estimates of functional ability has been questioned by some researchers. For example, Myers and Huddy (1985) found that institutionalized older adults were inaccurate in reporting current activities of daily living (ADL) and physical ability, and in estimating functional capabilities in activities they no longer performed. Similarly, Rubenstein, Schairer, Weiland, and Kane (1984) found that geriatric patients overestimated their functional ability. Kuriansky, Gurland, and Fleiss (1976) reported that affectively impaired older adults may underestimate their abilities. Sager et al. (1992) found that older adults both under- and overestimated their ability to complete activities of daily living compared to performance-based measures. In home settings, where older adults perform ADLs daily and where a change in functioning is less likely, self-reported ADLs have been shown to correlate highly with performance measures (Sager et al., 1992).

In addition to functional ability, some authors have reported that older adults' self-reports of memory impairment may not be accurate (e.g., Perlmutter, 1978; Rabbitt, 1982; Sunderland, Watts, Baddeley, & Harris, 1986; Zelinski, Gilewski, & Thompson, 1980). On a more positive note, Rodgers and Herzog (1987) suggested that older adults are no less accurate than younger adults in self-report survey-type information.

Since results of the aforementioned studies on accuracy of older adults' self-reports are mixed, broad generalizations as to accuracy of self-reports by older adults should be avoided. However, clinicians need to be alert to the factors that can influence self-report by older adults. For example, responses can be altered by affective response to acute illness, changes from previous levels of physical functioning occurring during hospitalization, and presence of acute or chronic cognitive impairment (Sager et al., 1992). Cognitively impaired elderly pose a special challenge to clinicians. Instruments are typically not validated for use with dementia patients (Sunderland et al., 1988). Some authors suggest that as levels of cognitive impairment increase, validity of self-report decreases (Sager et al., 1992). Clients with severe dementia may not be able to comprehend questions on the instruments or the nature of the information requested. In addition, older adults with dementia who deny memory loss also tend to deny the presence of other symptoms (Feher, Larrabee, & Crook, 1992). However, Feher, Larrabee, and Crook (1992) suggest that self-report instruments designed to measure mood may be utilized with older adults with mild-to-moderate dementia. These authors report that accurate self-report of recent mood requires only minimal memory ability.

One might conclude that some older adults under some conditions can be unreliable reporters. Nevertheless, self-report measures are an important source of data for geriatric assessment, especially for the relatively independent, "well" elderly (Morris & Boutelle, 1985). However, as with all age groups, such information should be considered in light of its potential limitations and combined with other sources of information.

Report by Other

The report-by-other methodology is typically used to supplement and/or verify information from other sources. External validation with other sources of information can be particularly important when denial or overreporting of symptoms is suspected or with unwilling or incapable individuals. Spouses, family members, and caregivers can be enlisted for assistance in the assessment of individuals. For example, significant others can provide invaluable information in large-scale surveys for planning service programs or new housing units, for demographic questionnaires, or as a part of clinical assessment procedures. Reports by others can also contribute to an expeditious assessment process. For example, a significant other can complete a questionnaire in a waiting room as the clinician interviews the older adult.

Limitations of report by other are similar to those of self-report and direct observation. When multiple reports are involved, there is always the issue of whose report constitutes the standard or is the most accurate. Several examples of disparities among reports can be found in the literature. Rubenstein et al. (1984) found that the discrepancy between the functional status of the subject and the rater's report was greater when a spouse responded rather than a child, another relative, or friend. They also found that nurses and community proxies tended to rate patients as more dysfunctional than suggested by more objective indices.

Report by other data is another rich source of geriatric assessment information. As with self-report information, one must consider the potential sources of influence and combine reports with information obtained from other information sources and methods.

Direct Observation

Direct observation is a method of assessment often used to quantify specific behaviors and activities of daily living. Older adults may be observed in natural settings or in similar contrived situations. The information obtained can be utilized for a variety of purposes (e.g., needs assessment, the planning of case management services, evaluation of functioning over time, admission planning for various living arrangements) (Morris & Boutelle, 1985).

There are several advantages of using direct observations. Direct observation can provide the most accurate information about an individual's behavior.

Observational methods are also useful for those older adults who are uncooperative, unavailable, or severely physically or mentally impaired and not amenable
to other assessment methods (Goga & Hambacher, 1977). In addition, simple
observational measurement systems are often easily taught. Institutional staff
members with little or no previous experience can be trained to become reliable
and accurate observers. Once staff are competent observers, resultant data can be
incorporated into cost-effective institution-wide systems to identify goals, track
behavior changes over time, and demonstrate facility patterns (Schnelle &
Traughber, 1983). Finally, idiosyncratic patterns of impairment in activities of
daily living caused by cognitive deficits can be noted with direct observations of
performance on specific tasks (Kapust & Weintraub, 1988).

The limitations of the direct observation methodology are both financial and
practical. Unfortunately, third-party payers currently provide no reimbursement
for direct observation assessment (Kapust & Weintraub, 1988). More complex
coding systems that provide richer sources of data may be too complicated or
demand too much time for caregiver implementation. In addition, direct observations of ADLs, such as bathing and toileting, may be too intrusive and aversive
to many older adults.

Interviews

The interview is the most frequently used assessment method (Haynes &
Jensen, 1979). A survey of clinical psychologists (Norcross, Prochaska, & Gallagher, 1989) revealed that the clinical interview was used by 96% of those
surveyed and occupied 39% of their assessment. These figures are not surprising. The interview is an extremely flexible and forgiving assessment method that
allows the clinician to observe behavior, ask a multitude of questions, explore
hypotheses, share information with the client, influence client behavior, and
adjust his or her own interviewing behavior as a continuous (cybernetic) function of the information obtained (Edelstein & Yoman, 1991). No other assessment
method offers such a range of functions.

The initial interview is typically the first contact between the clinician and
the client and the first critical link in the therapeutic process. No single standard
interview format exists, perhaps because of the many potential functions of
the interview and the many theoretical orientations of clinicians. Interviews
vary in structure, ranging from the very reliable, highly structured to unstruc-
tured interviews with unknown psychometric properties. Regardless of the form
taken by interviews, they all are intended to obtain accurate, reliable, and valid
information.

Adequacy of information obtained from an interview is, of course, partially
a function of its accuracy. The physical and psychological status of an older adult
can influence accuracy, as previously discussed, and must be considered when
deciding whether and how to use interview information. The length and complexity of the interview must be considered in light of the client's mental status
and physical stamina. Some older adults may tire in a matter of minutes, whereas

others may provide reliable information for hours. Several brief sessions may be required due to client fatigue or fluctuating cooperation. Virtually all of the considerations previously noted in the first section of this chapter about psychological and physiological considerations apply equally well to the interview.

Though interviews are subject to the same evaluative standards as other assessment methods, psychometric data are available for only the semistructured and structured interviews designed for specific populations and purposes (e.g., Comprehensive Assessment and Referral Evaluation, Gurland, Kuriansky, Sharpe, Simon, Stiller, & Burkett, 1977; Geriatric Mental State Schedule, Copeland et al., 1976). Many of these structured interviews have very good interrater and test—retest reliability. Though the comprehensiveness of these interviews is a strength, the considerable time required to administer them can challenge the attention and endurance of many older adults.

Interviewing older adults is not unlike interviewing younger adults. The same general interviewing strategies that are effective with younger adults are effective with older adults (e.g., establishing rapport, active listening, careful questioning). The content of the interview, of course, will vary with the client, nature of the client's presenting problems, physical and mental status of the client, and a host of other variables. While similarities exist among the behaviors of different-aged individuals, differences emerge as a function of the physiological and psychological considerations noted earlier. For example, older adults have been found to refuse to participate in surveys at a higher rate (e.g., DeMaio, 1980; Herzog & Rodgers, 1988), refuse to answer certain types of questions (e.g., Gergen & Back, 1966), and to respond "don't know" (Colsher & Wallace, 1989) more often than younger individuals. Older adults also tend to be more cautious when responding (Okun, 1976) and give more acquiescent responses (Kogan, 1961). In spite of the aforementioned findings, the interview can be a very effective assessment tool, particularly for older adults whose cognitive skills have not been severely compromised.

Computerized Assessment

Clinicians' increased familiarity with computers and programming, as well as the decreased cost of purchasing systems, has led to an abundance of computerized assistance for the assessor. Structured interviews, self-report, and report by other measures transferred to a computerized format can be administered, scored, and interpreted by programs. Innovative software is continually being invented and refined.

There are multiple advantages to utilizing computers in geriatric assessment. An obvious benefit is the savings of both time and money for the clinician and patient. Depth and dimension can be added to the clinical assessment without additional substantial cost. Several patients can be tested simultaneously by technicians. This allows the clinician to utilize time more efficiently by focusing more readily on specific problems or treatment areas in interviews (Alexander & Davidoff, 1990). In addition, the computer can store and process responses automatically, without engaging additional technicians (Alexander & Davidoff, 1990). Computerized assessment also ensures that interviews will be more consistent. Variability due to factors such as interviewer bias, fatigue, and emotional fluctuations can be eliminated (Alexander & Davidoff, 1990). A computer program can enrich assessments by measuring variables too fine or complex for the clinician and examine the relationship among vast numbers of variables. Finally, the computer allows greater flexibility and subdivision of questions based on the patients' response to answers of preceding questions (Alexander & Davidoff, 1990).

There are several limitations of computerized assessment. Computers may be intimidating or overwhelming to older adults, especially those who have had little past contact with computers. Programs can be written to select out respondents incapable of interacting adequately with computers, but most programs fail to make allowances for patients with cognitive difficulties, fluctuating cooperation from pharmacological side effects, fatigue, or emotional lability. Most tests were not validated with computer-assisted testing, so results may not be accurate (Alexander & Davidoff, 1990). In addition, computers have not been programmed to exercise the range of clinical judgment often necessary for clinical practice.

Computers are a valuable tool that can provide substantial savings in time, money, and effort for the geriatric clinician. However, the computer is merely complementary, and not a substitute for the decisions and judgments of a well-trained clinician.

MULTIDIMENSIONAL ASSESSMENT

"Health-care and social-service providers and organizations tend to specialize, but human beings are general entities with multidimensional functions, needs, and problems" (Janik & Wells, 1982, p. 45). Multidimensional assessment is a method of enhancing ideographic evaluation and treatment planning. The problems of older adults are typically multiple, multicausal, and have multidimensional symptom presentation. Multidimensional assessment is ideal for clinical geropsychologists and other social service or mental health professionals who work with older adults because it illuminates the disparate variables that play a role in the well-being of older adults (Janik & Wells, 1982). A thorough multidimensional assessment addresses physical health status, medication regimen, mental status, cognitive functioning, daily living skills (e.g., bathing, dressing, eating), level of stress, stress-coping skills, supportive and unsupportive social interactions, and economic or environmental resources (Fry, 1986; Gallagher, Thompson, & Levy, 1980; Martin, Morycz, McDowell, Snustad, & Karpf, 1985). Assets and/or liabilities in any or all of these domains can play a role in the presenting problems and treatment of older adult clients. The multidimensional approach softens rigid distinctions between assessment domains and between professional disciplines, resulting in a more integrated or holistic picture of the elderly client.

The importance of multidimensional assessment in the proper diagnosis and treatment of individuals is widely recognized. In present and past editions of the *Diagnostic and Statistical Manual of Mental Disorders*, the American Psychiatric Association has advocated a multiaxial approach that includes documentation of mental disorders, physical disorders, psychosocial stressors, and functional level (American Psychiatric Association, 1994). Research has shown that multidimensional assessment contributes to improved patient outcome in the following domains: improved diagnostic accuracy, more appropriate placement, decreased dependency, improved functional status (i.e., ADLs), more appropriate prescription and use of medications, improved coordination of services, improved emotional status and sense of well-being, and greater client satisfaction with services (e.g., Haug, Belgrave, & Gratton, 1984; Marcus-Bernstein, 1986; Martin et al., 1985; Moore, 1985; Rubenstein, 1983; Williams, Hill, Fairbank, & Knox, 1973). In recognition of the importance of multidimensional assessment, the Omnibus Reconciliation Act (OBRA, 1987) mandated regular, comprehensive assessment of functional, medical, psychosocial, and cognitive status of all nursing home residents (Morris et al., 1994).

Assessment Dimensions

Physical Health

Older adults have a higher incidence of medical and psychiatric disorders than do younger adults (Bressler, 1987) and often experience multiple, concurrent, acute and/or chronic conditions (Kane, Ouslander, & Abrass, 1989). Ouslander (1984) suggests that clinicians consider several points when assessing and developing interventions for older adults. First, psychiatric symptoms can be manifestations of physical illness. For example, common physical conditions among geriatric patients (e.g., hypothyroidism, diabetes, menopause, dementia, rheumatoid arthritis, pancreatic cancer, and nutritional deficiencies) sometimes present with symptoms of depression (Ouslander, 1984). Similarly, physical symptoms can be manifestations of psychiatric illness (e.g., sleep and appetite disturbance in major depression). Medical factors, such as drugs and hospital environments, can cause psychiatric symptoms (Ouslander, 1984). Adverse reactions to medications commonly prescribed for older adults can include confusion or delirium, depression, falls, gastrointestinal distress, postural hypotension, sexual dysfunction, sensory changes, and urinary incontinence, among others (Goodstein, 1985). A few medications, including corticosteroids and sympathomimetics, can even cause symptoms of acute mania or psychosis. Sensory impairments, like those described earlier in this chapter, are correlated with decreases in frequency and quality of social interaction, increased loneliness, depression (Marcus-Bernstein, 1986) and persecutory ideation (Christenson & Blazer, 1984).

An exhaustive assessment of a client's physical health status and medication regimen may be outside the expertise of the geropsychologist. However, the knowledgeable clinician can solicit information from a client or caregivers about the presence of physical disorders that are likely to be related to presenting problems and/or can consult in an interdisciplinary or multidisciplinary setting with medical personnel who are qualified to conduct thorough physical examinations.

Mental Status/Cognitive Functioning

Of all the tasks required in multidimensional assessment, identification of psychopathology and cognitive deficits are perhaps the most familiar to the psychologist. Within the context of multidimensional assessment, the psychologist is required to consider the interplay between mental and cognitive status and each of the other domains. For example, consider the case of a 75-year-old woman with rheumatoid arthritis and symptoms of possible early dementia who presents for assessment. Beyond assessing for presence of cognitive impairment, the psychologist could gather information to identify the potential source of her cognitive deficits. The psychologist could assess for depression, secondary to the chronic arthritis, which might impair her cognitive functioning. The psychologist also could investigate the degree to which cognitive impairments, pain, or depression interfere with the patient's ability to follow the medication and activity regimen prescribed for rheumatoid arthritis. As noted earlier, deviations from drug regimens sometimes lead to adverse reactions, including confusion and depression.

Activities of Daily Living

Optimal functioning from day to day requires a host of skills or behaviors of varying complexity (e.g., eating, grooming, dressing, using the telephone, shopping, using transportation, preparing meals, managing health and safety matters). Assessment of daily living skills or behaviors can provide valuable information in a multidimensional assessment. Level of functional capacity has been shown to have a strong positive correlation with subjective well-being and can be used as a predictor of overall health status, health service consumption (Shanas, 1974), and dementia (Lowenstein et al., 1989).

Initially the clinician must determine whether the current level of functional behavior or skill represents a change from a previous level of functioning. Changes in functional skills or behaviors are sometimes related to decrements in cognitive functioning, mental status, and/or physical health (Besdine, 1983) and thus provide a cue to the examiner that further assessment or intervention may be needed in these domains.

Alternatively, thorough assessment may reveal that an individual has always been deficient in a particular skill and that changes in functional status are a function of changes in environmental demands rather than loss of skill. For example, consider the case of a 76-year-old, depressed man who was recently widowed. During his 55-year marriage, his wife did all the shopping, cooking, cleaning, and managed all the household finances. Upon her death, he was faced not only with the loss of his lifetime companion but also with the need to assume many of the responsibilities once assumed by his wife. Understandably, he became overwhelmed. His children and physician took note of his apparent incapacitation and recommended that he be assessed for early signs of organic impairment. Assessment revealed that the man was cognitively intact, experiencing intense but normal grief, and lacked much of the knowledge and skill required to accomplish some important, instrumental daily activities. With some training and support, he was able to acquire the necessary skills and to adapt successfully to his new situation.

Stress and Coping

Although the multidimensional assessment literature traditionally does not address the need for the assessment of levels of stress and coping, ample literature suggests a strong relation between frequency and intensity of perceived stressors and mental and physical health status. Depression and anxiety (Rabkin, 1993), cardiovascular disease (Epstein & Perkins, 1988), gastrointestinal disorders (Sammons & Karoly, 1987), headaches (DeLongis, Folkman, & Lazarus, 1988), and more are positively correlated with various indices of stress. Furthermore, decreases in stress and/or improvements in coping strategies have been shown to decrease physical and mental health problems (Moos & Schaefer, 1993; Sammons & Karoly, 1987; Smith, 1993). Given the abundance and strength of these findings, the clinician would be remiss in not exploring intensity and frequency of stress and the adequacy of stress-coping abilities or resources present for an older adult client.

Social Support

Older adults with higher levels of perceived social support are typically mentally and physically healthier and live longer than do older adults with lower levels of social support. Social support can be obtained from a variety of sources (e.g., friends, family, co-workers, neighbors, professional caregivers) and can serve a variety of functions (e.g., material or instrumental aid, emotional support, guidance, affirmation, intimate interaction, love, esteem). Social support is believed to directly affect health as well as buffer against the harmful effects of stress.

Assessment of social support should address both the absolute number or frequency of contact with supportive others as well as the older adult's perception of the availability and adequacy of that support. Clinicians should be cautious of assuming that all social interactions are beneficial or that an older adult who is alone much of the time is lonely or needs or desires more social contact. Some social interactions produce more stress than they relieve (Rook, 1990). Individual differences in response to the environment argue for the need for idiographic assessment of social support status and needs.

Economic and Environmental Resources

The status of an older adult's economic and environmental resources is an important target of assessment. These resources include financial income, employment, debt load, insurance, access to needed health care, housing situation, access to appropriate nutrition, and availability of transportation.

Assessment of economic and environmental resources may provide information regarding the onset or maintenance of presenting problems. For example, Ms. N. was a 69-year-old woman who provided care for her bedridden husband, who had suffered a paralyzing stroke. In addition, she worked full time as a nurse and provided child care in the evening so that her daughter could complete her college degree. When she presented to a community mental health center, she was depressed and suicidal. Her caregiving responsibilities appeared, at first glance, to be the primary source of stress underlying her presentation. However, further questioning revealed that her husband had nearly $150,000 in unpaid medical bills, she had accumulated nearly $20,000 in credit card debt, she was getting frequent, threatening calls from creditors, and she was at risk of losing her home and automobile because of failure to make payments. She badly wanted to quit her job to provide full-time care for her increasingly ill husband, but her tremendous debt load prevented her from doing so. Whereas a typical intervention for a depressed caregiver might focus on accessing respite or support services or modifying maladaptive thoughts or beliefs, the most immediate goal for this caregiver was identification of strategies to minimize her debt and prevent her from losing her home and car.

In addition to revealing direct targets for intervention, assessment of economic and environmental resources may reveal factors that have the potential to prevent treatment from being effective. For example, older adults who are concerned about money may choose not to refill a prescription or may take medication less often than is prescribed. An older adult who shares a home with her children and grandchildren may have difficulty finding a quiet place to practice relaxation skills or may have difficulty implementing a new dietary regimen. A recommendation to increase social interactions by joining a local senior center is not likely to be followed if the older adult has no transportation to and from the senior center. If these factors are identified at the outset of treatment, they can be addressed and treatment failures can be minimized.

REVIEW OF SELECTED
ASSESSMENT INSTRUMENTS

A critical review of all psychological assessment instruments and methods used with older adults is beyond the scope of this chapter. In lieu of such a review, the authors surveyed the 212 members of the Section on Clinical Geropsychology of the American Psychological Association Division 12 (Clinical) to determine which assessment instruments and methods are most often used. The following categories of problem areas drawn primarily from the *DSM-III-R* were included in the survey: mood disorders, anxiety disorders, personality disorders, substance-related disorders, marital discord, adaptive functioning, dementia/amnestic/other cognitive disorders, schizophrenia and other psychotic disorders, sexual disorders, and behavior management problems. Ninety-seven individuals (46%) responded to the survey. In view of the fact that some of the 212 individuals surveyed probably do not perform clinical assessments, the return rate was considered acceptable for its intended function. The most frequently used instrument or method for each of these categories was determined, yielding the results presented in Table 3-1.

In the following section we examine the psychometric properties of the most frequently used instrument or method for each of the survey categories, with the exception of "behavior problems." The most frequently used method of assessing behavior problems was direct observation, which is discussed in the previous section.

Mood Disorders

The Geriatric Depression Scale (GDS) (Yesavage et al., 1983) was specifically designed to screen for depression in older adults. It was developed from a 100-item pool of yes/no questions, generated by researchers and clinicians in geriatric psychiatry and believed to have potential for distinguishing depressed from nondepressed older adults. The 100 items were administered to a sample ($n = 47$) of nondepressed, community-dwelling, older adults and older adults who were hospitalized for depression (age > 55 years). Thirty items with the highest and most significant correlation with the total 100-item score were combined to create the final version of the measure. Items were administered in a self-report format or read aloud to respondents.

Somatically focused items were excluded from the scale based on the empirical selection procedure described above, not on any theoretical considerations. It has been argued, however, that exclusion of somatic items represents one of the strengths of the GDS relative to other standardized measures of

Table 3-1. Frequently Used Assessment Instruments

Assessment category	Assessment instrument/method
Mood disorders	Geriatric Depression Scale
Anxiety disorders	MMPI-2
Personality disorders	MMPI-2
Substance-related disorders	CAGE
Marital discord	Locke-Wallace
Adaptive functioning	OARS
Dementia	Mini-Mental State Examination
Schizophrenia	MMPI-2
Sexual disorders	Sexual Interaction Inventory
Behavior management	Direct observation

depression; questions designed to assess the vegetative symptoms of depression are sometimes endorsed by nondepressed older adults who have experienced age-related or illness-related changes in sleep, appetite, energy or activity level, and so on, and thus increase the false-positive rate of depression measures.

Another strength of the GDS is the yes/no response format. This simple format results in a measure that is "comprehensible to older adults, takes less than five minutes to administer, and may be administered by nonphysicians" (Koenig, Meador, Cohen, & Blazer, 1988, p. 700). Some have argued that the simple format of the GDS requires less cognitive effort than is required for other commonly used measures of depression and thus that the GDS is perhaps more appropriate for cognitively impaired older adults (Norris, Gallagher, Wilson, & Winograd, 1987). This issue will be discussed further below.

Evidence for the reliability and validity of the GDS in community-dwelling, cognitively intact older adults has been found in several studies. Yesavage et al. (1983) found that the GDS scores correctly classified individuals as non-depressed, mildly depressed, and severely depressed. In their sample of 100 community-dwelling older adults, they found the GDS to be internally consistent (alpha = .94) and have high split-half reliability (r = .94). Gallagher, Slife, and Yesavage (cited in Yesavage et al., 1983) found that the GDS differentiated depressed from nondepressed elderly in a sample of physically ill, community-dwelling older adults.

The GDS appears to be a sensitive and specific measure for medically ill individuals. Norris, Gallagher, Wilson, and Winegrod (1987) found the GDS to exhibit 84% sensitivity in a medically ill sample (n = 68). Koenig, Meador, Cohen, and Blazer (1988) reported a sensitivity of 92% and specificity of 89% with medically ill elderly. Koenig, Meador, Cohen, and Blazer (1992) found that sensitivity and specificity were lower in medical inpatients who were more cognitively impaired or medically ill.

Evidence for the reliability and validity of the GDS for assessing depression in cognitively impaired older adults is mixed, with some studies finding support for its use with cognitive-impaired individuals (e.g., Parmelee, Katz, & Lawton, 1992) and others finding it insensitive with this population (e.g., Kaffonek et al., 1989). Feher, Larrabee, and Crook (1992) concluded that the GDS appears to be a valid instrument for mild-to-moderate depression among individuals with mild-to-moderate dementia.

In their recent review of depression assessment instruments for older adults, Pachana, Gallagher-Thompson, and Thompson (1994) concluded that "despite the limitations noted here, it seems to us that the GDS may well be the best all-around self-report depression scale available at present with utility across a broad range of geriatric populations" (p. 243).

Anxiety Disorders, Personality Disorders, and Schizophrenia

The MMPI-2 was the most frequently used instrument for the assessment of anxiety and personality disorders and schizophrenia and other psychotic disorders. The MMPI-2 was published in 1989 as a revised, restandardized, and expanded instrument. The normative sample consisted of 2,600 individuals between the ages of 18 and 84 years of age. Of those 60 and older, the sample included 134 males and 143 females; for ages 70 through 79, 55 males and 65 females; for ages 80 through 84, 9 males and 12 females. Though the relative numbers of individuals at each age level are consistent with age distribution figures from the 1980 census, they represent a relatively small absolute number of older adults.

Only two studies have addressed the psychometric properties of the MMPI-2 for older adults. Butcher et al. (1991) examined the need for separate norms for older men by contrasting scores of 1,459 men in the Normative Aging Study (age: $M = 61.27$, $SD = 8.37$) with those of 1,138 men from the MMPI Restandardization Study (age: $M = 41.71$, $SD = 15.32$). Subjects ranged in age from 40 to 91 years. The researchers found that "members of the NAS sample resembled the men of the MMPI-2 Restandardization sample both in the average and in the variance of their scores on the MMPI-2" (p. 363). The authors also examined within-sample age groups and found significant differences among the groups, with the older groups receiving higher scores on the D scale, and lower scores on the Pd and Ma scales.

Limitations of this study include use of almost exclusively white, middle-class men and cross-sectional data. The first limitation diminishes generalizability of these results, and the latter opens the door for cohort effects. Such comparisons among age groups may be insensitive to changes over the life-span (Aldwin, Spiro, Levenson, & Bossé, 1989). Although the researchers argue that the foregoing results do not suggest the need for separate norms for older adult males, the limitations imposed by the cross-sectional design preclude any definitive conclusions.

The second study to address older adult performance on the MMPI-2 was conducted by Spiro, Butcher, Levenson, Aldwin, and Bossé (1994). The investigators conducted a 5-year longitudinal study of 1,072 men, aged 40 to 88 years. Though the age range included adults over the age of 60, 80% of the men were between the ages of 50 and 69 and only 13 men were between the ages of 80 and 89. Statistically significant mean changes over time were found for 2 of 3 validity, 6 of 10 clinical, 3 of 7 supplementary, and 5 of 15 content scales. Changes in scores exceeded 1 T-score point for scales 1 to 3, 7, 8, and the Health Concerns Scale. In light of these results, and those of the first study, further examination of the validity and stability of the MMPI-2 with older adults is needed. The need to examine a more heterogenous sample of individuals (i.e., across genders, races, and ages above 60 years) also appears in order.

In light of the foregoing research, the jury appears to still be out as to whether the MMPI-2 is an appropriate measure for the assessment of anxiety disorders, personality disorders, schizophrenia, and related psychotic disorders. The MMPI enjoyed considerable success, which is probably why so many clinicians have shifted to the MMPI-2. We would caution clinicians who use the MMPI-2 with older adults that considerably more research is needed to establish this as a reliable and valid instrument for older adults.

Marital Discord

The Locke-Wallace Marital Adjustment Scale (a.k.a. Locke-Wallace Marriage Adjustment Scale, The Locke-Wallace Marital Adjustment Test) was developed in 1959. It is used by researchers and clinicians to classify married couples into high or low levels of adjustment (Cross & Sharpley, 1981). The scale was created by taking the 15 most significant items from existing adjustment scales. It was validated on a sample of 236 young, white, educated, Protestant couples. Split-half reliability (Spearman-Brown formula) was .90. The scale was considered valid because the mean adjustment score for a well-adjusted group (as reported by close friends) was significantly different from the mean score for a maladjusted group (Locke & Wallace, 1959).

More recent studies have found that the Locke-Wallace Marital Adjustment Scale is confounded by couples' desire to appear more well adjusted than they are (Hunt, 1978). Other studies have found that the scores of husbands and wives are moderately correlated ($r = .59$), suggesting that scores should be reported independently rather than compiled into a couple score (Hunt, 1978).

Although the Locke-Wallace Marital Adjustment Scale is more than 30 years old, it is referred to as "the most popular scale of marriage adjustment with well established validity and reliability" (Peterson & Miller, 1980, p. 248). No specific psychometric information is available for the Locke-Wallace Marital Adjustment Scale with older adults. It has, however, been used successfully through the years in the assessment of older adults (e.g., Carstensen, Gottman, & Levenson, 1994; Levenson, Carstenson, & Gottman, 1993; Levenson, Carstensen, & Gottman, 1994; Levenson & Gottman, 1983; Peterson & Miller, 1980).

Adaptive Behavior

The Older American Resources and Services methodology (OARS) (Pfeifer, 1975) is the oldest and most popular multidimensional assessment instrument and the one most frequently cited in our survey for assessing adaptive behavior. The OARS comprises two instruments, the Multidimensional Functional Assessment Questionnaire (MFAQ) and the Services Assessment Questionnaire (SAG). The MFAQ is designed to assess functional status and requires an interview by a trained professional that lasts approximately 45 to 60 minutes. The MFAQ contains 70 questions that are answered by the client, 10 questions answered by an informant, and 14 questions answered by the interviewer. Responses to the interview are rated on 6-point scales pertaining to the individuals well-being (1 = excellent functioning; 2 = severely impaired functioning) in the following categories: physical health, mental health (cognitive skill and psychological health), activities of daily living (physical and instrumental), social (time use and interaction with family and friends), and economic. Most of the questions are relevant to both community and institutional settings. Individual scores are obtained for each of these categories, although single scores can be obtained by summing the six category scores.

Psychometric evaluation of the MFAQ was based upon samples of 997 community residents age 65 and older, 98 individuals aged 65 and older presenting at a geriatric clinic with multiple problems, and 102 residents of nursing and rest homes, aged 65 and older. Interrater reliability estimates ranged from .67 to .87 across the five categories of functioning. Test–retest reliability over a 5-week period resulted in identical scores for 91% of the items. Validity was demonstrated by comparing scores on four of the five categories (social resources excluded) with ratings by professionals, yielding coefficients ranging from .60 for physical health to .83 for ADL (George, 1994). In addition, individuals living in the community, being seen in clinics, and living in institutions were compared, revealing the greatest impairment scores among institutionalized individuals and the least impairment among community-dwelling individuals not being seen in clinics.

Overall, the MFAQ of the OARS has much to recommend it, including a wealth of supportive research studies, normative data for older adults at various levels of functioning, good psychometric properties, and a comprehensiveness that lends itself well to both clinical and research settings. The only major shortcoming is the length of time required to administer the instrument.

Dementia/Amnestic Disorders

The Mini-Mental State Examination (MMSE) (Folstein, Folstein, & McHugh, 1975) was designed to provide a brief screening of mental abilities. It is the most widely used mental status assessment instrument and is available in many languages (Tombaugh & McIntyre, 1992). The main benefits of the instrument are the supplementary extensive research literature, ease of administration, short testing time (5 to 10 minutes), ability to screen for dementia, and ability to document cognitive change over time in patients with mild-to-moderate dementia. A score of 23 or less on the MMSE is generally accepted as indicative of cognitive impairment among individuals with average education and yields an approximate sensitivity of 87%. The highest levels of sensitivity have been reached with people with moderate-to-severe levels of dementia.

A cutoff of 27 has been recommended for individuals with greater than 16 years of education (Albert, 1994). Lower cutoff scores have been established for individuals with limited education. For individuals with less than 8 years of education, a cutoff of 17 has been recommended by Murden, McRae, Kaner, and Buckman (1991), who found a sensitivity of 81% and a specificity of 100% for dementia using this cutoff.

The sensitivity of the MMSE for general neurology and psychiatry patients usually is low, ranging from 21% to 76%, possibly because the MMSE fails to detect damage in the right hemisphere and the language items are too simple to detect mild impairment. The item requiring recall of three words, the pentagon copying task, serial sevens/WORLD item, and orientation to time questions appear to be the most sensitive to both normal aging and dementing illness.

Construct validation studies show that MMSE scores correlate highly with scores on other cognitive screening tests, and psychological and neurological measures tapping intelligence (e.g., Weschler Adult Intelligence Scale), memory (e.g., Wechsler Memory Scale), specific cognitive abilities (e.g., Trails B Test), and activities of daily living (e.g., Blessed Dementia Rating Scale). Internal consistency levels range from .68 and .77 with community samples to .96 with medical patients. Short-term (less than 1 or 2 years) test–retest reliability coefficients for both cognitively intact and impaired subjects range from .80 to .95 (Tombaugh & McIntyre, 1992). However, longitudinal test–retest assessments produce correlations of less than .50. Interrater reliability of the MMSE is .82.

There are several limitations of the MMSE. Scores are affected by demographic factors, especially age and education. The instrument lacks sensitivity to mild cognitive impairment, fails to adequately discriminate between individuals with mild Alzheimer's disease and normal older adults, and is insensitive to progressive changes occurring with severe Alzheimer's (Tombaugh & McIntyre, 1992). In addition, inconsistencies in administration, scoring, and interpretation of the MMSE are problematic.

In light of the foregoing, the MMSE should serve only as an initial screening device for cognitive impairment and should not serve as the sole determinant of a diagnosis of dementia. Finally, Tombaugh and McIntyre (1992) suggest three modifications to the administration instructions of the MMSE in order to standardize administration procedures. The interested reader is referred to the Tombaugh & McIntyre article for an elaboration of these recommended changes and a very comprehensive review of the MMSE literature.

Sexual Behavior

The Sexual Interaction Inventory (SII) was developed in 1974. It is a paper-and-pencil self-report inventory "for assessing the sexual adjustment and sexual satisfaction of heterosexual couples" (LoPiccolo & Steger, 1974, p. 585). The inventory consists of a list of 17 behaviors, each of which is addressed by 6 questions, yielding 102 questions. The 17 behaviors are presented in order from least invasive sexual behaviors to most invasive. Questions are answered on a 6-point Likert-type scale from *never* to *always* or from *extremely pleasant* to *extremely unpleasant*, as appropriate for the question. The test was validated on four samples of married couples, a total of 191 couples. All subjects were young, well educated, and recently married. Test–retest reliability coefficients ranged from .53 to .90 and internal consistency (Cronbach's alpha) ranged from .85 to .93. The SII was both sensitive and reliable when comparing the scores of dysfunctional couples with satisfied couples and when comparing pre- and post-treatment couples (LoPiccolo & Steger, 1974).

Several limitations of the SII have been noted. The first major limitation is the absence of psychometric information for use of the SII with older adults. That limitation notwithstanding, other concerns have been expressed about other features of the SII. D'Augelli-Frankel (1986) questioned the adequacy of the reliability and validity of the measure with younger adults. McCoy and D'Agostino's (1977) factor analysis of the SII revealed "sets of variables that are psychologically meaningless ... [and are] ... unstable between methods" (McCoy & D'Agostino, 1977, p. 30). The authors further noted that the design of the instrument made it difficult to perform a factor analysis regardless of whether the instrument was conceptually valid. Other researchers have reported that the nature of the SII prevents a factor analysis of the instrument (D'Agostino, McCoy, & Lacerda, 1976). D'Agostino et al. (1976) questioned the appropriateness of listing the 17 behaviors in a specific order, arguing that the 17-step progression from visually looking at each other to achieving orgasm through sexual intercourse may vary between individuals. They further noted that sexual activity does not necessarily follow a hierarchical course. D'Augelli-Frankel (1986) argued that not only is the hierarchical approach unnecessary in light of the scoring procedure, but it is also "sexist," as male behaviors are always first. In addition, the authors reported that the 17 items may not be adequately representative of sexual behaviors. In their conclusion, the authors questioned the value of measuring sexual function by asking questions regarding perceptions of sexual behaviors.

On the positive side, D'Augelli-Frankel (1986) noted that a strength of the SII is the effort made to evaluate certain responses in terms of *both* members of the dyad rather than assessing only one member. The author reported that this dyadic approach renders the device particularly helpful in the treatment of sexually dysfunctional couples.

Substance Abuse

The CAGE (Mayfield, McLeod, & Hall, 1974) is a four-item questionnaire designed to improve the detection rate of alcohol abuse with a brief, easily administered, sensitive, and valid instrument. The CAGE is a mnemonic for feeling one should *cut* down on drinking, being *annoyed* by people criticizing one's drinking, feeling bad or *guilty* about drinking, and drinking the first thing in the morning as an *eye* opener. The CAGE was initially presented at the 29th International Congress on Alcohol and Drug Dependence in 1970. The instrument was developed through interviews of 130 randomly selected general hospital patients (medical and surgical). The four resulting items were then administered to 166 male patients in an alcoholism rehabilitation center. No indication of the ages of these subjects was offered by the author (Ewing, 1984). However, in 1970, the author administered the CAGE questions to 48 "alcoholic patients" in treatment centers in England. Patient ages ranged from 23 to 61. Unfortunately, the results are not presented by age or age groups.

The first publication to more thoroughly examine the psychometric properties of the CAGE appeared in 1974 (Mayfield, McLeod, & Hall, 1974). The authors administered the CAGE to 366 patients of a Veterans' Administration hospital, with ages ranging from 19 to 75 years. Seventy-nine percent of the subjects were alcohol abusers and 21% were abstainers. The CAGE yielded no false-positive results, but identified only 37% of the alcoholics using a four-item criterion. When a two- or three-item criterion was used, the detection ostensibly improved. Unfortunately, the authors offered no data on the actual correct detection and false-positive rate using the two- or three-item procedure. No results were presented by age or age group.

Bush, Shaw, Cleary, Delbanco, and Aronson (1987) studied 521 patients below the age of 75 years who had been admitted to the orthopedic and medical services of Boston's Beth Israel Hospital during a 6-month period. Mean age of the CAGE-positive (one or more CAGE symptoms) patients was 48.9, and mean age of the CAGE-negative (no CAGE symptoms) patients was 50.26). All subjects completed a 25-item structured interview, which included the 4 CAGE items and the Michigan Alcoholism Screening Test (MAST). In addition, each patient's chart was examined to determine presence of any of the following diagnoses: alcohol withdrawal syndrome, alcohol withdrawal seizures, alcoholic pancreatitis, alcoholic hepatitis, alcoholic cardiomyopathy, and the Wernicke-Korsakoff syndrome. Patients were classified as alcohol dependent, alcohol abuser, or normal using *DSM-III* criteria. The prevalence of alcohol abuse was 20%. The CAGE questionnaire evidenced a sensitivity of 85% and a specificity of 89%. The data were not presented by age or age group.

Buchsbaum, Buchanan, Welsh, Centor, and Schnoll (1992) examined the sensitivity, specificity, receiver operating characteristic (ROC), and positive predictive value for CAGE scores of 0 to 4 for 323 patients 60 years or older. One hundred six patients (33%) met *DSM-III* criteria for a history of alcohol abuse, dependence, or problem drinking. Eighteen (16%) of the patients reported an active drinking problem. The ROC curve suggests that the CAGE is capable of distinguishing patients with a history of drinking from those without such a history. Sensitivity ranged from 1.0 for a CAGE score of 0 to .15 for a score of 4.0. Specificity ranged from 0 for a CAGE score of 0 to .995 for a CAGE score of 4.0. Positive predictive values ranged from .328 for CAGE scores of 0 to .94 for scores of 4. Different values for sensitivity, specificity, and positive predictive value were found for males and females. Positive predictive values also varied as a function of the prevalence of drinking problems and score on the CAGE. The authors recommend that one consider a score of 1 or more as positive. This criterion yields an 84% probability of a drinking problem in males and a 54% probability in females. Buchsbaum et al. (1992) also note that a criterion of 2 may be more appropriate for populations with a lower prevalence of drinking. The higher the prevalence, the lower the score that is necessary to lead to further investigation of drinking problems.

Though the data on the psychometric properties of the CAGE are limited, particularly with older adults, it does appear to be a useful gross screening instrument that can be followed with a more extensive interview and laboratory tests (e.g., Barbor, Kranzler, & Lauerman, 1987; Bernadt, Mumford, Taylor, Smith, & Murray, 1982).

SUMMARY

We have examined a variety of variables that could influence the assessment process and its outcome, including clinician biases and psychological and physiological variables. Though not an exhaustive review of such variables, this material should serve to sensitize the reader to the complexity of assessing older adults and many of the influential variables that the clinician should consider. We then discuss psychometric considerations that are important when considering the development or choice of assessment instruments and methods, with an eye to issues that are somewhat peculiar to older adults. The discussion of considerations for selecting assessment methods includes a brief review of the strengths and limitations of self-report, report by other, direct observation, interviews, and computerized assessment methods and consideration of the unique features of older adults that may interact with assessment methods. Discussion of the many advantages of multidimensional assessment emphasizes physical health, mental status, activities of daily living, stress and coping, social support, and economic and environmental resources. Finally, we present the results of a survey of clinical geropsychologists conducted for this chapter and review the psychometric properties of the most frequently used assessment instruments or methods.

We believe that this chapter offers the reader an overview of the most important issues associated with the assessment of older adults, as well as considerable practical information that can be translated directly into practice.

REFERENCES

Albert, M. S. (1994). Brief assessments of cognitive function in the elderly. In M. P. Lawton & J. A. Teresi (Eds.), *Annual review of gerontology and geriatrics: Focus on assessment techniques*, (Vol. 14, pp. 93–106). New York: Springer.

Aldwin, C., Spiro, A., III, Levenson, M. R. & Bossé, R. (1989). Longitudinal findings from the Normative Aging Study. I. Does mental health change with age? *Psychology and Aging, 4*, 295–306.

Alexander, J. E., & Davidoff, D. A. (1990). Psychological testing, computers, and aging. *International Journal of Technology and Aging, 3*(1) Spring/Summer, 47–56.

American Psychiatric Association. (1994). *Diagnostics and statistical manual of mental disorders* (4th ed.). Washington, DC: Author.

American Psychological Association (1985). *Standard for educational and psychological testing.* Washington, DC: Author.

Barbor, T. F., Kranzler, H. R., & Lauerman, R. J. (1987). Early detection of harmful alcohol consumption: Comparison of clinical laboratory and self-report screening procedures. *Addictive Behaviors, 14*, 139–157.

Bernadt, M. W., Mumford, J., Taylor, C., Smith, B., & Murray, R. M. (1982). Comparison of questionnaire and laboratory tests in the detection of excessive drinking and alcoholism. *Lancet, i*, 325–328.

Besdine, R. W. (1983). The educational utility of comprehensive functional assessment in the elderly. *Journal of the American Geriatrics Society, 31*, 651–656.

Bressler, R. (1987). Drug use in the geriatric patient. In L. Carstensen and B. Edelstein (Eds.), *Handbook of clinical gerontology* (pp. 152–174). New York: Pergamon Press.

Buchsbaum, D. G., Buchanan, R. G., Welsh, J., Centor, R. M., & Schnoll, S. (1992). Screening for drinking disorders in the elderly using the CAGE questionnaire. *Journal of the American Geriatrics Society, 40*, 662–665.

Bush, B., Shaw, S., Cleary, P., Delbanco, T., & Aronson, M. (1987). Screening for alcohol abuse using the CAGE questionnaire. *The American Journal of Medicine, 82*, 231–235.

Butcher, J. N., Aldwin, C. M., Levenson, M. R., Ben-Porath, Y. S., Spiro, A., & Bossé, R. (1991). Personality and aging: A study of the MMPI-2 among older men. *Psychology and Aging, 6*, 361–370.

Butler, R. (1969). Age-ism: Another form of bigotry. *The Gerontologist, 9,* 243–246.

Carstensen, L. L., Gottman, J. M., & Levenson, R. W. (1994). Emotional behavior in long-term marriage. *Psychology and Aging.*

Cavanaugh, J. C. (1993). *Adult development and aging* (2nd ed.). Belmont, CA: Brooks/Cole.

Christensen, R., & Blazer, D. (1984). Epidemiology of persecutory ideation in an elderly population in the community. *American Journal of Psychiatry, 141,* 1088–1091.

Colsher, P., & Wallace, R. B. (1989). Data quality and age: Health and psychobehavioral correlates of item nonresponse and inconsistent responses. *Journal of Gerontology: Psychological Sciences, 44,* P45–P52.

Copeland, J. R. M., Kelleher, M. J., Kellett, J. M., Gourlay, A. J., Gurland, B. J., Fleiss, J. L., & Sharpe, L. (1976). A semi-structured clinical interview for the assessment of diagnostic and mental state in the elderly: The Geriatric and Mental State Schedule. I. Development and reliability. *Psychological Medicine, 6,* 439–449.

Cross, D. G., & Sharpley, C. F. (1981). The Locke-Wallace Marital Adjustment Test reconsidered: Some psychometric findings as regards its reliability and factorial validity. *Educational and Psychological Measurement, 41,* 1303–1306.

D'Agostino, P. A., McCoy, N., & Lacerda, S. (1976). A critique of the item content and format of the Sexual Interaction Inventory. *Family Therapy, 3,* 217–228.

D'Augelli-Frankel, J. (1986). Sexual Interaction Inventory. *American Journal of Family Therapy, 14,* 165–170.

DeLongis, A., Folkman, S., & Lazarus, R. S. (1988). The impact of daily stress on health and mood: Psychological and social resources as mediators. *Journal of Personality and Social Psychology, 54,* 488–495.

DeMaio, T. (1980). Refusals: Who, where and why. *Public Opinion Quarterly, 44,* 223–233.

Dupree, L. E., & Patterson, R. L. (1985). Older adults. In M. Hersen and S. M. Turner (Eds.), *Diagnostic interviewing* (pp. 337–359). New York: Plenum Press.

Edelstein, B., & Yoman, J. (1991). Behavioral interviewing. In V. E. Caballo (Ed.), *Manual de tecnicas de terpaia y modificación de conducta.* Madrid: Interamerica.

Eisdorfer, C. (1968). Arousal and performance: Verbal learning. In G. A. Talland (Ed.), *Human aging and behavior* (pp. 189–216). New York: Academic Press.

Epstein, L., & Perkins, K. (1988). Smoking, stress, and coronary heart disease. *Journal of Consulting and Clinical Psychology, 56,* 342–349.

Ewing, J. A. (1984). Detecting alcoholism: The CAGE questionnaire. *Journal of the American Medical Association, 252,* 1905–1907.

Feher, E. P., Larrabee, G. J., & Crook, T. J. (1992). Factors attenuating the validity of the geriatric depression scale in a dementia population. *Journal of the American Geriatrics Society, 40,* 906–909.

Folstein, M. F., Folstein, S. E., & McHugh, P. R. (1975). Mini-mental state: A practical guide for grading the cognitive state of patients for the clinician. *Journal of Psychiatric Research, 12,* 189–198.

Freitag, C. B., & Barry, J. R. (1974). Interaction and interviewer bias in a survey of the aged. *Psychological Reports, 34,* 771–774.

Fry, P. S. (1986). *Depression, stress, and adaptations in the elderly: Psychological assessment and intervention.* Rockville, MD: Aspen.

Furry, C. A., & Baltes, P. B. (1973). The effect of age differences in ability on extraneous variables on the assessment of intelligence in children, adults, and the elderly. *Journal of Gerontology, 28,* 73–80.

Gallagher, D., Thompson, L. W., Levy, S. M. (1980). Clinical psychological assessment of older adults. In L. W. Poon (Ed.), *Aging in the 1980's* (pp. 19–40). Washington DC: American Psychology Association.

Gatz, M., & Pearson, C. G. (1988). Ageism revised and the provision of psychological services. *American Psychologist, 43,* 184–188.

George, L. K. (1994). Multidimensional assessment instruments: Present status and future prospects. In M. P. Lawton & J. A. Teresi (Eds.), *Annual review of gerontology and geriatrics* (Vol. 14, pp. 353–376). New York: Springer.

Gergen, K. J., & Back, K. W. (1966). Communication in the interview and the disengaged respondent. *Public Opinion Quarterly, 30*, 385–398.

Goga, J. A., & Hambacher, W. O. (1977). Psychologic and behavioral assessment of geriatric patients: a review. *Journal of the American Geriatrics Society, 25*(5), 232–237.

Goodstein, R. K. (1985). Common clinical problems in the elderly: Camouflaged by ageism and atypical presentation. *Psychiatric Annals, 15*, 299–312.

Graziano, A. M., & Raulin, M. L. (1989a). Data and the nature of measurement. In J. Rothman (Ed.), *Research Methods: A Process of Inquiry* (pp. 68–82). New York: Harper & Row.

Graziano, A. M., & Raulin, M. L. (1989b). Hypothesis testing, validity, and threats to validity. In J. Rothman (Ed.), *Research Methods: A Process of Inquiry* (pp. 153–177). New York: Harper & Row.

Greene, M. G., Adelman, R., Charon, R. & Hoffman, S. (1986) Ageism in the medical encounter: An exploratory study of the doctor–elderly patient relationship. *Language & Communication, 6*, 113–124.

Gurland, B. J. (1973). A broad clinical assessment of psychopathology in the aged. In C. Eisdorfer & M. P. Lawton (Eds.), *The psychology of adult development and aging* (pp. 343–377). Washington, DC: American Psychological Association.

Gurland, B. J., Kuriansky, J., Sharpe, L., Simon, R., Stiller, P., & Birkett, P. (1977–78). CARE: Rationale, development, and reliability. *International Journal of Aging and Human Development, 8*, 9–42.

Haug, M., Bellgrave, L. L., & Gratton, B. (1984). Mental health and the elderly: Factors in stability and change over time. *Journal of Health and Social Behavior, 25*, 100–115.

Hayes, P. M., Lohse, D., & Bernstein, I. (1991). The development and testing of the Hayes and Lohse Non-Verbal Depression Scale. *Clinical Gerontologist, 10*(3), 3–13.

Haynes, S., & Jensen, B. J. (1979). The interview as a behavioral assessment instrument. *Behavioral Assessment, 1*, 97–106.

Hayslip, B., & Kennelly, K. (1985). Cognitive and non-cognitive factors affecting learning among older adults. In D. B. Lumsden (Ed.), *The older adult as learner* (pp. 73–98). Washington, DC: Hemisphere.

Hayslip, B., Kennelly, K. J., & Maloy, R. M. (1990). Fatigue, depression, and cognitive performance among aged persons. *Experimental Aging Research, 16*, 111–115.

Hersen, M., & Van Hasselt, V. (1992). Behavioral assessment and treatment of anxiety in the elderly. *Clinical Psychology Review, 12*, 619–640.

Hertzog, C., & Schear, J. M. (1989). Psychometric considerations in testing the older person. In T. Hunt & C. J. Lindley (Eds.), *Testing older adults: A reference guide for geropsychological assessments* (pp. 24–50). Austin, TX: PRO-Ed.

Herzog, A. R., & Rodgers, W. L. (1988). Age and response rates to interview sample surveys. *Journal of Gerontology: Social Sciences, 43*, S200–S205.

Himmelfarb, S., & Murrell, S. A. (1983). Reliability and validity of five mental health scales in older persons. *Journal of Gerontology, 38*(3), 333–339.

Howell, D. C. (1992). The normal distribution. *Statistical Methods for Psychology* (3rd ed.). Boston: PWS Kent.

Hunt, R. A. (1978). The effect of item weighting on the Locke-Wallace Marital Adjustment Scale. *Journal of Marriage and the Family, 40*, 249–256.

Hunt, T. H., & Lindley, M. A. (1989). *Testing older adults*. Austin, TX: Pro-ed.

Hussian, R. A. (1981). *Geriatric psychology: A behavioral perspective*. New York: Van Nostrand Reinhold.

Janik, S. W., & Wells, K. S. (1982). Multidimensional assessment of the elderly client: A training program for the development of a new specialist. *Journal of Applied Gerontology, 1*, 45–52.

Kaffonek, S., Ettinger, W. H., Roca, R., Kittner, S., Taylor, N., & German, P. S. (1989). Instruments for screening for depression and dementia in a long-term care facility. *Journal of the American Geriatrics Society, 37*, 29–34.

Kane, M. J., Hasher, L., Stoltzfus, E. R., Zacks, R. T., & Connely, S. L. (1994). Inhibitory attentional mechanisms and aging. *Psychology and Aging, 9*(1), 103–112.

Kane, R. L., Ouslander, J. G., & Abrass, I. B. (1989). *Essentials of Clinical Geriatrics* (2nd ed.). New York: McGraw-Hill.

Kapust, L. R., & Weintraub, S. (1988). The home visit: Field assessment of mental status impairment in the elderly. *The Gerontologist, 28*(1), 112–115.

Kaszniak, A. (1990). Psychological assessment of the aging individual. In J. E. Birren & K. W. Schaie (Eds.), *Handbook of the psychology of aging* (3rd ed., pp. 427–445). New York: Academic Press.

Kennelly, K., Hayslip, B., & Richardson, S. (1985). Depression and helplessness-induced cognitive deficits in the aged. *Experimental Aging Research, 11,* 169–173.

Koenig, H. G., Meador, K. G., Cohen, H. J., & Blazer, D. G. (1988). Self-rated depression scales and screening for major depression in the older hospitalized patient with medical illness. *Journal of the American Geriatrics Association, 36,* 699–706.

Kogan, N. (1961). Attitudes towards old people in an older sample. *Journal of Abnormal and Social Psychology, 62,* 616–622.

Kuriansky, J. B., Gurland, B. J., & Fleiss, J. L. (1976). The assessment of self-care capacity in geriatric psychiatric patients by objective and subjective methods. *Journal of Clinical Psychology, 32*(1), 95–102.

Laidlaw, R. W., & Hamilton, M. A. (1937). A study of thresholds in apperception of passive movement among normal control subjects. *Bulletin of the Neurological Institute, 6,* 268–273.

Lawton, M. P., & Brody, E. M. (1969). Assessment of older people: Self-maintaining and instrumental activities of daily living. *The Gerontologist, 9,* 180–186.

Levenson, R. W., Carstensen, L. L., & Gottman, J. M. (1993). Long-term marriage: Age, gender, and satisfaction. *Psychology and Aging, 8*(2), 301–313.

Levenson, R. W., Carstensen, L. L., & Gottman, J. M. (1994). The influence of age and gender on affect, physiology, and their interrelations: A study of long-term marriages. *Journal of Personality and Social Psychology, 67*(1), 56–68.

Levenson, R. W., Gottman, J. M. (1983). Marital interaction: Physiological linkage and affective exchange. *Journal of Personality and Social Psychology, 45*(3), 587–697.

Locke, H. J., & Wallace, K. M. (1959). Short marital-adjustment and prediction tests: Their reliability and validity. *Marriage and Family Living, 21*(3), 251–255.

LoPiccolo, J., & Steger, J. C. (1974). The Sexual Interaction Inventory: A new instrument for assessment of sexual dysfunction. *Archives of Sexual Behavior, 3,* 585–595.

Lowenstein, D. A., Amigo, E., Duara, R., Guterman, R., Hurwitz, D., Berkowitz, N., Wilkie, F., Weinberg, G., Black,, B., Gittelman, B., & Eisdorfer, C. (1989). A new scale for the assessment of functional status in Alzheimer's disease and related disorders. *Journal of Gerontology, 55,* 114–121.

Marcus-Bernstein, C. (1986). Audiologic and nonaudiologic correlates of hearing handicap in black elderly. *Journal of Speech and Hearing Research, 29,* 301–312.

Margolis, E., Levy, B., & Sherman, F. T. (1981). Hearing disorders. In L. S. Libow & F. T. Sherman (Eds.), *The core of geriatric medicine.* St. Louis: C.V. Mosby.

Marmor, M. (1992). Normal age-related vision changes and their effects on vision. In E. Faye and C. Stuen (Eds.), *The aging eye and low vision* (pp. 6–16). New York: Lighthouse.

Martin, D. C., Moryzc, R. K., McDowell, J., Snustad, D., & Karpf, M. (1985). Community-based geriatric assessment. *Journal of the American Geriatric Society, 33*(9), 602–606.

Martin, R. L. (1990). Geriatric psychopharmacology: Present and future. *Psychiatric Annals, 20,* 682–694.

Mayfield, D., McLeod, G., & Hall, P. (1974). The CAGE questionnaire: Validation of a new alcoholism screening instrument. *American Journal of Psychiatry, 131,* 1121–1123.

McCoy, N. N., & D'Agostino, P. A. (1977). Factor analysis of the Sexual Interaction Inventory. *Archives of Sexual Behavior, 6,* 25–35.

Montamat, S. C., Cusack, B. J., & Vestal, R. E. (1989). Management of drug therapy in the elderly. *New England Journal of Medicine, 321,* 303–308.

Moore, J. T. (1985). Dysthymia in the elderly, 14th CINP Congress: Management of depression in late life. *Journal of Affective Disorders, Supplement 1,* 15–21.

Morris, J. N., Fries, B. E., Mehr, D. R., Hawes, C., Phillips, C., Mor, V., & Lipsitz, L. A. (1994). MDS Cognitive Performance Scale. *Journal of Gerontology: Medical Sciences, 49*(4), M174–M182.

Morris, W. W. & Boutelle, S. (1985). Multidimensional functional assessment in two modes. *The Gerontologist, 25*(6), 638–643.

Murden, R., McRae, T., Kaner, S., & Buckman, M. (1991). Mini-mental state exam scores vary with education in blacks and whites. *Journal of the American Geriatrics Society, 39,* 149–155.

Myers, A. M., & Huddy, L. (1985). Evaluating physical capabilities in the elderly: The relationship between ADL self-assessments and basic abilities. *Canadian Journal of Aging, 4*, 189–200.

Norcross, J. C., Prochaska, J. O., & Gallagher, K. M. (1989). Clinical psychologists in the 1980s: II. Theory, research and practice. *The Clinical Psychologist, 42*, 45–53.

Norris, J. T., Gallagher, D., Wilson, A. & Winograd, C. H. (1987). Assessment of depression in geriatric medical outpatients: The validity of two screening measures. *Journal of the American Geriatrics Society, 35*, 989–995.

Okun, M. (1976). Adult age and cautiousness in decision: A review of the literature. *Human Development, 19*, 220–233.

Ouslander, J. G. (1984). Psychiatric manifestations of physical illness in the elderly. *Psychiatric Medicine, 1*, 363–388.

Pachana, N. A., Gallagher-Thompson, D., & Thompson, L. W. (1994). Assessment of depression. In M. P. Lawton & J. A. Teresi (Eds.), *Annual review of gerontology and geriatrics*, (Vol. 14, pp. 234–256). New York: Springer.

Parmelee, P. A., Katz, I. R., & Lawton, P. (1992). Incidence of depression in long-term care settings. *Journal of Gerontology, 47*, 189–196.

Perlmutter, M. (1978). What is memory aging the aging of? *Developmental Psychology, 14*, 330–345.

Peterson, J. L., & Miller, C. (1980). Physical attractiveness and marriage adjustment in older America couples. *Journal of Psychology, 105*, 247–252.

Pfeiffer, E. (Ed.) (1975). *Multidimensional functional assessment: The OARS Methodology* (1st ed.). Durham, NC: Duke University Center for the Study of Aging and Human Development.

Poon, L., Crook, T., Gurland, B. J., Davis, K. L., Kaszniak, A., Eisdorfer, C. & Thompson, L. (Eds.). (1986). *Handbook for clinical memory assessment of older adults* (pp. 3–10). Washington, DC: American Psychological Association.

Rabbitt, P. (1982). Development of methods to measure changes in activities of daily living in the elderly. In S. Corkin, K. L. Davis, J. H. Growdon, E. Usdin, & R. J. Wurtman (Eds.), *Alzheimer's disease: A report of progress*. New York: Raven Press.

Rabkin, J. D. (1993). Stress and psychiatric disorders. In L. Goldberger & S. Breznitz (Eds.), *Handbook of stress: Theoretical and clinical aspects* (2nd ed., pp. 477–495). New York: Free Press.

Rodeheaver, D. (1990). Ageism. In I. A. Parham, L. W. Poon, & I. C. Siegler (Eds.), *Access: Aging curriculum content for education in the social-behavioral sciences* (pp. 7.1–7.43). New York: Springer.

Rodgers, W. L., & Herzog, A. R. (1987). Interviewing older adults: The accuracy of factual information. *Journal of Gerontology, 42*(4), 387–394.

Rook, K. S. (1990). Stressful aspects of older adults' social relationships: An overview of current theory and research. In M. A. P. Stephens, J. H. Crowther, S. E. Hobfoll, & D. L. Tennenbaum (Eds.), *Stress and coping in later-life families* (pp. 173–192). New York: Hemisphere.

Rubenstein, L. (1983). The clinical effectiveness of multidimensional geriatric assessment. *Journal of the American Geriatric Society, 31*(12), 758–762.

Rubenstein, L. Z., Schairer, C., Wieland, G. D., & Kane, R. (1984). Systematic biases in functional status assessment of elderly adults: Effects of different data sources. *Journal of Gerontology, 39*(6), 686–691.

Sager, M. A., Dunham, N. C., Schwantes, A., Mecum, L., Halverson, K., & Harlowe, D. (1992). Measurement of activities of daily living in hospitalized elderly: A comparison of self-report and performance-based methods, *Journal of the American Geriatrics Society, 40*, 457–462.

Sammons, M., & Karoly, P. (1987). Psychosocial variables in irritable bowel syndrome: A review and proposal. *Clinical Psychology Review, 7*, 187–204.

Schaefer, J., & Moos, R. (1993). Work stressors in health care: Context and outcomes. Special Issue: Work stressors in health care and social service settings. *Journal of Community and Applied Social Psychology, 3*, 235–242.

Schlenoff, D. (1989). Assessment of persons with motor disabilities. In T. Hunt, & C. J. Lindley (Eds.), *Testing older adults: A reference guide for geropsychological assessments* (pp. 122–134). Austin, TX: ProEd.

Schnelle, J. F., & Traughber, B. (1983). A behavioral assessment system applicable to geriatric nursing facility residents. *Behavioral Assessment, 5*, 231–243.

Shanas, E. (1974). Health status of older people: Cross national implications. *American Journal of Public Health, 64,* 261--263.

Shindell, S. (1989). Assessing the older adult with visual impairment. In T. Hunt, & C. J. Lindley (Eds.), *Testing older adults: A reference guide for geropsychological assessments* (pp. 135–149). Austin, TX: Pro-ed.

Spiro, A., Butcher, J., Levenson, M., Aldwin, C., & Bossé, R. (1994). *Personality change and stability over five years: The MMPI-2 in older men.* Manuscript submitted for publication.

Stones, M. J., & Kozma, A. (1989). Multidimensional assessment of the elderly via a microcomputer: The SENOTS program and battery. *Psychology and Aging,* March, *4*(1), 113–118.

Sunderland, A., Watts, K., Baddeley, A. D., & Harris, J. E. (1986). Subjective memory assessment and test performance in elderly adults. *Journal of Gerontology, 41*(3), 376–384.

Sunderland, T., Alterman, I. S., Yount, D., Hill, J. L., Tariot, P. N., Newhouse, P. A., Mueller, E. A., Mellow, A. M., & Cohen, R. M. (1988). A new scale for the assessment of depressed mood in demented patients. *American Journal of Psychiatry, 145*(8), 955–959.

Tinetti, M., & Powell, L. (1993). Fear of falling and low self-efficacy: A cause of dependence in elderly persons. *Journal of Gerontology, 48* (special issue), 35–38.

Tombaugh, T. N., & McIntyre, N. J. (1992). The mini-mental state examination: A comprehensive review. *Journal of the American Geriatric Society, 40,* 922–935.

Vernon, M. (1989). Assessment of persons with hearing disabilities. In T. Hunt, & C. J. Lindley (Eds.), *Testing older adults: A reference guide for geropsychological assessments* (pp. 150–162). Austin, TX: Pro-ed.

Vitalino, P. P., Breen, A. R., Albert, M. S., Russo, J., & Prinz, P. N. (1984). Memory, attention, and functional status in community-residing Alzheimer type dementia patients and optimally healthy aged individuals. *Journal of Gerontology, 39,* 58–64.

Whitbourne, S. K. (1985). *The aging body: Physiological changes and psychological consequences.* New York: Springer-Verlag.

Whitbourne, S. K., & Powers, C. B. (1996). Psychological perspectives on the normal aging process. In L. L. Carstensen, B. A. Edelstein, & L. Dornbrand (Eds.), *Handbook of the practice of clinical gerontology.* Beverly Hills, CA: Sage.

White, S., & Edelstein, B. (1991). Behavioral assessment and investigatory interviewing. *Behavioral Assessment, 13,* 245–264.

Williams, T. F., Hill, J. G., Fairbank, M. E., Knox, K. G. (1973). Appropriate placement of the chronically ill and aged: A successful approach by evaluation. *Journal of the American Medical Society, 226*(11), 1332–1335.

Wilson, L. A., Grant, K., Witney, P. M., & Kerridge, D. F. (1973). Mental status of elderly hospital patient's related to occupational therapist's assessment of activities of daily living. *Gerontologia Clinica, 15,* 197–222.

Winograd, I. R. (1984). Sensory changes with age: Impact on psychological well-being. *Psychiatric Medicine, 2,* 1–26.

Yesavage, J. A. (1986). The use of self-rating depression scales in the elderly. In Poon, L., T. Crook, B. J. Gurland, K. L. Davis, A. W. Kaszniak, C. Eisdorfer, & L. W. Thompson (Eds.), *Handbook for clinical memory assessment for older adults* (pp. 213–217). Washington, DC: American Psychological Association.

Yesavage, J. A., Brink, T. L., & Rose, T. L., Lum, O., Huang, V., Adey, M., & Leirer, V. O. (1983). Development and validation of a geriatric depression scale: A preliminary report. *Journal of Psychiatric Research, 17,* 37–49.

Zarit, J. M., & Zarit, S. H. (1987). Molar aging: The physiology and psychology of normal aging. In L. Carstensen & B. Edelstein (Eds.), *Handbook of clinical gerontology* (pp. 18–32). New York: Pergamon Press.

Zeiss, A. (1992, November). *What behavior therapy has to offer older adults.* Workshop presented at meeting of the Association for Advancement of Behavior Therapy. Boston, MA.

Zelinski, E. M., Gilewski, M. J., & Thompson, L. W. (1980). Do laboratory tests relate to self-assessment of memory ability in the young and old? In L. W. Poon, J. L. Fozard, L. S. Cermak, D. Arenberg, & L. W. Thompson (Eds.), *New directions in memory and aging: Proceedings of the George A. Talland memorial conference.* Hillsdale, NJ: Erlbaum.

CHAPTER 4

Clinical Neuropsychology of Older Adults

GEOFFREY TREMONT AND WILEY MITTENBERG

INTRODUCTION

Clinical neuropsychology is an empirically guided, applied discipline that seeks to identify behavioral correlates of central nervous system dysfunction (Lezak, 1983). It is particularly pertinent to older adults, who are at an increased risk for organic dysfunction and frequently present with cognitive complaints. Additionally, chronic medical illnesses and the extensive medication regimens of elderly individuals can compromise their mental status. The purposes of neuro-

---

GEOFFREY TREMONT • Department of Psychiatry and Behavioral Sciences, University of Oklahoma Health Sciences Center, Oklahoma City, Oklahoma 73142.   WILEY MITTENBERG • Center for Psychological Studies, Nova Southeastern University, Fort Lauderdale, Florida 33314.

Psychological Treatment of Older Adults: An Introductory Text, edited by Michel Hersen and Vincent B. Van Hasselt. Plenum Press, New York, 1996.

psychological assessment with the elderly (as with any age group) vary according to the referral question and patients' medical or psychiatric history. Often, differential diagnosis between the functional and organic nature of a person's disturbance is necessary, especially because neurological disorders can present with psychological symptoms or completely mimic psychiatric disorders (Lezak, 1983). Questions about legal or financial competency and the ability to function independently are also commonly encountered with the elderly. Finally, normal age-associated cognitive declines must often be distinguished from degenerative neurological disorders. This chapter will present a description of the neuropsychological changes associated with normal aging, common neuropsychological disorders in older adults, and the different neuropsychological approaches developed for distinguishing functional from organic disorders in the elderly.

NEUROPSYCHOLOGICAL CHANGES
IN NORMAL AGING

As the human body ages, alteration and deterioration of the cardiovascular, respiratory, immunological, and other organs systems occur. Thus, it is not surprising that the brain and the entire central nervous system are affected by aging. In this section, we will briefly discuss specific physiological changes that have been found in the normal aging brain (see Albert & Knoefel, 1994, for a complete review), cognitive changes associated with normal aging, and the theoretical explanations of cognitive decline.

Physiological Changes in Brain Structure and Function

The brain of an older adult displays average losses in peak weight of 7% to 8%, demyelination or loss of white matter, especially in frontal and subcortical regions (Miller, Alston, & Corsellis, 1980), atrophy with shrinking gyri and widening of sulci (Berg, 1988), and ventricular enlargement (Albert & Stafford, 1988). Neuronal loss has been found to average 40% in 90-year-old brains (Brody, 1978), with the greatest declines seen in frontal, temporal, and parietal regions (Kemper, 1984). Decreased interconnection in geriatric brains is evidenced by reduction of dendritic branching and declines in the neurotransmitter substances of acetylcholine, dopamine, and norepinephrine (Rogers & Bloom, 1985; Scheibel, 1992). Microscopic changes in elderly brains viewed on autopsy are characterized by the presence of neuritic (senile) plaques and neurofibrillary tangles, structures commonly associated with degenerative neurological disorders such as Alzheimer's disease (Jordan, 1971; Matsuyama & Nakamura, 1977). Mild declines in brain metabolism have been inferred from evidence of reduced regional cerebral blood flow and slowed glucose metabolism in older adults when compared to younger control subjects (Kuhl, Metter, Riege, & Hawkins, 1984; Metter, 1988). Electroencephalography studies of geriatric patients have consistently found diffuse slowing of the dominant alpha rhythm and the appearance of slow theta or delta waves (Wang & Busse, 1969). Taken as a whole, neurobiological findings in normal aging clearly indicate anatomical, neurochemical, microscopic, and electrical changes.

Cognitive Changes Associated with Normal Aging

Although the neurobiological literature implicates a clear association between aging and deteriorating changes in brain structure and function, it provides no information about an elderly individual's behavioral, psychological, and cognitive functioning. Neuropsychological studies with normal older adults address how central nervous system changes impact these functional abilities. In this section, we discuss specific cognitive declines associated with advancing age and their theoretical implications.

Studies of intellectual function in the elderly show greater declines in Performance IQ than Verbal IQ on the Wechsler Adult Intelligence Scale across the life-span (Botwinick, 1977). One explanation of these declines is posited by Horn and Cattell's (1967) model of fluid and crystallized abilities. The model suggests that verbal skills are overlearned—crystallized or emphasized—by educational experiences and thus affected little by advancing age (i.e., Verbal IQ). Nonverbal tasks that are more novel and unfamiliar to individuals appear more sensitive to aging (i.e., Performance IQ). Critics of the model have suggested that verbal-performance differences are artifactual, reflecting practice effects of different skills or decreased motor speed rather than neuropsychological declines (Mittenberg, Seidenberg, O'Leary, & DiGiulio, 1989; Storandt, 1977).

Normal older adults also show lower scores than younger subjects on tests of visual-spatial abilities. For example, the elderly perform worse on Block Design, Object Assembly, and Picture Completion subtests of the WAIS-R (Wechsler, 1981). Tests involving complex spatial organization, visual closure, and matching unfamiliar faces also show age-related declines (Benton, Eslinger, & Damasio, 1981; Read, 1988). One explanation of these visual-spatial impairments is the accelerated right hemisphere aging model, which proposes that elderly patients perform neuropsychological tasks in a manner that is similar to individuals with right hemisphere lesions (Goldstein & Shelly, 1981). Findings that structural changes in the central nervous system occur bilaterally and that neuropsychological testing results do not show lateralized patterns argue against the right hemisphere model (Benton et al., 1981; MacInnes, 1982).

An extensive literature has also examined memory problems in the elderly. Older adults show age-related deficits when material is presented in a rapid manner with a tachistoscope, suggesting that older people need greater stimulus exposure time to encode information (Cerella, Poon, & Fozard, 1982). These results contrast with studies of attention (immediate memory span), which indicate little to no effect of aging (Botwinick, 1977). The most consistent memory deficits found among healthy older individuals involve storing learned material in memory (secondary memory). Research evidence has indicated that normal elderly subjects may not process information thoroughly and appear to use inefficient strategies to remember (Perlmutter & Mitchell, 1982). Training these subjects in more a efficient system offers only short-term effects, with individuals reverting back to inefficient methods quickly (Scogin & Bienias, 1988). Finally, memory retrieval problems in normal geriatric subjects have been studied through a comparison of recognition and recall abilities. Recognition (i.e., selecting remembered material when given choices) consistently exceeds recall (i.e., having to freely generate learned material) across ages; however, greatest differences between the two abilities are seen in older adults (Kazniak, Poon, & Riege, 1986).

Consistent declines in normal aging on tests sensitive to frontal lobe functions has led researchers to posit a frontal-deficit hypothesis (Albert & Kaplan, 1980; Hochanadel & Kaplan, 1984; Mittenberg et al., 1989). The model suggests that as people age, they often perform more poorly on tests sensitive to frontal lobe lesions and make errors suggestive of frontal lobe dysfunction (Albert & Kaplan, 1980). These tests tap a number of so-called executive functions such as problem solving, shifting of mental sets, inhibitory behavior, and verbal and nonverbal fluency. Mittenberg et al. (1989) examined the efficacy of the right hemisphere and frontal models by comparing the performance of a group of healthy older adults to a control group of younger subjects on a number of neuropsychological tests, tapping lateralized functions of the frontal, temporal, and parietal lobes. Their results indicated no hemispheric differences between age groups, arguing against accelerated right hemisphere aging. The highest correlations were found between age and tests sensitive to both right and left frontal lobe function, supporting the frontal deficit model. Further evidence for the frontal hypothesis comes from neurological studies implicating structural and functional changes in the frontal lobe with normal aging (e.g., Gerard & Weisberg, 1986) and findings of increased concrete reasoning, perseveration, and slowed thought processes among healthy geriatric subjects (Botwinick, 1977).

Overall, findings from the neurological and neuropsychological research on aging clearly indicate structural and functional deterioration of the central nervous system. Much of the current research points to decline in the frontal lobe region, which is consistent with findings indicating age-related losses of white matter in regions of the brain that complete myelination late in development, such as the frontal lobes (Miller et al., 1980). Age-associated declines in cognitive function add to an already complicated differential diagnosis, as will be seen in the next section.

COMMON NEUROPSYCHOLOGICAL
DISORDERS IN OLDER ADULTS

As individuals age, they are at greater risk for developing disorders of the central nervous system (Roth, 1980). Additionally, age and acquired brain damage interact, in that severity of deficits increases with advancing age (Lezak, 1983). Finally, neurological disorders in the elderly (and in fact at all ages) often present with associated psychological symptomatology or mimic actual psychiatric disturbances. In this section, we will discuss common neurological disorders in older adults, their incidence, etiology, clinical presentation, and course.

Alzheimer's Disease

Alzheimer's Disease (AD), also known as dementia of the Alzheimer's type, is a progressive deteriorating condition affecting the central nervous system at the microscopic level. It accounts for 70% of dementia cases, making it the most common dementing illness (Malaspina, Quitkin, & Kaufmann, 1994). One large study, utilizing criteria established by the National Institute of Neurological and Communicative Disorders and Stroke (NINCDS) and the Alzheimer's Disease and Related Disorders Association (ADRDA; for criteria see McKhann et al., 1984), found rates for the disorder of 3% for 65- to 74-year-olds, 18.7% for 75- to 85-year-olds, and 47.2% for individuals age 85 or older (Evans et al., 1989). Women are at a slightly greater risk of developing AD than men (Rocca, Amaducci, & Schoenberg, 1986).

Etiology

The cause of AD remains unknown, but research has identified multiple possible etiologies of the disorder (see review by Wurtman, Corkin, Ritter-Walker, & Growdon, 1990). Specific microscopic neuropathological changes have been identified, including the presence of neurofibrillary tangles, neuritic plaques, and granuvacuolar bodies. These changes are seen to a lesser degree in normal aging, consistent with the hypothesis that AD may represent an acceleration of the aging process. However, another interpretation of these findings is that aging may place an individual at greater risk of developing AD (Adams & Victor, 1977). Similar neuropathological findings in AD and older Down's syndrome patients suggest a genetic defect in chromosome 21 (Glenner & Wong, 1984). However, a number of studies searching for such a defect have failed to detect it (Malaspina et al., 1994), leaving the causal role of genetics in AD unclear. There is also some indication of a familial pattern in AD, with a slightly increased risk of the disorder among first-degree relatives of an individual diagnosed with AD ranging from 3.8% to 14.4% (Amaducci, Fratiglioni, & Rocca, 1986). This familial subtype may be associated with early-onset AD (before age 65; Heston, 1988). However, this may be an artifactual finding, since family studies are complicated by the usual late onset of the disorder, which can result in probands dying from other diseases before AD appears. Finally, twin studies have demonstrated equal concordance rates (40%) and highly discrepant ages at onset among monozygotic and dizygotic twins (ranging from 6 to 15 years), implicating a strong environmental influence on the emergence of AD (e.g., Cook, Schneck, & Clark, 1981; Kay, 1989). Aluminum toxicity has been proposed as a possible etiology of AD. Aluminum is toxic to the central nervous system and has been found in high levels in neurofibrillary tangles of AD brains, but no causal links have been established (Perl & Brody, 1980). Other findings suggest reduced production of acetylcholine and degeneration of cholinergic neurons as a cause of AD (Coyle, Price, & DeLong, 1983). However, pharmacological intervention focused on increasing cholinergic activity has not been shown to significantly improve cognitive function (Bartus, Dean, Beer, & Lippa, 1982). Finally, a viral etiology has also been posited because some degenerative disorders, such as Creutzfeldt-Jakob's disease, are virally transmitted. However, research with animals has not found any transmission of AD neuropathology and no direct evidence of infection is seen in humans.

Clinical Features and Course

Diagnosis of AD is generally made as definite or probable, with definite diagnosis requiring histopathological evidence of AD from biopsy or autopsy (McKhann et al., 1984). Computed tomography (CT) scan abnormalities do not usually appear until middle stages of the disease and are characterized by diffuse atrophy and ventricular enlargement. Cognitive symptoms of AD include intellectual decline, deficits in learning new information, impaired naming and receptive language function, visual-spatial deficits, and poor judgment Cummings, 1994). Intact functions in AD patients include motor and sensory skills, attentional abilities, and verbal fluency, which do not become impaired until very late in the disease process. According to the *Diagnostic and Statistical Manual of Mental Disorders* (4th ed.; *DSM-IV*; American Psychiatric Association, 1994), AD is diagnosed when a memory impairment and one other specific cognitive impairment is present. These deficits must represent a decline from previously higher functioning and must interfere with social or occupational functioning. Exclusionary criteria involve the presence of other central nervous system dysfunction, systemic illness associated with dementia, and delirium that is concomitant with the dementia symptoms. *DSM-IV* also requires specification of early (before age 65) versus late onset and the presence of complicating factors such as delirium, delusions, or depressed mood.

In early stages of the illness, psychological symptoms may predominate, and careful neuropsychological assessment is necessary for differential diagnosis. General personality changes, such as reduced emotional responsiveness and energy level, difficulty initiating activity, loss of interest and enthusiasm, and decreased affection, are common in AD patients (Petry, Cummings, & Hill, 1989). Delusions have been noted to occur in as many as 50% of AD patients, with the most frequent appearance during the middle stages of the disease (Wragg & Jeste, 1989). Common delusional themes include persecution, infidelity of one's spouse, abandonment, theft, and not recognizing one's own home (Reisberg, Borenstein, & Salob, 1987). Hallucinations can also occur in AD but less frequently than delusions. According to one study, visual hallucinations are most often reported, typically involving deceased persons, intruders, and animals (Mendez, Martin, & Smith, 1990). Symptoms of depression, anxiety, and mood lability occur in a large portion of AD patients (Cummings, Miller, Hill, & Neshkes, 1987). Differential diagnosis between AD and depression must frequently be made. Often, depressed geriatric patients present with a pseudodementia or depression characterized by cognitive dysfunction. Some features that may distinguish pseudodementia from AD include abrupt onset and rapid progression of symptoms, complaints of cognitive problems, and variable performance on neuropsychological tests (Kaplan & Sadock, 1991). Neuropsychological examination is essential in making the distinction between depression and early AD.

AD is characterized by insidious onset with a steady decline in function. Once the disorder is diagnosed, the average life expectancy is 7 years, with 30% living more than 10 years, and a small percentage surviving more than 20 years (Walton, 1977). Researchers have highlighted stages of the disease (e.g., Strub & Black, 1981). In initial stages, the patient usually displays mild IQ declines, significant memory impairment, anomia, constructional dyspraxia, depression, anxiety, and mild agitation. During this stage, neurodiagnostic examination is typically normal. Middle stages are characterized by decreased depression, fluent aphasia, inability to perform mathematical calculations, apraxia, indifference to disease, and personality changes. An EEG during this period may show mild slowing and possible atrophy on CT scan. Final stages of the disease involve complete loss of cognitive function, no speech output or echolalia, urinary incontinence, and motor rigidity. AD patients' deaths usually occur as a result of pneumonia, urinary tract infection, or other age-related disease such as heart disease or cancer (Cummings, 1994).

Vascular Dementia

Vascular dementia, also known as multiinfarct dementia (MID), results from cerebrovascular disease and is the second most common form of dementia, accounting for 8% to 35% of diagnosed cases (Cummings & Benson, 1992). It can easily be misdiagnosed as AD, and therefore we will highlight throughout this section some of its distinguishing features. Vascular dementia is characterized by a stepwise deterioration of cognitive function with patchy areas of intact abilities. Onset usually occurs after age 50. It is more common in men than women, especially with onset before age 70 (Ladurner, Iliff, & Lechner, 1982). Risk factors for vascular dementia include aging and any of the risk factors for stroke such as diabetes, hypertension, heart disease, and cigarette smoking (Schoenberg, 1988; Loeb, 1980).

Etiology

Vascular dementia can result from numerous types of cerebrovascular disease (see review by Mirsen & Hachinski, 1988). The most common cause of vascular dementia is multiple cerebral infarctions or dead brain tissue resulting from insufficient oxygen supply secondary to blocked or reduced blood flow to that area. The severity of dementia appears to be related to the number and location of the infarcts. Small infarcts in subcortical white matter (also called lacunar infarcts) have also been implicated as a cause of dementia (Hachinski,

Lassen, & Marshall, 1974). There is some controversy over how often subcortical infarctions are involved in causing dementia; this subject awaits further investigation (Brust, 1988). Whether they are cortical or subcortical, infarcts can usually be detected on CT scan and even better through magnetic resonance imaging (MRI). Another less common cause of vascular dementia is Binswanger's disease (also known as subcortical arteriosclerotic encephalopathy), which involves white matter degeneration secondary to arteriosclerosis (hardening) of small arteries in subcortical regions (Cummings & Benson, 1992).

Clinical Features and Course

Although vascular dementia usually presents with a rapid onset, its presentation can resemble AD, making differential diagnosis important. The patient often has a history of cardiovascular disease or other risk factors previously mentioned. The patient is also noted to have a stepwise deterioration, referring to abrupt declines in functioning associated with vascular changes. The usual features of vascular dementia include psychological symptomatology, motor disturbance, and neuropsychological impairments. *DSM-IV* (American Psychiatric Association, 1994) requires the presence of a dementia (see AD for a description), and either focal neurological signs and symptoms or neurodiagnostic evidence of cerebrovascular disease that is judged to be related to the behavioral presentation. Focal neurological signs include the presence of primitive reflexes not commonly displayed by adults (e.g., extensor plantar response), pseudobulbar palsy, motor weakness, and gait disturbances. These patients frequently present depression as initial symptoms. In fact, as many as 60% of these patients would meet diagnostic criteria for major depression (Cummings, 1988). The most common depressive symptoms include sadness, psychomotor retardation, and somatic complaints (Cummings, 1994). Personality changes are less common in vascular dementia than AD. However, emotional lability is frequently present and, in addition, MID patients often experience nocturnal confusion. As with AD, delusional ideation is common and has been identified in up to 50% of vascularly demented patients (Cummings et al., 1987).

Neuropsychological findings in vascular dementia are seen as "patchy," with areas of intact functioning. Declines in intellectual and memory function are associated with vascular dementia, but scores frequently fluctuate and losses are not as large as seen in AD (Perez et al., 1975). Numerous investigations indicate greater impairments in verbal fluency in vascular dementia patients than AD patients and better performance by MID patients on naming tasks than AD patients (Hier, Hagenlocker, & Shindler, 1985; Powell, Cummings, Hill, & Benson, 1988). Other specific neuropsychological findings can depend on the number of specific location of infarcts. Subcortical infarctions (lacunar and Binswanger's disease) are associated with motor slowing, memory impairments, and frontal lobe findings (Cummings & Benson, 1992). Cortical features can involve impairments in complex skills of language, visual-spatial, and memory abilities.

As stated previously, the onset of vascular dementia is usually abrupt, and the course is characterized by plateaus of stable functioning and then large declines. As with larger strokes, focal deficits may appear suddenly and resolve just as quickly. Without treatment, patients with vascular dementia may experience further small occlusions as well as larger strokes, which can cause severe neurological symptoms (e.g., hemiparesis) or even death.

Alcoholic Dementia

Alcoholic dementia is associated with long-term alcohol abuse and is believed to be a direct effect of alcohol on the central nervous system. Although the disorder occurs in only 3% to 7% of alcoholics, cognitive impairments have been observed in up to 50% to 70% of chronic alcoholic patients (Charness, Simon, & Greenberg, 1989). The amount of alcohol necessary to produce alcohol dementia has been estimated to be 150 ml of absolute alcohol per day over a 10- to 15-year period, which would be equivalent to two bottles of wine, 7 pints of beer, or one-half bottle of distilled spirits (Cummings & Benson, 1983). The disorder is distinguished from another alcohol-related disorder, Wernicke-Korsakoff's syndrome, which is characterized by a severe amnestic impairment secondary to a vitamin deficiency (i.e., thiamine). There is some debate in the current literature about the relationship between the two conditions; however, they are both the result of heavy alcohol use (Brandt & Butters, 1986).

Etiology

Alcohol dementia is clearly associated with chronic ingestion of large quantities of alcohol, but the cause of the disorder has yet to be delineated. Hypothetical mechanisms have been proposed through empirical study and will be briefly presented here (see review by Parsons, 1994). The most parsimonious explanation of the relationship between alcohol and cognitive impairment is that the neurotoxic effect of alcohol directly alters brain tissue and causes cerebral atrophy. CT scans of alcoholic patients with dementia indicate extensive and severe cortical atrophy (especially in frontal regions) and EEG findings indicate diffuse slowing of brain activity (Cummings & Benson, 1983). However, the amount of ethanol intake has not consistently been correlated with neuropsychological test results or findings with neurodiagnostic techniques (Cutting, 1982). This finding may be due to confounding factors such as age and length of abstinence prior to examination, which show relatively strong relationships to neurological and neuropsychological results. Additionally, some researchers have suggested that alcoholics' proneness to head injury, liver disease, and nutritional deficiencies may explain consistent neuropsychological impairments in this population (Cutting, 1982; Loberg, 1986). Sex differences have been noted, with women developing dementia after a much shorter period of alcohol abuse (Cutting, 1982). Like theories on cognitive changes in normal aging, explanations of the neurological findings seen in chronic alcoholism implicate accelerated aging, deterioration of the right hemisphere, frontal-subcortical, or diffuse brain regions (Loberg, 1986). More work needs to be done, but the frontal-subcortical hypothesis currently seems to have the most support from radiological and neuropsychological studies.

Clinical Features and Course

The initial presentation of a patient with alcohol dementia can be easily mistaken for a psychiatric disturbance. Patients may display poor hygiene, impaired judgment, attentional difficulties, and general slowed thought processes (Strub & Black, 1981). Forgetfulness, motor slowing, perseveration, and poor attention can also be present (Lishman, 1990). The cognitive deficits associated with alcoholic dementia can range from mild to total confusion. Depression is commonly associated with alcoholism, which may further mask the neurological impairment. Other associated medical illnesses, such as peripheral neuropathy and cirrhosis, may provide evidence for the presence of alcohol dementia. Neuropsychological testing shows impairments on nonverbal intellectual abilities, short-term memory function, and verbal fluency (Blusewicz, Dustman, Schenkenberg, & Beck, 1977). Tests of frontal lobe function often reveal poor abstraction, difficulty shifting mental sets, and perserveration (Lishman, 1990). Alcohol dementia can be distinguished neuropsychologically from AD by the infrequent presence of visuoconstructionàl impairments among alcoholic patients. Interestingly, however, alcohol abuse has been identified as a risk factor for late-onset AD (Fratiglioni, 1993). Alcoholic dementia can be distinguished from Wernicke's encephalopathy because memory impairment and language disturbances are not as severe in alcoholic dementia.

The course of alcoholic dementia will depend on the behavior of the patient. In patients who abstain from alcohol no progression of cognitive impairments would be expected. Further, some studies indicate at least partial reversibility of the cognitive impairments and neuroradiological findings in abstinent patients (Carlen, Wortzman, Holgate, & Rankin, 1978; Cutting, 1982). Research into the neuropsychological reversibility of the disorder has shown that a large percentage of abstinent patients improve, but apparently not to premorbid levels (O'Leary, Radford, Chaney, & Schau, 1977; Page & Linden, 1974).

Cerebral Neoplasms

Cerebral neoplasms or central nervous system tumors can arise from a myriad of cell types found in the brain and its protective layers, as well as through metastatic processes from other locations in the body. Ten percent of all neoplasms develop in the central nervous system and account for 2% of cancer-related deaths (Kurtzke, 1984). The likelihood for the development of tumors in the body increases with advancing age; however, the frequency of cerebral neoplasms declines after middle age (Katzman & Rowe, 1992). The most common tumors in older adults are glioblastomas, meningiomas, neurilemmomas, and metastatic processes, which account for 82% of tumors in adults over the age of 60 (Katzman & Rowe, 1992). Additionally, patients who are 50 and younger show median survival rates that are two times greater following surgery for cerebral neoplasms than adults age 60 and older (Kornblith, Wicker, & Casady, 1987). Thus, brain tumors may be less common in older adults, but appear to be associated with a poorer prognosis.

Etiology

Numerous classification systems have been developed for brain tumors, identifying their cell type, location, and rate of growth. Among adults, 80% of brain tumors are classified as primary, originating in the brain, and 20% metastatic, carried to the central nervous system from other primary sites in the body (Price, Goetz, & Lovell, 1994). The classification system of malignant versus benign is less valuable with cerebral neoplasms because even slowly growing masses labeled as benign can produce severe dysfunction or even death secondary to increased intracranial pressure, compressed brain tissue, or edema (Reitan & Wolfson, 1992). The specific causal mechanisms of brain tumors have not been confirmed. Hypotheses about their etiology propose genetic factors, physical trauma, chemical carcinogens, and viruses (Reitan & Wolfson, 1992). Gliomas, which arise from glial cells inside the brain, are the most common type of tumor at all ages and can range from rapid and invasive (i.e., glioblastoma or grade 4 to 5 astrocytoma), usually resulting in death within a few months, to slow growing and invasive (i.e., grade 1 astrocytoma), resulting in death after approximately 5 years (Lezak, 1983). Meningiomas, also common in older adults, are slow growing, well-encapsulated tumors that develop in the meninges (outer protective surface of the brain). Surgical removal is usually very effective with these neoplasms. One study reported that 96% of patients undergoing surgery for meningiomas survived 1 year after surgery and 63% survived after 15 years (Reitan & Wolfson, 1992). The most common metastatic tumors that travel to the brain are lung and breast cancer (Price et al., 1994). The final category of cerebral neoplasms common in the elderly is neurilemmomas, which develop in the area of the cranial nerves, most commonly near the acoustic nerve (i.e., acoustic neuromas).

Clinical Features and Course

Many cerebral neoplasms can present with psychological symptoms in conjunction with neurological signs or as the only manifestation of the lesion (Strub & Black, 1981). Indeed, central nervous system tumors can completely mimic psychiatric disturbances and make distinguishing functional and organic symptoms impossible (referred to as neurologically silent; Price et al., 1994). Large-sample studies have reported that 51% to 78% of patients with cerebral tumors display psychiatric symptoms (Keschner, Bender, & Strauss, 1938; Schlesinger, 1950). Another investigation found that 15% of brain tumor patients were hospitalized for psychiatric disorders (Williams, Bell, & Gye, 1974). The most common types of psychological disturbances include depression, psychosis, and personality changes, with the majority (88%) of tumor patients displaying emotional symptoms having tumors located in the frontal, temporal, or limbic regions (Williams et al., 1974). A recent study with older brain tumor patients (ages 66 to 87) displaying primarily psychiatric symptoms found that 93% had lesions located in the frontal lobe (Fulton, Duncan, & Caird, 1992). Commonly associated neurological signs and symptoms include headache, vomiting, seizures, papilledema, and acute confusional state, with the last symptom easily being misattributed as psychiatric disorder. Focal neurological deficits, such as aphasia or sensory impairments, can occur, depending the size and velocity of the lesion. Cerebral neoplasms can be best detected by neuropsychological examination, CT, or MRI.

Neuropsychological examination is useful to identify the level of cognitive dysfunction associated with the lesion and provide pre- and postsurgical information about a patient's status. Cognitive features of brain tumors vary with the location, size, and growth rate of the lesions (Reitan & Wolfson, 1992). For example, slow-growing, well-encapsulated tumors may produce subtle cognitive and psychological changes as a result of pressure effects, whereas rapidly growing invasive tumors may produce acute confusional symptoms and focal neurological signs associated with increased intracranial pressure and destruction of tissue. Specific symptomatology has been identified for common locations of cerebral neoplasms. Frontal lobe neoplasms are associated with behavioral symptoms of depression, apathy, euphoria, lack of social graces, and personality changes and relatively few neurological symptoms, whereas temporal lobe tumors commonly produce seizure activity, hallucinations, depression, psychosis, and personality change (Strub & Black, 1982).

Symptoms of brain tumors usually develop over several months and are slowly progressive. Once symptoms appear, the course of tumors such as glioblastomas and metastatic processes is rapidly progressive, and death usually occurs within several months. Other slow-growing encapsulated tumors such as meningiomas can be successfully removed through surgery, and the prognosis for long-term survival is favorable (Reitan & Wolfson, 1992). Often, cognitive and behavioral symptoms of cerebral neoplasms do not become obvious until the lesion is quite large (Price et al., 1994).

Head Trauma

Head trauma is a major public health concern in the United States, with two million head injuries occurring annually and the cost to society estimated at $25 billion yearly. The most common causes of head injuries are motor vehicle accidents (50%), falls (21%), assaults and violence (12%), and sports and recreation accidents (10%) (U. S. Department of Health and Human Services, 1989). Mild head injury accounts for most trauma and can be especially difficult to manage because of the lack of neurological findings but frequent psychiatric and emotional sequelae. The majority of head injuries occur in children and young adults, but with increasing age physical and neurological factors may place the older adult especially at risk for falls (Wolfson, 1992). Further, a considerable amount of evidence has accumulated indicating that elderly head-injured patients have poorer recovery, longer periods of unconsciousness and posttraumatic amnesia, greater neuropsychological impairment, and increased mortality than younger head trauma patients (e.g., Bricolo, Turazzi, & Feriotti, 1980; Jeannett & Teasdale, 1977; Long & Schmitter, 1992; Russell & Smith, 1961).

Etiology

Head injuries can be generally classified as open or closed. Open head injury refers to penetration of the skull by an object or force such as a bullet. Damage to the brain occurs at the site of penetration, and localized neurological findings usually will be present. In closed head injury, there is no breech of the skull but rather rapid rotation and movement of the brain against bony structures inside the skull that cause the damage. Injury from closed head trauma can result from a number of factors. With this type of injury, pressure waves can travel through the brain, causing contusions and damage to regions opposite the point of impact (i.e., contra-coup injury). Edema or swelling of the cerebral cortex can also result from closed head injury, which can cause further damage to brain tissue (Lezak, 1983). Microscopic axonal tearing and shearing that results from the twisting and rotating of the brain on impact is also responsible for the effects of head injury. Finally, a complication of head injury may be hematoma, which can act like space-occupying lesion, displacing brain tissue and often requiring surgical evacuation.

Clinical Features and Course

Severity of head trauma is generally estimated, based on length of unconsciousness, CT scan abnormalities, and duration of posttraumatic amnesia. Classification is often done for research purposes and differs slightly between studies. In general, mild head injury is usually characterized by a very short duration of unconsciousness or no loss of consciousness, posttraumatic amnesia of 0 to 24 hours, and normal findings on CT scan. Moderate head injury involves some unconsciousness, posttraumatic amnesia of 1 to 7 days, and possible edema on CT scan. In severe head injury, there usually is an extended period of unconsciousness, a long duration of posttraumatic amnesia (> 7 days), and CT scan abnormalities such as hematoma and severe edema. Recovery from head injury occurs rapidly following injury and levels off, so that by 24 months most recovery has taken place (Leigh, 1979).

Head injury patients can present with almost any type of psychiatric symptom, making differentiation of functional from organic components almost impossible for the general clinician. For example, damage to the frontal lobes (an area highly vulnerable to damage from head injuries) can result in frontal lobe syndrome. This disturbance is characterized by relatively intact cognitive function and severe personality and behavioral changes such as apathy, impulsiveness, lability of affect, irritability, and manic states (Silver, Hales, & Yudofsky,

1994). Additionally, posttraumatic epilepsy occurs in approximately 15% of patients with head injuries and is associated with psychosis, especially with the seizure focus in the temporal lobes (McKenna, Kane, & Parrish, 1985). Depression and anxiety are very common following head injury and can be a reaction to injury and associated deficits or can occur because of cortical damage, especially to limbic and frontal structures (Ross & Stewart, 1987). Because motor vehicle accidents account for the majority of head traumas, patients can develop phobias or posttraumatic stress reactions to the accident (Silver et al., 1994). Individuals who have suffered mild injuries often present in psychiatric settings with post-concussion syndrome. Symptoms include headache, vertigo, depression, anxiety, concentration difficulty, memory problems, trouble thinking, blurred vision, fatigue, irritability, photophobia, and increased sensitivity to noise (Binder, 1986). The disorder has been recently included in the *DSM-IV* (American Psychiatric Association, 1994) with criteria set for further study. Usually, no corresponding neurological abnormalities are present, and neuropsychological evaluation shows little to no impairment. The disturbance usually resolves within 3 months following injury, but some patients can experience symptoms for months or even years following the trauma.

Overall, neuropsychological findings in head-injured patients vary with severity of injury and time since injury. Impairments in intellectual and memory function, problem solving, reasoning, abstracting, and processing information predominate (Levin, Benton, & Grossman, 1982). As previously noted, geriatric head-injured patients have a poorer prognosis than their younger counterparts and are most susceptible to neurological complications because of their age.

DIFFERENTIAL DIAGNOSIS OF FUNCTIONAL AND ORGANIC DISORDERS

An obvious difficulty of working with older adults is the differentiation of neurological and psychiatric illness, as highlighted by our discussion of common neuropsychological disorders in the elderly. To make the distinction, a neuropsychological evaluation is necessary, often in conjunction with neurological examination and other neurodiagnostic procedures. A patient referred for neuropsychological examination can be evaluated using a number of approaches. These methods vary not only in the instruments utilized, but also in their focus and the level of training and knowledge required to implement them. In this section, we will discuss three common approaches to neuropsychological examination and their usefulness in older adult disorders.

Halstead-Reitan Neuropsychological Battery

The most commonly used neuropsychological battery is the Halstead-Reitan Neuropsychological Battery (HRNB). It originated as a set of tests designed to measure "biological intelligence" and distinguish patients with frontal lobe damage from other brain-damaged and normal individuals (Halstead, 1947). The battery was modified and adapted by Reitan to distinguish all brain-damaged patients from normal persons (Reitan & Wolfson, 1985). The HRNB is composed of numerous tests of adaptive ability and problem solving, which measure psychomotor, visuospatial, and abstract reasoning abilities. Also included in the battery are brief tests of language, motor, and sensory functions. Additionally, the Wechsler scales and the Minnesota Multiphasic Personality Inventory (MMPI) are often included to assess intellectual and personality functions.

Five of the tests in the battery most sensitive to central nervous system dysfunction yield seven scores, which can be compared to cutoff scores to calculate an impairment index. The impairment index provides information about the severity of brain dysfunction, ranging from no dysfunction (.1) to severe dysfunction (1.0). A cutoff of >.4 is used as an indicator of brain impairment (Reitan & Wolfson, 1985). The impairment index from the HRNB has been shown to have a high level of discriminant efficiency, correctly classifying (brain damaged or not) 73% to 89% of patients (Hevern, 1980). Additionally, the HRNB does as well and at times better than neurodiagnostic techniques in identifying brain dysfunction (Snow, 1981). Numerous studies have shown strong age effects on tests that comprise the HRNB, with large percentages of normal older adults being classified as brain damaged (Heaton, Grant, & Matthews, 1986; Moehle & Long, 1989). These results suggest that caution must be used when interpreting results for older adults. Refined normative data are available for this purpose (Heaton, Grant, & Matthews, 1991; Russell & Starkey, 1993).

Luria-Nebraska Neuropsychological Battery

A. R. Luria, a respected Russian neuropsychologist and brain-behavior theorist, conducted highly individualized assessments with his patients. He was not interested in scores that patients obtained but rather observed qualitative aspects of the patient's performance (Luria, 1974). Based on her observations and study of Luria's techniques, Christensen (1979) published materials and questions for neuropsychological assessment. Golden, Hammeke, and Purisch (1980) standardized these materials, added their own items, and developed the Luria-Nebraska Neuropsychological Battery (LNNB). Items were chosen based on their ability to discriminate between brain-impaired, psychiatric, and normal control patients. Form I of the battery is comprised of 269 items that yield 11 clinical scores representing different aspects of functioning such as motor, expressive speech, memory, arithmetic, and intellectual processes. A pathognomonic scale is also included, which is comprised of items from the other scales that are most closely associated with brain damage. Localization scales have also been derived to identify focal aspects of central nervous system lesions. The battery takes approximately 2½ hours to administer, possibly longer with older or impaired patients. Each item on the LNNB is scored on a 3-point scale, with 0 indicating no impairment; 1, borderline impairment; and 2, definite central nervous system impairment.

Standardized rules of interpretation based on scale elevations within an age and education context are used to determine the extent of cognitive impairment (Golden et al., 1980). Using these rules for the LNNB yields rates ranging from 88% to 93% for correct classification of brain-damaged, psychiatric, and normal patients (Golden et al., 1980). Additionally, the LNNB is highly correlated with the HRNB and shows slightly better discriminant efficiency rates (Kane, Parsons, & Goldstein, 1985). The battery has been criticized because clinical scales are composed of heterogenous items that may not reflect functions indicated by their labels (Crosson & Warren, 1982). The LNNB has been shown to be highly discriminative in geriatric populations and may be an excellent tool for diagnosing central nervous system dysfunction in the elderly. One final word of caution about the LNNB is that although the scale has standardized interpretive rules, the diagnostic and prognostic information derived from the battery cannot be accurately integrated without extensive neuropsychological experience and knowledge.

Functional Systems Approach

The most complex approach to neuropsychological assessment is the functional systems approach, also known as the flexible approach. Standardized tests are selected for use based on a patient's presenting problem, age, and medical/psychiatric history. This approach is most closely associated with Muriel Lezak, whose comprehensive text is standard in the field (Lezak, 1983). She points out that "by adapting the examination to the patient rather than the other way around, the examiner can answer the examination questions most fully at the least cost and with greatest benefit to the patient" (Lezak, 1983, p. 98). A thorough knowledge of neuropsychological assessment devices, relevant research literature, test result patterns, and differential diagnosis are essential when utilizing a flexible battery. Comparisons are often made between this technique and the experimental method because the examiner generates hypotheses about the patient and then systematically investigates each one through the testing process.

The flexibility of the approach occurs on a continuum, from adding one or two tests to a battery to selecting all tests based on the patient's presentation, or even selecting tests based on performance on earlier tasks. Lezak (1983) recommends that a basic or core battery that assesses the major functions of the individual be administered initially and that decisions regarding further testing be decided based on test results. Others propose that tests should be selected to measure each functional aspect of the brain. For example, Bigler (1988) proposes that a neuropsychological examination should include measures of intelligence, motor function, language, visuospatial skills, memory, sensory abilities, and personality function. Extensive neuropsychological experience is required to construct batteries, and interpretation of test results can become quite complex. A flexible approach may be quite helpful in the neuropsychological assessment of older adults because of its adaptation to physical limitations of patients and its emphasis on differential diagnosis.

· SUMMARY

In this chapter, we have presented important neuropsychological considerations in older adult populations. It is clear that normal aging causes predictable declines in cognitive function, just as it does in physical capabilities. Results from examinations of intellectual, memory, and other abilities must be interpreted in light of these changes. Our discussion of common neuropsychological disorders in the elderly has highlighted how these illnesses can often mimic functional disorders. We caution against ruling out neurological illness because a patient does not display obvious cognitive deficits. As we suggest, in the early stages many neurological disorders will not show clear neurological signs, and deficits will only become apparent on careful neuropsychological examination. The geriatric patient's medical and psychiatric history must be obtained to provide clues to his or her current presenting problem. We have presented a brief overview of approaches to neuropsychological assessment, including two common neuropsychological batteries and the functional systems approach. Each approach has its associated strengths and weaknesses and each requires extensive neuropsychological experience and knowledge. As the population of older adults burgeons, and as people live longer, the need for neuropsychological assessment will also increase.

REFERENCES

Adams, R. D., & Victor, M. (1977). *Principles of neurology*. New York: McGraw-Hill.

Albert, M. L., & Knoefel, J. E. (1994). Clinical neurology of aging (2nd ed.). New York: Oxford University Press.

Albert, M. S., & Kaplan, E. (1980). Organic implications of neuropsychological deficits in the elderly. In L. W. Poon & J. L. Fozard (Eds.), *New directions in memory and aging* (pp. 403–432). Hillsdale, NJ: Erlbaum.

Albert, M. S., & Stafford, J. L. (1988). Computed tomography studies. In M. S. Albert & M. B. Moss (Eds.), *Geriatric neuropsychology* (pp. 211–227). New York: Guilford Press.

Amaducci, L. A., Fratiglioni, L., Rocca, W. A., Fiesch, C., Livrea, P., Pedore, D., Bracco, L., Lippi, A., Gando, C., Bino, G., Prencipe, M., Bonatti, M. L., Girotti, F., Carella, F., Tavolato, B., Ferla, S., Lenzi, G. L., Gambi, A., Grigoletto, F., & Schoenberg, B. S. (1986). Risk factors for clinically diagnosed Alzheimer's disease: A case-control study of an Italian population. *Neurology, 36*, 922–931.

American Psychiatric Association (1994). *Diagnostic and statistical manual of mental disorders* (4th ed.). Washington, DC: Author.

Bartus, R. T., Dean, R. L., III, Beer, B., & Lippa, A. S. (1982). The cholinergic hypothesis of geriatric memory dysfunction. *Science, 217*, 408–417.

Benton, A. L., Eslinger, P. J., & Damasio, A. R. (1981). Normative observations on neuropsychological test performances in old age. *Journal of Clinical Neuropsychology, 3*, 33–42.

Berg, L. (1988). The aging brain. In R. Strong, W. G. Wood, & W. J. Burke (Eds.), *Central nervous disorders of aging: Clinical intervention and research* (pp. 1–16). New York: Raven Press.

Bigler, E. D. (1988). *Diagnostic clinical neuropsychology*. Austin, TX: University of Texas Press.

Binder, L. M. (1986). Persisting symptoms after mild head injury: A review of the postconcussive syndrome. *Journal of Clinical and Experimental Neuropsychology, 8*, 323–346.

Blusewicz, M. J., Dustman, R. E., Schenkenberg, T., & Beck, E. L. (1977). Neuropsychological correlates of chronic alcoholism and aging. *Journal of Nervous and Mental Disease, 165*, 348–355.

Botwinick, J. (1977). Intellectual abilities. In J. E. Birren & K. W. Schaie (Eds.), *Handbook of the psychology of aging* (pp. 580–605). New York: Van Nostrand Reinhold.

Brandt, J., & Butters, N. (1986). The alcoholic Wernicke-Korsakoff syndrome and its relationship to long-term alcohol abuse. In I. Grant & K. M. Adams (Eds.), *Neuropsychological assessment of neuropsychiatric disorders* (pp. 441–477). New York: Oxford University Press.

Bricolo, A., Turazzi, S., & Feriotti, G. (1980). Prolonged posttraumatic unconsciousnesss. *Journal of Neurosurgery, 52*, 625–634.

Brody, H. (1978). Cell counts in cerebral cortex and brainstem. In R. Katzman, R. D. Terry, & K. L. Bick (Eds.), *Alzheimer's disease: Senile dementia and related disorders* (pp. 345–352). New York: Raven Press.

Brust, J. C. M. (1988). Vascular dementia is overdiagnosed. *Archives of Neurology, 45*, 799–801.

Carlen, P. L., Wortzman, G., Holgate, R. C., & Rankin, J. G. (1978). Reversible cerebral atrophy in recently abstinent chronic alcoholics measured by computed tomography scans. *Science, 200*, 1076–1078.

Cerella, J., Poon, L. W., & Fozard, J. L. (1982). Age and iconic read-out. *Journal of Gerontology, 37*, 197–202.

Charness, M. E., Simon, R. P., & Greenberg, D. A. (1989). Ethanol and the nervous system. *New England Journal of Medicine, 321*, 442–454.

Christensen, A. L. (1979). *Luria's neuropsychological investigation*. New York: Spectrum.

Cook, R. H., Schneck, S. A., & Clark, D. B. (1981). Twins with Alzheimer's disease. *Archives of Neurology, 38*, 300–301.

Coyle, J. T., Price, D. L., & DeLong, M. R. (1983). Alzheimer's disease: A disorder of cortical cholinergic innervation. *Science, 219*, 1184–1190.

Crosson, B., & Warren, R. L. (1982). Use of the Luria-Nebraska Neuropsychological Battery in aphasia: A conceptual critique. *Journal of Consulting and Clinical Psychology, 50*, 22–31.

Cummings, J. L. (1988). Depression in vascular dementia. *Journal of Clinical Psychiatry, 10*, 209–231.

Cummings, J. L. (1994). Neuropsychiatric aspects of Alzheimer's disease and other dementing illnesses. In S. C. Yudofsky & R. E. Hales (Eds.), *Textbook of neuropsychiatry* (pp. 605–620). Washington, DC: American Psychiatric Press.

Cummings, J. L., & Benson, D. F. (1992). *Dementia: A clinical approach* (2nd ed.). Boston: Butterworths.

Cummings, J. L., Miller, B., Hill, M. A., & Neshkes, (1987). Neuropsychiatric aspects of multi-infarct dementia and dementia of the Alzheimer type. *Archives of Neurology, 44*, 389–393.

Cutting, J. (1982). Alcohol dementia. In D. F. Benson, & D. Blumer (Eds.), *Psychiatric aspects of neurologic disease* (Vol. 2, pp. 149–165). New York: Grune & Stratton.

Evans, D. A., Funkenstein, H. H., Albert, M. S., Scherr, P. A., Cook, N. R., Chown, M. J., Hebert, L. E., Hennekens, C. H., & Taylor, J. O. (1989). Prevalence of Alzheimer's disease in a community population of older persons: Higher than previously reported. *Journal of the American Medical Association, 262*, 2551–2556.

Fratiglioni, L. (1993). Epidemiology of Alzheimer's disease: Issues of etiology and validity. *Acta Neurologica Scandinavica, 87*, 1–70.

Fulton, J. D., Duncan, G., & Caird, F. I. (1992). Psychiatric presentation of intracranial tumour in the elderly. *International Journal of Geriatric Psychiatry, 7*, 411–418.

Gerard, G., & Weisberg, L. A. (1986). MRI periventricular lesions in adults. *Neurology, 36*, 998–1001.

Glenner, G. G., & Wong, C. W. (1984). Alzheimer's disease and Down's syndrome: Sharing of a unique cerebrovascular amyloid fibril protein. *Biochemical and Biophysical Research Communication, 122*, 1131–1135.

Golden, C. J., Hammeke, T. A., & Purisch, A. D. (1980). *The Luria-Nebraska Neuropsychological Battery manual*. Los Angeles: Western Psychological Services.

Goldstein, G., & Shelly, C. (1981). Does the right hemisphere age more rapidly than the left? *Journal of Clinical Neuropsychology, 3*, 65–78.

Hachinski, V. C., Lassen, N. A., & Marshall, J. (1974). Multi-infarct dementia: A cause of mental deterioration in the elderly. *The Lancet, 2*, 207–209.

Halstead, W. C. (1947). *Brain and intelligence*. Chicago: University of Chicago Press.

Heaton, R. K., Grant, I., & Matthews, C. G. (1986). Differences in neuropsychological test performance associated with age, education, and sex. In I. Grant & K. W. Adams (Eds.), *Neuropsychological assessment of neuropsychiatric disorders* (pp. 100–120). New York: Oxford University Press.

Heaton, R. K., Grant, I., & Matthews, C. G. (1991). *Comprehensive norms for an expanded Halstead-Reitan Battery: Demographic corrections, research findings, and clinical applications.* Odessa, FL: Psychological Assessment Resources.

Heston, L. L. (1988). Morbid risk in first-degree relatives of persons with Alzheimer's disease. *Archives of General Psychiatry, 38,* 1085–1090.

Hevern, V. W. (1980). Recent validity studies of the Halstead-Reitan approach to clinical neuropsychological assessment: A critical review. *Clinical Neuropsychology, 2,* 49–61.

Hier, D. B., Hagenlocker, K., & Shindler, A. G. (1985). Language disintegration in dementia: Effects of etiology and severity. *Brain and Language, 25,* 117–133.

Hochanadel, G., & Kaplan, E. (1984). Neuropsychology and normal aging. In M. L. Albert (Ed.), *Clinical neurology of aging* (pp. 231–244). New York: Oxford University Press.

Horn, J. L., & Cattell, R. B. (1967). Age differences in fluid and crystallized intelligence. *Acta Psychologica, 26,* 107–129.

Jeanett, B., & Teasdale, G. (1977). Aspects of coma after severe head injury. *Lancet, 1,* 878–881.

Jordan, S. W. (1971). Central nervous system. *Human Pathology, 2,* 561.

Kaplan, H. I., & Sadock, B. J. (1991). *Synopsis of psychiatry* (6th ed.). Baltimore: Williams & Wilkins.

Kane, R. L., Parsons, O. A., & Goldstein, G. (1985). Statistical relationships and discriminative accuracy of the Halstead-Reitan, Luria-Nebraska, and Wechsler IQ scores in the identification of brain damage. *Journal of Clinical and Experimental Neuropsychology, 7,* 211–223.

Katzman, R., & Rowe, J. W. (1992). *Principles of geriatric neurology.* Philadelphia: F. A. Davis.

Kay, D. W. K. (1989). Genetics, Alzheimer's disease and senile dementia. *British Journal of Psychiatry, 154,* 311–320.

Kazniak, A. W., Poon, L. W., & Riege, W. (1986). Assessing memory deficits: An information-processing approach. In L. W. Poon (Ed.), *Handbook for clinical memory assessment of older adults* (pp. 168–188). Washington, DC: American Psychological Association.

Kemper, T. (1984). Neuroanatomical and neuropathological changes in normal aging and in dementia. In M. L. Albert (Ed.), *Clinical neurology of aging* (pp. 9–52). New York: Oxford University Press.

Keschner, M., Bender, M. B., & Strauss, I. (1938). Mental symptoms associated with brain tumor: A study of 530 verified cases. *Journal of the American medical Association, 110,* 714–718.

Kornblith, P. L., Wicker, M. D., & Casady, J. R. (1987). *Neurologic oncology.* Philadelphia: J. B. Lippincott.

Kuhl, D. E., Metter, E. J., Riege, W. H., & Hawkins, R. A. (1984). The effects of normal aging on patterns of local cerebral glucose utilization. *Annals of Neurology, 15,* 133–137.

Kurtzke, J. F. (1984). Neuroepidemiology. *Annals of Neurology, 16,* 265–277.

Ladurner, G., Iliff, L. D., & Lechner, H. (1982). Clinical factors associated with dementia in ischaemic stroke. *Journal of Neurology, Neurosurgery, and Psychiatry, 45,* 97–101.

Leigh, D. (1979). Psychiatric aspects of head injury. *Psychiatric Digest, 40,* 21–33.

Levin, H. S., Benton, A. L., & Grossman, R. G. (1982). *Neurobehavioral consequences of closed head injury.* New York: Oxford University Press.

Lezak, M. (1983). *Neuropsychological assessment* (2nd ed.). New York: Oxford University Press.

Lishman, W. A. (1990). Alcohol and the brain. *British Journal of Psychiatry, 156,* 635–644.

Loberg, T. (1986). Neuropsychological findings in the early and middle phases of alcoholism. In I. Grant & K. M. Adams (Eds.), *Neuropsychological assessment of neuropsychiatric disorders* (pp. 415–440). New York: Oxford University Press.

Loeb, C. (1980). Clinical diagnosis of multi-infarct dementia. In L. Amaduci, A. N. Davidson, & P. Antuono (Eds.), *Aging of the brain and dementia* (pp. 251–260). New York: Raven Press.

Long, C. J., & Schmitter, M. E. (1992). Cognitive sequelae in closed head injury. In C. J. Long & L. K. Ross (Eds.), *Handbook of head trauma: Acute care to recovery.* New York: Plenum Press.

Luria, A. (1974). *The working brain.* London: Penguin.

MacInnes, (1982). *Aging and its relationship to neuropsychological and neurological measures.* Paper presented at the National Academy of Neuropsychology, Atlanta, GA.

Malaspina, D., Quitkin, H. M., & Kaufmann, C. A. (1994). Epidemiology and genetics of neuropsychiatric disorders. In S. C. Yudofsky & R. E. Hales (Eds.), *Textbook of neuropsychiatry* (pp. 187–226). Washington, DC: American Psychiatric Press.

Matsuyama, H., & Nakamura, S. (1977). Senile changes in the brain in the Japanese: Incidence of Alzheimer's neurofibrillary change and senile plaque. In R. Katzman, R. D. Terry, & K. L. Bick (Eds.), *Alzheimer's disease: Senile dementia and related disorders* (pp. 287–297). New York: Raven Press.

McKenna, P. J., Kane, J. M., & Parrish, K. (1985). Psychotic syndromes in epilepsy. *American Journal of Psychiatry, 142,* 895–904.

McKhann, G., Drachman, D., Folstein, M., Katzman, R., Price, D., & Stradlin, E. M. (1984). Clinical diagnosis of Alzheimer's disease: Report of the NINCDS-ADRDA work group under the auspices of the Department of Health and Human Services task force on Alzheimer's disease. *Neurology, 34,* 939–944.

Mendez, M. F., Martin, R. J., & Smith, K. A. (1990). Psychiatric symptoms associated with Alzheimer's disease. *Journal of Neuropsychiatry and Clinical Neuroscience, 2,* 28–33.

Metter, E. J. (1988). Positron tomography and cerebral blood flow studies. In M. S. Albert & M. B. Moss (Eds.), *Geriatric neuropsychology* (pp. 228–261). New York: Guilford Press.

Miller, A. K. H., Alston, R. L., & Corsellis, J. A. N. (1980). Variations with age in the volumes of grey and white matter in the cerebral hemispheres of man: Measurements with an image analyzer. *Neuropathology and Applied Neurobiology, 6,* 119–132.

Mirsen, T., & Hachinski, V. (1988). Epidemiology and classification of vascular and multiinfarct dementia. In J. S. Meyer, J. Marshall, H. Lechner, & J. F. Toole (Eds.), *Vascular and multi-infarct dementia* (pp. 61–76). Mount Kisco, NY: Futura.

Mittenberg, W., Seidenberg, M., O'Leary, D. S., & DiGiulio, D. V. (1989). Changes in cerebral functioning associated with normal aging. *Journal of Clinical and Experimental Neuropsychology, 11,* 918–932.

Moehle, K. A., & Long, C. J. (1989). Models of aging and neuropsychological test performance decline with aging. *Journal of Gerontology: Psychological Sciences, 44,* 176–177.

O'Leary, M. R., Radford, L. M., Chaney, E. F., & Schau, E. J. (1977). Assessment of cognitive recovery in alcoholics by use of the Trail Making Test. *Journal of Clinical Psychology, 33,* 579–582.

Page, R. D., & Linden, J. D. (1974). "Reversible" organc brain syndrome in alcoholics: A psychometric evaluation. *Quarterly Journal of Studies on Alcohol, 35,* 98–107.

Parsons, O. A. (1994). Determinants of cognitive deficits in alcoholism: The search continues. *The Clinical Neuropsychologist, 8,* 39–58.

Perez, F. I., Rivera, V. M., Meyer, J. S., Gay, J. R. A., Taylor, R. C., & Matthew, N. T. (1975). Analysis of intellectual and cognitive performance in patients with multi-infarct dementia, vertebrobasilar insufficiency with dementia, and Alzheimer's disease. *Journal of Neurological and Neurosurgical Psychiatry, 38,* 533–540.

Perl, D. P., & Brody, A. Z. (1980). Alzheimer's disease: X-ray spectrometric evidence of aluminum accumulation in neurofibrillary tangle-bearing neurons. *Science, 208,* 297–299.

Perlmutter, M., & Mitchell, D. B. (1982). The appearance and disappearance of age differences in adult memory. In F. I. M. Craik & S. Trehub (Eds.), *Aging and cognitive processes* (pp. 127–143). New York: Plenum Press.

Petry, S., Cummings, J. L., & Hill, M. A. (1989). Personality alterations in dementia of the Alzheimer's type. *Archives of Neurology, 45,* 1187–1190.

Powell, A. L., Cummings, J. L., Hill, M. A., & Benson, F. (1988). Speech and language alterations in multi-infarct dementia. *Neurology, 38,* 717–719.

Price, T. P. R., Goetz, K. L., & Lovell, M. R. (1994). Neuropsychiatric aspects of brain tumors. In S. C. Yudofsky & R. E. Hales (Eds.), *Textbook of neuropsychiatry* (pp. 473–498). Washington, DC: American Psychiatric Press.

Read, D. E. (1988). Age-related changes in performance on a visual-closure task. *Journal of Clinical and Experimental Neuropsychology, 10,* 451–466.

Reisberg, B., Borenstein, J., & Salob, S. P. (1987). Behavioral symptoms in Alzheimer's disease: Phenomenology and treatment. *Journal of Clinical Psychiatry, 48,* 9–15.

Reitan, R. M., & Wolfson, D. (1985). *The Halstead-Reitan Neuropsychological Battery: Theory and clinical interpretation.* Tucson, AZ: Neuropsychology Press.

Reitan, R. M., & Wolfson, D. (1992). *Neuroanatomy and neuropathology: A clinical guide for neuropsychologists.* Tucson, AZ: Neuropsychology Press.

Rocca, W. A., Amaducci, L. A., & Schoenberg, B. S. (1986). Epidemiology of clinically diagnosed Alzheimer's disease. *Annals of Neurology, 19*, 415–424.

Rogers, J., & Bloom, F. E. (1985). Neurotranmitter metabolism and function in the aging central nervous system. In C. E. Finch & E. L. Schneider (Eds.), *Handbook of the biology of aging* (2nd ed., pp. 645–691). New York: Van Nostrand Reinhold.

Ross, E. D., & Stewart, R. S. (1987). Pathological display of affect in patients with depression and right frontal brain damage: An alternative mechanism. *Journal of Nervous and Mental Disease, 176*, 165–172.

Roth, M. (1980). Aging of the brain and dementia: An overview. In L. Amaducci, A. N. Davison, & P. Antuono (Eds.), *Aging of the brain and dementia*. New York: Raven Press.

Russell, E. W., & Starkey, R. I. (1993). *Halstead-Russell Neuropsychological evaluation system*. Los Angeles: Western Psychological Services.

Russell, W. R., & Smith, A. (1961). Postraumatic amnesia in closed head injury. *Archives of Neurology, 5*, 4–17.

Scheibel, A. B. (1992). Structural changes in the aging brain. In J. E. Birren, R. B. Sloane, & G. Cohen (Eds.), *Handbook of mental health and aging* (2nd ed., pp. 147–173). New York: Academic Press.

Schlesinger, B. (1950). Mental changes in intracranial tumors and related problems. *Confinia Neurologica, 10*, 225–263.

Schoenberg, B. S. (1988). Epidemiology of vascular and multi-infarct dementi. In J. S. Meyer, J. Marshall, H. Lechner, J. F. Toole (Eds.), *Vascular and multi-infarct dementia* (pp. 47–60). Mount Kisco, NY: Futura.

Scogin, F., & Bienas, J. L. (1988). A three-year follow-up of older adult participants in a memory-skills training program. *Psychology and Aging, 3*, 334–337.

Silver, J. M., Hales, R. E., & Yodofsky, S. C. (1994). Neuropsychiatric aspects of traumatic brain injury. In S. C. Yudofsky & R. E. Hales (Eds.), *Textbook of neuropsychiatry* (pp. 363–396). Washington, DC: American Psychiatric Press.

Snow, W. G. (1981). A comparison of frequency of abnormal results in neuropsychological vs. neurodiagnostic procedures. *Journal of Clinical Psychology, 37*, 22–28.

Storandt, M. (1977). Age, ability level, and method of administering and scoring the WAIS. *Journal of Gerontology, 32*, 175–178.

Strub, R. L., & Black, F. W. (1981). *Organic brain syndromes: An introduction to neurobehavioral disorders*. Philadelphia: F. A. Davis.

U. S. Department of Health and Human Services (1989). *Interagency head injury task force report*. Washington, DC: U. S. Government Printing Office.

Walton, J. N. (1977). *Brain's diseases of the nervous system* (8th ed.). New York: Oxford University Press.

Wang, H. S., & Busse, E. W. (1969). EEG of healthy old persons—A longitudinal study: 1. Dominant background activity and occipital rhythm. *Journal of Gerontology, 24*, 419–426.

Wechsler, D. (1981). *Wechsler Adult Intelligence Scale—Revised*. New York: Psychological Corporation.

Williams, S. E., Bell, D. S., & Gye, R. S. (1974). Neurosurgical disease encountered in a psychiatric service. *Journal of Neurology, Neurosurgery, and Psychiatry, 37*, 112.

Wolfson, L. (1992). Falls and gait. In R. Katzman & J. W. Rowe (Eds.), *Principles of geriatric neurology*. Philadelphia: F. A. Davis.

Wragg, R. E., Jeste, D. V. (1989). Overview of depression and psychosis in Alzheimer's disease. *American Journal of Psychiatry, 45*, 64–69.

Wurtman, R. J., Corkin, S., Ritter-Walker, E., & Growdon, J. H. (1990). *Alzheimer's disease*. New York: Raven Press.

CHAPTER 5

Medical Assessment

BENOIT H. MULSANT AND BRUCE A. WRIGHT

INTRODUCTION

Although the association between specific mental disorders and physical disorders is discussed in the relevant chapters of Part II, this chapter presents a brief overview of the comprehensive medical assessment that every older adult presenting with a mental problem should receive. Such an assessment often plays an important role in the diagnostic process and treatment planning of late-life mental disorders because of the complex interaction between psychological and physical problems in the elderly (Cohen-Cole & Stoudemire, 1987). As in younger persons, initial manifestations of a medical problem may be predominantly "psychological" (e.g., hypothyroidism with complaints of fatigue and low motivation). A known or unknown underlying medical disorder may di-

BENOIT H. MULSANT AND BRUCE A. WRIGHT • Division of Geriatrics and Neuropsychiatry, Western Psychiatric Institute and Clinic, Department of Psychiatry, University of Pittsburgh School of Medicine, Pittsburgh, Pennsylvania 15213.
Psychological Treatment of Older Adults: An Introductory Text, edited by Michel Hersen and Vincent B. Van Hasselt. Plenum Press, New York, 1996.

rectly produce an organic mental syndrome (e.g., a dementia due to vitamin B_{12} deficiency). The psychological and physiological stress associated with a significant medical illness (e.g., a myocardial infarction) or surgical procedure (e.g., coronary artery bypass) can trigger onset of a nonorganic mental disorder (e.g., a major depressive disorder). Finally, the comorbid occurrence of physical and mental problems (in particular depression) has been associated with increased somatization, as if mental disorders amplify the experience of discomfort that arises from physical illnesses (Mulsant et al., 1994; Waxman, McCreary, Weinrit, & Carner, 1985). For these reasons, older adults presenting with psychological distress or with a psychiatric problem (in particular of late onset) deserve a thorough medical assessment. One of the primary goals of this work-up is to determine whether the presenting mental problem is directly caused by a physical illness. Following the fourth edition of the *Diagnostic and Statistical Manual of Mental Disorders* (*DSM-IV*; American Psychiatric Association, 1994), identification of a causative physical disorder establishes a diagnosis of Mental Disorder Due to a General Medical Condition (referred to as Organic Mental Disorder in *DSM-III-R*; APA, 1987). Usefulness of the medical assessment goes beyond the diagnostic stage; even when there is no specific treatment for the identified causative illness (e.g., Alzheimer's disease), a thorough medical work-up will often detect concurrent treatable conditions that exacerbate psychological and behavioral problems (Mulsant & Thornton, 1990). In addition, for all late-life mental disorders, the medical assessment will provide management guidelines, since comorbid medical problems may significantly constrain, interfere with, or even prevent behavioral, psychological, or pharmacological interventions. The first and second sections of this chapter review the role of the medical history and physical examination; the third section describes the laboratory tests most commonly obtained. For almost all older adults, the medical assessment described below can and should be performed on an outpatient basis (Martin, Morycz, McDowell, Snustad, & Karpf, 1985).

MEDICAL HISTORY

A detailed history is probably the single most important procedure in the medical assessment of an older adult. If the patient is cognitively impaired, the history should be obtained from both the patient and a reliable informant close to the patient. Previous medical records should be obtained and reviewed. Based on all available information, a comprehensive list of all past and current medical problems (including surgical interventions) should be established. Similarly, a list of all prescription and over-the-counter medications should be generated. Particular attention should be paid to the temporal relationship between onset, exacerbation, or remission of mental and physical problems, since identification of a temporal association is a major factor in establishing an etiological relationship (APA, 1994). For instance, when evaluating a demented patient, identification of specific medical events at or around the time of onset of cognitive impairment may directly point to a specific cause or class of causes: a fall or an accident with or without a recognized head trauma may have induced a subdural hematoma. A hospitalization raises the possibility of administration of general anesthesia, an intubation, or a major blood loss associated with an hypoxic encephalopathy. The prescription of a new drug for any medical problem, even minor, may be responsible for delirium or chronic drug intoxication. When evaluating a person presenting with a first depressive episode, initiation of a beta-blocker antihypertensive medication a few weeks prior to onset of depressive symptoms would support a diagnosis of Substance-Induced Mood Disorder with Depressive Features; similarly, occurrence of the same depressive symptoms following a stroke would support a diagnosis of Mood Disorder Due to Cerebrovascular Disease, with Major-Depressive-Like Episode.

Old or apparently inactive medical problems can be germane to current mental problems: a remote gastrectomy can be the cause of a current vitamin B_{12} deficiency and its neuropsychiatric sequelae. A history of thyroid disease, with or without treatment, can be the cause of current hypothyroidism. Finally, a past history of venereal disease (including, obviously, syphilis), tuberculosis, or fungal infection should prompt the clinician to consider a diagnosis of chronic meningitis. Identification of known risk factors will also help in establishing a specific diagnosis. For instance, in a demented patient, a history of hypertension, stroke, or peripheral vascular disease supports a diagnosis of Vascular Dementia (Hachinski et al., 1975), a remote history of head trauma is a statistical risk factor for a Dementia of the Alzheimer's Type, while a history of intravenous drug abuse, blood product transfusion, or recurrent venereal disease should alert the clinician to the possibility of Dementia Due to HIV Disease.

PHYSICAL EXAMINATION

The physical examination can confirm information obtained during the history, or sometimes it reveals additional etiological clues, such as an elevated blood pressure, a carotid or cardiac murmur (risk factors for cerebrovascular disease), tender and thickened temporal arteries (consistent with giant cell arteritis), a stiff neck (suggestive of meningitis), a goiter (indicative of thyroid disease), or an abdominal scar (compatible with a remote gastrectomy). A thorough neurological examination, including an assessment of vision and hearing, is critical in older adults. Vision and hearing deficits have been implicated as causes of some late-life mental disorders (e.g., late-onset Schizophrenia [Mulsant & Gershon, 1993]) or as results of other late-life mental disorders (e.g., Dementia of the Alzheimer's Type [Hinton, Sadun, Blanks, & Miller, 1986; Steffes & Thralow, 1987]). In addition, sensory deficits interfere with performance and interpretation of neuropsychological testing (Corbin & Eastwood, 1986). The neurological examination can detect focal neurological signs compatible with previous strokes or multiple sclerosis, or it can suggest an unsuspected space-occupying lesion. A gait disturbance early in the course of a dementia makes a diagnosis of Dementia of the Alzheimer's Type unlikely and should prompt the search for another dementing disorder, in particular normal pressure hydrocephalus and subdural hematoma. A cranial or peripheral neuropathy may be an important clue for the identification of some toxic or metabolic disorders, for instance Wernicke-Korsakoff syndrome, vitamin B_{12} deficiency, recurrent hypoglycemia, or heavy metal intoxication (Cummings & Benson, 1992). Presence of extrapyramidal signs (EPS) may indicate evidence of one of the extrapyramidal disorders (e.g., Parkinson's, Huntington's, Wilson's or Lewy body disease, or progressive nuclear palsy) that have been associated with mood, psychotic, and cognitive disorders. However, EPS also have been associated with Alzheimer's disease (Funkenstein et al., 1993). Orofacial and other dyskinetic movements supporting a diagnosis of Tardive Dyskinesia are suggestive of a history of psychosis and neuroleptic treatment (Roose, Glassman, & Dalack, 1989; Sweet et al., 1995).

LABORATORY ASSESSMENT

In addition to a careful medical history and physical examination, laboratory tests are often helpful in detecting medical causes of psychiatric symptoms. In particular, considering the high social and economic costs involved in the management of a demented person, customary etiological investigation of a dementia includes a complete battery of diagnostic tests to exclude as definitely as possible a reversible or arrestable dementing disorder. Typically, the following laboratory tests are performed: metabolic profile (including serum electrolytes, BUN, creatinine, glucose, calcium, magnesium, and phosphate), complete blood count with differential, liver function tests, thyroid function tests, vitamin B_{12} and folate, serology for syphilis, erythrocyte sedimentation rate, urinalysis, chest radiograph, electrocardiogram, and central nervous system imaging (magnetic resonance imaging [MRI] or computed tomography [CT] when MRI is not available or is contraindicated). Additional tests (e.g., electroencephalogram [EEG] or lumbar puncture [LP]) are ordered as indicated by the history, mental status, and physical examination. It is reasonable to perform such a dementia work-up not only in demented patients but also in any older adult presenting with a late-onset mental disorder. In addition, some of these laboratory tests must be obtained at baseline and monitored longitudinally when administering psychotropic medications.

Metabolic Profile

A metabolic screen includes serum sodium, potassium, chloride, bicarbonate, blood urea nitrogen (BUN), creatinine, glucose, calcium, magnesium, and phosphate and is useful in detecting metabolic disorders such as acid–base disorders, electrolyte disturbances, endocrinopathies, and renal failure, which may cause a variety of psychiatric symptoms. In particular, alterations in sodium, glucose, calcium, or BUN frequently cause mental status changes ranging from mild nonspecific cognitive impairment to frank delirium. A metabolic screen can also identify the surreptitious use of medications. Notable examples include the hyponatremia and/or hypokalemia often seen in individuals who abuse laxatives and diuretics.

Monitoring of the metabolic screen is also useful in older patients receiving psychotropic medications. During lithium therapy, electrolytes and renal function should be regularly monitored. Although some controversy exists over the actual nephrotoxic potential of lithium, the serum creatinine level can help to estimate a patient's creatinine clearance. However, an older adult with a decreased muscular mass may have a normal serum creatinine despite a significant reduction in renal function (Pollock et al., 1992). Thus, measurement of the creatinine clearance based on a 24-hour urine collection may be necessary in the elderly. In some older depressed patients, serotonin-specific reuptake inhibitors (SSRI) such as fluoxetine (Prozac), sertraline (Zoloft), or paroxetine (Paxil) may induce a syndrome of inappropriate secretion of antidiuretic hormone (SIADH), resulting in severe hyponatremia (Druckenbrod & Mulsant, 1995). Thus, a significant change in mental status should prompt a rechecking of serum electrolytes.

Complete Blood Count with Differential

An altered white blood cell (WBC) count or hemoglobin and hematocrit reading may indicate hematological or systemic disease processes, including anemia and infection. The mean corpuscular volume (MCV) can assist in determining the etiology of anemia. A megaloblastic anemia (increased MCV) may be associated with a deficiency of B_{12} or folate and is relatively common in chronic alcoholics and malnourished persons. A microcytic anemia (decreased MCV) is usually associated with iron deficiency or lead poisoning. Perturbations of the WBC count can be secondary to acute or chronic (occult) infections or various blood dyscrasias.

Several psychotropic medications affect the WBC count. Lithium often induces a benign, reversible elevation of the WBC count (leukocytosis), usually in the range of 10,000 to 13,000 cells per cubic millimeter. Lithium-induced leukocytosis is not associated with a left-shift of the WBC count. Carbamazepine (Tegretol) and clozapine (Clozaril), on the other hand, can precipitate more serious hematological changes. Carbamazepine is often associated with a benign decrease in WBC count and rarely (less than 1 in 20,000 treated patients) with more serious blood dyscrasias, including agranulocytosis and aplastic anemia. Clozapine is more frequently associated with hematological alterations. Up to 1% of patients receiving this agent develop severe agranulocytosis, and elderly people may be at even higher risk (Alvir et al., 1993). For these reasons, patients receiving carbamazepine or clozapine should have periodic CBC counts, especially at the first sign of any infection. It is currently impossible to prescribe clozapine in the United States without obtaining a weekly CBC count. Finally, the WBC count can be elevated in the neuroleptic malignant syndrome (NMS). A CBC (and CPK level) should be obtained in any patient receiving antipsychotic medication who has a change in mental status or physical examination suggestive of NMS.

Liver Function Tests

Mental status examination changes associated with liver disease can range from generalized malaise and lethargy to gross encephalopathy. Liver function tests (LFTs) are frequently elevated secondary to alcohol consumption, hepatitis, cirrhosis, liver metastasis, or iatrogenic causes. An elevation of gamma glutamyl transpeptidase (GGTP) is the most sensitive evidence of acute liver damage due to recent alcohol ingestion. The recent consumption of alcohol may also result in an increase of both liver transaminases (AST/SGOT and ALT/SGPT), but AST tends to be more markedly elevated with hepatic damage secondary to alcohol. A hepatitis screen is occasionally useful for evaluating psychopathology; it should be obtained in all patients with significant risk factors for hepatitis (e.g., numerous transfusions, IV drug abuse), with a previous history of hepatitis, or with unexplained elevations of LFTs.

Baseline LFTs should be evaluated prior to starting psychotropic medications that can cause elevation of LFTs, such as tacrine (Cognex), neuroleptics, some anticonvulsants, tricyclic antidepressants, and benzodiazepines. Tacrine, a cholinesterase inhibitor prescribed to some patients with a Dementia of the Alzheimer's Type (Small, 1992), induces reversible elevations of transaminases in 20% to 30% of treated patients. Thus, LFTs need to be monitored weekly for 4 months and monthly thereafter (Committee on Aging: Group for the Advancement of Psychiatry, 1994). Antipsychotics, especially chlorpromazine (Thorazine), may induce a reversible cholestatic jaundice. The anticonvulsants carbamazepine and phenytoin (Dilantin) occasionally precipitate an idiosyncratic hepatitis. Less commonly, tricyclic antidepressants and benzodiazepines affect liver functions. However, it is useful to obtain LFTs prior to starting tricyclic antidepressants, SSRIs, or benzodiazepines, since patients with liver damage may not metabolize these drugs adequately.

Thyroid Function Tests (TFTs)

Abnormalities of the hypothalamic–pituitary–thyroid axis are associated with a variety of psychiatric symptoms, including anxiety, depression, psychosis, or cognitive impairment, even in the absence of obvious physical signs or symptoms of hypothyroidism or hyperthyroidism. Psychiatric patients suffering from hypo- or hyperthyroidism generally do not respond to psychotropic treatment unless their thyroid dysfunction is corrected. Furthermore, psychotropic medications can increase the cardiotoxicity of hyperthyroidism. Therefore, thyroid functions should be evaluated at least once in an older person presenting with a mental problem. "Standard" TFTs include measurement of thyroxine (T_4), triiodothyronine (T_3), T_3 resin uptake (T_3RU), and thyroid-stimulating hormone (TSH).

Lithium induces either clinical or subclinical hypothyroidism in 10% to 15% of treated patients. Elders and women tend to be more prone to lithium-induced hypothyroidism, and these abnormalities are often associated with increased antithyroid antibodies, suggesting a predisposition to lithium-induced thyrotoxicity. Baseline TFTs should be obtained prior to initiating lithium therapy and at least twice per year thereafter.

Vitamin B$_{12}$ and Folate

A deficiency in vitamin B$_{12}$ or folate can result in a broad range of neuropsychiatric symptoms, most notably dementia. The dementia associated with B$_{12}$ or folate deficiency may be reversible if detected early. In addition, pernicious anemia, due to vitamin B$_{12}$ deficiency secondary to decreased intrinsic factor, frequently presents with depressive symptoms. Since the neuropsychiatric abnormalities associated with vitamin B$_{12}$ or folate deficiencies have been described in the absence of anemia or of a macrocytosis (Lindenbaum, Healton, & Savage, 1988), serum level of vitamin B$_{12}$ and red blood cell folate should be checked in any older patient presenting with significant mental problems.

Serology for Syphilis

At the turn of the century, about 50% of the patients in state mental hospitals were suffering from syphilitic dementia paralytica. The antibiotic treatment of syphilis and subsequent prevention of its tertiary form have eliminated a major cause of dementia. However, incidence of syphilis is again rising, and the possibility of neurosyphilis should always be considered when evaluating psychiatric symptoms. The most common methods to screen for syphilis are the RPR (rapid plasma reagin) and VDRL (Venereal Disease Research Laboratory) tests. These tests commonly produce false-positives (especially in the presence of other infections or connective tissue diseases), and they are not always sensitive enough to detect an infection of the central nervous system. To confirm a positive RPR or VDRL, a more sensitive test, the FTA-ABS (fluorescent treponema antibody absorbed test) should be performed.

Erythrocyte Sedimentation Rate

The erythrocyte sedimentation rate (ESR) is essentially a highly sensitive but nonspecific indication of tissue inflammation. Elevations of the ESR are seen with various pathological processes, including infectious, hematological, and connective tissue diseases. ESR can also be elevated by smoking. A markedly elevated ESR (i.e., above 40 mm/hr) in a demented or depressed elderly person raises the possibility of giant cell (temporal) arteritis, a disease that responds readily to corticosteroids but that can cause significant disability if untreated (Cummings & Benson, 1992).

Urinalysis

A urine sample should be obtained for baseline urinalysis and microscopic examination of the urine sediment after centrifugation. These simple tests are useful in screening not only for nephrological/urological problems, but also for endocrinological (e.g., diabetes) and infectious disorders. In particular, urinalysis offers a simple way to rule out an occult urinary tract infection, a frequent cause of confusion, agitation, or frank delirium in institutionalized elderly persons.

Chest Radiograph

A chest radiograph can be useful, since it can detect pulmonary and heart diseases such as pneumonia, chronic obstructive pulmonary disease, congestive heart failure, tuberculosis, primary lung cancer, and lung metastases, which are quite prevalent in the elderly and which often present with significant changes in mental status. Likewise, pulse oximetry or arterial blood gases may help to further assess pulmonary function and blood oxygenation.

Electrocardiogram

In an older person, an electrocardiogram (ECG) can be of value in detecting cardiac diseases (e.g., arrhythmia, myocardial infarction) associated with central nervous system hypoxia and cognitive impairment. More importantly, baseline and serial ECGs are often required to monitor the potential cardiotoxicity of many psychotropic medications, in particular tricyclic antidepressants (Rosen, Sweet, Pollock, & Mulsant, 1993).

Neuroimaging

The primary purpose of neuroimaging in psychiatry is to detect structural lesions of the central nervous system. A computed tomography (CT) scan involves exposure to x-rays, produces axial images of the CNS, and is indicated for the detection of tumors, infarcts (especially acute hemorrhagic infarcts), subdural hematomas, central nervous system calcification, and abscesses. The value of the CT scan is limited if the lesions of interest have a volume of less than 1 cm^3 or are close to bony structures. In these instances, magnetic resonance imaging (MRI) is of more benefit. Also, MRI does not involve exposure to radiation and is more specific than CT scanning in detecting white matter lesions. Overall, MRI has become the preferred form of neuroimaging, but it is not always available and is contraindicated in the presence of ferrous foreign bodies (e.g., shrapnel, aneurysm clips, pacemaker, and some metallic prosthetic valves). Neuroimaging is indicated in any person who experiences onset of a psychotic, affective, or cognitive disorder after age 45 or who presents with a disorder refractory to treatment or concurrent focal neurological deficits (Cummings & Benson, 1992; Martin, Miller, Kapoor, Karpf, & Boller, 1987). However, as emphasized by Cummings and Benson (1992) neuroimaging "is most valuable to support or confirm a clinical diagnosis" (p. 356). This may change in the near future, as functional neuroimaging techniques replace or complement CT and MRI scanning, but as of 1996, functional MRI, magnetic resonance spectroscopy (MRS), positron emission tomography (PET), and single photon emission computed tomography (SPECT) are still mostly limited to research settings.

Other Laboratory Tests

Electroencephalogram

The electroencephalogram (EEG) can provide helpful etiological information in the evaluation of some older adults presenting with mental status changes, in particular cognitive impairment of fairly recent onset (days or weeks) or acute cognitive deterioration occurring in the context of an established dementia. Presence of spike or sharp spike wave activity can confirm a suspected seizure disorder or reveal an occult one. Focal slowing may indicate a space-occupying lesion. In rare cases, a pathognomonic EEG pattern can establish a diagnosis of Creutzfeldt-Jakob disease, heavy metal poisoning, hepatic encephalopathy, or subacute sclerosing panencephalitis. EEG also has considerable value in identifying delirium or metabolic or toxic dementia. Finally, a relatively normal EEG in a patient with a rapidly progressive dementia supports a diagnosis of Major Depressive Disorder with cognitive impairment.

Lumbar Puncture and Cerebrospinal Fluid Examination

The role of the lumbar puncture (LP) and cerebrospinal fluid (CSF) examination is more limited. Several studies have concluded that an LP should be performed in demented patients with at least one of the following characteristics: age under 55 years, rapid onset or progression of dementia, headache or signs and symptoms of meningeal irritation, fever, positive syphilis serology, leukocytosis or infiltrate on chest radiographs, other evidence of infection by *Mycobacterium tuberculosis*, *Cryptococcus neoformans*, or other fungus (Becker, Feussner, Mulrow, Williams, & Vokaty, 1985; Hammerstrom & Zimmer, 1985).

Miscellaneous Tests

Other diagnostic tests are restricted to specific cases. For instance, a dynamic radioisotope cisternography is necessary to establish a diagnosis of normal pressure hydrocephalus. Polysomnography, or sleep studies, are mostly used to verify the presence of a primary sleep disorder (e.g., sleep apnea syndromes), but demonstration of a characteristic pattern of polysomnographic changes (i.e., decreased sleep efficiency, decreased delta wave sleep, decreased rapid eye movement [REM] latency, REM shift toward the beginning of the night, and increased REM intensity) can sometimes be used to support a diagnosis of Major Depressive Disorder. Finally, even though prevalence of alcoholism, illicit drug use, and human immunodeficiency (HIV) infection decreases with advancing age, these conditions may present with a variety of psychiatric symptoms and thus should always be considered possibilities. Breathalyzer (or blood alcohol level) and urine drug screen should be obtained in any person suspected of alcohol abuse, intoxication, or dependence. HIV testing should be performed in older patients with risk factors for HIV infection or with atypical presentations (e.g., early dementia).

SUMMARY

In summary, since psychological and physical problems often interact in a complex fashion in late life, all older adults presenting with a significant mental health problem should receive a thorough medical assessment. Its most important component is a detailed history from both the patient and a reliable informant. A physical examination confirms information obtained during the history and can reveal additional etiological clues. Selected laboratory tests complement the history and physical examination.

One of the primary goals of this assessment is to determine whether the presenting mental problem is directly caused by a physical illness. Even when this is not the case, a thorough medical work-up often detects concurrent treatable physical conditions that exacerbate psychological and behavioral problems. This comprehensive assessment also plays an important role in treatment planning, since it provides management guidelines when comorbid medical conditions constrain or interfere with behavioral, psychological, or pharmacological interventions.

REFERENCES

Alvir, J. M. J., Lieberman, J. A., Safferman, A. Z., & Schaaf, J. A. (1993). Clozapine-induced agranulocytosis: Incidence and risk factors in the United States. *New England Journal of Medicine, 329*, 162–167.

American Psychiatric Association. (1987). *Diagnostic and statistical manual of mental disorders* (3rd ed., revised). Washington, DC: Author.

American Psychiatric Association. (1994). *Diagnostic and statistical manual of mental disorders* (4th ed.). Washington, DC: Author.

Becker, P. M., Feussner, J. R., Mulrow, C. D., Williams, B. C., & Vokaty, K. A. (1985). The role of lumbar puncture in the evaluation of dementia: The Durham Veterans Administration/Duke University study. *Journal of the American Geriatrics Society, 33*, 392–396.

Cohen-Cole, S. A., & Stoudemire, A. (1987). Major depression and physical illness. *Psychiatric Clinics of North America, 10*, 1–17.

Committee on Aging: Group for the Advancement of Psychiatry. (1994). Impact of tacrine in the care of patients with Alzheimer's disease: What we know one year after FDA approval. *American Journal of Geriatric Psychiatry, 2*, 285–289.

Corbin, S. L., & Eastwood, M. R. (1986). Sensory deficits and mental disorders of old age: Causal or coincidental associations? *Psychological Medicine, 16*, 251–256.

Cummings, J. L., & Benson, D. F. (1992). *Dementia: A clinical approach.* Boston: Butterworth-Heinemann.

Druckenbrod, R., & Mulsant, B. H. (1995). Fluoxetine-induced syndrome of inappropriate antidiuretic hormone secretion. *Journal of Geriatric Psychiatry and Neurology, 7*, 225–258.

Funkenstein, H. H., Albert, M. S., Cook, N. R., West, C. G., Scherr, P. A., Chown, M. J., Pilgrim, D., & Evans, D. A. (1993). Extrapyramidal signs and other neurologic findings in clinically diagnosed alzheimer's disease. A community-based study. *Archives of Neurology, 50*, 51–56.

Hachinski, V. C., Iliff, L. D., Zlihka, E., Du Boulay, G. H., McAllister, V. L., Marshall, J., Russell, R. W. R., & Symon, L. (1975). Cerebral blood flow in dementia. *Archives of Neurology, 32*, 632–637.

Hammerstrom, D. C., & Zimmer, B. (1985). The role of lumbar puncture in the evaluation of dementia: The University of Pittsburgh study. *Journal of the American Geriatrics Society, 33*, 397–400.

Hinton, D. R., Sadun, A. A., Blanks, J. C., & Miller, C. A. (1986). Optic-nerve degeneration in Alzheimer's disease. *New England Journal of Medicine, 315*, 485–487.

Lindenbaum, J., Healton, E. B., & Savage, D. G. (1988). Neuropsychiatric disorders caused by cobalamin deficiency in the absence of anemia or microcytosis. *New England Journal of Medicine, 318*, 1720–1728.

Martin, D. C., Miller, J., Kapoor, W., Karpf, M., & Boller, F. (1987). Clinical prediction rules for computed tomographic scanning in senile dementia. *Archives of Internal Medicine, 147*, 77–80.

Martin, D. C., Morycz, R. K., McDowell, B. J., Snustad D., & Karpf, M. (1985). Community-based geriatric assessment. *Journal of the American Geriatrics Society, 33*, 602–606.

Mulsant, B. H., & Gershon, S. (1993). Neuroleptics in the treatment of psychosis in late life. A rational approach. *International Journal of Geriatric Psychiatry, 8*, 979–992.

Mulsant, B. H., Sweet, R. A., Rifai, A. H., Pasternak, R. E., McEachran, A., & Zubenko, G. S. (1994). The use of the Hamilton rating scale for depression in elderly patients with cognitive impairment and physical illness. *American Journal of Geriatric Psychiatry, 2*, 220–229.

Mulsant, B. H., & Thornton, J. E. (1990). Alzheimer disease and other dementias. In M. E. Thase, B. A. Edelstein, & M. Hersen (Eds.), *Handbook of outpatient treatment of adults: Nonpsychotic mental disorders.* (pp. 353–388). New York: Plenum Press.

Pollock, B. G., Perel, J. M., Altieri, L. P., Kirshner, M., Fasiczka, A. L., Houck, P. R., & Reynolds, C. F., III. (1992). Debrisoquin hydroxylation phenotyping in geriatric psychopharmacology. *Psychopharmacology Bulletin, 28*, 163–168.

Roose, S. P., Glassman, A. H., & Dalack, G. W. (1989). Depression, heart disease, and tricyclic antidepressants. *Journal of Clinical Psychiatry, 50*, 12–16.

Rosen, J., Sweet, R., Pollock, B. G., & Mulsant, B. H. (1993). Nortriptyline in the hospitalized elderly: Tolerance and side-effect reduction. *Psychopharmacological Bulletin, 29*, 327–331.

Small, G. W. (1992). Tacrine for treating Alzheimer's disease. *Journal of the American Medical Association, 268*(18), 2564–2565.

Steffes, R., & Thralow, J. (1987). Visual field limitation in the patient with dementia of the Alzheimer's type. *Journal of the American Geriatrics Society, 35*, 198–204.

Sweet, R. A., Mulsant, B. H., Gupta, B., Rifai, A. H., Pasternak, R. E., McEachran, A., & Zubenko, G. S. (1995). Duration of neuroleptic treatment and prevalence of tardive dyskinesia in late life. *Archives of General Psychiatry, 52*, 478–486.

Waxman, H. M., McCreary, G., Weinrit, R. M., & Carner, E. A. (1985). A comparison of somatic complaints among depressed and non-depressed older persons. *Gerontologist, 25*, 501–507.

CHAPTER 6

Competence and Other Legal Issues

C. V. Haldipur and Marilyn S. Ward

CHAPTER OUTLINE

Introduction	Guardianship
Definition of the Term	Competence to Consent to Research
Ethical and Legal Background	Testamentary Capacity
Assessment of Competence	Summary
Advance Directives	References

> I am a very foolish, fond old man,
> Fourscore and upward, not an hour more or less,
> And, to deal plainly,
> I fear I am not in my perfect mind.
> —King Lear

INTRODUCTION

Sophocles, the great Greek poet and playwright, it is said, was brought into court in his dotage by his son and charged with being incompetent to manage his own affairs. The aged tragedian's defense was to recite to the jurors passages from a play he had recently written. How could a man who could write such fine poetry not be competent? The case was dismissed, the complainant fined, and the poet triumphant (Hamilton, 1942).

C. V. Haldipur and Marilyn S. Ward • Department of Psychiatry, State University of New York Health Science Center, Syracuse, New York 13210.

Psychological Treatment of Older Adults: An Introductory Text, edited by Michel Hersen and Vincent B. Van Hasselt. Plenum Press, New York, 1996.

From extant court documents, it is possible to glean the methods by which individuals were declared *non compos mentis* (not of sound mind) in medieval England. Neugebauer (1979) points out that the records indicate that the English government conducted mental status examinations using "commonsense, naturalistic criteria of impairment" (p. 477). Evidence suggests strongly that examinations were designed to measure and test the subject's orientation, memory, and intellect. For instance, to determine competence of a woman in 14th-century England, she was asked to name the town she was in, give the number of days in a week, and figure simple tests of arithmetic. Later, in English courts it was common to ask subjects to recognize coins and perform simple numerical functions in relation to these coins or in the abstract. These examinations were the forerunners of the mental status examination modern-day clinicians use in their practice.

DEFINITION OF THE TERM

From medieval to modern times, issues of competence have been determined by a judge. However, realities of clinical practice require mental health practitioners to make their own assessments of patients' likely competence (Appelbaum & Gutheil, 1991). White (1959) used the term competence to refer to "an organism's capacity to interact effectively with its environment" (p. 297). In this chapter, however, the term will be used in its conventional legal sense: to connote decision-making capacity. All of us, then, were born incompetent and will most likely lose our decision-making capacity for some period in the future. In late adulthood, incompetence may be relatively brief when it occurs due to delirium or depression, or it can be permanent and irreversible when due to dementia. And because delirium, depression, and dementia occur more frequently in older adults, clinicians are often required to assess competence when working with patients in this age group. This chapter, therefore, will focus extensively on competence rather than on other legal issues in clinical practice. In a clinical context, it may become necessary to ensure that the patient is competent to consent to medical or psychological treatment; in forensic settings clinicians are called upon to determine a person's competence to make a contract, execute a will, or stand trial.

The statements "Mr. A is incompetent" and "Ms. B is competent" are incomplete. Competence is always for a task; we speak of competence to do something specific. And yet it is not a mere synonym for ability. Because we cannot run the Boston marathon or play the saxophone, might one say that we are incompetent to run the marathon and to play the saxophone? Competence usually involves mental and volitional rather than physical activities (Culver & Gert, 1982). But not all of us are capable of mental activities such as solving quadratic equations. It would be misleading to say that one is incompetent to perform the specific task unless one were in a position in which it was expected to have that mental ability. Thus, a mathematician may be said to be incompetent to solve a quadratic equation; and a psychologist or a psychiatrist, incompetent to do psychotherapy. It should also be noted that a person may be competent to make a certain decision at a particular time but incompetent at another point in time. There are, of course, individuals in irreversible coma or with severe dementia who remain incompetent. Furthermore, just as persons are more or less intelligent or athletic, persons are more or less competent to perform a task. Thus, the ability continuum runs from full mastery through various levels of partial proficiency to complete ineptitude (Beauchamp & Childress, 1994); for example, an intelligent and knowledgeable patient who has been in therapy for a long time may be more qualified to consent to a specific treatment modality, say, to taking psychotropic medication than a patient involuntarily committed for the first time to a state psychiatric hospital. However, for practical reasons, we need a threshold level below which a person is declared incompetent, even though a continuum of abilities underlies the performance of tasks.

Since competence is always for a specific task, one may be confronted with a clinical situation where an individual may be competent in one area and not the other. Even with individuals in irreversible coma or severe dementia, who could be considered globally incompetent, it may be prudent to consider competence for each specific task. It is not unusual to come across patients who are competent to consent to, say, admission to a nursing home but not to certain modalities of treatment or to execute a will. In the psychiatric field, involuntarily committed psychiatric patients are deemed *de jure* competent to refuse medications, and in many states only courts can authorize medication over the patients' objections.

What capacities are necessary for an individual to be competent to decide about health care or financial matters? Although there are clear differences in capacities necessary for competence in health care and financial matters, it may be possible to generalize about certain basic, necessary capacities. The individual must have the capacity, first, to understand and communicate and, second, to reason and deliberate. Buchanan and Brock (1990) add that the individual must have "a set of values or conception of what is good that is at least minimally consistent, stable, and affirmed as his or her own" (p. 25). As we shall note later in this chapter, assessment of competence, whenever possible, should incorporate testing for the presence of these capacities.

It may appear from the foregoing discussion that there are objective and value-free standards for judging competence. Although there are tests with high interrater agreement in judging whether an individual is irrational or is experiencing memory problems, competence judgments, Beauchamp and Childress (1994) point out, have a distinctive normative role in qualifying or disqualifying the person for certain decisions or actions; and though the tests used are empirical, normative judgments determine how the test will be used to sort out persons into the two classes of competent and incompetent. "They are normative because they concern how persons ought to be or may permissibly be treated" (p. 133). Indeed, in hospital practice the question of competence is usually raised when individuals decline to accept treatment recommended by their physicians.

ETHICAL AND LEGAL BACKGROUND

One way to approach and understand the importance of competence to clinicians is through moral reasoning. One could, for instance, argue that whatever the conditions of patients, their right to refuse treatment should be accepted even if it is not in their best interest. This would be a libertarian position, albeit an extreme one. Do we, as clinicians, have an obligation to prevent patients from self-destructive acts? At the other extreme, an argument could be made for paternalism, where professionals act as they deem fit in the circumstances. Moral and ethical disputes can be expressed in terms of rights, duties, and values. Clinicians have obligations and duties to patients; this is the deontological (Greek *deon*, obligation) school of ethical thought. It is such theoretical bases that constitute current ethics, with its emphasis on duties and obligations that in some instances would translate into an obligation or duty to assess competence. A case can then be made that if the harm done by treatment refusal far outweighs the benefits, clinicians have an obligation not to honor the refusal until the patient's competence is assessed. Increasingly, it is being acknowledged that patients have a right to accept or refuse treatment but that when questions arise about patient competence clinicians have an obligation to assess competence and seek legal counsel.

The shift from medical paternalism to respect for individual autonomy has been gradual and parallels the importance placed on individual freedom and liberties in Western social and political thought. Laws meant to guarantee individual civil liberties and political rights are often invoked to protect patient autonomy in clinical situations. The notion that individual freedom and liberty are important and should not be abridged unless the rights of others are constrained was enunciated by the philosopher John Stuart Mill in 1859. One school of ethical thought, utilitarian philosophy, derives from his writings. "Utility," he writes, "... holds that actions are right in proportion as they tend to promote happiness, wrong as they tend to produce the reverse of happiness" (Mill, 1977, p. 80). Individuals, he argues, can act in their best interest when they know what enhances their personal happiness and can act freely based on this knowledge. However, people do not always act in their best interest. The doctrine, he wrote, is meant to apply "only to human beings in the maturity of their faculties." Mill (1956), reflecting his Victorian sensibilities, also left out of consideration "those backward states of society in which the race itself may be considered as in its nonage" (p. 14). The important point to be gleaned from his writing is that Mill, a champion of liberty, acknowledged that there may be exceptions to the general injunction to respect individual freedom and autonomy. "Those who are in a state to require being taken care of by others must be protected against their own actions as well as against external injury" (Mill, 1956, p. 13). Would this utilitarian, or "greatest happiness," principle help a clinician deal with a terminally ill patient contemplating suicide by refusing life-saving treatment to escape a life of chronic pain and disability?

Despite the move away from paternalism toward respect for individual autonomy, it is acknowledged that paternalism has a place in certain situations and for some persons. There is universal agreement that children, before they attain maturity, lack competence to consent or refuse treatment or to execute a will. Laws requiring seat belts and licenses to practice certain professions and, in psychiatric practice, allowing civil commitments of the mentally ill based on *parens patriae* principle are clearly paternalistic in purpose. Dworkin (1977) defines such paternalism as "roughly the interference with a person's liberty of action justified by reasons referring exclusively to the welfare, good, happiness, needs, interests or values of the person being coerced" (p. 191). Thus, there may be justification for preventing an individual from jumping from a building with the belief that he will float in the air or for preventing an elderly person from giving all her money away to a favorite charity in the false belief that she inherited a large fortune. Of particular interest to clinicians is the recent popularity of living wills and proxy decision making, where individuals may in anticipation of future incompetence express and request consent or refusal for specific treatment. This is often referred to as the "Odysseus" or "Ulysses contract." Ulysses, you may recall from the Greek myth, commanded his men to tie him to the mast and refuse all future orders to be set free because he was aware of the power of the Sirens to enchant men with their songs. Later in the chapter we shall return to living wills and health care proxy.

Competence is a major issue for mental health professionals. Individuals in psychological treatment may have their competence called into question. However, it is the doctrine of informed consent, which has gained importance in the past three decades, that has made competence a major issue for clinicians. It is not always acknowledged that physicians and other health care workers withhold and conceal from their patients most relevant information about the diagnosis, treatment and its possible adverse effects, and prognosis. Hippocrates himself had the following advice to physicians: "perform all this calmly and adroitly, concealing most things from the patient while you are attending to him." The Nuremberg trials and subsequent court decisions in the United States, Canada, and Western Europe have made the pendulum shift from medical paternalism to respect for patients and ensuring their participation in decisions affecting their lives. But such ideals of the individual's autonomy, particularly the emphasis on patient participation, presupposes a capacity for such acts. No one suggests that infants or young children can truly participate in their treatment, and doubts may arise about the capacity of some older delirious or demented adults to participate meaningfully in their treatment. Thus, it is difficult, if not impossible, to advocate for patient autonomy or the doctrine of informed consent without, in some way, addressing the issue of competence. There are, of course, societies, such as Japan, that place emphasis on the interests of the group or the family over individual autonomy. There is, for instance, the *hogasha* system, which designates a family member of the mentally ill individual to consent or refuse treatment, constituting a guardianship of sorts for the patient. However, as Appelbaum (1994) notes, Japan, too, is "falling under the sway of approaches to mental health law that emphasize the value of individual rights" (p. 635).

The doctrine of informed consent creates dilemmas because it tries to balance two very different set of values: on the one hand there is the health and well-being of the individual, and on the other the principle of autonomy or the individual's right to self-determination. Although many recent court decisions have focused on clinicians' responsibility to disclose all relevant information to patients and thereby keep clinical encounters free from coercion, more and more frequently, especially when working with the elderly, questions arise about competence to consent or refuse treatment. The doctrine of informed consent has the legal imprimatur in case law. Thus, philosophers and clinicians are not alone in their interest in the doctrine; competence to consent or refuse treatment is ultimately determined in a court of law. Perhaps the most succinct and trenchant statement concerning this subject has been made by Justice Cardozo: "Every human being of adult years and sound mind has a right to determine what shall be done with his own body ..." (cited in Roth, 1982, p. 350). The statement has two important caveats: first, the person must be of adult years and, second, the person must be of sound mind. By what criteria does one judge an individual to be of sound mind? Who should determine whether the person is of sound mind? One needs to bear in mind that individuals of sound mind may, on occasions, act and decide irrationally and not in their own interest. Situations in which rational persons act or wish to act against their best interest present particularly challenging circumstances for clinicians and courts, as when an otherwise intelligent and rational person refuses life-sustaining blood transfusion on religious grounds.

There is presumption of competence in adults. Adults, *de jure*, are considered competent to consent or refuse treatment and to enter into a contract or execute a will unless they are determined to be incompetent at a court hearing. Children and adolescents up to a certain age (usually specified by law) are considered to be incompetent to consent or refuse treatment and to enter into a contract or execute a will. Clinicians are often called upon to render an opinion about a patient's *de facto* competence as a prelude to, or instead of, a formal legal review. Such opinions, of course, lack the force of law.

When competent patients make irrational choices, clinicians should make every effort to persuade them to reconsider their decisions. Brock and Wartman (1990) offer a taxonomy of irrational treatment choices. There may be, for instance, cultural, religious, or moral reasons for the choice. "Distinguishing irrational preferences from those that express different attitudes, values and beliefs can be difficult in both theory and practice" (p. 1599). Truly irrational choices are not sufficient reason to override patients' choices; one's only possible recourse is through courts.

Therapeutic relationships are not static but dynamic and go through various stages as the treatment progresses. It would be difficult in such relationships to obtain informed consent for each modality of treatment or tests during the treatment period. A patient truly must be competent and give consent freely after receiving appropriate information. But rather than adhere to a single standard of competence, a "sliding scale" is suggested that requires an increasingly more stringent standard as the consequences of the patient's decision embody more risk (Drane, 1984, 1985). The standard of competence, in other words, will depend on the dangerousness of the decision. The least stringent standard of competence to give valid consent applies to those decisions that are not dangerous and are in the patient's best interest. An example would be of a patient who is critically ill with a life-threatening disease; the treatment available is not very risky and there are few alternatives. The most stringent and demanding standard is reserved for dangerous decisions; for example, when the diagnosis is not in doubt, available treatment is effective and treatment refusal will result in death. Buchanan and Brock (1990) also advocate that the required level of decision-making competence be placed on a sliding scale from low to high in accordance with the risk. But Beauchamp and Childress (1994) recommend that "only the *required standards of evidence* [italics added] for decision making competence should be placed on a sliding scale" (p. 141).

Clinicians should remember that competence or incompetence need not be permanent. Indeed, clinicians should always rule out and treat underlying psychopathology before declaring any person to be competent or incompetent, unless, of course, there is compelling evidence that the individual suffers from a proven irreversible condition. Declaring someone competent or incompetent calls for clinicians to use not just one's skills in testing but clinical skills as well. The following case may be illustrative: a chronically medically ill male patient was refusing a standard treatment offered by his physician. On formal testing there appeared to be no evidence of psychosis. He understood the nature of his illness and the consequences of not treating the condition. The senior clinician on the case was about to declare the patient competent to decline the treatment when a trainee suggested transferring the patient to a psychiatric unit to rule out depression. The patient's physician agreed, since nothing could be one on the medical ward. Although the senior mental health clinician was not convinced about the diagnosis of depression, he agreed to the transfer at the trainee's insistence. With intensive daily psychotherapy and antidepressant medication the patient showed marked improvement in his attitude and, subsequently, voluntarily consented to treatment.

ASSESSMENT OF COMPETENCE

The need for a clinical assessment of competence arises in circumstances where there is some suspicion that a mental or physical disability is interfering with the individual's ability to make rational decisions. Much of the literature on assessment of competence deals specifically with the ability to make health care decisions. According to Levitte and Thornby (1989), evaluation of competence is a much more frequent reason for referral of older patients for psychiatric consultation than it is for younger patients. In their study population, the elderly were also much more likely to be referred for evaluation of competency for nonmedical decision making. Among patients referred to a consult-liaison psychiatric service for competency evaluation, organic mental disorder was found to be much more prevalent than in a control group referred for other types of psychiatric evaluation (Golinger & Fedoroff, 1989). Competence in a medical context is generally defined as the ability to give informed consent. There is evidence that the elderly are at increased risk of deficits in the skills needed to give informed consent, especially in the areas of memory and comprehension (Taub, 1980). The incidence of dementia rises with age, with a corresponding increase in the likelihood of incompetence. A low educational level also seems to raise the likelihood of incompetence.

Informed consent consists of three elements: competency to consent, voluntariness, and information. Although this discussion is focused on competency, issues of voluntariness and information do arise in clinical practice. Competency assessment may be requested in a case where it becomes clear that the patient has not been provided with all the relevant information necessary to make a decision. For example, an elderly patient may refuse a surgical procedure because of a mistaken estimate of the risks of surgical versus medical treatment for a given condition. Subtle and not-so-subtle issues of coercion also arise, and vulnerability to outside influence may be a factor that needs to be assessed. This can be an issue for the elderly person who is dependent on a family member for survival and who may feel that there is little choice but to accede to the caregiver's wishes.

In 1982, the President's Commission for the Study of Ethical Problems in Medicine and Biomedical and Behavioral Research issued its report on the topic of informed consent. The commission stated three necessary criteria for decision-making capacity: (1) possession of a set of values or goals, (2) the ability to communicate and to understand information, and (3) the ability to reason and deliberate about one's choices (Kaplan & Price, 1989).

Roth, Meisel, and Lidz (1977) classified proposed tests for competency as follows: (1) evidencing a choice, (2) "reasonable" outcome of choice, (3) choice based on "rational" reasons, (4) ability to understand, and (5) actual understanding. They also noted that decisions about competency do not exist in a vacuum and depend on the risk–benefit ratio of any proposed treatment and the patient's decision to refuse or accept the treatment. This has been elaborated into the sliding scale concept of competency mentioned earlier. For example, the taking of a blood sample for a routine laboratory test is associated with the risk of discomfort and a possible hematoma and the benefit of assistance in diagnosis. Thus, a low threshold of competence, such as mere assent, might be acceptable in this circumstance. This framework also takes into account the consequences of the patient's decision. In situations where a patient is refusing a treatment with low risk and high benefit for a life-threatening condition, the threshold for competency would be quite high. For example, if a previously healthy patient refused antibiotic treatment for bacterial meningitis, this decision would be heavily scrutinized. This does allow a competent patient to make irrational treatment decisions, provided the decision-making process is rational.

The problem of defining rationality in this context is a thorny one. Brock and Wartman (1990) state that the ideal rational patient weighs the risks and benefits of alternative treatments, including no treatment, according to personal values and selects the treatment alternative that best promotes those values. These authors point out several types of irrationality in medical decision making that are not based on the kinds of mental disabilities that we are accustomed to thinking about. These include a bias toward thinking in the short term, feelings of invulnerability, fear of pain or other unpleasant aspects of medical treatment, and effects related to the way medical decisions are framed by the practitioner. However, rationality is very much in the eye of the beholder, and patients may later view decisions to forego treatment during the course of an acute illness as irrational. This problem may be particularly important in an elderly population according to Pomerantz and deNesnera (1991), who present examples of two elderly men who declined treatment while in delirious states, partly because of the intensive and uncomfortable nature of the treatment involved. When their conditions improved, both expressed satisfaction that they had been treated.

Appelbaum and Grisso (1988) have classified legal standards for competency to consent to treatment into four categories: (1) the ability to communicate a choice, (2) the ability to understand information about a treatment decision, (3) the ability to appreciate the situation and its consequences, and (4) the ability to manipulate information rationally. This represents a hierarchy of tests, with the ability to manipulate information rationally being the most stringent standard and that of communicating a choice being the one most protective of patient autonomy. They suggest that the evaluator begin by asking questions that deal with the patient's abilities in each of the four areas. For example, in assessing the ability to communicate a choice, the examiner would ask the patient to make a choice about a proposed treatment based on the information given and then would judge the stability of that choice over time. Memory deficits and extreme ambivalence may make the patient unable to meet this standard. The ability to understand information can be assessed by asking the patient to repeat it back in his own words. Again, memory deficits can cause significant problems regarding this standard. Every effort should be made to overcome sensory and educational deficits in communicating information to the patient. Appreciation of the situation is evaluated by asking the patient her concept of her illness, the need for treatment, and likely outcomes of treatment. Denial of illness can have a significant impact on the patient's ability to meet this standard. Rational manipulation of information is evaluated by asking the patient to explain his chain of reasoning in reaching the treatment decision he elected. Some authors stress the need for a full clinical evaluation in assessing patient competency, including making any applicable diagnosis of a condition listed in *Diagnostic and Statistical Manual of Mental Health Disorders* (*DSM-IV*) and administering the Folstein Mini-Mental State Examination (Janofsky, 1990; Kaplan & Price, 1989). The need for assessing psychodynamic factors in patient decision making has also been stressed, as has been the need for assessing interfering emotional states and pathological motivations (Appelbaum & Roth, 1981; Mahler & Perry, 1988). Appelbaum and Roth also point out the need to get information from collateral sources, to assess what information has actually been given to the patient (it may well have been incomplete), to be aware of the fluctuation of the patient's mental status over time, and to be cognizant of the effects of the setting (such as cultural factors or dislike of the health care provider). At least one standardized instrument for assessing patients' competence to make treatment decisions has been developed (Janofsky, McCarthy, & Folstein, 1992), and its authors suggest it be used as a screening test. It has been noted that standardized instruments alone are probably not a sufficiently accurate way to make final clinical decisions about competence (Rutman & Silberfeld, 1992).

No single diagnosis automatically implies incompetence to make health care decisions. Conditions that can lead to at least temporary impairment in decision-making ability include drug intoxication, metabolic and nutritional disturbances, head injury, infectious disease, sensory loss, hypoxia, cerebrovascular disease, and psychiatric disorders (Farnsworth, 1989). When possible, correctable conditions that interfere with competence should be treated. Certain diagnoses are of particular concern in evaluating the elderly patient. As previously noted, the first is organic brain disease in general and senile dementia in particular. The incidence of dementing illness increases with age, reaching 45.2% in the population over 85 in one study (Evans et al., 1989). An elderly person's verbal skills may be preserved relative to performance skills, and an incapacitating degree of dementia can thus be masked from a casual examiner. More controversial is the effect of depressive illness on competency, as cognitive skills generally remain intact. It is estimated that major depressive illness affects 3% to 5% of older adults (Blazer, 1990). Some authors contend that existing standards for competency are skewed toward cognitive capacity, with a relative neglect of affective issues (Bursztajn, Harding, Gutheil, & Brodsky, 1991). In a depressed state, the patient may be unable to appreciate benefits or be overly concerned about risks. At the extreme, the depressed patient may refuse life-sustaining treatment based on the perception that life is no longer worth living, and the clinician is left to judge whether this is a realistic, rational perception (Sullivan & Youngner, 1994). For example, a frail elderly patient with difficulty communicating due to a stroke may stop eating and drinking and may decline antidepressant medications and a feeding tube. To mental health clinicians, this apparent desire to die may in and of itself represent a mental condition justifying treatment, on an involuntary basis if necessary. Depressive symptoms of helplessness, hopelessness, guilt, and anhedonia are particularly likely to hinder patients' perceptions of their medical situations. Although physical illness is a frequent precipitant for depression, terminally ill patients are unlikely to desire death in the absence of depression (Brown, Henteleff, Barakat, & Rowe, 1986). The depressed elderly may not be truly autonomous agents in the sense that informed consent theory demands.

Other criticisms of the assessment of competency using the informed consent model center on its emphasis on autonomy at the expense of the interpersonal context of real-life decision making (Jecker, 1990). This analysis suggests that patient autonomy cannot be viewed outside the context of the patient's intimate relationships. Family members often play a large role in the medical care of elderly patients, and patients' decisions about health care may have far-reaching effects on the family as a whole. Jecker points out that the marginally competent patient may look incompetent on clinical evaluation yet be able to make decisions consistent with their lifetime values and experience in collaboration with family members. Berlin and Canaan (1991) also point out that when treatment decisions for possibly incompetent patients were presented to courts, the court frequently turned around and recommended that clinicians consult the family. In their examples, competence problems were reframed as family systems problems, and the original competency issue became irrelevant. Families persuaded patients to accept realistic treatment alternatives. Some writers state that clinicians have an ethical and legal obligation to try to persuade competent patients to accept indicated treatment, using the family for leverage if necessary (Kapp, 1992).

One of the most contentious decisions facing elderly patients and their families is the decision to give up independent living and/or move into a nursing home. This situation does not readily lend itself to an informed consent type of analysis. Many people when competent will say that they never want to go into a nursing home regardless of the circumstances, and the family members may say they will never put their increasingly disabled relative in a nursing home. When the possibility of placement actually has to be considered, the patients, families, and health care professionals are likely to have competing interests. A narrow assessment of a patient's ability to make a decision about where to live will rarely be helpful. Rather, full consideration of the entire situation, including the level of care that would be best for the patient, the ability and willingness of significant others to meet patient needs, and patient's currently and previously expressed wishes about placement, should take place (Meier & Cassel, 1986).

What avenues are available to the clinician treating the incompetent patient? In an emergency situation, there is a presumption that a reasonable patient would want treatment to preserve life or health in the absence of previously expressed wishes to the contrary. Therefore, the clinician should generally proceed with lifesaving treatment. Providers should also attempt to ascertain whether the patient has executed some sort of advance directive (discussed later), which may provide guidance about the patient's wishes regarding treatment. There is some support for the provision of routine types of treatment despite patient incompetence. This might include treatments such as diets or wound and skin care and treatments with pain medications and antibiotics. Generally, a substitute decision maker will be needed to make major decisions for the incompetent patient. If the patient has not designated this person in advance, tradition dictates that the clinician go to a family member to make decisions for the patient. In its 1982 report, the President's Commission endorsed this practice, and some states have codified it. However, family dynamics can make this problematic, and in some situations courts and legislatures have mandated more formal procedures (Schwartz & Roth, 1989). The clinician has the option of going to court, either to have a guardian appointed for the patient (see below) or to obtain a court order for a specified course of treatment. This is obviously expensive and time consuming, as well as impractical in a rapidly evolving clinical situation. There also are realistic limitations to what types of treatment can be delivered to the incompetent patient without physical cooperation. For example, a family member may authorize dental care for an incompetent elderly patient, but it may be impossible to deliver this without some level of cooperation from the patient. Due to the nature of the treatment, the incompetent patient will be unable to engage in many forms of psychotherapeutic treatment.

Some states have experimented with alternatives to guardianship for health care decision making for the incompetent patient. In 1985, New York initiated a surrogate decision-making program for persons with mental disabilities who resided in state-operated or state-licensed facilities (Herr & Hopkins, 1994). The program provides for decision making about major medical treatment, which is considered to be interventions where general anesthesia is necessary or where there is a significant risk or invasion of bodily integrity. A major advantage of the program was the substantial decrease in time that decisions were rendered. The court system was reported to take an average of 135 days to reach a decision, whereas the program usually rendered a decision in 14 days. The program was designed for situations in which no other appropriate surrogate decision maker was available.

It should also be noted that special procedures may apply for certain kinds of treatment. For example, a guardian's consent is frequently not adequate for some types of psychiatric treatment (In re Guardianship of Richard Roe III, 1981). Court authorization is often needed for treatments such as psychotropic medication, electroconvulsive therapy and psychiatric hospitalization. In addition, involuntary psychiatric treatment generally cannot take place outside the context of involuntary hospitalization. In most states, commitment to a psychiatric hospital does not imply incompetence to make treatment decisions. Clinicians involved in these areas need to be familiar with local statutes and case law. Involuntary commitment has been increasingly limited as a way of dealing with the incompetent elderly patient with a dementing illness, and some states explicitly forbid dementia as a grounds for involuntary civil commitment (Parry, 1994).

ADVANCE DIRECTIVES

In 1976, Americans became familiar with the story of Karen Ann Quinlan, a young woman who had lapsed into a persistent vegetative state after ingesting a combination of prescription medications and alcohol and subsequently sustaining a cardiopulmonary arrest. Her parents fought a court battle to allow discontinuation of mechanical ventilation, which was thought to be sustaining her life. The story led to a debate about the appropriateness of life-sustaining treatment in such cases and about how such treatment decisions should be made. By 1991, more than 40 states had enacted living will statutes, which generally applied only to terminally ill patients and to certain types of treatments, such as those considered "extraordinary" (Annas, 1991).

An early variant of the advance directive is the do-not-resuscitate (DNR) order, limiting use of cardiopulmonary resuscitation. Hospitals have formulated policies ensuring that competent patients must consent prior to a DNR order and that in the case of incompetent patients a surrogate must consent. At least one state enacted legislation codifying this type of policy. As a practical matter, most DNR decisions are made by surrogates, as the patient is often incompetent by the time the physician brings up the matter, even though patients who have DNR orders are generally competent at the time of hospital admission (LaPuma, Orentlicher, & Moss, 1991).

In 1990, the U.S. Supreme Court issued its decision in the Cruzan case, the only right-to-die case that it has decided to this point. A clear majority of the court held that a competent patient has the right to refuse medical treatment, including life-sustaining medical treatment, and that this right has a constitutional basis under a liberty interest based in the due process clause of the Fourteenth Amendment (*Cruzan v. Missouri Department of Health*, 1990). Five justices upheld Missouri's right to require clear and convincing evidence of an incompetent person's wishes prior to withdrawing life-sustaining treatment. On December 1, 1991, the Patient Self-Determination Act of 1990 went into effect. This federal statute requires all health care institutions receiving federal funding (Medicare or Medicaid) to provide patients with written information describing patient's right to make decisions about medical care, to refuse treatment, and to formulate advance directives. The information must also describe the institution's policies about these matters. The law is intended to encourage adults to prepare written documents about their wishes about medical care, particularly concerning end-of-life treatment (Wolf et al., 1991). By this means, it is hoped that competent patients can exercise their autonomy even after they become incompetent. It is estimated that approximately 10% of American have executed an advance directive of some sort.

Legislation about advance directives generally describes two types: the living will and the health care proxy. The living will states the competent patient's treatment preferences in various medical situations and takes effect when the patient becomes incompetent. A major criticism of the living will is that it is very difficult to anticipate the kinds of medical situations that will occur in one's life. A related criticism is that a person's view of illness when well may differ significantly from that when ill. The health care proxy is a person appointed by the patients to make health care decisions for them should they later become incompetent. The proxy is expected to make decisions based on his or her interpretation of what the patient would have wanted if competent. Ideally, the proxy will be someone with whom the patient has discussed his or her values, views about different types of medical care, and preferences about end-of-life treatment.

A great deal has been written about the desirability of encouraging patients to execute advance directives if they wish to do so. According to one study (Emanuel, Barry, Stoeckle, Ettelson, & Emanuel, 1991), the general public is interested in executing advance directives but perceives that their physician is the one who should initiate any discussion of this issue. They advocate the use of a structured interview format to explore these issues with patients. The interview specifies four possible incompetency scenarios and several types of medical treatments (Emanuel & Emanuel, 1989). These include cardiopulmonary respiration, mechanical ventilation, artificial nutrition, surgery, renal dialysis, cancer chemotherapy, diagnostic tests, transfusion, antibiotics, and pain medications. They also point out that advance planning is relevant to young, healthy people as well as to older people with health problems. However, execution of an advance directive cannot be a precondition for admission to a nursing home or other health care facility. Respect for autonomy dictates that individuals have the choice to make their wishes about health care be known as they see fit. In addition, completion of an advance directive can decrease anxiety about death and increase feelings of control (LaPuma et al., 1991).

Many criticisms have been leveled at living wills and health care proxies. As noted, making out a living will involves trying to anticipate what types of medical situations may occur in one's future life, which is a difficult task. Most state living will statutes specify that the directive is only triggered by a terminal condition or a persistent vegetative state; these conditions are not necessarily those that occur frequently in clinical practice with the elderly. Concern has been raised about the demented patient who prior to incompetence has left a directive that life-sustaining treatment be withheld but after incompetence appears to enjoy life. Some feel that, in this situation, the patient's best interests should take precedence over any advance directive on the subject (Wolf et al., 1991). Concern has also been raised over the clinician's accuracy in diagnosing triggering conditions, particularly the persistent vegetative state (Steinbock, 1989). There is also no practical way to ensure that the treating physician adheres to the living will. Another scenario may be a patient in an emergency room, where none of the treatment providers has any way of knowing that the patient has a living will or health care proxy. In one study involving nursing home residents, the written advance directive was successfully delivered to the hospital in only 25 of 71 cases (Danis et al., 1991), even though the nursing home is a location where there is generally a high level of awareness about advance directives.

Health care proxies have been criticized on the grounds that they frequently do not make truly substituted judgments but merely do what they think is best for the patient. Studies have pointed out a low degree of concordance between patients' judgments and surrogates' judgments (Seckler, Meier, Mulvihill, & Cammer Paris, 1991), although family members do better than physicians in this area. Of course, patients do not necessarily want their directives followed to the letter. In a study of dialysis patients 31% wanted to give their surrogates "complete leeway" in following their directives (Seghal et al., 1992). The patients also varied in how much they wanted their surrogates to weigh various factors in decision making, such as pain, quality of life, indignity of treatment, financial impact of treatment on the family, and religious beliefs.

Ethical criticism of advance directives, particularly with regard to the elderly, has been proposed on the grounds that they could be used in an attempt to limit costs. There is some concern that patients may be asked to sign directives to limit care with little understanding of what they are signing (LaPuma et al., 1991). Of course, they can also be used to maximize "high-tech," expensive care. In a Minnesota case, a family requested that their relative remain on a respirator in a persistent vegetative state, and a court supported their decision (Angell, 1991).

As a practical manner, advance directives have not been shown to decrease costs for end-of-life care (Emanuel & Emanuel, 1994).

Advance directives were originally conceived as a way to make end-of-life decisions for people who had permanently lost decision-making capacity. Since that time, there has been some exploration of using advance directives to make other types of medical decisions in the context of temporary incompetence, such as major mental illness. At least one state, Minnesota, has a law that permits a patient to write a directive expressing wishes regarding the future use of psychotropic medication and electroconvulsive therapy (Weiner & Wettstein, 1993). This has been used for the so-called Ulysses contract, in which a patient authorizes specified treatments in case of a future mental illness, even if the patient should object at that future time. Other states have laws that are silent on this issue. In California, use of a health care proxy to consent for mental hospitalization, electroconvulsive therapy, and psychosurgery is expressly forbidden (Sales, 1993). A major limitation on the use of advance directives in psychiatric settings is that they are very likely to conflict with already-existing state laws and procedures. However, it is likely that a detailed directive or a designated proxy's views would have some weight with a court considering the issue of whether to treat a psychiatric patient over her objection.

GUARDIANSHIP

Guardianship as an institution can be traced back to Roman times, and its original intent was to conserve the property of the ward (Brakel, Parry, & Weiner, 1985). At that point, guardianship of the person did not exist. In British law, the right and duty of the King to protect people who were mentally impaired and their property extends at least back until the 13th century. This duty was usually exercised by transferring custodial authority to private individuals, who were then responsible to the Crown. The courts inquired into areas, such as intellect, orientation, memory, personal habits, and judgments, in making guardianship decisions (Neugebauer, 1979). In the United States, the duty to protect the mentally impaired devolves to the state and is based on the doctrine of *parens patriae.*

Guardianships have traditionally been divided into those of property and those of the person. A guardianship of property is frequently called a conservatorship. All of the states have statutes allowing a substitute decision maker, generally called a guardian, to be appointed to make decisions for an incompetent person, generally called a ward (Kapp, 1992). The recent trend is for guardianships to be limited to specific areas of incapacity and for alternatives to be used when possible. As noted, guardianship may be sought when medical decisions must be made for an incompetent person. However, a full guardianship entails a complete loss of many basic rights, such as the right to contract and the right to vote. Thus, many commentators feel that it should be reserved for situations in which there is no other alternative.

Guardianship proceedings most frequently involve the elderly, and usually the guardian appointed is a family member (Bulcroft, Kielkopf, & Tripp, 1991). The petition for guardianship is most often initiated by a family member, usually on the grounds that the person is unable to care for himself or his property. In the proceedings reviewed by Bulcroft et al., all the petitions for guardianship were granted despite rather scanty evidence. Although some of the potential wards were opposed to the proposed guardianship, none of them contested it legally. It also appeared that the main reason for most petitions was to preserve the estate of the potential ward.

In 1987, the Associated Press published its study of the nation's guardianship system and concluded that it was "a dangerously burdened and troubled system" (cited in Kapp, 1992). The American Bar Association (1989) issued recommendations aimed at improving the system. These included exploration of alternatives to guardianship, data collection and evaluation, clear and objective standards for incapacity, standards for guardianship agencies, and a variety of procedural recommendations. These developments led to widespread statutory changes that were intended to protect potential wards against unnecessary guardianships. Procedural changes included the following requirements: a specific statement about the type of incapacity in the petition; that the proposed ward be present at the hearing; that the proposed ward have a lawyer to act as his or her advocate; and a neutral investigation by the court. In a study of the effects of these procedural changes, specific petitions were more likely to lead to a recommendation of a limited guardianship, as were evaluations by a neutral fact finder. Proposed wards who hired their own attorneys to contest the guardianship were more likely to receive limited or no guardianship (Keith & Wacker, 1993).

Standards for guardianship vary somewhat by state. Some jurisdictions require that specified disabilities be present, such as mental illness or physical disability. Most states require that the proposed ward "lacks sufficient understanding or capacity to make or communicate responsible decisions" (Anderer, 1990). In some statutes, functional impairment in the sense of inability to care for self or property is mentioned. Mental health professionals are sometimes specified as those who are to do competency assessments for guardianship. Recently, many commentators have suggested a much more thorough assessment than would be necessary for evaluating a more specific competency, and some states require a functional evaluation. It is recommended that the evaluator attempt to obtain informed consent to the evaluation before beginning and only to proceed if the evaluation is likely to serve the interests of the person being evaluated (Pepper-Smith, Harvey, Silberfeld, Stein, & Rutman, 1992). At least one standard assessment of functional capacity has been developed (Saunders & Simon, 1987). This type of assessment can be completed only with the assistance of someone who knows the person well. In addition to medical and psychiatric diagnoses, it calls for assessment of behavior and receptive, expressive, and written communications. Also to be investigated are orientation and health care skills: for example, ability to take medication independently, ability to indicate pain, and ability to remember and keep appointments. Ability to consent to medical care is included, as is the ability to conduct legal business. Inclusion of examples of the person's functional abilities is encouraged. This type of assessment also provides for evaluation of possible alternatives to guardianship as well as potential guardians and their relationships with the proposed ward.

As noted above, guardianship has become the least-favored means of dealing with the needs of an incompetent person, and some state laws explicitly demand that all other options be explored first. One common alternative is the durable power of attorney. "Durable" means that the power of attorney survives the incompetence of the person who executes it. Ideally, the person who is prepared for possible future incompetence prepares a document transferring the authority to make certain types of decisions to an agent, such as a friend or relative. The transfer of authority can take place immediately or at the time the person becomes incompetent (Kapp, 1992). The health care proxy laws mentioned earlier are a variant of the durable power of attorney, and prior to their enactment ordinary durable powers of attorney were sometimes used for medical decision making. One particularly attractive characteristic of the durable power of attorney is its flexibility. A disadvantage is that a guardian is at least theoretically subject to review and monitoring by the appointing court, whereas an appointed agent is not.

Another alternative to guardianship in the area of financial management is the appointment of a representative payee, with or without the consent of the person whose funds are involved. The payee is usually involved in managing funds from either an entitlement or retirement program, such as Social Security or veterans' benefits. Like guardianship, the representative payee system affects the elderly more than others (Kapp, 1992). It has also been criticized for lack of accountability.

Most states have also developed adult protective services. The purpose of these services is to enable adults at risk (which includes many elderly adults) to live safely in the community. Ideally, the social services agency involved in providing the services has a wide range of options, such as homemaker services, home health services, a variety of supportive living arrangements, guardianships, and institutional care if absolutely necessary (Weiner & Wettstein, 1993). A social service agency may be empowered to intervene in the life of an elderly person without his consent and without the procedural safeguards present in the guardianship process (Kapp, 1992). These services are generally modeled after child protective services and would appear to have the same vulnerability to excessive caseloads.

COMPETENCE TO CONSENT TO RESEARCH

Another area in which competence becomes important for the older patient is when she is asked to participate in research. This aspect of competence was first recognized in the Nuremberg Code, which was the first recognized set of principles for ethical standards for research. The code was a response to the atrocities committed by the Nazis in pursuit of what were allegedly research ends. It states that voluntary consent of the subject is needed for the pursuit of research, and the subject "should have the legal capacity to give consent" (cited in Appelbaum & Roth, 1982). Since that time, a variety of guidelines and regulations have been promulgated on the ethical conduct of research. This was given added impetus by widely publicized abuses occurring in this country, such as the Tuskegee syphilis study. All are based on the following principles: (1) the subject must have volunteered on the basis of having had all of the information necessary for the decision to be an informed one; (2) the subject should be allowed to withdraw from the research at any time; (3) all unnecessary risks should be eliminated and, if feasible, animal studies should precede those on humans; (4) the benefits of the experiment to the subject or to society, preferably to both, should outweigh the risks to the subject; and (5) an experiment should be conducted only by qualified researchers (Kapp, 1992, p. 240). Federal regulations have led to the development of institutional review boards, which are bodies that review and approve research within the institution.

The criteria for competency to consent to research are similar to those for informed consent in general, and the same issues with respect to the sliding scale apply. The possible standards in order of increasing stringency are (1) evidencing a choice, (2) factual understanding of the issues, (3) rational manipulation of information, and (4) actual appreciation of the nature of the situation (Appelbaum & Roth, 1982). However, since enrollment in a research study is not primarily intended to benefit the individual enrollee, heightened scrutiny of the issues surrounding consent occurs. There is also an assumption that certain groups, such as prisoners and those who are mentally disabled, are at increased risk of being taken advantage of in the consent process (Delano & Zucker, 1994) because of mental status and the inherently coercive nature of institutional settings. Some would include the elderly as a class of potential subjects needing special protection. However, this view stigmatizes the elderly as inherently mentally disabled and decreases their autonomy. It has been pointed out that if appreciation of the situation is used as the standard, many "normal" people would not meet it. Appelbaum and Roth (1982) give examples of studies in which subjects did not understand that they were part of an investigation, were not aware of the risks of a study drug despite explanations, and believed that a placebo was therapeutically active despite explanations indicating otherwise.

Are the elderly at increased risk for incompetence to consent to research? As noted, older subjects with low educational levels and vocabulary skills were at high risk not to understand informed consent materials (Taub, 1986), although better-educated older subjects did as well as younger subjects. A low educational level of older subjects is likely to persist into the future, as 37% of individuals who were between 55 and 64 in 1982 did not complete high school. Some studies report decreases in cognitive flexibility, recall and recognition, memory storage and retrieval, and judgment with age. Stanley and Stanley (1987), for example, studied competency of elderly medical patients by presenting them with hypothetical research scenarios that involved varied risk-benefit ratios and then compared their responses with those of younger patients. Elderly patients did exhibit reduced comprehension of the risk-benefit information presented but generally made equally reasonable decisions about participation despite a reduced quality of reasoning.

For the study of certain conditions, there is no alternative to using human subjects deemed incompetent. The most relevant example of this in an elderly population is the study of Alzheimer's disease, for which a valid animal model does not exist (High, 1992). In the case of the incompetent subject, consent of the legally authorized surrogate must be obtained. It has been argued that surrogates ought to be restricted in the type of research they can consent to on behalf of their wards. For example, the guidelines of the National Institute on Aging propose that surrogates be authorized only to consent to minimal risk studies or to those with greater than minimal risk that offer some realistic possibility of benefit (Stanley, 1983). As we move into an era in which risky treatments of potential therapeutic benefit are being developed, such as tacrine, problems of surrogate consent will multiply.

TESTAMENTARY CAPACITY

Another area of competence of increased relevance to the elderly is that of testamentary capacity, which is competence to make out one's will. Although a person can make out a will at any time, it is frequently a task that people postpone until late in life. In addition, changes to the will, known as codicils, may become necessary as circumstances change. Usually, a person's testamentary capacity is not questioned until she dies and some living person is upset about the contents of the will. Partly because of the increased number of medical conditions that can affect competence, will challenges have become more and more common (Redmond, 1987). With this in mind, potential testators are increasingly turning to mental health professionals to provide evidence of testamentary capacity.

Generally, wills can be challenged only on the following grounds: (1) the will was executed improperly; (2) the will is fraudulent; (3) the testator lacked capacity at the time the will was executed; and (4) the testator was subject to undue influence (*Money*, September 1993, pp. 92–102). The case presented in *Money* is of an 82-year-old widower who died 7 months after leaving all of a considerable estate to a waitress who served him meals in a diner. Within a few months, no fewer than five people had stepped forward to contest the will. It points out that challenges are most likely in situations where there are frequent, seemingly arbitrary will changes and in situations where natural heirs are disinherited.

Lack of capacity and undue influence are issues around which the mental health practitioner can give useful information for future legal use (Spar & Garb, 1992). The standard for testamentary capacity varies somewhat by state, but in general the testator must understand that he is making a will, must know the nature and extent of his property, and must know "the natural objects of his bounty," or those who might be expected to benefit from the will. To do an accurate assessment, the evaluator must know the extent and nature of the testator's assets and the identities of possible heirs. A structured mental status examination should be conducted, and some commentators suggest videotaping the evaluation to preserve evidence of competence for future review. Information from collateral sources is always important to supplement findings about cognitive capacity and to clarify the testator's goals and values. Undue influence is the overriding of the testator's free will by another, usually someone who benefits directly. Inquiry in this area must delve into the testator's personal relationships, particularly those with the alleged influencer. It has been pointed out that it is probably easier to influence anyone whose chronic physical or mental illness has placed them in a dependent position.

The elderly person who wishes to arrange for the orderly disposition of assets after death should be referred to an attorney experienced in these matters. The mental health professional who does this type of evaluation must be sure to have all of the relevant information, including the possible agendas of whoever wanted the evaluation. If the professional is approached to do an evaluation by someone other than the testator or the testator's lawyer, suspicions should be aroused (Redmond, 1987).

SUMMARY

As we have seen, the decision-making capacity of the older individual is more likely to be called into question than that of the younger counterpart. This is due to increased prevalence of debilitating disease, particularly dementia, with age, as well as to stereotypes about aging. Although in theory every person is competent until declared legally incompetent by a judge, in practice clinicians must frequently make judgments about a patient's ability to make decisions in a competent manner. In more paternalistic times, professionals simply did what they thought was best for the patient. Considerations of patient autonomy as well as potential legal liability dictate a more cautious approach to the possibly incompetent patient.

We have not addressed every type of incompetence that may be relevant to the older person. The person who is arrested for a crime may be found incompetent to stand trial or to waive legal rights. A potential witness may be incompetent to testify. These are relatively specialized areas of inquiry. In addition, we have not discussed civil commitment in detail, as it is not currently a primary means of dealing with incompetency.

We emphasize again that, in the clinical setting, competency is not an all-or-nothing affair, nor is it something that necessarily remains constant with time. Competency is only one factor in the ability to give informed consent, and it is not always independent of voluntariness and information delivery. Even for the legally incompetent patient, current preferences and previously expressed values should be considered in decision making. A patient who is not competent to make complex medical decisions may be competent to designate a proxy to do so. Older persons should be made aware of their options to make provisions for future incompetence, including durable powers of attorney and living wills.

Finally, the incompetent older person is at risk for abuse and neglect in our society. As treatment providers, our obligations may go beyond the psychological and extend to ensuring that the person is provided with basic necessities, medical care, and financial and legal services.

REFERENCES

American Bar Association (1989). *Guardianship: An agenda for reform*. Washington, DC: American Bar Association.

American Psychiatric Association. (1994). *Diagnostic and statistical manual of mental disorders* (4th ed.). Washington, DC: Author.

Anderer, S. (1990). *Determining competency in guardianship proceedings*. Washington, DC: American Bar Association.

Angell, M. (1991). The case of Helga Wanglie: A new kind of "right to die" case. *New England Journal of Medicine, 325*(7), 511–512.

Annas, G. J. (1991). The health care proxy and the living will. *New England Journal of Medicine, 324*(17), 1210–1213.

Appelbaum, P. S. (1994). Law and psychiatry: Mental health law and ethics in transition. A report from Japan. *Hospital and Community Psychiatry, 45*, 635–644.

Appelbaum, P. S., & Grisso, T. (1988). Assessing patients' capacities to consent to treatment. *New England Journal of Medicine, 319*(25), 1635–1638.

Appelbaum, P. S., & Gutheil, T. G. (1991). *Clinical handbook of psychiatry and the law*. Baltimore: Williams & Wilkins.

Appelbaum, P. S., & Roth, L. H. (1981). Clinical issues in the assessment of competency. *American Journal of Psychiatry, 138*(11), 1462–1467.

Appelbaum, P. S., & Roth, L. H. (1982). Competency to consent to research: A psychiatric overview. *Archives of General Psychiatry, 39*(8), 951–958.

Beauchamp, T. L., and Childress, J. F. (1994). *Principles of biomedical ethics* (4th ed.). New York: Oxford University Press.

Berlin, R. M., & Canaan, A. (1991). A family systems approach to competency evaluations in the elderly. *Psychosomatics, 32*(3), 349–354.

Blazer, D. G. (1990). Epidemiology of psychiatric disorders and cognitive problems in the elderly. In R. Michels (Ed.), *Psychiatry* (Vol. 3, chap. 21, p. 5). Philadelphia: Lippincott.

Brakel, S. J., Parry, J., & Weiner, B. A. (1985). *The mentally disabled and the law* (3rd ed.). Chicago: American Bar Foundation.

Brown, J. H., Henteleff, P., Barakat, S., & Rowe, C. J. (1986). Is it normal for terminally ill patients to desire death? *American Journal of Psychiatry, 143*(2), 208–211.

Brock, D. W., & Wartman, S. A. (1990). When competent patients make irrational choices. *New England Journal of Medicine, 322*(22), 1595–1599.

Buchanan, A. E., & Brock, D. W. (1990). Deciding for others: The ethics of surrogate decision making. New York: Cambridge University Press.

Bulcroft, K., Kielkopf, M. R., & Tripp, K. (1991). Elderly wards and their legal guardians: Analysis of county probate records in Ohio and Washington. *The Gerontologist, 31*, 156–164.

Bursztajn, H. J., Harding, H. P., Gutheil, T. G., & Brodksy, A. (1991). Beyond cognition: The role of disordered affective states in impairing competence to consent to treatment. *Bulletin of the American Academy of Psychiatry and the Law, 19*(4), 383–388.

Culver, C. M., & Gert, B. (1982). *Philosophy in medicine: Conceptual and ethical issues in medicine and psychiatry*. New York: Oxford University Press.

Cruzan v. Missouri Department of Health, 110 S. Ct. 2841, 1990.

Danis, M., Southerland, L. I., Garrett, J. M., Smith, J. L., Heilema, F., Pickard, C. G., Egner, D. M., & Patrick, D. L. (1991). A prospective study of advance directives for life-sustaining care. *New England Journal of Medicine, 324*(13), 882–888.

Delano, S. J., & Zucker, J. L. (1994). Protecting mental health research subjects without prohibiting progress. *Hospital and Community Psychiatry, 45*(6), 601–603.

Drane, J. F. (1984). Competency to give informed consent: A model for making clinical assessments. *Journal of the American Medical Association, 252*(7), 925–927.

Drane, J. F. (1985). The many faces of competency. *Hastings Center Report* (April), 17–21.

Dworkin, G. (1977). Paternalism. In S. J. Reiser, A. J. Dyke, & W. J. Curran (Eds.), *Ethics in Medicine: Historical Perspectives and Contemporary Concerns.* Cambridge: Massachusetts Institute of Technology.

Emanuel, E. J., & Emanuel, L. L. (1994). The economics of dying: The illusion of cost savings at the end of life. *New England Journal of Medicine, 330*(8), 540–544.

Emanuel, L. L., & Emanuel, E. J. (1989). The medical directive: A new comprehensive advance care document. *Journal of the American Medical Association, 261*(22), 3288–3293.

Emanuel, L. L., Barry, M. J., Stoeckle, J. D., Ettelson, L. M., & Emanuel, E. J. (1991). Advance directives for medical care—A case for greater use. *New England Journal of Medicine, 324*(13), 889–895.

Evans, D. A., Funkenstein, H. H., Albert, M. S., Scherr, P. A., Cook, N. R., Chown, M. J., Hebert, L. E., Hennekens, C. H., & Taylor, J. O. (1989). Prevalence of Alzheimer's disease in a community population of older persons—Higher than previously reported. *Journal of the American Medical Association, 262*(18), 2551–2556.

Farnsworth, M. G. (1989). Evaluation of mental competency. *American Family Physician, 39*(6), 182–190.

Golinger, R. C., & Fedoroff, J. P. (1989). Characteristics of patients referred to psychiatrists for competency evaluations. *Psychosomatics, 30*(3), 296–299.

Hamilton, E. (1942). *The Greek Way.* New York: Norton.

Herr, S. S., & Hopkins, B. L. (1994). Health care decision making for persons with disabilities: An alternative to guardianship. *Journal of the American Medical Association, 271*(13), 1017–1022.

High, D. M. (1992). Research with Alzheimer's disease subjects: Informed consent and proxy decision making. *Journal of the American Geriatrics Society, 40,* 950–957.

In re Guardianship of Richard Roe III, 383 Mass. 728, 370 N.E. 2d 40, 1981.

Janofsky, J. S. (1990). Assessing competency in the elderly. *Geriatrics, 45*(10), 45–48.

Janofsky, J. S., McCarthy, R. J., & Folstein, M. F. (1992). The Hopkins competency assessment test: A brief method for evaluating patients' capacity to give informed consent. *Hospital and Community Psychiatry, 43*(2), 132–136.

Jecker, N. S. (1990). The role of intimate others in medical decision making. *The Gerontologist, 30*(1), 65–71.

Kaplan, K. H., & Price, M. (1989). The clinician's role in competency evaluations. *General Hospital Psychiatry, 11,* 397–403.

Kapp, M. B. (1992). *Geriatrics and the law: Patient rights and professional responsibilities.* New York: Springer.

Keith, P. M., & Wacker, R. R. (1993). Implementation of recommended guardianship practices and outcomes of hearings for older persons. *The Gerontologist, 33*(1), 81–87.

LaPuma, J., Orentlicher, D., & Moss, R. J. (1991). Advance directives on admission: Clinical implications and analysis of the patient self-determination act of 1990. *Journal of the American Medical Association, 266*(3), 402–405.

Levitte, S. S., & Thornby, J. I. (1989). Geriatric and nongeriatric psychiatry consultation: A comparison study. *General Hospital Psychiatry, 11,* 339–344.

Mahler, J., & Perry, S. (1988). Assessing competency in the physically ill: Guidelines for psychiatric consultants. *Hospital and Community Psychiatry, 39*(8), 856–861.

Meier, D. E., & Cassel, C. K. (1986). Nursing home placement and the demented patient: A case presentation and ethical analysis. *Annals of Internal Medicine, 104,* 98–105.

Mill, J. S. (1956). *On liberty.* Indianapolis, IN: Bobbs-Merrill.

Mill, J. S. (1977). Utilitarianism. In S. J. Reiser, A. J. Dyck, & W. J. Curran (Eds.), *Ethics in medicine: Historical perspectives and contemporary concerns.* Cambridge: Massachusetts Institute of Technology.

Neugebauer, R. (1979). Medieval and early modern theories of mental illness. *Archives of General Psychiatry, 36*, 477–483.

Parry, J. (1994). Survey of standards for extended involuntary commitment. *Mental and Physical Disability Law Reporter, 18*(3), 329–336.

Pepper-Smith, R., Harvey, W. R. C., Silberfeld, M., Stein, E., & Rutman, D. (1992). Consent to a competency assessment. *International Journal of Law and Psychiatry, 15*, 13–23.

Pomerantz, A. S., & deNesnera, A. (1991). Informed consent, competency, and the illusion of rationality. *General Hospital Psychiatry, 13*, 138–142.

Redmond, F. C. (1987). Testamentary capacity. *Bulletin of the American Academy of Psychiatry and the Law, 15*(3), 247–256.

Roth, L. H. (1982). Competency to consent to or refuse treatment. In L. Grinspoon (Ed.), *Psychiatry 1982*, Washington, DC: American Psychiatric Press.

Roth, L. H., Meisel, A., & Lidz, C. W. (1977). Tests of competency to consent to treatment. *American Journal of Psychiatry, 134*(3), 279–284.

Rutman, D., & Silberfeld, M. (1992). A preliminary report on the discrepancy between clinical and test evaluations of competence. *Canadian Journal of Psychiatry, 37*(11), 634–639.

Sales, G. N. (1993). The health care proxy for mental illness: Can it work and should we want it to? *Bulletin of the American Academy of Psychiatry and the Law, 21*(2), 161–179.

Saunders, A. G., & Simon, M. M. (1987). Individual functional assessment: An instruction manual. *Mental and Physical Disability Law Reporter, 11*(1), 60–70.

Schwartz, H. I., & Roth, L. H. (1989). Informed consent and competency in psychiatric practice. In A. Tasman, R. E. Hales, & A. J. Frances (Eds.). *Review of Psychiatry* (Vol. 8.). Washington, DC: American Psychiatric Press.

Seckler, A. B., Meier, D. E., Mulvihill, M., & Cammer Paris, B. E. (1991). Substituted judgment: How accurate are proxy predictions? *Annals of Internal Medicine, 115*(2), 92–98.

Seghal, A., Galbraith, A., Chesney, M., Schoenfeld, P., Charles, G., & Lo, B. (1992). How strictly do dialysis patients want their advance directives followed? *Journal of the American Medical Association, 267*(1), 59–63.

Spar, J. E., & Garb, A. S. (1992). Assessing competency to make a will. *American Journal of Psychiatry, 149*(2), 169–174.

Stanley, B. (1983). Senile dementia and informed consent. *Behavioral Sciences and the Law, 1*(4), 57–71.

Stanley, B., & Stanley, M. (1987). Competency and informed consent in geriatric psychiatry. In *Geriatric psychiatry and the law*. New York: Plenum Press.

Steinbock, B. (1989). Recovery from persistent vegetative state?: The case of Carrie Coons. *Hastings Center Report* (July/August), 14–15.

Sullivan M. D., & Youngner, S. J. (1994). Depression, competence and the right to refuse lifesaving medical treatment. *American Journal of Psychiatry, 151*(7), 971–978.

Taub, H. A. (1980). Informed consent, memory, and age. *The Gerontologist, 20*(6), 686–690.

Taub, H. A. (1986). Comprehension of informed consent for research: Issues and directions for future study. *IRB: A Review of Human Subjects Research, 8*, 7–10.

Weiner, B. A., & Wettstein, R. M. (1993). *Legal issues in mental health care*. New York: Plenum Press.

White, R. W. (1959). Motivation reconsidered: The concept of competence. *Psychological Review, 66*(5), 297–333.

Wolf, S. M., Boyle, P., Callahan, D., Fins, J. J., Jennings, B., Nelson, J. L., Barondess, J. A., Brock, D. W., Dresser, R., Emanuel, L., Johnson, S., Lantos, J., Mason, D. R., Mezey, M., Orentlicher, D., & Rouse, F. (1991). Sources of concern about the patient self-determination act. *New England Journal of Medicine, 325*(23), 1666–1671.

CHAPTER 7

Treatment in Residential Settings

LOUIS D. BURGIO, ELLEN M. COTTER, AND ALAN B. STEVENS

CHAPTER OUTLINE

Introduction	Activity Programs
Behavior Therapy	Visual Art Therapy
Reality Orientation	Music Therapy
Reminiscence Therapy	Pet Therapy
Movement Therapies	Summary
Milieu Therapy	References

INTRODUCTION

Geriatric behavioral disturbances present numerous difficulties for both the staff and the residents of nursing homes and other geriatric long-term care settings. Examples of these problematic behaviors include behavioral excesses, such as agitation, wandering, disruptive vocalization (DV) and physical aggression, and various behavioral deficits. Behavioral deficits, also referred to by geriatric health care professionals as "excess deficits" (Brody, Kleban, Lawton, & Silverman, 1971), are symptoms of functional incapacity greater than that warranted by actual organic impairment. Such deficits can range from an absence of ambulation when the capability exists to urinary incontinence with no identifiable

LOUIS D. BURGIO, ELLEN M. COTTER, AND ALAN B. STEVENS • Center for Aging, Division of Gerontology and Geriatric Medicine, and Department of Psychology, University of Alabama at Birmingham, Birmingham, Alabama 35294.
Psychological Treatment of Older Adults: An Introductory Text, edited by Michel Hersen and Vincent B. Van Hasselt. Plenum Press, New York, 1996.

medical cause. Estimates of the prevalence of disruptive behaviors in nursing homes vary, depending on method of reporting and presence of dementia, but studies have found that between 64% (Zimmer, Watson, & Treat, 1984) and 83% of nursing home residents exhibit disruptive behaviors (Swearer, Drachman, O'Donnell, & Mitchell, 1988). It is further estimated that 73% of demented nursing home residents display at least one, if not several, aberrant behaviors (Cohen-Mansfield, 1986). Consequently, there is great interest among geriatric health care professionals in developing interventions for managing these behaviors.

Pharmacotherapy, usually with neuroleptic medications, has traditionally been used to manage geriatric behavioral disturbances. However, recent changes in federal nursing home regulations (Omnibus Budget Reconciliation Act, 1987) prohibit use of psychoactive drugs as the sole means of controlling these behaviors (American Health Care Association, 1990). The OBRA regulations aside, there appears to be little compelling evidence supporting use of pharmacotherapy for treating geriatric behavioral disturbances. A recent meta-analysis concluded that only one in five patients appears to benefit from pharmacotherapy (Schneider, Pollock, & Lyness, 1990). Furthermore, long-term use of neuroleptic drugs has been associated with severe and often irreversible side effects when used with older adults (Butler, Burgio, & Engel, 1987; Ray, Federspiel, & Schaffner, 1980). In sum, although pharmacotherapy is still widely used to treat geriatric behavioral disturbances, professionals agree that it should no longer be the treatment of choice. Instead, psychosocial and environmental interventions are being recommended for use with geriatric patients in residential settings (Burgio & Burgio, 1986; Carstensen, 1988; Jencks & Clausen, 1991).

This chapter provides an overview of the major forms of nonpharmacological therapies presently used to treat disruptive behaviors in geriatric residential settings. Not all of the therapeutic interventions described in this chapter target behavior problems directly; rather, their goal is to provide a more stimulating environment that should prevent behavior problems from occurring. Although some of these interventions may not be practical for widespread use, many of these treatments can be implemented with minimal resources by existing nursing home staff and can easily be incorporated into current activity programs; for example, reality orientation can be incorporated into almost any other activity. The therapies outlined herein will be discussed in terms of their defining characteristics and applicability to various behavioral problems.

Finally, it should be noted that research on psychosocial interventions used for reducing disruptive behaviors in residential settings is in its infancy. Few methodologically sound evaluative studies have been published, although several clinical trials are ongoing. Typically, published empirical evaluations of therapeutic interventions lack proper control procedures and rely on either staff reports of behavioral functioning or global outcome measures with questionable psychometric properties. Additionally, researchers have failed to include process measures that establish proper implementation of the therapeutic interventions. We will address these and other methodological problems in our discussion of specific studies presented below.

BEHAVIOR THERAPY

Behavior therapy has been the most thoroughly evaluated and successful form of treatment for remediating geriatric behavioral disturbances. As mentioned above, changes in nursing home regulations now make it more difficult to use neuroleptics as the only means of controlling geriatric behavioral disturbances. These changes, combined with increased knowledge about pharmacotherapy's risks, have led to a regulatory recommendation for attempting behavior management techniques whenever pharmacotherapy is being considered for behavioral control (Burgio & Bourgeois, 1992; Carstensen, 1988; Jencks & Clausen, 1991). Behavior therapy has the potential for not only improving resident behavior but also maintaining these improvements over time (Burgio & Burgio, 1986; Carstensen, 1988; Hussian & Davis, 1985; McEvoy, 1989). Successful applications have been reported for problems such as physical aggression (Vaccaro, 1988), verbal aggression (Spayd & Smyer, 1988), excess disability (Hoodin & Fatis, 1989; Lichtenberg, 1990), DV (Baltes & Lascomb, 1975; Wanlass & Culver, 1990), and wandering (Hussian, 1981).

Behavior therapy involves changing the frequency, duration, and/or intensity of specific problem behaviors or sets of behaviors by modifying the environmental antecedents and consequences of those behaviors (Rapp, Flint, Herrmann, & Proulx, 1992). Because the factors that trigger inappropriate behaviors may vary among residents, and because the consequences that affect these behaviors may also vary from resident to resident (Burgio & Bourgeois, 1992), behavioral interventions are usually tailored to individual residents. Behavioral interventions require clearly identified target behaviors and an analysis of the related antecedents and consequences. Some of the proposed antecedents for geriatric behavioral disturbances include overstimulation or understimulation, aversive behaviors of other residents, and pain (Burgio & Bourgeois, 1992; Cariaga, Burgio, Flynn, & Martin, 1991; Hussian & Davis, 1985). Problem behaviors may also be maintained through staff attention, escape from responsibility or an undesired activity, or a combination of both antecedents and consequences (Burgio & Bourgeois, 1992; Hussian & Davis, 1985).

Differential reinforcement of other behavior (DRO) is a relatively simple behavioral technique that has been used to decrease occurrence of inappropriate behavior in elderly nursing home residents. In this procedure, a reinforcer (usually staff attention) is provided to the resident if the target inappropriate behavior has not occurred for a certain period of time or if the resident has exhibited an appropriate behavior that is incompatible with the occurrence of the inappropriate behavior. Lundervold and Jackson (1992) present a case study of a physically aggressive Huntington's patient. A functional analysis suggested that the aggression was sparked by staff requests and maintained by negative staff attention. The intervention, consisting of DRO and contingent 5-minute physical restraint, was effective in decreasing the rate of physical aggression.

Systematic antecedent manipulations have also been attempted with behaviorally disturbed residents. In light of literature suggesting that DV may be related to understimulation (see Burgio & Lewis, in press, for a brief review), Burgio and colleagues provided different forms of auditory and tactile stimulation to nursing home residents who displayed DV. In this research, DV was considered to include "screaming, cursing, complaining, negativism, moaning, paranoid verbalization, repeated requests for attention, repetitious words or sentences, singing outside of an organized activity, and self-talk regardless of volume" (Burgio et al., 1994a). Auditory stimulation consisted of music, environmental sounds (such as ocean sounds), or auditory amplification of ambient sounds in the surrounding nursing home environment. Auditory stimulation was delivered via a portable headset radio/cassette tape player (for music and environmental sounds) or a small microphone placed on the resident (for amplification). Tactile stimulation consisted of the resident being given either a teddy bear or a teddy bear into which had been inserted a commercially available, battery-operated vibrator. While all stimulus conditions were associated with lower levels of DV in at least some of the residents, not all conditions were equally effective, nor did every resident tested respond well to treatment. In short, while providing sensory stimulation may decrease the frequency of inappropriate behaviors, there are significant intersubject differences in responsiveness (Burgio, Scilley, Hoar, Washington, & Tunstall, 1993).

Although there are no available clinical trials on behavior therapy with behaviorally disturbed elderly individuals, these techniques have been used extensively in nursing home environments and demonstrated to be effective for treating various behavioral deficits and excesses in small intrasubject studies. Studies show that professionals and consumers find behavior therapy acceptable for use with elderly individuals when compared with pharmacotherapy (Burgio & Sinnott, 1989, 1990; Burgio, Janosky, Sinnott, & Hohman, 1992; Burgio, Sinnott, Janosky, & Hohman, 1992, 1995b; Burgio, Hardin, Sinnott, Janosky, & Hohman, 1995a).

There are difficulties associated with use of behavior therapy with elderly individuals. Staff require special training to implement behavior therapy techniques, and in light of the high turnover rate of nursing home staff, such training would need to be conducted regularly. It is also possible that a resident's medical problems could preclude effective intervention. Despite the demonstrated long-term effectiveness of behavior therapy, it is not uncommon to find a temporary increase in disruptive behaviors with initiation of behavior therapy. This exacerbation, though temporary, can discourage staff from using the technique. Even more problematic, the relationship between the behavior and the environment may be complex, and it may take considerable "trial and error" to determine the antecedents and consequences of a particular behavior.

A major complication involves the necessity to apply the techniques in a consistent manner over a rather lengthy period of time. Successful application of behavior management techniques in nursing homes requires the use of staff management techniques in which institutional staff are provided with ongoing performance monitoring and feedback. Burgio and Burgio (1990) proposed a Behavior Supervisor Model for use in the nursing home setting. This model is a multicomponent system that involves defining staff responsibilities, monitoring their performance, and providing consequences (e.g., rewards) based on the evaluation. Frequently, direct-care staff monitor their own performance and are in turn evaluated by their supervisors. It has been demonstrated that the effects of staff management procedures can be maintained over a period of 6 months if evaluative feedback is provided to the staff (see Burgio & Scilley, 1994).

REALITY ORIENTATION

In Reality Orientation (RO), the interventionist attempts to orient confused residents to the present time and place by repeatedly providing reminders of the residents' surroundings (Folsom, 1968). RO can be conducted either on its own or in the context of other activities. This section will focus only on RO as a singular intervention. Subsequent sections of this chapter will discuss RO as a component of other therapies.

RO was originally designed as an autonomous intervention that could be implemented in two variations. Twenty-four-hour RO, as its name implies, is conducted throughout the day and evening, and all staff–resident interactions provide opportunities for its use. For example, during resident care activities, staff can use RO by using the resident's name frequently, by reminding the resident about current events or activities, or by asking pertinent questions such as "What's my name?" or "Today is Thursday—what do we usually do on Thursday?" Twenty-four-hour RO can also be incorporated into the daily stream of activities through the use of external memory aids such as calendars and posted reminders of information (e.g., the season, current president, time of next meal, and setting). This type of RO has the benefit of being easy to implement and use as well as inexpensive and adaptable to the needs of the staff and residents. However, researchers have found that it may be difficult at times to find age-appropriate reminders for certain events. Some holidays such as Christmas or Easter may involve child-oriented themes, and other holidays such as Halloween provide few opportunities for adult expression.

RO classes constitute an alternative method of presenting orienting information to residents. RO classes are generally implemented through a structured group that meets on a regular basis. In this group, certain topics such as seasons, holidays, life events (e.g., birthdays of fellow residents), and some news events (e.g., local news or international events of interest) are discussed and put into context of the residents' current lives. RO classes can incorporate other types of therapies (e.g., music, art) to convey this information and are compatible with the use of 24-hour RO both in and out of the structured group setting.

Conclusive evaluations of RO have been hampered by apparent inconsistencies as to the desired behavioral outcomes of RO therapy. Improved orientation to one's environment appears to be the most frequently cited benefit of RO (Burton, 1982), but the concept of improved orientation is not well defined apart from rote memorization of orienting information. Although RO has also been suggested as a possible treatment for problematic behaviors such as agitation and wandering, its effectiveness as an intervention for these problems is unproven

(Burton, 1982; Ferrario, Cappa, Molaschi, Rocco, & Fabris, 1991; Gropper-Katz, 1987; Hussian, 1987). Few RO studies have assessed behavioral changes due to therapy. As a result, even fewer studies have demonstrated positive behavioral changes or even an overall improvement in the level of behavioral functioning with participation (Powell-Proctor & Miller, 1982). Additionally, frequent attempts at reorientation can highlight residents' deficits, which may undermine self-esteem and possibly lead to confrontative and disruptive behavior (Newton & Lazarus, 1992).

Although many studies have purported to examine the efficacy of RO, unsound methodologies prohibit a clear interpretation of these results. Inadequate control procedures are common in this research. In many studies, the active component of the treatment could be staff attention; however, the nonspecific effects of increased staff attention in the experimental group have not been evaluated in control groups (Burton, 1982). On a similar note, reported benefits of RO therapy could result from nonspecific rather than specific effects of the techniques used (Newton & Lazarus, 1992). This possibility further emphasizes the need for control procedures. Furthermore, standardized instruments are rarely used to measure the effectiveness of RO, and the instruments developed specifically to measure RO effects are rarely tested for reliability and validity, either within or across experiments (Burton, 1982). Global outcome measures lacking sensitivity are frequently the sole indicators of an intervention's efficacy. For example, one study used a Reality Orientation Information Sheet that assessed subjects' orientation and ability to perform basic bodily functions (Citrin & Dixon, 1977). Cross-sample comparisons are problematic because subject selection criteria are sometimes unclear (in particular, the concepts of disorientation and confusion are not universally defined) and because the lack of standardized outcome instruments precludes comparison of the significance of behavioral change (Burton, 1982; Gropper-Katz, 1987).

A study conducted by Ferrario et al. (1991) provides representative examples of some additional problems in RO research. Ferrario and colleagues treated 13 nursing home residents with hourly classroom sessions, five times a week, for 24 weeks. Six residents served as controls, but experimental procedures for the control group are not described. Significant improvements in orientation (as measured by the Clifton Assessment Scale and the Multidimensional Observation Scale for Elderly Subjects) occurred in the experimental group after 24 weeks. However, the authors acknowledge that their sample was a "rather homogeneous population" due to exclusion of "noisy or violent patients, severely incontinents [sic]," and people receiving psychoactive medications (subjects were mildly demented). Use of RO with this high-functioning and, apparently, well-behaved population may not be generalizable to more typical nursing home residents.

REMINISCENCE THERAPY

Reminiscence therapy uses structured reminiscing as a vehicle for resolving life's unfinished conflicts. The goal of this therapy is to place an elderly individual's life experiences in perspective (Goldwasser, Auerbach, & Harkins, 1987; Lappe, 1987). Reminiscence groups are structured groups that meet on a regular basis in the residential facility. Topics discussed typically relate to the past in some way. Examples include aspects of childhood, love and marriage, other life events such as education or jobs, and some news events of the past (including commemorative anniversaries of historical events). It has been suggested that older adults' use of reminiscence is a developmentally appropriate and natural activity, for it adds a sense of closure to one's life and thus helps the reminiscer prepare for death (Butler, 1961). Like RO, it can be used singularly and be integrated naturally throughout the course of daily care, or it can be used as one component of a multicomponent intervention.

Reminiscence therapy has been suggested as a potentially effective treatment for agitation, confusion, wandering, and affective disorders (Goldwasser et al., 1987). Anecdotal reports suggest that reminiscence therapy provides additional benefits for the "well-being" of the facility residents. Specifically, reminiscence groups can provide a feeling of community and increased self-esteem by demonstrating to residents that other people see their past as interesting and that they share similar experiences. As a result of such increased community and self-esteem, residents may then increase participation in activities and improve the quantity and quality of their social interactions (Lappe, 1987; Lesser, Lazarus, Frankel, & Havasy, 1981; Orten, Allen, & Cook, 1989). It has also been suggested that reminiscence therapy may, by allowing its participants to discuss pleasant past experiences, help the resident to compensate for a less gratifying present life situation (Newton & Lazarus, 1992).

Determining the efficacy of reminiscence therapy is difficult due to inadequate outcome measures, unspecified control procedures, and the wide variety of desired outcomes reported in the research literature. Even a study with meticulous subject selection criteria and a 16-week course of reminiscence group therapy (Orten et al., 1989) failed to control for the effects of increased staff attention in the treatment group. Additionally, this study did not use validated measures to assess memory, orientation, and social behaviors. Results of the Orten et al. (1989) study suggested changes in social behavior for one of the three experimental groups. In attempting to explain these results, the investigators noted that the different leaders of the three experimental groups had different levels of experience with reminiscence groups and the target population. These shortcomings affect the reader's confidence in the results of this particular study.

Similar methodological problems prohibit conclusive findings in a study that compared musically cued reminiscence, verbally cued reminiscence, and musical activity alone (Smith, 1986). Subjects received two cycles of therapy (e.g., a session of musically cued reminiscence, a session of verbally cued reminiscence, and a session of musical activity; then the entire sequence was repeated), and the three experimental groups differed only in the order in which they received treatment. While varying the order of receipt of therapy appears to control for order effects, it is unclear what effects are produced by presenting the therapy in cycles. Results indicated that only the Mini-Mental State Exam (MMSE) language subscale improved significantly at post-test for the two reminiscence groups. The musical activity group improved significantly on the total

MMSE score (overall cognitive performance). None of the groups experienced improved orientation and attention.

Studies using more methodologically sound procedures fail to demonstrate many of the proposed benefits of reminiscence therapy. Goldwasser et al. (1987) provided nursing home residents with either reminiscence therapy, a non-reminiscence support group, or no treatment and then examined the effects of group membership on cognitive, affective, and behavioral functioning. The reminiscence group showed a decline in self-reported depression after treatment, but no effects on MMSE scores or performance of activities of daily living (ADL) were noted. Baines, Saxby, and Ehlert (1987) used a crossover design to compare RO and reminiscence therapy and found that residents who received RO prior to reminiscence therapy improved on measures of awareness, behavioral problems, and orientation; however, residents who received reminiscence therapy before RO showed little change on these measures and more closely resembled a no-treatment control group. These results suggest that reminiscence therapy alone is not sufficient to improve the functioning of residents with impaired cognitive functioning, and that RO may facilitate reminiscence therapy by providing a current context for interpreting past experiences (Baines et al., 1987). It has also been suggested that people who are unable to change their present life situations may experience a temporary decrease in life satisfaction if they talk about unresolved issues of the past (Hewett, Asamen, Hedgespeth, & Dietch, 1991).

MOVEMENT THERAPIES

The benefits of physical exercise are well known. Exercise can improve physical health, reduce stress, alleviate depression, and possibly improve cognitive functioning and reduce behavioral disturbances in elderly adults (Mullins, Nelson, & Smith, 1987; Short & Leonardelli, 1987). Exercise therapy is also a feasible intervention for most nursing homes. Exercise programs can be adapted to accommodate various abilities and needs (e.g., even wheelchair-bound residents can usually engage in rhythmic arm and leg movements) and while it is unlikely that geriatric residents will be able to engage in high-impact aerobics, there are many natural opportunities for movement therapies in nursing homes. Exercise can even be "disguised" in the form of craft activities, pet care, or dance, thus increasing its face validity and improving the likelihood of resident participation (Mullins et al., 1987). In conjunction with music therapy, RO, and reminiscence, it also provides opportunities for social interaction and group cooperation. Most importantly, exercise programs reduce the negative side effects of immobility.

Mobility in geriatric nursing home residents can be limited by physical disabilities, environmental barriers, and restrictive administrative policies. In fact, excessive movements associated with agitation or wandering are actively discouraged by the staff of these facilities. Physical restraint is a controversial intervention often used to reduce behavioral excesses. Wandering is the most frequently exhibited behavioral excess, but disruption of medical treatment and assaults on other residents and staff are also common problems. A growing body of evidence indicates that physical restraints are an ineffective intervention for these behavioral disturbances. Additionally, use of physical restraints appears to have negative consequences on the physical health and social behavior of residents (Evans & Strumpf, 1989; Folmar & Wilson, 1989). Conversely, interventions that encourage movement or physical exercise appear to be a more appropriate intervention for behavioral excesses such as wandering. Rader (1987) implemented a 1-hour program of exercise, music, and touch conducted three times a week to reduce wandering behavior in nursing home residents. According to Rader (1987), participation in the program resulted in a decrease in wandering. She also notes decreased use of physical restraints with use of this program; however, no empirical data are reported. Providing residents with a secure place to wander is another technique used to increase exercise and decrease disruptive behavior. Secure wandering space can include inner corridors, a patio, and both indoor and outdoor winding paths (Ohta & Ohta, 1988).

Although their effectiveness is questionable, therapeutic exercise programs have been proposed as an intervention for behavioral disturbances other than wandering. In a study of a therapeutic exercise program, Rabinovich and Cohen-Mansfield (1992) found no significant benefits of a physical exercise program for Alzheimer's disease (AD) patients in a nursing home. The activities used in this study were manipulation of a large beach ball and simple arm and leg exercises. However, "participation" and "nonparticipation" were determined solely by proximity to the activity and not by actual engagement with the materials. Subjects in the exercise group failed to demonstrate improvement in six categories of agitated behavior. Although other cognitive or psychological changes associated with exercise have been suggested (e.g., Short & Leonardelli, 1987), these studies are replete with methodological limitations—small sample size, no control groups, insignificant results—that preclude definitive conclusions regarding the beneficial effects of exercise therapy.

MILIEU THERAPY

Whether or not milieu therapy is utilized formally, all therapy must occur in the context of a supportive milieu. The concept of the milieu encompasses not only the physical features of the environment but also the manner in which the facility's staff and residents interact, the ideals of the institution, and the internal world of the resident (Winnett, 1989). As such, the goals of milieu therapy focus on improving the quality of the individual's interactions with the environment. These goals include improved orientation to reality as a natural outcome of involvement in the environment, learning or relearning self-care and social skills, and taking on normal social roles within the facility's community. Milieu therapy is generally accomplished by providing an environment that facilitates orientation to and active involvement in the setting (Coons & Spencer, 1983; Winnett, 1989).

Sometimes, resident behavior can be changed by making simple modifications in the physical environment. For example, placing masking tape grids on glass doors or windows appears to decrease the occurrence of wandering (Hussian & Brown, 1987). Marking resident room doors with distinctive colors or painting colored paths on the floor can help confused residents find their rooms or locate key places such as the restroom or lounge (Hussian, 1988). Rearranging placement of chairs in a recreation room into a circle rather than rows may increase the quality of social interactions with other residents (Ingstad & Gotestam, 1987; Sommer & Ross, 1958).

Research assessing benefits of milieu therapy has yielded varied results. Steer and Boger (1975) assigned 20 medically infirm elderly residents each to a new hospital ward, an open ward, a semiclosed ward, or a closed ward and found that the latter wards were most effective in improving social and activity of daily living (ADL) functioning. Interestingly, the residents described as "most regressed" responded best to treatment, although criteria for determining functional ability are unclear. A study with a similar population, using a "normal-treatment" control group and an experimental group who received work therapy and social therapy, found that the experimental group improved on the nurse-rated Self-Care Personal Neatness Evaluation and on unspecified measures of social competence. This group also decreased on measures of irritability and "retardation" (Mullins & Overstreet, 1984). Ingstad and Gotestam (1987) implemented milieu therapy by turning resident chairs in common areas toward each other, providing more activities for the residents, and extending meal times. As reported by staff, communication and activity levels of residents improved, although appropriateness of eating behaviors decreased slightly. Staff attitudes regarding patient care were also assessed and found to improve; however, the measures used in this study were not standardized.

Disruptive residents may benefit from having their daily schedules altered or by being allowed to make more choices regarding their preferred activities. Both of these alternatives can be considered forms of milieu therapy. Nursing home residents seldom have control over their schedules and activities, and merely offering a choice of activities has been found to improve behavior. Langer and Rodin (1976) attempted to increase choice-making behavior in nursing home residents by emphasizing residents' responsibility for themselves (a control group heard similar information stressing the staff's responsibility for them). The experimental group reported that they were happier and more active following the intervention; these residents also were rated by staff as being more alert, more social, and more involved in facility activities than residents in the control group. However, these residents reported no increase in perceived control over their lives. Pohl and Fuller (1980) assessed cognitively intact residents' perceptions of the choices they were allowed to make about their food, schedule, and other activities. Frequency of social interaction and dimensions of morale were also measured. Results indicated that perceived control over decision making was a significant contributor to reported feelings of good morale. The effects of allowing the resident to have more control over his or her daily schedule include increased compliance, fewer behavioral problems, and improved orientation to the environment. In these cases, the staff and resident worked together to design a daily schedule for the resident that is more compatible with his or her own needs but also sensitive to the other duties of the staff (Brown, 1991).

Forming generalizations from this research is problematic because, as discussed above, the physical environment is not the sole component of milieu therapy. Many aspects of the milieu are appropriate targets for intervention; however, implementing milieu therapy is not a standardized procedure. Furthermore, standardized outcome measures have not been generated, although improved social interaction appears to be a common goal in milieu therapy research. Self-care and ADL functioning have also frequently been the targeted outcomes.

Cautionary considerations associated with milieu therapy are few and mainly occur when the physical environment undergoes some kind of modification. Making extensive renovations of the physical environment of a facility can be quite expensive, and there is no guarantee that such changes will have any beneficial effect on the residents' functioning. In fact, data suggest that some residents will become more confused and may exhibit a temporary increase in disruptive behaviors following changes in their physical environments (Sommer & Ross, 1958).

ACTIVITY PROGRAMS

Activity programs are an integral component of the care provided in residential settings. Typically, activity programs provide residents with opportunities for positive social interaction, which may in turn promote greater self-esteem, decrease the risk of depression, and reduce behavioral disturbances. Several activities have been labeled as "therapies" and conducted within activity programs. A review of the three most frequently cited activity programs—visual arts, music, and pet programs—fails to provide conclusive evidence of their positive benefits.

Visual Art Therapy

Art therapy has long been used with various age groups in residential settings. Art therapy can be used in conjunction with RO and reminiscence therapy to provide a meaningful context for participation. Many potential benefits of the various art therapies have been reported. It has been suggested that having an entertaining activity available for participation can induce residents to at least temporarily decrease frequency of wandering. By incorporating RO techniques, art therapy can increase residents' orientation to their environment (Bumanis & Yoder, 1987). Anger and aggression may be displaced through artistic expression or the provision of a quiet, pleasant activity. Similarly, art therapies can decrease agitation by providing soothing stimuli (Bright, 1987). Art therapies can give residents an opportunity to produce something to which others can react, thus improving residents' social interactions and, potentially, the "artist's" own self-esteem (Wald, 1986).

The visual arts (e.g., painting, drawing, sculpture) provide many opportunities for self-expression, as well as a quiet and reflective activity that can be individualized to the skills and needs of the participants (Kornreich, 1988; Wald, 1986). For example, physical limitations in fine motor control or flexibility may prevent residents from working effectively with clay, although they may still be able to hold a paintbrush. It has been suggested that art therapy can uncover the presence of mental illness or organic brain damage and help residents gain a sense of control over the progress of their illness by allowing them to depict visually the progression and characteristic symptoms of the disease (e.g., perseveration and disorganization in Alzheimer's disease; Kornreich, 1988; Mango, 1992; Wald, 1986).

Music Therapy

Music therapy is one of the most frequently used therapeutic activities in nursing homes. It is responsive to residents' needs and abilities and easily incorporated into the surroundings. Music therapy can be as simple as aides singing with residents during care or as involved as conducting structured music groups. Even tuning a radio to a resident-preferred station can function as a form of therapy. Residents who can sing or play musical instruments are able to rediscover musical abilities and possibly perform for the enjoyment of others. Finally, it has been suggested that music therapy can provide exercise through the use of rhythmic movement. Additionally, staff have been reported to benefit from participation in music therapy (Bright, 1987).

Unfortunately, evaluative studies of music therapy fail to support many of the hypothesized social and behavioral effects of treatment. For example, Pollack and Namazi (1992) claimed a 24% increase in social behavior and a 14% decrease in nonsocial behavior following six music therapy sessions, but lack of a control group and questionable overlap among behavioral categories prevent clear interpretation of these results. Millard and Smith (1989), using an intrasubject reversal design, reported increased verbal participation and social behavior (as measured by the categories "Sitting" and "Walking with Others") following a group singing exercise. Additionally, staff reports of resident behaviors such as standing still, talking to self, and smiling were affected by participation, although the direction of change is unclear. Subject selection was limited to residents with a diagnosis of AD or probable AD in the "middle" stages of decline. Criteria for diagnosis are not specified. Bright (1987) provided an abundance of anecdotal data suggesting the usefulness of music therapy for decreasing staff stress and improving behavioral disturbances. However, the connection between music therapy and staff stress was not clear, and data were not provided to support the claim of music therapy's beneficial effects on resident behaviors.

Other proposed benefits of music therapy include increased orientation to the environment, generic improvement of difficult behaviors, and increased attention. Many of the studies carried out to examine these effects have small subject populations (fewer than 10 subjects per study or experimental group), raising questions of adequate statistical power. Additionally, determination of functioning is not consistent across studies, and descriptive terms are vague (e.g., "relatively high functioning"). More importantly, though, many of the claimed effects of music therapy have not held up to empirical scrutiny. Although gains in orientation are frequently noted, these gains are often not significant (e.g., Bumanis & Yoder, 1987). Clair and Bernstein (1990) described maintenance of structured music therapy over 15 months, but the three subjects in this study appeared to participate mostly by sitting still and watching others; social interaction was almost nonexistent. Christie (1992) reported improvements in orientation following music therapy in subjects grouped together either because they had similar levels of cognitive functioning (not specified) or because they had expressed an interest in music therapy. This subject selection confound creates difficulties in interpreting results. Smith-Marchese (1994) provided a 6-week therapeutic music program for 10 nursing home residents in the middle to late stages of AD. This program consisted of a series of 10-minute audio selections of nature sounds, classical music, hymns, and popular songs of the early 1900s. Participants were rated on a Reality Orientation Scale to indicate their orientation to self, others, time, and place as well as on a Sociability Scale that rated the participants' eye contact, facial expressions, body language, and verbal communication. Comparison of pre- and postintervention ratings on these instruments found a significant improvement on the Reality Orientation Scale and a trend toward improvement on the Sociability Scale. However, the global nature of these measures and the lack of a control group prohibit clear demonstration of the value of this intervention.

Pet Therapy

Pet therapy can be implemented in many different forms. Each type of pet therapy has its own special considerations, and pet therapy carries with it many potential benefits and risks apart from those associated with other therapeutic activities.

One form of pet therapy involves a mascot, in which the entire ward, home, or unit shares one pet. It has been suggested that caring for an animal can help increase residents' involvement with their environment and can provide a common activity that will improve group cohesion. However, jealousy can result if the mascot prefers one resident over another, and not all residents may be physically or cognitively able to care for an animal (Brickel, 1986; McCulloch, 1985).

Another form of pet therapy has been termed pet visitation. Pet visitation involves regular visits from animals who do not live at the facility. Although pet visitation may involve a staff member or relative visiting with his or her own personal pet, it is preferable to have the visiting animals come from shelters and brought by trained volunteers. One drawback of pet visitation is that the same animals might not be available at all visits, disrupting the continuity and the animal-resident bonding process. Furthermore, jealousy may again occur if a visiting pet does not get to spend equal amounts of time with all interested residents (Brickel, 1986; McCulloch, 1985).

Some facilities are able to support residents' personal pets. While personal pets can improve morale (McCulloch, 1985), they can also be problematic. A pet that the resident owned prior to institutionalization may be inappropriate for inclusion in the facility because of size or temperament. For residents who did not previously have pets, matching with appropriate pets can be difficult. Some residents may be unable to interact properly with or care for a pet. Although animals such as fish or turtles require less commitment than dogs or cats, they also provide fewer opportunities for meaningful interaction. If a particular pet does not bond with its "owner," the owner may feel hurt and inadequate (Brickel, 1986; McCulloch, 1985).

Many positive benefits have been claimed for pet therapy. Pet therapy can increase the frequency and quality of social interactions between residents and individuals who stop to comment on the animal or who help with the animal's care (Haughie, Milne, & Elliott, 1992; McCulloch, 1985). Haughie et al. (1992) used direct observation and a nurses' rating scale and found that residents exhibited more spontaneous interactions in the presence of a pet than they did without the pet or with a photograph of themselves with a pet. A resident who is responsible for regular care of a pet may become better oriented to the environment because he or she must be aware of the animal's needs and regularly scheduled activities, such as walks, feeding, and health care. It has been suggested that taking care of an animal can increase feelings of self-esteem and can provide nonjudgmental companionship for a lonely resident. Walking a dog can be a good form of exercise, and having an animal in the surroundings provides sensory stimulation. Pet therapy has also been used as a topic of discussion in RO and reminiscence therapy sessions (Brickel, 1986; Gammonley & Yates, 1991; McCulloch, 1985).

However, the pet therapy research is fraught with methodological problems. Available data from pet therapy projects are mostly anecdotal or, at best, use case study methods. Few empirical data have been generated to date (e.g., Gammonley & Yates, 1991). Those studies that do supply quantitative data use behavior rating scales with questionable reliability and validity, untested observation scales, and no maintenance of effects across settings, people, or behaviors (Haughie et al., 1992). The beneficial effects of pet therapy on physiological measures and physical well-being are widely known (Brickel, 1986), but pet therapy's utility for modifying psychological and behavioral functioning is documented less consistently (Brickel, 1986).

In addition to the concerns outlined above, there are some general issues that need to be considered before a pet therapy program is implemented. Staff or residents may suffer from allergies and thus may be unable to participate in a pet therapy program. Some residents and staff may be afraid of certain animals, particularly large dogs. Some animals may bite or scratch, especially if not handled properly, and the possibility of disease transmission is one that many nursing homes do not want to risk. Finally, keeping an animal in a residential facility can be expensive and can require a significant time commitment by staff (Brickel, 1986; McCulloch, 1985; Schantz, 1990).

SUMMARY

There are many available options for treating geriatric behavioral disturbances in institutional settings. However, although the data on behavioral techniques appear promising, the evaluative literature shows little to no support for most other forms of therapy. While anecdotal reports and some experimental studies provide evidence for the potential usefulness of pet therapy, music therapy, RO, and reminiscence therapy, these results are preliminary, at best. Many of these nonbehavioral studies are poorly designed and executed, preventing clear interpretation of results. The techniques and outcome measures used in these studies are often not standardized, and the generalizability of the treatments is uncertain. Moreover, many of these treatments involve considerable investment of time, training, and money, with questionable payoff.

In contrast, through numerous intrasubject studies (see Burgio & Bourgeois, 1992, for a review), behavior therapy has been shown to be an effective treatment for many types of geriatric behavioral disturbances. Behavior therapy can be implemented with existing staffing patterns and without extensive investment of money, although staff will require training in the techniques and supervisors will need to oversee their use. When executed appropriately, the effects of behavior therapy appear to be maintained over time (Burgio et al., 1994b). An important next step is to ascertain whether the efficacy of behavior therapy techniques will withstand the rigors of clinical trial methodology. Successful completion of sound clinical trials of behavior therapy techniques is necessary prior to wider dissemination of these promising techniques with elderly individuals.

REFERENCES

American Health Care Association (1990). *The Long-Term Care Survey: Regulations, Forms, Procedures, Guidelines.* Washington DC: CAT# 4697/UBP/2.5k/7/90.

Baines, S., Saxby, P., & Ehlert, K. (1987). Reality orientation and reminiscence therapy: A controlled cross-over study of elderly confused people. *British Journal of Psychiatry, 151,* 222–231.

Baltes, M. M., & Lascomb, S. L. (1975). Creating a healthy institutional environment for the elderly via behavior management. *International Journal of Nursing Studies, 12,* 5–12.

Brickel, C. M. (1986). Pet-facilitated therapies: A review of the literature and clinical implementation considerations. *Clinical Gerontologist, 5,* 309–332.

Bright, R. (1987). The use of music therapy and activities with demented patients who are deemed "difficult to manage." The elderly uncooperative patient. [Special issue]. *Clinical Gerontologist, 6,* 131–144.

Brody, E. M., Kleban, M. H., Lawton, M. P., & Silverman, H. A. (1971). Excess disabilities of mentally impaired aged: Impact of institutionalized treatment. *Gerontologist, 11,* 124–133.

Brown, F. (1991). Creative daily scheduling: A nonintrusive approach to challenging behaviors in community residences. *Journal of the Association for Persons with Severe Handicaps, 16,* 75–84.

Bumanis, A., & Yoder, J. W. (1987). Music and dance: Tools for reality orientation. "You bring out the music in me": Music in nursing homes. [Special issue]. *Activities, Adaptation and Aging, 10,* 23–35.

Burgio, L. D., & Bourgeois, M. (1992). Treating severe behavior disorders in geriatric residential settings. *Behavioral Residential Treatment, 7,* 145–168.

Burgio, L. D., & Burgio, K. L. (1986). Behavioral gerontology: Application of behavioral methods to the problems of older adults. *Journal of Applied Behavior Analysis, 19,* 321–328.

Burgio, L. D., & Burgio, K. L. (1990). Institutional staff training and management: A review of the literature and a model for geriatric long-term care facilities. *International Journal of Aging and Human Development, 30,* 287–302.

Burgio, L. D., & Lewis, T. (in press). Functional analysis and intervention in geriatric settings. In A. Repp & R. Horner (Eds.), *Functional analysis of problem behavior: From effective assessment to effective support.* Pacific Grove, CA: Brooks/Cole.

Burgio, L. D., & Scilley, K. (1994). Caregiver performance in the nursing home: The use of staff training and management procedures. *Seminars in Speech and Language, 15,* 313–322.

Burgio, L. D., & Sinnott, J. (1989). Behavioral treatments and pharmacotherapy: Acceptability ratings for elderly individuals. *Journal of Gerontology: Psychological Sciences, 44,* 3–8.

Burgio, L. D., & Sinnott, J. (1990). Behavioral treatments and pharmacotherapy: Acceptability ratings by elderly individuals in residential settings. *Gerontologist, 30,* 811–816.

Burgio, L. D., Janosky, J., Sinnott, J., & Hohman, M. J. (1992). Acceptability of behavioral treatments and pharmacotherapy for geriatric behavioral disturbances: A comparison among health care professionals and consumer groups. *Verhaltenstherapie, 2,* 237–243.

Burgio, L. D., Sinnott, J., Janosky, J., & Hohman, M. J. (1992). Physicians' acceptance of behavioral treatments and pharmacotherapy for behavioral disturbances in older adults. *Gerontologist, 32,* 546–551.

Burgio, L., Scilley, K., Hoar, T., Washington, C., & Tunstall, A. (1993). Behavioral interventions for disruptive vocalizations in elderly nursing home residents with dementia. *Gerontologist, 33,* 110.

Burgio, L. D., Scilley, K., Hardin, J. M., Janosky, J., Bonino, P., Slater, S. C., & Engberg, R. (1994a). Studying disruptive vocalization and contextual factors in the nursing home using computer-assisted real-time observation. *Journal of Gerontology: Psychological Sciences, 49,* P230–P239.

Burgio, L. D., McCormick, K. A., Scheve, A. S., Engel, B. T., Hawkins, A., & Leahy, E. (1994b). The effects of changing prompted voiding schedules in the treatment of urinary incontinence in nursing home residents. *Journal of the American Geriatrics Society, 42,* 315–320.

Burgio, L. D., Hardin, M., Sinnott, J., Janosky, J., & Hohman, M. J. (1995a). Acceptability of behavioral treatments and pharmacotherapy for behaviorally disturbed older adults: Ratings of caregivers and relatives. *Journal of Clinical Geropsychology, 1,* 19–31.

Burgio, L. D., Sinnott, J., Janosky, J., & Hohman, M. J. (1995b). Nurses' acceptance of behavioral treatments and pharmacotherapy for behavioral disturbances in older adults. *Applied Nursing Research, 8*(4), 174–181.

Burton, M. (1982). Reality orientation for the elderly: A critique. *Journal of Advanced Nursing, 7,* 427–433.

Butler, F., Burgio, L., & Engel, B. (1987). A behavioral analysis of geriatric nursing home patients receiving neuroleptic medication: A comparative study. *Journal of Gerontological Nursing, 13,* 15–19.

Butler, R. N. (1961). The life review: An interpretation of reminiscence in the aged. *Psychiatry, 26,* 65–76.

Cariaga, J., Burgio, L., Flynn, W., & Martin, D. (1991). A controlled study of disruptive vocalizations among geriatric residents in nursing homes. *Journal of the American Geriatrics Society, 39,* 501–507.

Carstensen, L. L. (1988). The emerging field of behavioral gerontology. *Behavior Therapy, 19,* 259–281.

Christie, M. E. (1992). Music therapy applications in a skilled and intermediate care nursing home facility: A clinical study. *Activities, Adaptation & Aging, 16,* 69–87.

Citrin, R. S., & Dixon, D. N. (1977). Reality orientation, a therapy for psychogeriatric patients: A controlled study. *Gerontologist, 16,* 69–76.

Clair, A. A., & Bernstein, B. (1990). A preliminary study of music therapy programming for severely regressed persons with Alzheimer's-type dementia. *Journal of Applied Gerontology, 9*, 299–311.

Cohen-Mansfield, J. (1986). Agitated behaviors in the elderly: II. Preliminary results in the cognitively deteriorated. *Journal of the American Geriatrics Society, 34*, 722–727.

Coons, D. H., & Spencer, B. (1983). The older person's response to therapy: The in-hospital therapeutic community. *Psychiatric Quarterly, 55*, 156–172.

Evans, L. K., & Strumpf, N. E. (1989). Tying down the elderly: A review of the literature on physical restraint. *Journal of the American Geriatrics Society, 36*, 65–74.

Ferrario, E., Cappa, G., Molaschi, M., Rocco, M., & Fabris, F. (1991). Reality orientation therapy in institutionalized elderly patients: Preliminary results. *Archives of Gerontology and Geriatrics*, suppl. 2, 139–142.

Folmar, S., & Wilson, H. (1989). Social behavior and physical restraints. *Gerontologist, 29*, 650–653.

Folsom, J. (1968). Reality orientation for the elderly mental patient. *Journal of Geriatric Psychiatry, 1*, 291–307.

Gammonley, J., & Yates, J. (1991). Pet projects: Animal assisted therapy in nursing homes. *Journal of Gerontological Nursing, 17*, 12–15.

Goldwasser, A. N., Auerbach, S. M., & Harkins, S. W. (1987). Cognitive, affective, and behavioral effects of reminiscence group therapy on demented elderly. *International Journal of Aging and Human Development, 25*, 209–222.

Gropper-Katz, E. I. (1987). Reality orientation research. *Journal of Gerontological Nursing, 13*, 13–18.

Haughie, E., Milne, D., & Elliott, V. (1992). An evaluation of companion pets with elderly psychiatric patients. *Behavioral Psychotherapy, 20*, 367–372.

Hewett, L. J., Asamen, J. K., Hedgespeth, J., & Dietch, J. T. (1991). Group reminiscence with nursing home residents. *Clinical Gerontologist, 10*, 69–72.

Hoodin, F., & Fatis, M. (1989). Differential reinforcement to reduce excessive requests for toileting assistance of a geriatric nursing home resident. *Clinical Gerontologist, 9*, 15–29.

Hussian, R. A. (1981). *Geriatric psychology: A behavioral perspective.* New York: Van Nostrand Reinhold.

Hussian, R. A. (1987). Wandering and disorientation. In L. L. Carstensen & B. A. Edelstein (Eds.), *Handbook of clinical gerontology* (pp. 177–189). New York: Pergamon.

Hussian, R. A. (1988). Modification of behaviors in dementia via stimulus manipulation. *Clinical Gerontologist, 8*, 37–43.

Hussian, R. A., & Brown, D. C. (1987). Use of two-dimensional grid patterns to limit hazardous ambulation in demented patients. *Journal of Gerontology, 42*, 558–560.

Hussian, R. A., & Davis, R. L. (1985). *Responsive care: Behavioral interventions with elderly persons.* Champaign, IL: Research Press.

Ingstad, P. J., & Gotestam, K. G. (1987). Staff attitude changes after environmental changes on a ward for psychogeriatric patients. *International Journal of Social Psychiatry, 33*, 237–244.

Jencks, S. F., & Clausen, S. B. (1991). Managing behavior problems in nursing homes. *Journal of the American Medical Association, 265*, 502–503.

Kornreich, S. (1988). An Alzheimer patient's use of art as a form of constancy. *Pratt Institute Creative Arts Therapy Review, 9*, 29–39.

Langer, E. J., & Rodin, J. (1976). The effects of choice and enhanced personal responsibility for the aged: A field experiment in an institutional setting. *Journal of Personality and Social Psychology, 34*, 191–198.

Lappe, J. M. (1987). Reminiscing: The life review therapy. *Journal of Gerontological Nursing, 13*, 12–16.

Lesser, J., Lazarus, L. W., Frankel, R., & Havasy, S. (1981). Reminiscence group therapy with psychotic geriatric inpatients. *Gerontologist, 21*, 291–296.

Lichtenberg, P. A. (1990). Reducing excess disabilities in geropsychiatric inpatients: A focus on behavioral problems. Mental health in the nursing home. [Special issue]. *Clinical Gerontologist, 9*, 65–76.

Lundervold, D. A., & Jackson, T. (1992). Use of applied behavior analysis in treating nursing home residents. *Hospital and Community Psychiatry, 43*, 171–173.

Mango, C. (1992). Emma: Art therapy illustrating personal and universal images of loss. *Omega, 25*, 259–269.

McCulloch, M. J. (1985). Pets in therapeutic programs for the aged. *Journal of the Delta Society, 2,* 34–44.

McEvoy, C. (1989). Behavioral treatment. In J. Cummings & B. Miller (Eds.), *Alzheimer's disease: Treatment and long-term management* (pp. 207–224). New York: Marcel Dekker.

Millard, K. A. O., & Smith, J. M. (1989). The influence of group singing therapy on the behavior of Alzheimer's disease patients. *Journal of Music Therapy, 26,* 58–70.

Mullins, C. S., Nelson, D. L., & Smith, Doris A. (1987). Exercise through dual-purpose activity in the institutionalized elderly. *Physical and Occupational Therapy in Geriatrics, 5,* 29–39.

Mullins, D. W., & Overstreet, L. L. (1984). Effects of milieu therapy on the chronically ill geriatric patient. *American Corrective Therapy Journal, 38,* 115–118.

Newton, N. A., & Lazarus, L. W. (1992). Behavioral and psychotherapeutic interventions. In J. E. Birren, R. B. Sloane, & G. D. Cohen (Eds.), *Handbook of mental health and aging* (2nd Ed.). (pp. 699–719). San Diego: Academic Press.

Ohta, R. J., & Ohta, B. M. (1988). Special units for Alzheimer's disease patients: A critical look. *Gerontologist, 28,* 803–808.

Orten, J. D., Allen, M., & Cook, J. (1989). Reminiscence groups with confused nursing center residents: An experimental study. *Social Work in Health Care, 14,* 73–86.

Pohl, J., & Fuller, S. (1980). Perceived choice, social interaction, and dimensions of morale of residents in a home for the aged. *Research in Nursing and Health, 3,* 147–157.

Pollack, N. J., & Namazi, K. H. (1992). The effect of music participation on the social behavior of Alzheimer's disease patients. *Journal of Music Therapy, 29,* 54–67.

Powell-Proctor, A., & Miller, J. S. (1982). Reality orientation: A critical appraisal. *British Journal of Psychiatry, 140,* 457–463.

Rabinovich, B. A., & Cohen-Mansfield, J. (1992). The impact of participation in structured recreational activities on the agitated behavior of nursing home residents: An observational study. *Activities, Adaptation & Aging, 16,* 89–98.

Rader, J. (1987). A comprehensive staff approach to problem wandering. *Gerontologist, 27,* 756–760.

Rapp, M. S., Flint, A. J., Herrmann, N., & Proulx, G. (1992). Behavioural disturbances in the demented elderly: Phenomenology, pharmacotherapy and behavioural management. *Canadian Journal of Psychiatry, 37,* 651–657.

Ray, W. A., Federspiel, C. F., & Schaffner, W. (1980). Antipsychotic drug use in nursing homes: Evidence of misuse. *American Journal of Public Health, 70,* 485–491.

Schantz, P. M. (1990). Preventing potential health hazards incidental to the use of pets in therapy. *Anthrozoos, 4,* 14–23.

Schneider, L. S., Pollock, V. E., & Lyness, S. A. (1990). A meta-analysis of controlled trials of neuroleptic treatment in dementia. *Journal of the American Geriatrics Society, 38,* 553–563.

Short, L., & Leonardelli, C. A. (1987). The effects of exercise on the elderly and implications for therapy. *Physical and Occupational Therapy in Geriatrics, 5,* 65–73.

Smith, G. H. (1986). A comparison of the effects of three treatment interventions on cognitive functioning of Alzheimer patients. *Music Therapy, 6,* 41–56.

Smith-Marchese, K. (1994). The effects of participatory music on the reality orientation and sociability of Alzheimer's residents in a long-term care setting. *Activities, Adaptation and Aging, 18,* 41–55.

Sommer, R., & Ross, H. (1958). Social interaction on a geriatrics ward. *International Journal of Social Psychiatry, 4,* 128–133.

Spayd, C. S., & Smyer, M. A. (1988). Interventions with agitated, disoriented, or depressed residents. In M. A. Smyer, M. D. Cohn, & D. Brannon (Eds.), *Mental health constitution in nursing homes* (pp. 123–141). New York: New York University Press.

Steer, R. A., & Boger, W. P. (1975). Milieu therapy with psychiatric medically infirm patients. *Gerontologist, 15,* 138–141.

Swearer, J. M., Drachman, D. A., O'Donnell, B. F., & Mitchell, A. L. (1988). Troublesome and disruptive behaviors in dementia: Relationships to diagnosis and disease severity. *Journal of the American Geriatrics Society, 36,* 784–790.

Vaccaro, F. J. (1988). Application of operant procedures in a group of institutionalized aggressive elderly subjects. *Psychology and Aging, 3,* 22–28.

Wald, J. (1986). Art therapy for patients with dementing illnesses. *Clinical Gerontologist, 4,* 29–40.
Wanlass, W., & Culver, S. (1990). Behavior modification in a demented nursing home patient. Paper presented at the annual meeting of AGS/AFAR, May, 1990, Atlanta, GA.
Winnett, R. L. (1989). Long-term care reconsidered: The role of the psychologist in the geriatric rehabilitation milieu. *Journal of Applied Gerontology, 8,* 53–68.
Zimmer, J. G., Watson, N. G., & Treat, A. (1984). Behavioral problems among patients in skilled nursing facilities. *American Journal of Public Health, 76,* 1118–1121.

PART II

SPECIFIC DISORDERS AND PROBLEMS

CHAPTER 8

Anxiety-Based Disorders

RON ACIERNO, MICHEL HERSEN, AND VINCENT B. VAN HASSELT

CHAPTER OUTLINE

Introduction
DSM-IV Anxiety Disorder Subtypes
  Specific Phobia
  Agoraphobia
  Social Phobia
  Generalized Anxiety Disorder
  Panic Disorder
  Obsessive Compulsive Disorder
  Posttraumatic Stress Disorder
  Anxiety Disorders Due to a General
    Medical Condition
Case Identification and Presenting
  Complaints
History

Other Relevant History
Selection of Psychological Treatment
  Anxiety Reduction Strategies
  The Present Case: Prescriptive
    Assessment
  Treatment Selection
Concurrent Medical Treatment
  The Present Case
Course of Treatment
Follow-Up
Overall Evaluation
Summary
References

INTRODUCTION

Barlow (1988) describes anxiety as a "diffuse cognitive-affective structure [at the heart of which] is high negative affect composed of various levels and combinations of activation and arousal, perceptions of lack of control over future events, and shifts in attention to self-evaluative concerns" (p. 235). Along slightly different lines, Wolpe (1990) operationally defines anxiety as "the individual

RON ACIERNO • Department of Psychiatry and Behavioral Sciences, Medical University of South Carolina, Charleston, South Carolina 29425-0742. MICHEL HERSEN AND VINCENT B. VAN HASSELT • Center for Psychological Studies, Nova Southeastern University, Fort Lauderdale, Florida 33314.
Psychological Treatment of Older Adults: An Introductory Text, edited by Michel Hersen and Vincent B. Van Hasselt. Plenum Press, New York, 1996.

organism's characteristic pattern of autonomic responses to noxious stimulation" (p. 23). While the former description emphasizes anxiety's subjective aspects, the latter highlights its overtly measurable (i.e., physiologic) correlates. Importantly, both conceptualizations refer to an experience that is quite common in the general population. Moreover, anxiety is often an appropriate and functional response to a dangerous or frightening situation (e.g., being physically attacked), and facilitates performance of behaviors (e.g., rapid escape) necessary to the survival of an organism. In contrast, excessive or inappropriately experienced anxiety is considered psychopathological when it no longer serves a purpose but instead results in functional impairment.

The construct of anxiety is particularly relevant to older adults, who typically experience high levels of environmental, physical, and psychological stress. Indeed, loss of economic productivity, reduced health and vocational status, diminished visual and auditory acuity, decreased sensory/motor coordination and sexual responsiveness, reduced cognitive functioning, and loss of spouse, friends, relatives, and other sources of social support occur more frequently in older than in younger adults. Not surprisingly, anxiety disorders in the elderly appear to be more prevalent than any other class of psychopathology (Sheikh, 1992). Specific risk factors for developing anxiety in old age include being female, divorced, or widowed, or having low income, high blood pressure, or cardiac or gastrointestinal complications (Eaton & Keyl, 1990; Himmelfarb & Murrell, 1984). Conflicting prevalence estimates of anxiety and anxiety disorders in older adults exist, with some surveys revealing an increased level of anxiety with age (Brickman & Eisdorfer, 1989; Himmelfarb & Murrell, 1984; Uhlenhuth et al., 1983) and others showing a decrease (Myers et al., 1984). Reasons for disparate prevalence estimates are multifold. First, assessment devices employed to measure anxiety in the elderly were not developed specifically for that population (Hersen & Van Hasselt, 1992; Sheikh, 1991), and low reported rates of anxiety may be a function of inadequate or inappropriate application of these indices. Moreover, failure to account for specific changes in anxiety presentation that accompany the aging process potentially increases the incidence of "false negatives," or overlooked cases of anxiety in general surveys. Burvill (1987), for example, points out that data from the large, federally funded Epidemiologic Catchment Area (ECA) survey cited above may significantly underestimate the prevalence of anxiety in older adults because presence of Generalized Anxiety Disorder (GAD) was not consistently assessed. This is particularly problematic when one considers that GAD is among the three most frequently reported psychological disorders in the elderly by primary care physicians (Thompson, Mitchell, & House, 1989), and because the Diagnostic Interview Schedule (DIS), a structured clinical interview employed by ECA researchers to obtain diagnoses, may not be an appropriate measure of anxiety for older adults, particularly when administered by lay interviewers. Second, several investigators have noted that presentation of anxiety in the elderly, as in children, lacks the clear interdiagnostic specificity found in younger adults (Anthony & Aboraya, 1992; Gurian & Miner, 1991). That is, while multiple symptoms of anxiety may exist in an older patient, this symptom cluster may fail to meet any specific *Diagnostic and*

Statistical Manual of Mental Disorders (*DSM-IV*; American Psychiatric Association, 1994) diagnostic cutoff criteria for an anxiety disorder. Third, for many older adults, a lack of familiarity with psychological problems and generational/cultural prohibitions toward disclosure of psychological disorders (Weiss, 1994) act singly or in combination to cause underreporting of anxiety symptomatology. Further, a substantial number of older adults (and their physicians) seem to accept increased anxiety as a natural consequence of aging (Gurian & Miner, 1991; McCarthy, Katz, & Foa, 1991) and are thus hesitant to seek treatment for what they consider to be an expected and unrelievable condition. Finally, even if older adults do not actively deny existence of anxiety symptoms, they may often mistake them for signs of physical illness (Busse, 1975) and seek treatment from medical, rather than psychological, sources. Interestingly, this misattribution is somewhat justified, in that while a very weak linear relationship exists between anxiety level and age per se, a clear relationship exists between anxiety and medical illness, for which older adults are obviously at an increased risk (Gurian & Miner, 1991; Himmelfarb & Murrell, 1984). Overall, however, it is generally agreed that 10% to 20% of older adults experience clinical levels of anxiety and would benefit from treatment (Himmelfarb & Murrell, 1984; Matt, Dean, Wang, & Wood, 1992; Sheikh, 1992).

DSM-IV ANXIETY DISORDER SUBTYPES

Specific Phobia

While prevalence estimates of specific disorders vary greatly across surveys and geographical areas (e.g., Meyers et al., 1984), phobic disorders (specific phobia, agoraphobia, and social phobia) appear to be the most common psychological illness in older females (6.1% population prevalence) and the second most common psychological disorder in older males (2.9% population prevalence) (Meyers et al., 1984; Thyer et al., 1985). The *DSM-IV* defines a specific phobia as "a persistent fear of clearly discernible, circumscribed objects or situations" (p. 405, APA, 1994). In order to receive the diagnosis of specific phobia, exposure (or even anticipated exposure) to feared stimuli must consistently elicit marked and unreasonable anxiety. Moreover, individuals are required to avoid phobic objects, or endure such stimuli with high levels of distress, even though they recognize that their fear is excessive or irrational. Finally, avoidance or anticipatory anxiety must be of sufficient magnitude to impair social or vocational functioning. The estimated risk of developing specific phobia for the first time after age 65 (late onset) is surprisingly high (4.29%) (Eaton et al., 1989) and does not diminish with increased age. In contrast to individuals with other anxiety disorders, incidence of additional diffuse anxiety symptomatology and depression is not elevated in specific phobic individuals, and a vast majority of older adults with specific phobias do not seek treatment. Interestingly, while animal fears are the most represented specific phobia in younger adults, increasingly large numbers of elderly residing in urban settings report fears of crime and victimization and, consequently, evince pervasive avoidance of the outdoors after dark (Clarke & Lewis, 1982).

Agoraphobia

Agoraphobia appears to be the second most prevalent form of phobia in older adults (Blazer, George, & Hughes, 1991) and occurs both in isolation or secondary to panic (panic with agoraphobia appears to be more common in individuals who present for treatment (Weisman et al., 1986). A *DSM-IV* diagnosis of agoraphobia is assigned when an individual markedly avoids, or endures with excessive fear, situations in which aid is unavailable or escape might be difficult. Often, development of agoraphobic avoidance follows the experience of an unexpected (e.g., "uncued") panic attack. Importantly, avoidance behavior must not be attributed to another anxiety disorder (such as specific phobia, in which a clear "cue" is present). Finally, and of particular relevance to older adults, agoraphobic avoidance must not be the result of a medical condition, and if a medical condition is present, the extent of avoidance or fear must clearly exceed that which is warranted.

Social Phobia

Social phobia does not appear to be highly prevalent in older adults; however, the nature of this disorder likely contributes to reduced estimates of its occurrence. Note that social phobia is not analogous to extreme shyness (which appears to be related to Avoidant Personality Disorder). Rather, in social phobia, interpersonal situations involving exposure to possible scrutiny of others, such as public speaking, dancing, or eating in a restaurant, reliably elicit anxiety and fears of humiliation or embarrassment. Anxiety produced by these situations is often intense and may result in a panic attack. Further, a *DSM-IV* diagnosis of social phobia requires that patients recognize the excessive or unreasonable quality of their fear. Older adults who suffer from debilitating medical conditions that produce overt symptoms, such as visible tremors associated with Parkinson's disease or slurred speech associated with frontal/temporal lobe strokes, may avoid interpersonal situations in response to social-evaluative fears and are thus at increased risk for developing the disorder.

Generalized Anxiety Disorder

While ECA survey data indicate that specific phobia is the most common anxiety disorder among older adults, other sources (Dubovsky, 1990; Uhlenhuth et al., 1983) report that Generalized Anxiety Disorder (GAD) is equally, if not more, prevalent. GAD is characterized by excessive and pervasive anxiety, worry, and apprehension about real and potential life events (e.g., finances, health) occurring on the majority of days over a 6-month period. Moreover, the uncontrollable quality associated with apprehensive worry in this disorder must result in clinically significant distress and impaired social or occupational functioning. In addition, multiple somatic correlates of anxiety (e.g., restlessness, fatiguability, muscle tension, sleep disturbance) must be present. Note that several symptoms of GAD overlap greatly with symptoms found in mood disorders. Indeed, in both young adult and elderly populations, generalized anxiety is often accompanied by depression (Sheikh, 1992; Wolpe, 1990) and may represent an independent mixed-anxiety depression subtype. Increases in intensity and frequency of stressful life events experienced by older adults logically appear to place them at high risk for developing GAD, although this hypothesis has yet to be empirically verified.

Panic Disorder

According to ECA data, prevalence of panic disorder in adults over 65 years of age is only 0.1% (George et al., 1988). *DSM-IV* defines panic disorder as the experience of several unexpected panic attacks, or the occurrence of at least two attacks followed by severe anticipatory anxiety or fear of future attacks for at least 1 month. Panic attacks are arbitrarily defined as the sudden onset (within 10 minutes) of at least 4 of 13 cognitive and somatic anxiety symptoms, including, but not limited to, intense fear of dying or losing control, tachycardia, dyspnea, dizziness, choking, and shortness of breath. Note that panic attacks may be experienced with other anxiety disorders during exposure to feared objects or situations. In these cases, panic is "cued" and "expected," and a diagnosis of panic disorder is not warranted.

As with most other anxiety-related psychopathology, females are at greater risk of developing panic disorder than males. Interestingly, and in contrast to most other anxiety disorders, there appear to be two "peaks" at which risk of developing panic disorder is greatest: the late 20s and the late 50s (Anthony & Aboraya, 1992). Moreover, the disorder is particularly resilient and persists for decades if untreated (Raj, Corvea, & Dagon, 1993). In light of these two facts, it appears that ECA prevalence estimates of panic disorder may be too low. Indeed, Raj, Corvea, and Dagon (1993) surveyed 540 older adults presenting for treatment at a geriatric psychiatric clinic and found the prevalence of panic disorder to be 9.4%. Although these authors obtained their sample from a clinical population, the observed rate of panic far exceeds that which was predicted by ECA investigators. Therefore, older adults with a history of anxiety attacks should be thoroughly assessed for the disorder, particularly in light of possible risks associated with panic (e.g., heart attack) in the elderly (Coryell, Noyes, & House, 1986).

Obsessive Compulsive Disorder

Obsessive Compulsive Disorder (OCD) is less prevalent in older (1%) than in younger (2.5%) adults (George et al., 1988; Robins et al., 1984) with women affected to a greater extent than men. OCD rarely remits in the absence of treatment (Jenike, 1991), and its existence for several decades in a particular individual is not uncommon. The *DSM-IV* diagnosis of OCD is assigned when either obsessions *or* compulsions are present and cause significant distress or functional impairment. Obsessions are defined as recurrent, intrusive thoughts or urges that produce extreme anxiety. Individuals diagnosed with OCD recognize that their obsessions are the irrational product of their own minds and actively attempt to suppress them. (Note that excessive worry about real-life events—as in GAD—does not constitute obsessional behavior.) In contrast, compulsions are repetitive, patterned motor behaviors that regularly follow obsessions and serve to significantly reduce distress or symbolically "prevent" some dreaded event with which they are not truly causally related. The majority of compulsions involve either washing (e.g., hands, countertops, floors) or checking (e.g., stove, door locks, medicine dosage) behaviors. However, forgetfulness resulting from impaired concentration (as in GAD) or memory (as in Alzheimer's) often results in repeated checking and should be distinguished from OCD. Indeed, existing treatments for each of these disorders are different.

Posttraumatic Stress Disorder

Systematic studies of the prevalence and course of Posttraumatic Stress Disorder (PTSD) have not yet been performed, and the effect of age on presentation of this disorder is largely unknown. PTSD is among the few *DSM-IV* diagnoses to specify a particular etiological component, namely, proximate exposure to a traumatic event that presented a serious threat to the physical integrity of oneself or others. A diagnosis of Posttraumatic Stress Disorder is made when, following exposure, an individual develops symptoms of reexperiencing, avoidance, and hyperarousal. Specific symptoms include nightmares, flashbacks, repetitive thoughts concerning the event, intense distress in the presence of cues associated with the event, social withdrawal, increased alertness and vigilance, and difficulties in sleep and concentration (Lipovsky, 1991). Moreover, these symptoms must be of at least 1 month duration following the traumatic event. The estimated population prevalence of PTSD in young adults is 1% (Famularo, Kinscherff, & Fenton, 1990) or slightly greater than that of schizophrenia.

Anxiety Disorders Due to a General Medical Condition

An exceptionally strong relationship between physical illness and anxiety in older adults has been demonstrated (Arling, 1987; Turnbull, 1989) and warrants additional comment. Anxiety may be produced either as a direct concomitant of a medical condition or medical treatment (e.g., hypothyroidism) or indirectly as a consequence of significant life changes associated with a physical disorder. As such, thorough etiological assessment prior to implementation of any intervention (psychological or medical) is indicated. However, the considerable degree of symptomatic overlap between psychogenic anxiety and medical disorders (Gurian & Miner, 1991), particularly in the presence of depression (Starkstein et al., 1990), makes this an exceptionally difficult task. Indeed, Sklar (1978) noted that fully 44% of his sample of patients with gastrointestinal disorders presented with somatic anxiety symptoms representing true medical, rather than psychological, disorders. Importantly, anxiety experienced as a result of medical illness can take the form of any previously discussed disorder, and in many cases, both psychological and medical treatments are indicated. Additional organic and pharmacological factors associated with anxiety or anxietylike presentations are listed in Table 8-1.

CASE IDENTIFICATION
AND PRESENTING COMPLAINTS

The following brief case example illustrates assessment and treatment of anxiety in an older adult who was seen at the Nova Southeastern Community Clinic for Older Adults. The patient, Mario, was an 83-year-old, married, Italian-American male in relatively good physical condition. He resided with his wife of over 50 years in a southern Florida mobile home village populated almost exclusively by older adults. Members of this community formed a large, close-knit social network, with which Mario and his wife had been actively involved. Although he walked with the aid of a cane, Mario had retained an exceptionally vigorous life-style, walking daily around his neighborhood and riding a three-wheel bike with his wife whenever the temperature was not prohibitively hot. In addition, he was a talented wood carver and regularly created small sculptures for his friends and family. Moreover, despite the fact that he was totally blind in one eye and had only limited vision in the other, he continued to drive his automobile when accompanied by his wife, who in effect directed him through traffic and around pedestrians.

Approximately 4 months prior to his presentation at our outpatient clinic for older adults, Mario suffered what he believed to be a heart attack while sleeping in his reclining chair. Upon awakening, he was unable to arise from the chair or call for help and experienced intense feelings of dread and panic. Eventually, his wife found him and rushed him to the emergency room. Following several days in the hospital (no evidence of heart failure was found), he returned home but continued to suffer from pervasive anxiety and discomfort, particularly when he was seated. Indeed, he reported that he could not remain in a chair for longer than a minute before he was overwhelmed with anxiety and felt compelled to stand, at which point his anxiety immediately dissipated. In addition, both he and his wife noted that his level of daily activity had diminished dramatically. He indicated that he could no longer participate in activities that required sitting, and as a result, he and his wife no longer attended church or the weekly neighborhood potluck lunches he had enjoyed tremendously. Further, he was unable to watch a movie in a theater or on television at home, play cards, carve sculptures, or visit with neighbors. He reported that although he was

Table 8-1.   Pharmacological and Organic Factors
Associated with Anxiety or Anxietylike Presentations

Cardiopulmonary/vascular	Endocrinological
Myocardial infarction	Cardinoid syndrome
Mitral valve prolapse	Cushing's syndrome
Paroxysmal atrial tachycardia	Hypothermia
Hypoxia	Hyperthermia
Hypertension	Postmenstrual syndrome
Cardiac arrhythmias	Insulinoma
Asthma	Hypoglycemia
Pneumonia	Hyperkalemia
Anemia	Pharmacological
Neurological	Akathisia
Epilepsy	Alcohol withdrawal
Multiple sclerosis	Sedative withdrawal
Dementia	Anticholinergic drugs
Delirium	Caffeine/cocaine
Huntington's disease	Steroids
CNS infection	Vitamin deficiency
Postconcussion syndrome	Sympathomimetics

extremely restless, he became dizzy or lightheaded following minimal exertion and fatigued quite easily. He had great trouble sleeping through the night, and woke intermittently, returning to bed only after having paced about his mobile home for several hours. During the day, he experienced severe muscle tension and backache and no longer walked around the neighborhood or rode his bike with his wife. Moreover, he suffered from stomach pains and diarrhea and reported that he had to urinate more frequently than in the past. He complained that he could not concentrate or maintain focused attention on projects he initiated (e.g., reading a newspaper) and derived very little pleasure from once-reinforcing activities. In addition to his progressively worsening anxiety symptoms, he complained that feelings of sadness and worthlessness had become increasingly prominent in the month preceding his presentation for treatment. Finally, he worried frequently that he would die from another heart (anxiety) attack and that his wife would "be left penniless," even though discussion of their financial position revealed that this was not the case. Since his hospitalization, Mario had been maintained on lorazepam (Ativan) (4 mg), a high-potency benzodiazepine; however, he indicated that the drug did little to ameliorate his anxiety. Notably, Mario was unable to sit during the entire 2-hour interview.

To more thoroughly delineate the parameters of Mario's psychopathology, a comprehensive assessment battery comprised of a structured interview and standardized measures of anxiety, depression, assertiveness, marital adjustment, memory, and intelligence was administered. Specific tests included the (1) Structured Clinical Interview for *Diagnostic and Statistical Manual of Mental Disorders* (3rd ed., revised; *DSM-III-R*) (SCID), (2) State-Trait Anxiety Inventory,

(3) Beck Anxiety Inventory, (4) Beck Depression Inventory, (5) Geriatric Depression Scale, (6) Wolpe-Lazarus Assertiveness Scale, (7) Marital Adjustment Scale, (8) Michigan Alcoholism Screening Test, (9) Logical Memory and Visual Reproduction subtests of the Wechsler Memory Scale—Revised, and (10) Block Design and Vocabulary subtests of the Wechsler Adult Intelligence Scale—Revised. On the basis of the SCID, Mario received diagnoses of GAD and specific phobia (fear of confinement in the form of sitting), with secondary Major Depression developing within the past month. These diagnoses were supported by scores on all indices of anxiety and depression. Although several symptoms of panic disorder were present, this diagnosis was not assigned because Mario's feelings of impending panic did not occur unexpectedly. Performance on tests of assertiveness, intelligence, and memory was within normal limits, and there was no evidence of substance abuse. Notably, Marital Adjustment Scale scores were well above average (see Table 8-2 for actual test scores). During the interview and testing, Mario was somewhat quiet and deferential but possessed a subtle sense of humor and was exceptionally engaging.

HISTORY

As mentioned, onset of Mario's pathology occurred approximately 4 months prior to his presentation for treatment. He indicated that he had experienced similar symptoms only once before, following his son's death from cancer the previous year. At this time, he suffered a panic attack immediately upon learning that his son had died and remained extremely anxious over the next several days. In fact, his level of distress was so great that he ceased participation in all activities outside his home and was unable to board a plane to the Northeast to attend his son's funeral. However, these symptoms dissipated within 2 weeks and did not return until he experienced what he thought to be a heart attack 8 months later (the present episode). Mario was hospitalized for several days following this "attack." Although hospital tests revealed no evidence of cardiopulmonary distress, the staff physician ordered that he be restricted to bed rest at the hospital, under observation, for 3 days. Mario indicated that he was not continually informed of his medical status or the doctor's recommendations and, as a result, became increasingly agitated and confused. Because of his repeated attempts to arise and dress himself, staff members were eventually required to restrain him with straps. He reported that he became terribly anxious in response to his disorientation and realization that he was again unable to arise, to the extent that his desire to stand and walk became overwhelming. His general level of anxiety did not diminish upon discharge from the hospital, and he began to fear situations in which standing was difficult. Moreover, he sat on only on the edge of chairs and stood immediately when he perceived any somatic or affective anxiety cues. His wife noted that he spent the majority of each day standing or pacing around the house. Importantly, he reported that his anxiety was temporarily reduced when he stood.

Table 8-2. Pretreatment Scores on Standardized Tests of Psychopathology, Memory, and Intelligence

Assessment index	Result
Structured Clinical Interview for *DSM-III-R*	Generalized Anxiety Disorder, Specific Phobia, Major Depression
State-Trait Anxiety Inventory	State: 63* Trait: 46*
Beck Anxiety Inventory	Score: 20*
Beck Depression Inventory	Score: 29*
Geriatric Depression Scale	Score: 18*
Wolpe-Lazarus Assertiveness Scale	Score: 10*
Locke-Wallace Marital Adjustment Scale	Score: 127**
Michigan Alcoholism Screening Test	Score: 0**
Wechsler Memory Scale—Revised (Subtests)***	Logical Memory I: 82 II: 79, Visual Reproduction I: 92 II: 81
Wechsler Adult Intelligence Scale—Revised***	Full Scale IQ est. based on Block Design and Vocabulary: 83

*Indicates significant pathology.
**Indicates significantly positive result.
***Indicates norms unavailable for this age group.

Although remaining seated produced the most acute distress, Mario also worried excessively about his health and financial status. He reported that his anxiety in response to these somewhat obsessive ruminations was reduced only when he verified that his pulse was within normal limits or confirmed that no arithmetic errors had been made in his bank account. Mario also remarked that his level of anxiety was particularly high during the evening hours, when he became extremely bored and frustrated.

Other Relevant History

Mario was the fourth of nine children in a traditional Italian family. He reported that his early family life was extremely rewarding and that he was particularly close to his siblings and mother. Further, he indicated that his relationship with his father was also quite good, although his interactions with him were restricted because his father was employed in two full-time jobs. No significant negative childhood events or psychopathology were reported.

Mario was the father of three children (two males and a female), all of whom were married with children of their own. Although he reported that his relationships with his children were excellent and interactions with them were consistently enjoyable, Mario noted that since moving to Florida, he was able to visit them only about twice per year. Mario was still obviously greatly disturbed by the death of his youngest son (at age 55) and reported tearfully that he felt terribly guilty because he did not attend the funeral.

SELECTION OF
PSYCHOLOGICAL TREATMENT

A plethora of empirically validated anxiety-reduction strategies for younger adults currently exist. In contrast, very few studies employing similar treatments with older adults have been conducted. However, preliminary case study data indicate that there are more similarities than differences in treatment response between age groups (e.g., Garrison, 1978; Rowan, Holburn, Walker, and Siddique, 1984; Thyer, 1981). Interventions found effective with younger adults are therefore likely to be effective with the majority of older adults (Wisocki, 1991). Nevertheless, several age-related procedural modifications are recommended and include (1) increased treatment duration, particularly when new physical (e.g., muscle relaxation) or social skills are being taught; (2) concomitant reduced treatment intensity, especially when using techniques that induce high levels of anxiety (e.g., exposure-based strategies); (3) consideration of cultural and generational factors affecting performance of therapy assignments (e.g., during sensate focus training); and (4) adaption of a strongly prescriptive approach to therapy (consistent with expectations of patients who are very familiar with the medical model of treatment).

In general, older patients require a relatively greater number of learning trials to acquire new anxiety-reduction behaviors than younger adults. This may be attributed to the following: (1) older adults, by definition, tend to evince more extensive psychopathological learning histories than similarly diagnosed younger adults and (2) reductions in visual spatial coordination and muscle control that accompany the aging process increase the difficulty with which new behavioral repertoires are acquired. In support of this conclusion, Garfinkel (1979) noted that number of sessions needed by elderly patients to become proficient in progressive muscle relaxation was nearly twice that required by younger adults. Regarding the second point, weakened health status and increased risk for development of cardiopulmonary complications in many older adults contraindicate the repeated or intense application of those procedures that intentionally produce high levels of anxiety and fear (e.g., flooding). Further, it has been demonstrated that exceptionally intense anxiety-provoking interventions, while often effective, result in unacceptably high rates of treatment attrition, particularly in agoraphobics (Janssen & Ost, 1982). Along different lines, thoughtful consideration of cultural/generational characteristics of older adults in treatment greatly facilitates establishment of a strong therapeutic relationship and enables elderly patients to develop trust and confidence in (often younger) therapists. Treatment providers must be cognizant of the fact that discussion of personal problems or public expression of fear (typically part of every psychological interview) are strongly forbidden in many cultures and may elicit severe anxiety in some older adults. Relatedly, adoption of a relatively prescriptive approach to psychotherapy (see Hersen & Ammerman, 1994) with geriatric populations routinely allays many of the fears triggered by the relatively novel psychotherapy experience. Indeed, anxiety-disordered older adults presenting for treatment routinely expect their therapist to fulfill a role similar to that of their medical doctor and may become even more anxious if their therapist adopts an entirely nondirective stance. In contrast, clinical experience indicates that a directive approach frequently results in greater treatment compliance and gains.

Anxiety Reduction Strategies

Progressive Muscle Relaxation

Progressive Muscle Relaxation (PMR), originally developed by Jacobson (1938), is perhaps the most widely used of all behavioral treatment techniques. PMR derives it theoretical justification from the fact that autonomic responses associated with muscle relaxation are the opposite of those caused by anxiety (Wolpe, 1990). In the procedure, patients are taught to detect muscle tension and replace this tension with relaxation. This is achieved through systematic constriction and release of several specific sets of muscles that comprise the human body (Bernstein & Borkovec, 1973). Typically, therapists will first model the procedure, tensing an isolated group of muscles for about 7 seconds, followed by about 15 to 20 seconds of relaxation. Patients are then instructed to tense their muscles as the therapist had done, followed by complete relaxation of those muscles. During tension and release cycles, the patient's attention is directed to the qualitatively different muscular sensation associated with each phase of the procedure. Diaphragmatic breathing and guided positive imagery are often employed to augment relaxation. Once patients can effectively relax specific sets of muscles (e.g., fingers and hands, biceps, triceps), more diffuse groupings are used (e.g., hands and arms, upper chest and neck) until finally, the patient can relax his or her entire body at will. In younger adults, the procedure routinely involves four or five weekly therapist-directed sessions complemented by 30 minutes of daily self-directed practice. Importantly, lower "doses" of training appear to be ineffective (Borkovec & Sides, 1979). Further, as mentioned earlier (Garfinkel, 1979), older adults regularly require 8 to 10 weeks of training in PMR to achieve states of deep muscle relaxation. Note that exercises involving muscle tensioning are contraindicated in older patients suffering from arthritis, osteoporosis, or other painful medical conditions. For these individuals, imagined muscle tension followed by relaxation appears to be almost as effective as the standard procedure (Scogin, Rickard, Keith, & Wilson, 1992)

Support for the efficacy of PMR in reducing anxiety in the elderly is provided by DeBerry (1982), DeBerry, Davis, and Reinhard (1989), and Scogin et al. (1992). In these studies, PMR proved to be as effective as cognitive restructuring and meditation training in reducing overall levels of general anxiety. Further, Yesavage, Sheikh, Tanke, & Hill (1988) found that PMR improved short-term recall in older adults whose concentration was presumably negatively affected by high levels of anxiety. However, PMR is infrequently employed in isolation (Craske, Rapee, & Barlow, 1992) and is relatively ineffective in treating fear or anxiety elicited by specific stimuli (as occurs in agoraphobia, social phobia, OCD, and specific phobia).

Applied Relaxation

Applied Relaxation (AR) differs from PMR in that patients are taught not only to relax their muscles but to actively apply this state of relaxation to those specific situations and stimuli known to produce anxiety. The procedure typically begins with standard PMR training. Once patients are able to voluntarily induce relaxation, however, they practice applying this state to a variety of behaviors, such as waiting in a line, walking, sitting in an uncomfortable chair, or talking to others. This active form of relaxation is then gradually applied imaginally or in role-play format to specific fear-producing situations. Finally, applied relaxation during exposure to actual anxiety-producing stimuli is encouraged and practiced. Note that in contrast to extinction-based procedures, in which a conditioned fear response is gradually inhibited through repeated nonreinforcement during exposure trials, AR replaces a conditioned response of fear (sympathetic arousal) with a new response of relaxation (parasympathetic arousal). That is, in AR, patients learn to associate specific stimuli with relaxation rather than anxiety. AR has the added benefit of being proactive, in that a specific coping behavior (i.e., relaxation) is employed to overcome anxiety. This is in contrast to the more passive stance adopted by some of the simple extinction-based exposure treatments described below. Ost (1988) has found AR to be significantly more effective than simple PMR in reducing panic attacks when relaxation is applied to interoceptive cues associated with panic. In addition, AR has been used successfully in the treatment of specific and social phobias (Ost, Lindahl, Sterner, & Jerremalm, 1984). Unfortunately, no treatment outcome studies employing AR with older adults have been reported.

Systematic Desensitization

Systematic Desensitization (SD) is based on the concept of reciprocal inhibition: the diminution of one response (anxiety) by the excitation of another, directly incompatible response (relaxation) (Wolpe, 1958). Standard SD contains three primary components: (1) PMR training, (2) anxiety hierarchy construction, and (3) systematic application of muscle relaxation to imaginal hierarchy items. Although relaxation is routinely employed to inhibit anxiety in SD, additional antianxiety responses exist, and include assertiveness and sexual arousal (Wolpe, 1990). Anxiety hierarchies or "thematically related lists of anxiety-stimuli, ranked according to the amount of anxiety they evoke" (Wolpe, 1990, p. 160) may involve internal (e.g., feelings of panic) or external (e.g., spiders) stimulus situations, or combinations of the two. Detailed and specific hierarchy items (e.g., "going to an office party with Mary, John, and Denise") are preferable to general items (e.g., "groups of people") and facilitate relatively more powerful counterconditioning effects by increasing the salience of anxiety-producing stimuli. Since this specificity may restrict therapeutic generalization, multiple hierarchies are regularly required to overcome anxiety in a particular patient.

In addition to hierarchical item specificity, the increasing anxiety-eliciting potential of successive hierarchical items should be evenly spaced and gradual.

This spacing is facilitated by assigning a relative value of anxiety to each item via the Subjective Units of Discomfort Scale (SUDS) or some similar anxiety "thermometer." During hierarchy construction, patients are asked to generate the most anxiety-producing stimulus possible and assign it a SUDS value of 100. Absolute calm is given a SUDS value of 0. As patient and therapist generate new hierarchy items, a relative SUDS value is assigned to each. Incremental values of hierarchy items should be spaced at about five to ten SUDS in order to facilitate step-wise reciprocal inhibition of progressively greater anxiety-evoking stimuli. The concept of graduated, incremental exposure is integral to systematic desensitization and is based on the finding that, if a minor anxiety response associated with a particular stimulus is reciprocally inhibited by relaxation, consecutive items in the hierarchy will elicit less anxiety than they otherwise would have (Wolpe, 1958). As a result, a constant level of relaxation will effectively reciprocally inhibit the anxiety responses of stimuli that would have otherwise exceeded relaxation's anxiety-inhibiting potential (Wolpe & Flood, 1970).

To initiate the process of systematic desensitization (after at least four sessions of PMR training), patients induce a state of muscle relaxation and provide a SUDS rating of their basal anxiety level (usually between 0 to 20 SUDS). Patients then attempt to vividly imagine the first hierarchy item and indicate, by raised finger, when the image is clear. After about 7 seconds of exposure, the therapist instructs the patient to (1) stop the scene, (2) report the number of SUDS the scene aroused, and (3) relax. After about 30 seconds of relaxation, the procedure is repeated with the same scene until the patient reports that the SUDS level experienced during exposure is approximately equal to that reported during baseline, at which point the next scene in the hierarchy is desensitized. Typically, scene presentations continue after 30-second intervals of relaxation if consistent SUDS reductions are evident. Normally, each scene requires about four repetitions to bring the SUDS level down to baseline, but some scenes may require a great many more (Wolpe, 1990). Repeated exposure to an item yielding successively lower SUDS ratings is indicative of improvement through inhibition of anxiety. Subtle variations of the procedure are often warranted for some patients. For example, extremely frightening scenes may require shorter presentation times and longer interscene intervals. In addition, the content of some scenes may determine the length of imaginal exposure—a clap of thunder will likely require less time to imagine than interacting with peers at an office party (Wolpe, 1990).

The relatively nonaversive nature of SD makes it particularly well suited for use with older adults. In addition, progression through the hierarchy is almost completely patient controlled, and the potential for exacerbating anxiety responses through sensitization (i.e., exposure resulting in increased, rather than decreased fear) is minimal.

Exposure

Exposure treatments have as their theoretical basis the process of extinction or the diminution of the probability of occurrence of a conditioned response following repeated nonreinforced exposure to a conditioned stimulus. Almost without exception, effective treatments for anxiety disorders will, at some point, involve exposure to anxiety-producing stimuli. The method by which exposure is incorporated into these interventions, however, varies greatly along the following parameters: (1) medium of stimulus presentation (i.e., imaginal vs. in vivo), (2) intensity of stimulus presentation (graded vs. full), and (3) purity of stimulus presentation (pure extinction vs. addition of coping strategies).

Exposure may take place in either imaginal or in vivo formats. Systematic desensitization (discussed above) and flooding are the two primary types of imaginal exposure strategies. In flooding, patients are instructed to imagine, in extremely vivid detail, the most aversive aspects of their anxiety-producing stimuli. Often, patient-narrated audiotapes depicting aversive stimuli are employed to enhance visual imagery. Exposure trials typically last from 30 minutes to several hours. As expected, exceptionally high levels of anxiety are produced during these trials; however, repeated exposure results in a diminution or extinction of fear responses. Importantly, both therapist and patient should be aware of the fact that initial exacerbations, rather than reductions, in anxiety often occur as a result of flooding. Premature termination of exposure trials, through escape or, in the case of OCD, compulsive behavior may actually result in sensitization or increased anxiety in response to conditioned stimuli. Obviously, high potential for attrition exists with this procedure, and its use with frail or medically unstable older adults is not justified. Flooding has been used successfully to treat specific phobias and PTSD; however, its effectiveness with social phobia and agoraphobia is less well established (Emmelkamp & Wessills, 1975).

Imaginal exposure techniques, such as systematic desensitization and flooding, are indicated in instances where in vivo exposure is inappropriate or impossible to implement (e.g., PTSD). However, level of stimulus salience achieved by in vivo exposure is typically greater than that produced by imaginal exposure. As such, in vivo exposure often results in more "efficient" extinction of conditioned anxiety responses. In vivo exposure is routinely performed in a graded format, with exposure to mildly anxiety-producing stimuli preceding exposure to stimuli that elicit great fear. The degree to which stimulus intensity is varied (i.e., highly graded to full exposure) is determined, in large part, by the individual characteristics of each patient, with high "doses" of stimulus exposure (and hence anxiety) producing relatively more rapid treatment response than lower doses. As noted above, high-intensity exposure treatments are associated with very large attrition rates (Barlow, 1988). Further, prolonged intense exposure to anxiety-producing stimuli regularly results in significant elevations of heart rate and blood pressure and may pose unacceptable health risks for some older adults. Therefore, exposure treatments should be graded so as to produce significant, but not overwhelming, levels of anxiety.

Fortunately, in vivo exposure is amenable to several forms of graduation. Indeed, anything that serves to reduce the level of fear associated with anxiety-producing stimuli can be considered a grading component. Most commonly, a hierarchy of feared objects or situations, analogous to the imaginal hierarchy employed in SD, is used. Alternatively, exposure can be graded by the proximity of a significant other or therapist. This form of graduation incorporates positive reinforcement (provided by significant other or therapist) into the extinction process and increases the likelihood that exposure exercises will be practiced between sessions (Barlow, O'Brien, & Last, 1984). Relatedly, addition of relaxation and coping strategies (i.e., impurities), while largely ineffective in reducing anxiety beyond that produced by exposure alone (Barlow, 1988), appear to diminish fear levels during exposure trials. Importantly, these techniques are also quite effective in increasing self-efficacy and feelings of control, which in turn serve to increase the probability that intersession exposure exercises will be performed and that treatment gains will be maintained (Marshall, 1985). Additional modulation of exposure is achieved simply by altering the duration and frequency of extinction trials; however, theoretical ramifications of this form of graduation must be considered. According to conditioning postulates, extinction occurs only when an individual remains in the presence of feared stimuli until the anxiety eliciting potential of those stimuli begins to diminish. In effect, a new response, that of less fear, is learned. If a patient is permitted to leave an anxiety-producing situation before his or her level of anxiety begins to decrease, no learning occurs, and the stimulus will continue to elicit fear. Moreover, the patient will be negatively reinforced for avoiding the feared stimulus, and escape behaviors will increase. Temporal grading, therefore, should not be used in isolation.

While employed less extensively with noninstitutionalized older adults, operant procedures are effective in increasing compliance with exposure-based treatment regimens (Agras, Leitenerg, & Barlow, 1968; O'Brien, 1978; Williamson & Ascione, 1983). Frequently, contingent reinforcement in the form of social attention or praise is delivered by significant others when subjects remain in anxiety-producing situations for progressively longer durations. Formal contingency contracting for increased exposure to anxiety-producing stimuli has also been employed with anxious older adults through marital therapy contracts (Rowan et al., 1984).

Obviously, in vivo exposure treatment can be implemented in a variety of formats. However, Barlow (1988) notes that potential for successful outcome is maximized when exposure exercises are (1) graded, (2) patient controlled, (3) moderately anxiety-producing, and (4) practiced frequently between sessions. In older adults, such interventions have proved efficacious in the treatment of specific phobia (Thyer, 1981), agoraphobia (Garrison, 1978), GAD (Garfinkel, 1979), and OCD (Rowan et al., 1984).

Cognitive Treatment

While less effective than exposure-based treatments (Biran & Wilson, 1981), cognitive therapy for anxiety is indicated in those instances where a cognitive etiology has been established (Acierno, Hersen, & Ammerman, 1994; Hersen, 1981; Wolpe, 1977), as is frequently the case in specific phobia, social phobia, and GAD. Cognitive treatments include Rational Emotive Therapy (RET) (Ellis &

Dryden, 1987), Focal Cognitive Therapy (FCT) for panic (Beck, Sokal, Clark, Berchick, & Wright, 1992), Self-Instructional Training (SIT) (Meichenbaum, 1974), Self-Efficacy Enhancement (Williams, Turner, & Peer, 1985), and Thought Stopping (Wolpe, 1990). In RET, patients are taught that their response (i.e., anxiety) to a particular stimulus or event is determined in large part by underlying beliefs they hold about that stimulus or event. Therefore, treatment is directed to identify and alter "irrational" beliefs that ultimately produce anxiety. For example, a socially phobic individual who feels that she cannot eat in front of others may infer that if she choked or gagged on her food, she would receive overwhelming disapproval and condemnation from those strangers around her, with the underlying belief that such social disapproval is exceptionally horrible and indicates that she is worthless. The RET therapist will point out that anxiety is a natural consequence of such an irrational belief (i.e., that others *must* approve of me at all times), but that, in fact, the belief is not necessarily a natural consequence of the situation and therefore is amenable to change. Substitution of a new, benign belief (e.g., "Although I prefer that others approve of me, my self-worth is not wholly determined by their approval") is thought to result in reduced anxiety. Note that it is the general belief of worthlessness based on other's disapproval, rather than the overt inference that others will disapprove of me if I gag, that is targeted for change.

In contrast, patients receiving Beck's FCT for panic are taught that catastrophic cognitions (e.g., "I'm having a heart attack") generated in response to somatic symptoms (e.g., mild heart rate increase) are actually inappropriate misattributions of benign physiological states, and serve to exacerbate precisely those interoceptive cues patients fear. Continued catastrophic misattribution and subsequent intensification of interoceptive stimuli may eventually culminate in a panic attack. As a result, FCT is directed toward altering catastrophic cognitions, thereby disrupting the vicious cycle of increasing anxiety. Beck et al. (1992) have found FCT to be highly effective in reducing frequency and intensity of anxiety attacks in patients diagnosed with panic disorder (although the procedure was complemented by interoceptive exposure exercises).

In contrast to RET and FCT, Meichenbaum's SIT combines exposure with therapist modeling and cognitive-behavioral coping strategies. In this treatment, therapists first model appropriate self-talk aloud while undergoing exposure to feared stimuli. Typical self-statements are "I am handling this well; I am remaining calm; I am controlling the situation and my anxiety." Next, patients, aided by therapist prompts, engage in exposure exercises, utilizing similar overtly verbal coping self-statements. After patients begin to demonstrate competency using self-statements, clinician prompts are faded. Finally, the patient fades his or her verbal self-prompts as well, first to whispers, and then to completely covert self-talk. In this manner, a coping style is adopted that enables patients to endure relatively greater lengths of exposure with gradually increasing independence.

In Self-Efficacy treatment (Williams et al., 1985), therapists facilitate patient completion of "mastery experiences" (i.e., exposure tasks), which are thought to increase perceptions of self-efficacy and confidence while simultaneously reducing anxiety. Mastery exercises are typically graded, modeled by the clinician, and involve therapist guidance and support. Although the technique appears quite similar to standard exposure-based interventions, relatively greater emphasis is placed on teaching patients to make internal, rather than external, attributions of success. Indeed, proponents of Self-Efficacy theory maintain that performance success in the absence of concomitant increases in self-efficacy will have little impact on overall levels of anxiety. To date, not studies of Self-Efficacy treatment with older adults have been published.

Thought-Stopping "is a method of changing cognitive behavior that ... does not depend on changing the meaning of words or interpretation of situations" (Wolpe, 1990, p. 129). This procedure is most frequently employed to reduce intrusive obsessional thoughts found in OCD and the obsessive worry characteristic of GAD. Interestingly, the technique is somewhat analogous to the behavioral procedure of response prevention/interruption used to eliminate compulsive behavior. In Thought-Stopping, patients are trained to interrupt incipient thoughts (e.g., I won't be able to pay next month's bills) as they begin by exclaiming aloud "Stop!" or some other similar vocal command, followed immediately by the substitution of a competing benign thought for the intrusive cognition (e.g., I always pay my debts in a timely fashion). As the occurrence of intrusive thoughts is diminished, self-commands are faded to the subvocal level. No reports regarding efficacy of Thought Stopping with older adults have been published; however, the relatively nonaversive nature of this treatment, and the ease with which it is applied to repetitive anxiety-producing thoughts, justifies its use with this population.

The Present Case: Prescriptive Assessment

Although several effective interventions for anxiety exist, appropriate selection of any psychological treatment presupposes adequate assessment of the patient's psychopathology. Comprehensive assessment necessarily includes measurement of (1) symptoms, (2) etiology, (3) maintaining factors, and (4) subject characteristics and history. Symptoms are composed of the tripartite response classes of motoric behavior, cognitive behavior, and affective/physiological behavior. In the present case, Mario's affective, cognitive, and behavioral symptoms were easily assessed through a structured clinical interview and several standardized questionnaires. Physiological responses indicative of anxiety and autonomic arousal included muscle tension and pain, gastrointestinal distress, dizziness, and fatigue. Anxiety-related cognitions were evident from Mario's repeated self-statements (e.g., "I will surely have an anxiety attack if I sit in a chair"), as well as from his persistent and excessive worry about his health and financial status. In addition, anxiety-induced cognitive impairments (relatively more prominent in older adults) were evident and included difficulties in concentration and attention. Motoric symptoms of anxiety included pervasive avoidance of several stimulus situations that reliably produced fear (i.e., activities that required sitting). Additional motoric symptoms were evident in Mario's frequent escape behaviors, which functioned to reduce anxiety. These ranged from obvious tendencies to flee situations in which he felt physically restrained (e.g., sitting in a deep chair) by standing and pacing, to rather subtle escape from excessive financial and health-related worries by repeatedly checking his bank account and heart rate.

Knowledge of the etiological pathway of a disorder enhances the efficacy with which specific treatments are applied. A conditioning etiology of fear appeared to best explain the origin of Mario's pathological anxiety. Specifically, an exceptionally potent aversive stimulus, involuntary immobility, was *twice* paired with sitting. Indeed, during the first aversive conditioning trial, Mario very likely suffered a panic attack, followed by the inability to stand. Two days later, he again became acutely anxious while reclining and was unable to escape, this time because he was strapped to his hospital bed. As a result of its association with aversiveness, sitting itself came to elicit severe anxiety. Moreover, several second-order conditioned stimuli (e.g., slightly increased heart rate, muscle tension) were also associated with the frightening event and acquired anxiety-eliciting potential. Contact with these higher-order conditioned stimuli occurred in a wide variety of situations, resulting in pervasive and seemingly free-floating anxiety. The primacy of a conditioning over a cognitive etiology was further supported by the fact that Mario did not actually believe he would be harmed by sitting in the chair. Rather, he simply feared the autonomic sensations of panic he "knew" would come as a result remaining seated. However, multiple etiological pathways are often present and responsible for psychopathology in a given individual. And, there was some evidence to support cognitive contributions to Mario's anxiety, particularly in the origin of his more pervasive health and financial fears. For example, in the 82 years prior to his presentation for treatment, Mario had never suffered from any significant anxiety symptomatology. As a result, his panic was disturbingly unfamiliar and interpreted by him as clear and indisputable evidence that his death was imminent. He simply did not possess the experience or cognitive learning history to know that panic and extreme autonomic arousal are not necessarily indicative of impending death. While a conditioning etiology provides some insight into the causes of Mario's anxiety when he engaged in any activity that required sitting, a cognitive or misinformational explanation facilitates understanding of why Mario so severely curtailed his level of physical activity and participation in once enjoyable activities.

Measurement of factors that maintain anxiety is accomplished by identifying discriminative stimuli and/or contingencies in a patient's natural environment that perpetuate or reliably elicit problem behaviors. Assessment of maintaining variables includes (1) identification of antecedents and consequences of the target behavior, (2) specification of the effects of the target behavior on significant others (e.g., spouse, parents, friends) and their responses to these effects, and (3) determination of environmental stimuli that vary as a function of the target behavior. In Mario's case, the most salient discriminitive stimulus for anxiety was clearly confinement in a chair from which standing was difficult. However, Mario was able to delineate additional anxiety-triggering antecedent stimuli, including thoughts about his health and finances, small or confined rooms from which exit was difficult (though not elevators), increases in his pulse, and medical visits to the hospital. Following incidental exposure to all these stimuli, Mario engaged in varied forms of avoidance behavior that served to reduce his anxiety. These behaviors both prevented extinction of conditioned anxiety responses and negatively reinforced escape tendencies. As a result, probability that escape behaviors would be performed in the future (thereby precluding extinction) increased. Specifically, to reduce the anxiety experienced while seated, Mario would immediately stand; to reduce anxiety in response to negative or catastrophic cognitions about his finances or health, he would quickly check his bank book or take his pulse; and to reduce anxiety elicited by small or crowded rooms, he would leave and return home.

The response of Mario's spouse to these avoidance behaviors also was of interest. Rather than insisting he remain in an anxiety-provoking situation, his wife quickly facilitated escape. Moreover, she attempted to calm and comfort him each time he felt anxious. She indicated that she did not engage in similar attentive behaviors when he was actually attempting to expose himself to anxiety-producing situations (e.g., playing cards with her while seated) because she "didn't want to ruin it with too much commotion." Therefore, it appeared that Mario received differential reinforcement from his spouse for behaving anxiously.

Mario also noted that he "felt himself" only when talking to his children on the phone. Indeed, he reported that, while conversing with his daughter, he often was able to remain seated for several minutes at a time, but quickly arose when he "realized that [he] was sitting and began to experience anxiety." Upon further inspection, it became apparent that other factors also served to modulate his level of anxiety. He indicated that he was less anxious in the company of his friends, who would typically visit him for brief periods several mornings each week. Not surprisingly, he reported that although she reduced rather than exacerbated his anxiety, he always seemed to experience more panic symptoms when in the company of his wife than when alone. Finally, he noted that his anxiety was relatively more intense at night before bed, "when the only thing to do was worry about what could go wrong." In summary, Mario's anxiety appeared to have been maintained by several factors, including avoidance of and escape from anxiety-producing stimuli before extinction of the fear response could occur, negative reinforcement of avoidance behavior through reduction of aversiveness, differential positive reinforcement from his spouse when he suffered from anxiety symptomatology, and repeated negative cognitions regarding his future health and financial status.

Delineation of relevant subject characteristics and history facilitates appropriate application and refinement of psychological interventions. This is particularly the case with older adults, for whom factors such as physical health, marital status, prior treatment successes, and cultural background play a relatively more significant role. As noted, Mario was a first-generation Italian male with traditional mores against admitting weaknesses or seeking help, especially of a psychological nature. Moreover, he was very unfamiliar with both psychopathology and psychotherapy. Indeed, he had experienced neither for the first

82 years of his life. As a result, presenting for treatment itself was somewhat anxiety provoking. In addition, Mario and his wife had a very close and interdependent relationship. They accompanied each other during all regular medical appointments, and they rarely engaged in social activities apart from one another. Further, Mario, like the majority of older adults, was very familiar with the medical model of health care, in which treatment providers assume a highly directive stance. In terms of specific physical characteristics, Mario's ability to safely tolerate prolonged intense anxiety was questionable. Additionally, though cognitive functioning was within normal limits, his capacity to generate highly affective imagery was limited.

Treatment Selection

Following a thorough medical examination in which no physical pathology was established to account for Mario's anxiety symptoms, prescriptive selection and application of psychological treatment was initiated. As mentioned, etiological assessment revealed that Mario's fears were primarily of a conditioning origin but also contained cognitive components. Therefore, both extinction-based treatments and cognitively oriented interventions were chosen. Moreover, it was hypothesized that contingencies of reinforcement maintained his anxiety. As such, existing reinforcement contingencies were targeted for modification.

Because Mario's capacity to generate affective imagery was limited (he reported that he could imagine anxiety-producing situations but did not "feel" the anxiety), in vivo exposure strategies were chosen over imaginal techniques in order to increase stimulus salience and facilitate sufficient generalization of treatment effects. Additionally, in light of Mario's advanced age and somewhat frail physical status, highly aversive strategies were rejected in favor of relatively less intrusive interventions. Specifically, graded in vivo exposure was applied to his most functionally impairing fear (i.e., sitting in a chair for extended durations), as well as to secondary fears that seemed to produce generalized anxiety (i.e., health and financial issues). Individual grading and coping components included duration of continuous exposure, presence of significant other and/or therapist during exposure trials, and use of self-efficacy enhancement and SIT coping strategies. Typically, Mario practiced remaining seated in a reclining chair in the therapist's office with both therapist and wife present, for progressively longer intervals. This form of exposure produced significant, but not overwhelming, anxiety. Exposure to secondary health and financial fears was performed through prolonged discussions of possible negative ramifications of increased heart rate and financial insecurity. Again, these discussions elicited considerable, but not unbearable, anxiety. To eliminate negative reinforcement resulting from escape or avoidance in response to increased distress during exposure trials, Mario was strongly persuaded to remain seated or continue to participate in aversive discussions about his health or finances until his anxiety began to diminish. Further, Mario was taught to monitor and terminate avoidance behavior in the form of standing, measuring his heart rate, or verifying the balance of his bank account. Daily intersession homework was assigned and consisted of repeated exposure trials of progressively longer duration (beginning with 30 seconds), for which he remained seated in his reclining chair with his wife present. In addition, previously reinforcing activities that required sitting were scheduled in a graded format (e.g., sitting in church in the last row for 1 minute, watching part of a billiards game at the community clubhouse) and performed daily. These activities had the dual benefit of reducing anxiety through extinction and improving Mario's overall mood by increasing the density of positive reinforcement received as a function of his increased behavior.

Simple exposure exercises were augmented by operant procedures. Importantly, reinforcement in the form of social attention by Mario's wife and therapist was made contingent on his performance of behavioral exposure exercises. Moreover, Mario's wife was instructed to withhold rather than increase attentiveness when he engaged in avoidance behavior in the form of standing and pacing or checking his pulse or bank book. A contract delineating these contingencies was created and contained operationalized definitions of both appropriate and inappropriate behaviors, as well as descriptions of the reinforcers to be provided by his wife upon successful completion of exposure exercise or termination of avoidance behaviors. Specific reinforcers included playing cards for 30 minutes, receiving a back rub for 10 minutes, choice of meal at dinner or lunch, among others. Behavioral contracts were signed by Mario, his wife, and the therapist and revised as needed each week.

Although PMR is often employed as a coping strategy to reduce anxiety during exposure treatments, the procedure elicited severe anxiety in Mario. (Relaxation-induced anxiety is not an uncommon occurrence and may be associated with the relatively novel sensation of "letting go" that regularly precedes muscle relaxation.) Therefore, cognitive techniques, including SIT, self-efficacy enhancement, and rational disputation were used for this purpose. SIT was particularly effective in enabling Mario to prolong his exposure to feared stimuli so that effective extinction of anxiety responses could occur. Moreover, his sense of mastery over feared situations was increased as a function of these progressively greater performance successes. Cognitive restructuring through corrective information and disputation were employed to counter Mario's erroneous beliefs that anxiety and its typical physiological correlates were indicative of imminent heart attack and death.

CONCURRENT MEDICAL TREATMENT

Medication is often an appropriate and helpful adjunctive therapy in the treatment of anxiety-based disorders. However, recent data indicate that older adults are frequently inappropriate recipients of anxiolytic drugs. Indeed, "irrespective of the etiology of anxiety, the over 65 group disproportionately is the largest consumer of ... anti-anxiety pharmacological agents" (Hersen & Van Hasselt, 1992, p. 620). While they comprise only 12% of the population, older adults ingest twice the quantity of over-the-counter and prescription drugs as their younger counterparts (King, Van Hasselt, Segal, & Hersen, 1994). Current popular anxiolytic medications include benzodiazepines, azapirones, beta-blockers, and antidepressants. Benzodiazepines, including oxazepam, loraze-pam, diazepam, alprazolam, are the most frequently prescribed antianxiety agents in the elderly. Fifty percent of nursing home patients (Allen, 1986) and 37% of general outpatients (Beers et al., 1988) are maintained on this class of drugs. While precautions are in order when using benzodiazepines with patients of any age, geriatric patients evince an increased potential for benzodiazepine toxicity resulting from or exacerbated by (1) increased central nervous system sensitivity and reduced renal excretion capability, (2) comorbid medical conditions (e.g., Parkinson's disease), (3) polypharmacy and increased sensitivity to drug interactions, and (4) medication noncompliance (Salzman, 1991). Indeed, a study performed in Great Britain revealed that 10% of a sample of consecutive geriatric hospital admissions were in response to adverse drug reactions (Williamson & Chopin, 1980). In addition to increased risk for toxicity, older adults seem to suffer more severe side effects as a result of benzodiazepine use than do younger adults, including sedation, reduced coordination, lethargy, depressed mood, disorientation, impaired memory, and attentional deficits (Keuthen, 1991). Not unexpectedly, older adults maintained on benzodiazepines appear to be at increased risk for injury resulting from falls (Ray et al., 1987). In light of these dangers, Cutler and Narang (1984) and Stoudemire and Moran (1993) recommend reducing benzodiazepine dosage levels by 50% in order to compensate for increased drug half lives associated with reduced kidney and liver functioning in the aged. Such dosage adjustment is justified by the fact that the half-life of diazepam's metabolite in an 80-year-old is approximately 90 hours, compared to about 20 hours in a 20-year-old (Sheikh, 1992). Further, if benzodiazepines are to be prescribed, drugs with shorter half-lives, such as alprazolam, are recommended but carry with them increased risk of withdrawal upon discontinuation, particularly in older adults (Weiss, 1994). Clearly, benzodiazepines should be used only to reduce exacerbations of acute anxiety over very short periods of time, particularly since their long-term efficacy has not been demonstrated, and they may actually inhibit the effects of exposure-based treatments (Barlow, 1988).

Azapirones (of which buspirone is currently available) are nonsedating serotonin agonists that produce significantly fewer side effects than benzodiazepines. Moreover, no clinically significant drug interactions or withdrawal effects are associated with their use (Stoudemire & Moran, 1993). Notably, buspirone appears to be as effective an anxiolytic as the benzodiazepines for those older adults who have not yet been maintained on benzodiazepines. However, its effectiveness is significantly diminished for individuals who have used benzodiazepines in the past (this may be due to the fact that no sedation side effects associated with benzodiazepines are present with buspirone). While effectiveness of buspirone with older adults has not been strongly established (e.g., Singh & Beer, 1988), its use appears to be preferable to that of benzodiazepines.

Beta-blockers, including propranolol and atenolol, are used frequently in the treatment of performance anxiety and appear to be effective in ameliorating somatic correlates of anxiety such as tachycardia and perspiration. However, beta-blockers do little to eliminate feelings of fear or dread (Markovitz, 1993). While beta-blockers produce fewer side effects than benzodiazepines, they have been implicated as the source of nightmares, hallucinations, and sleep disturbances in some individuals taking the drug.

Antidepressant medications, such as imipramine, fluoxetine, and clomipramine, have proven moderately effective in reducing anxiety symptoms, particularly those resulting from panic and OCD in younger adults. The anxiolytic properties of antidepressant medications appear to be enhanced in instances where depressed mood and anxiety co-occur (Stoudemire & Moran, 1993). However, side effects such as cognitive impairment and weight loss or gain are associated with antidepressant usage. Although the antianxiety properties of antidepressants have been evaluated with younger adults, similar research has not been conducted with geriatric populations.

From the above review it should be apparent that, in contrast to actual practice, long-term treatment of anxiety in the elderly by benzodiazepines is to be avoided if at all possible. Alternate pharmacological interventions, including buspirone for general anxiety, beta-blockers for somatic anxiety correlates, and antidepressants for mixed anxiety-depression presentations, produce fewer side effects and have some clinical and empirical support. None of the psychopharmacological interventions for anxiety appears to be as effective as exposure-based psychological treatments. However, adjunctive use of anxiolytic medication is often justified in instances where patients are exceedingly anxious and cannot consistently engage in exposure exercises. In these situations, medication can facilitate performance of in vivo exposure by reducing anxiety to manageable levels. Buspirone and propranolol appear to be particularly well suited for use with behavior therapy because they are nonsedating and do not impair attention or concentration. Stimulus salience is thus maintained at high levels during exposure trials, thereby permitting extinction or reciprocal inhibition of anxiety responses. Similarly, antidepressant medication may facilitate participation in psychological treatments for anxiety by increasing interest and motivational levels in lethargic and fatigued patients.

The Present Case

Predictably, Mario had been maintained on lorazepam, a high-potency, intermediate-acting (half-life in young adults of 14 hours) benzodiazepine for the 4 months prior to his presentation for treatment with little or no reduction in anxiety. Moreover, he reported several symptoms associated with benzodiazepine sedation (e.g., fatigue, dizziness, poor coordination) that indicated he was at increased risk for both benzodiazepine toxicity and injury from a fall. However, he expressed no desire to stop taking lorazepam; rather, he feared that termination of the drug would exacerbate his anxiety. Therefore, it was agreed that he would neither increase nor decrease his dosage during his initial treatment at our clinic. This had the dual benefit of allaying his somewhat justified concerns about intensified anxiety after terminating the benzodiazepine and increasing the confidence with which causal attributions of therapeutic change in response to psychological therapy were made.

Had Mario not been maintained on benzodiazepines for the 4 months prior to his presentation at our clinic, buspirone may have been an appropriate pharmacological adjunct to psychological treatment. However, this option was not chosen because patients first maintained on benzodiazepines do not respond well to buspirone. Alternately, Mario's recent increase in depressive symptomatology may have justified use of adjunctive antidepressant medications. Indeed, clinical knowledge suggests that antidepressant medication is often effective in "energizing" otherwise lethargic individuals, thereby enhancing motivation and facilitating performance of behavioral exposure exercises. However, Mario indicated that he preferred to forego ingesting additional medication until behavioral anxiety-reduction techniques were attempted.

COURSE OF TREATMENT

Since treatment involving discussion of personal psychopathology and weaknesses was a unique and anxiety-provoking experience for Mario, initial sessions were devoted to establishing a strong therapeutic relationship in which the therapist's respect of his age and familial status, two major defining characteristics of traditional Italian males, was emphasized. This format reduced Mario's anxiety about psychotherapy while simultaneously elevating his self-esteem and confidence, thereby increasing the likelihood of self-disclosure and treatment success. Similarly, in response to his lack of familiarity with psychotherapy, explicit rationales for all treatment procedures were provided and treatment techniques were implemented only after obtaining Mario's explicit approval. Because he and his wife functioned almost exclusively as a marital unit, rather than independently, she was invited (and she expected) to participate in all treatment sessions and assignments. Consistent with Mario's expectations, the therapist adopted a directive stance in which prescriptive instructions and assignments were given in order to ameliorate anxiety.

As mentioned, highly graded in vivo exposure was employed to eliminate Mario's primary fear of being confined in a reclining chair. Specifically, Mario was informed that, through its association with aversiveness (i.e., his "attack"), remaining seated had acquired the power to elicit anxiety. Moreover, just as fear of confinement had been learned, its unlearning was also possible; however, effective treatment required the production and endurance of some discomfort and anxiety. Initial exposure trials were performed for very brief periods in a chair from which escape was not difficult, thereby minimizing experienced anxiety, maximizing the potential for success, and increasing his overall sense of self-efficacy. Additionally, both therapist and spouse were present during exposure episodes and provided descriptive reinforcement for his efforts. For the first few sessions, exposure trials occurred exclusively in the context of the office.

However, to further assure generalization of treatment effects, several sessions were also conducted in Mario's home, complemented by daily self-exposure exercises. Mario was able to complete most office and home exposure exercises with only moderate levels of anxiety. Importantly, graded exposure was intensified only following successful performance of extinction trials. At no point during treatment was Mario's level of anxiety permitted to increase past moderate levels. In session, this was achieved through the use of repeated SUDS reports made by Mario to the therapist every few minutes during exposure trials.

In addition to anxiety elicited by sitting, more generalized anxiety, manifested as pervasive health and financial worries, was also targeted for reduction through highly graded exposure. For these areas, the therapist pointed out that Mario's pattern of repeatedly monitoring his heart rate or bank account was an inappropriate and disruptive form of avoidance behavior used to reduce anxiety, in much the same way refusing to remain seated in a chair permitted him to avoid anxious feelings. Repeated exposure to these somewhat obsessive concerns that was not followed by escape (in the form of monitoring) would eventually result in a diminution of anxiety. Therefore, Mario was instructed to gradually reduce the frequency with which he engaged in health or finance monitoring behaviors, with increasingly longer durations between each episode of monitoring (i.e., avoidance), beginning at once per half-hour and eventually ending in once per day. Mario's wife assisted in these extinction exercises by providing reinforcement for successful efforts. As with earlier graded exposure trials, Mario had little difficulty enduring exposure (i.e., not taking his pulse) to these general fears and worries.

In final sessions, exposure trials were significantly intensified in order to solidify treatment effects achieved at that point. Specifically, Mario practiced remaining in a multiposition, full reclining chair for the entire office session. In addition, somewhat exaggerated discussions of possible negative effects of increased heart rate and financial insecurity were conducted. In this manner, positive treatment effects were "overlearned" and a resistance to relapse was induced. Importantly, intensification of exposure also occurred gradually, and Mario had few problems overcoming anxiety during these trials.

In addition to graded exposure-based treatment, several sessions with Mario and his wife were devoted to illustrating effects of existing reinforcement contingencies on overt anxiety-related behavior. Importantly, inappropriate contingencies were targeted for modification. In particular, Mario's spouse was taught to provide positive, descriptive reinforcement whenever she noticed he was acting without fear or anxiety. In contrast, she was instructed to withhold reinforcement in the form of attention and concern whenever he engaged in anxiety-related behaviors. Both Mario and his wife agreed to implement these new contingencies in order to reduce inadvertent reinforcement of inappropriate anxious behavior. Indeed, consent from both parties is typically an essential component in such marital contingency contracts and prevents partners from developing extreme resentment or anger toward one another. As mentioned, both desired behaviors and specific reinforcers were operationalized. Desired behaviors included rehearsal of daily exposure assignments (defined in session each week), discussion of health or finances without checking his pulse or bankbook, walking outside, sitting in his chair while watching television or playing cards, and attending church. Reinforcers provided by his spouse included attention in the form of neck rubs, discussion of topics of his choosing, preparation of a meal of his choice, and "kissing sessions." The contingency contract was reviewed weekly and altered as needed. Mario noted that the contract served as a constant reminder of "What I need to do to get better" and that his wife's exceptionally strong contingent reinforcement and support for nonanxious behavior enabled him to withstand much greater levels of anxiety during daily exposure exercises than he otherwise would have. Note that the overall emphasis on this contract was reinforcement of positive, rather than punishment of negative, behaviors.

Further generalization of treatment effects was achieved through scheduling of previously reinforcing activities. Mario and his wife were instructed to plan, each day, at least one activity that they had enjoyed in the past but were currently avoiding. In initial sessions, activities were chosen that were of brief duration and that did not elicit high levels of anxiety, such as playing cards while seated or watching a short television show. As treatment progressed, however, previously reinforcing activities that required sitting for gradually increasing time periods were selected. Specific activities included attending church services and picnics for progressively longer durations, watching a feature-length movie in a theater, and participating in neighborhood potluck lunches. Notably, scheduling of reinforcing activities (rather than simple suggestion or exhortation to engage in these activities) resulted in further generalization of treatment effects as well as an elevation of Mario's affective state. As before, Mario's wife was taught to reinforce both his attempts to schedule exposure activities and his performance during actual trials.

Though prompted by the therapist and encouraged by his wife, Mario's progress through treatment was largely self-controlled. Importantly, treatment was implemented so that success rather than failure or disappointment resulted at each stage of increasingly intense exposure. Operant procedures were effective in increasing the consistency with which intersession extinction trials were performed by increasing Mario's level of motivation. Generalization of successful session performance was assured by recruiting Mario's spouse as an active treatment facilitator and by conducting treatment sessions in Mario's true home environment. Finally, maintenance of treatment gains was assured through the use of very intense exposure, also provided in a graded format, during final treatment sessions.

FOLLOW-UP

Approximately 3 months after treatment termination, an informal follow-up session was conducted in Mario's home. Previously employed treatment techniques were reviewed. Behavioral observation during exposure trials revealed that all gains had been maintained. Similar positive results were reported by

Mario and confirmed by his wife and daughter during a 6-month follow-up telephone contact. Importantly, Mario did not exhibit any new anxiety symptomatology. Successful long-term outcome was expected because Mario had been purposefully familiarized with the rationale and generalized application of each treatment strategy, in addition to his training in specific techniques. He was thus able to effectively detect, assess, and counter anxiety and avoidance behaviors at their inception. Indeed, Mario reported that he experienced two episodes of increased anxiety related to specific medical concerns after leaving treatment (one episode was triggered when his wife suffered a severe laceration on her leg; the other was in response to his severe shortness of breath and dizziness following a bike ride on a particularly hot day) but was able to rapidly eliminate anxiety by engaging in exposure (in the first instance, by repeatedly looking at his wife's swollen leg and in the second, by imagining himself gagging) without concomitant escape behaviors (e.g., avoiding visual contact with his wife's leg, making repeated doctor's appointments for her). Mario also indicated that he no longer suffered from depressive symptoms and had continued to maintain his active, premorbid life-style.

OVERALL EVALUATION

In evaluating Mario's case, special consideration is given to the effectiveness with which specific treatment techniques were prescriptively chosen to ameliorate particular aspects of his psychopathology. As mentioned, successful use of prescriptive interventions (Hersen & Ammerman, 1994) presupposes comprehensive assessment of problem areas, including measurement of symptoms, etiology, maintaining factors, and subject characteristics and history. Symptomatic presentation was thoroughly evaluated through multiple standardized questionnaires and structured interviews and produced diagnoses of GAD, specific phobia, and major depression. Moreover, focused behavioral assessment revealed that etiological pathways were primarily of a conditioning origin, but that certain cognitive misconceptions existed and contributed to Mario's anxiety. Further, it was determined that anxiety was maintained by existing reinforcement contingencies that facilitated escape and avoidance while preventing extinction of fear responses. Finally, consideration of subject factors and history, including Mario's age, cultural background, and familiarity with psychotherapy, permitted establishment of a strong therapeutic relationship and refinement of treatment techniques so that chances of successful outcome were maximized.

The prescriptive treatments chosen as a function of this thorough assessment included graded exposure provided in a variety of formats, activity scheduling, marital contingency contracting, and cognitive restructuring. Treatment response was quite positive, as reflected by patient, significant other, and therapist report. Importantly, Mario was educated in both the rational and application of specific antianxiety strategies, with the result that he was able to adapt and utilize previously learned techniques to problems that developed during the 6-month follow-up. Overall, then, it appears that prescriptive treatment of

Mario's GAD was quite successful; however, this contention would have been significantly strengthened through the use of repeated rather than only pretreatment standardized dependent measures.

SUMMARY

Older adults routinely experience high levels of environmental, physical, and psychological stress and are thus at increased risk for developing anxiety disorders. Indeed, anxiety in the elderly appears to be more prevalent than any other type of psychopathology and is frequently found in the form of specific phobias or GAD. However, anxiety is often overlooked in older populations, either because clinicians and patients are unfamiliar with its presentation in the elderly because the condition is considered to be intractable or of a physical origin. Recently, measurement and treatment of anxiety disorders in older adults has received increased attention, and interventions found to be effective with younger adults are undergoing evaluation with aged individuals. Importantly, the potential for successful application of these treatments is maximized when thorough assessments are conducted and treatments are modified to meet specific requirements of older adults. Such modifications include longer treatment durations, lowered aversiveness levels, and increased consideration of generational and sociocultural aspects of each patient. As with younger adults, exposure-based treatments, including systematic desensitization, in vivo graded exposure, and applied relaxation, appear to be most effective in ameliorating anxiety in older adults. Cognitive strategies are useful in maintaining motivation for treatment and facilitating effective performance of exposure exercises. Psychopharmacological interventions are less effective than psychological treatments and are associated with increased abuse and misuse potential. However, benzodiazepines and azapirones can be used as effective initial adjunctive treatments when acute anxiety levels produced by graded exposure-based interventions threaten to overwhelm patients. Overall, psychological assessment and treatment of anxious older adults are at the nascent stage. Therefore, further research is needed in order to refine existing knowledge and dispel misconceptions about anxiety in the elderly.

REFERENCES

Acierno, R., Hersen, M., & Ammerman, R. (1994). Overview of the issues in prescriptive treatments. In M. Hersen & R. T. Ammerman (Eds.), *Handbook of prescriptive treatments for adults* (pp. 3–27). New York: Plenum Press.

Agras, W. S., Leitenerg, H., & Barlow, D. H. (1968). Social reinforcement in the modification of agoraphobia. *Archives of General Psychiatry, 19*, 423–427.

Allen, R. M. (1986). Tranquilizers and sedative/hypnotics: Appropriate use in the elderly. *Geriatrics, 41*, 75–88.

American Psychiatric Association. (1994). *Diagnostic and statistical manual of mental disorders* (4th ed.). Washington, DC: Author.

Anthony, J. C., & Aboraya, A. (1992). The epidemiology of selected mental disorders in later life. In J. E. Birren, R. B. Sloane, & G. D. Cohen (Eds.), *Handbook of mental health and aging* (2nd ed., pp. 28–73). New York: Academic Press.

Arling, G. (1987). Strain, social support, and distress in old age. *Journal of Gerontology, 42*, 107–113.

Barlow, D. H. (1988). *Anxiety and its disorders: The nature and treatment of anxiety and panic.* New York: Guilford Press.

Barlow, D. H., O'Brien, G. T., & Last, C. G. (1984). Couples treatment of agoraphobia. *Behavior Therapy, 15*, 41–58.

Beck, A. T., Sokal, L., Clark, D. A., Berchick, R., & Wright, F. (1992). A crossover study of focused cognitive therapy for panic disorder. *American Journal of Psychiatry, 149*, 778–783.

Beers, M. Avorn, J., Soumerai, S. B., Everitt, D. E., Sherman, D. S., & Salem, S. (1988). Psychoactive medication use in intermediate-care facility residents. *Journal of the American Medical Association, 260*, 3016–3020.

Bernstein, D. A., & Borkovec, T. D. (1973). *Progressive relaxation: A manual for the helping professions.* Champaign, IL: Research Press.

Biran, M., & Wilson, G. T. (1981). Treatment of phobic disorders using cognitive and exposure methods: A self-efficacy analysis. *Journal of Consulting and Clinical Psychology, 49*, 886–899.

Blazer, D., George, L. K., & Huges, D. (1991). The epidemiology of anxiety disorders: An age comparison. In C. Salzman & B. D. Lebowitz (Eds.), *Anxiety in the elderly: Treatment and research* (pp. 17–30). New York: Springer.

Borkovec, T. D., & Sides, J. K. (1979) Critical procedural variables related to the physiological effects of progressive relaxations: A review. *Behaviour Research and Therapy, 17*, 119.

Brickman, A. L., & Eisdorfer, C. (1989). Anxiety in the elderly. In E. W. Busse & D. G. Blazer (Eds.), *Geriatric psychiatry.* Washington, DC: American Psychiatric Press.

Burvill, P. W. (1987). An appraisal of the NIMH Epidemiologic Catchment Area Program. *Australian and New Zealand Journal of Psychiatry, 21*, 175–184.

Busse, E. (1975). Aging and psychiatric diseases in late life. In M. Reiser (Ed.), *American handbook of psychiatry.* New York: Basic Books.

Clarke, A. H., & Lewis, M. J. (1982). Fear of crime among the elderly. *British Journal of Criminology, 232*, 49.

Coryell, W., Noyes, R., & House, J. (1986). Mortality among outpatients with anxiety disorders. *American Journal of Psychiatry, 143*, 508–510.

Craske, M. G., Rapee, R. M., & Barlow, D. H. (1992). Cognitive-behavioral treatment of panic disorder, agoraphobia, and generalized anxisty disorder. In S. M. Turner, K. S. Calhoun, & H. E. Adams (Eds.), *Handbook of clinical behavior therapy* (2nd ed., pp. 39–66). New York: Wiley.

Cutler, N. R., & Narang, P. K. (1984). Implications of dosing tricyclic antidepressants and benzodiazepines in geriatrics. *Psychiatric Clinics of North America, 7*, 845–861.

DeBerry, S. (1982). The effects of meditation-relaxation on anxiety and depression in a geriatric population. *Psychotherapy, Theory, Research, & Practice, 19*, 512–521.

DeBerry, S., Davis, S., & Reinhard, K. E. (1989). A comparison of meditation-relaxation and cognitive/ behavioral techniques for reducing anxiety and depression in a geriatric population. *Journal of Geriatric Psychiatry, 22*, 231–247.

Dubovsky, S. L. (1990). Generalized anxiety disorder: New concepts and psychopharmacologic therapies. *Journal of Clinical Psychiatry, 51*(suppl), 3–10.

Eaton, W. W., & Keyl, P. M (1990). Risk factors for the onset of DIS/DSM-III agoraphobia in a prospective, population-based study. *Archives of General Psychiatry, 47*, 819–824.

Eaton, W. W., Kramer, M., Anthony, J. C., Dryman, A., Shapiro, S., & Locke, B. (1989). The incidence of specific DIS/DSM-III mental disorders: Data from the NIMH Epidemiologic Catchment Area Program. *Acta Psychiatrica Scandinavica, 79*, 163–178.

Ellis, A., & Dryden, W. (1987). *The practice of rational emotive therapy.* New York: Springer.

Emmelkamp, P. M., & Wessels, H. (1975). Flooding in imagination vs. flooding in vivo: A comparison with agoraphobics. *Behaviour Research and Therapy, 13*, 7–15.

Famularo, R., Kinscherff, R., & Fenton, T. (1990). Symptom differences in acute and chronic presentation of childhood PTSD. *Child Abuse and Neglect, 14*, 439–444.

Garfinkel, R. (1979). Brief behavior therapy with an elderly patient: A case study. *Journal of Geriatric Psychiatry, 12,* 101–109.

Garrison, J. (1978). Stress management for the elderly: A psychoeducational approach. *Journal of the American Geriatrics Society, 26,* 397–403.

George, L. K., Blazer, D. G., Winfield-Laird, I., Leaf, P. J., & Fischbach, R. L. (1988). Psychiatric disorders and mental health service use in later life: Evidence from the ECA Program. In J. Brody & G. L. Maddox (Eds.), *Epidemiology and aging* (pp. 189–219). New York: Springer.

Gurian, B. S., & Miner, J. H. (1991). Clinical presentation of anxiety in the elderly. In C. Salzman & B. D. Lebowitz (Eds.), *Anxiety in the elderly: Treatment and research* (pp. 31–44). New York: Springer.

Hersen, M. (1981). Complex problems require complex solutions. *Behavior Therapy, 2,* 15–29.

Hersen, M., & Ammerman, R. T. (Eds.). (1994). *Handbook of prescriptive treatments for adults.* New York: Plenum Press.

Hersen, M., & Van Hasselt, V. B. (1992). Behavioral assessment and treatment of anxiety in the elderly. *Clinical Psychology Review, 12,* 619–640.

Himmelfarb, S., & Murrell, S. A. (1984). The prevalence and correlation of anxiety symptoms in older adults. *Journal of Psychology, 116,* 159–167.

Jacobson, E. (1938). *Progressive relaxation.* Chicago: University of Chicago Press.

Jansson, L., & Ost, L. G. (1982). Behavioral treatments for agoraphobia: An evaluative review. *Clinical Psychology Review, 2,* 311–336.

Jenike, M. A. (1991). Geriatric obsessive-compulsive disorder. *Journal of Geriatric Psychiatry and Neurology, 4,* 34–39.

Keuthen, N. (1991). Medication and the aging organism: A guide for the non-prescribing clinician. In P. A. Wisocki (Ed.), *Handbook of clinical behavior therapy with the elderly client.* New York: Plenum Press.

King, C. J., Van Hasselt, V. B., Segal, D. L., & Hersen, M. (1994). Diagnosis and assessment of substance abuse in older adults: Current strategies and issues. *Addictive Behaviors, 19,* 41–55.

Markowitz, P. J. (1993). Treatment of anxiety in the elderly. 145th Annual Meeting of the American Psychiatric Association: Anxiety: Special problems and new approaches (1992, Washington, DC). *Journal of Clinical Psychiatry, 54*(suppl), 64–68.

Marshall, W. L. (1985). The effects of variable exposure in flooding therapy. *Behavior Therapy, 16,* 117–135.

Matt, G. E., Dean, A., Wang, B., & Wood, P. (1992). Identifying clinical syndromes in a community sample of elderly persons. *Psychological Assessment, 4,* 174–184.

McCarthy, P. R., Katz, I. R., & Foa, E. B. (1991). In C. Salzman & B. D. Lebowitz (Eds.), *Anxiety in the elderly: Treatment and research* (pp. 197–209). New York: Springer.

Meichenbaum, D. (1974). Self-instructional strategy training: A cognitive prosthesis for the aged. *Human Development, 17,* 273–280.

Myers, J. K., Weissman, M. M., Tischler, G. L., Holzer, C. E., Leaf, P. J., et al. (1984). Six-month prevalence of psychiatric disorders in three communities: 1980–1982. *Archives of General Psychiatry, 41,* 959–970.

O'Brien, J. (1978). The behavioral treatment of a 30-year smallpox obsession and handwashing compulsion. *Journal of Behavior Therapy and Experimental Psychiatry, 9,* 365–368.

Ost, L. G. (1988). Applied relaxation vs. progressive relaxation in the treatment of panic disorder. *Behaviour Research and Therapy, 26,* 13–22.

Ost, L. G., Lindahl, I. L., Sterner, U., & Jerremalm, A. (1984). Exposure in vivo vs. applied relaxation in the treatment of blood phobia. *Behaviour Research and Therapy, 22,* 205–216.

Raj, B. A., Corvea, M. H., & Dagon, E. M. (1993). The clinical characteristics of panic disorder in the elderly: A retrospective study. *Journal of Clinical Psychiatry, 54,* 150–155.

Ray, W. A., Griffin, M. R., Schaffner, W., Baugh, D. K., & Melton, L. J. (1987). Psychotropic drug use and the risk of hip fracture. *New England Journal of Medicine, 316,* 363–369.

Robins, L. N., Helzer, J. E., Weissman, M. M., Orvaschel, H., Gruenberg, E., Burke, J. D., et al. (1984). Lifetime prevalence of specific psychiatric disorders in three sites. *Archives of General Psychiatry, 38,* 381–389.

Rowan, V. C., Holburn, S. W., Walker, J. R., & Siddique, A. (1984). A rapid multi-component treatment for an obsessive compulsive disorder. *Journal of Behavior Therapy and Experimental Psychiatry, 15*, 347–352.

Salzman, C. (1991). Pharmacological treatment of the anxious elderly patient. In C. Salzman & B. D. Lebowitz (Eds.), *Anxiety in the elderly: Treatment and research* (pp. 149–173). New York: Springer.

Scogin, F., Rickard, H. C., Keith, S., Wilson, J., et al. (1992). Progressive and imaginal relaxation training for elderly persons with subjective anxiety. *Psychology and Aging, 7*, 419–424.

Sheikh, J. I. (1991). Anxiety rating scales for the elderly. In C. Salzman & B. D. Lebowitz (Eds.), *Anxiety in the elderly: Treatment and research* (pp. 251–266). New York: Springer.

Sheikh, J. I. (1992). Anxiety and its disorders in old age. In J. E. Birren, R. B. Sloane, & G. D. Cohen (Eds.), *Handbook of mental health and aging* (2nd ed., pp. 410–432). New York: Academic Press.

Singh, A. N., & Beer, M. (1988). A dose range-finding study of buspirone in geriatric patients with symptoms of anxiety. *Journal of Clinical Psychopharmacology, 8*, 67–68.

Sklar, M. (1978). Gastrointestinal diseases in the aged. In W. Reichel (Ed.), *Clinical aspects of aging*. Baltimore: Williams & Wilkins.

Starkstein, S. E., Cohen, B. S., Fedoroff, P., Parikh, R. M., Price, T. R., & Robinson, R. (1990). Relationship between anxiety disorders and depressive disorders in patients with cerebrovascular injury. *Archives of General Psychiatry, 47*, 246–251.

Stoudemire, A., & Moran, M. G. (1993). Psychopharmacologic treatment of anxiety in the medically ill elderly patient: Special considerations. 144th Annual Meeting of the American Psychiatric Association: Treatment strategies for complicated anxiety (1991, New Orleans, LA). *Journal of Clinical Psychiatry, 54*(suppl), 27–33.

Thompson, T., Mitchell W., & House, M. (1989). Geriatric psychiatry patient's care by primary care physicians. *Psychosomatics, 30*, 65–72

Thyer, B. (1981). Prolonged in vivo exposure therapy with a 70 year old woman. *Journal of Behavior Therapy and Experimental Psychiatry, 12*, 69–71.

Thyer, B., Parrish, R. J., Curtis, G. C., Nesse, R. M., & Cameron, O. G. (1985). Ages of onset of DSM-III anxiety disorders. *Comprehensive Psychiatry, 23*, 113–122.

Turnbull, J. M. (1989). Anxiety and physical illness in the elderly. Symposium: Anxiety: The silent partner (1989, San Francisco, CA). *Journal of Clinical Psychiatry, 50*(11, suppl), 40–45.

Uhlenhuth, E. H., Balter, M. B., Mellinger, G. D., Cisin, H., & Clinthorne, J. (1983). Symptom checklist syndromes in the general population: Correlations with psychotherapeutic drug use. *Archives of General Psychiatry, 40*, 1167–1173.

Weiss, K. J. (1994). Management of anxiety and depression syndromes in the elderly. *Journal of Clinical Psychiatry, 55*(suppl), 5–12.

Weissman, M. M., Leaf, P., Blazer, D. G., Boyd, J., & Florio, L. (1986). The relationship between panic disorder and agoraphobia: An epidemiological perspective. *Psychopharmacology Bulletin, 43*, 787–791.

Williams, S. L., Turner, S. M., & Peer, D. F. (1985). Guided mastery and performance desensitization treatments for severe acrophobia. *Journal of Consulting and Clinical Psychology, 53*, 237–247.

Williamson, D. S., & Ascione, F. R. (1983). Behavioral treatment of the elderly. *Behavior Modification, 7*, 583–610.

Williamson, J., & Chopin, J. M. (1980). Adverse reactions to prescribed drugs in the elderly: A multicenter investigation. *Age and Aging, 9*, 73–80.

Wisocki, P., A. (1991). Behavioral gerontology. In P. A. Wisocki (Ed.), *Handbook of clinical behavior therapy with the elderly client*. New York: Plenum Press.

Wolpe, J. (1958). *Psychotherapy by reciprocal inhibition*. Stanford, CA: Stanford University Press.

Wolpe, J. (1977). Inadequate behavior analysis: The Achilles heel of outcome research in behavior therapy. *Journal of Behavior Therapy and Experimental Psychiatry, 8*, 1–3.

Wolpe, J. (1990). *The practice of behavior therapy* (4th ed.). New York: Pergamon Press.

Wolpe, J., & Flood, J. (1970). The effect of relaxation on the galvanic skin response to repeated phobic stimuli in ascending order. *Journal of Behavior Therapy and Experimental Psychiatry, 1*, 195.

Yesavage, J. A., Sheikh, J., Tanke, E. D., & Hill, R. (1988). Response to memory training and individual differences in verbal intelligence and state anxiety. *American Journal of Psychiatry, 145*, 636–639.

CHAPTER 9

Late-Life Depression

LEAH P. DICK AND
DOLORES GALLAGHER-THOMPSON

DESCRIPTION OF THE DISORDER

Mrs. B is a 64-year-old retired teacher who is caring for her husband with Alzheimer's disease. He has required care for 5 years. Mrs. B took an early retirement from teaching high school English 4 years ago when her husband's health severely declined. She reports a good relationship with her husband and their two children. Mrs. B is visiting her rheumatologist because of leg pain from her arthritis and

LEAH P. DICK AND DOLORES GALLAGHER-THOMPSON • Geriatric Research, Education, and Clinical Center, Veterans Affairs Medical Center, Palo Alto, California 94304, and Stanford University School of Medicine, Stanford, California 94305.

Psychological Treatment of Older Adults: An Introductory Text, edited by Michel Hersen and Vincent B. Van Hasselt. Plenum Press, New York, 1996.

sleeping difficulties due to the discomfort. The physician comments that her tone of voice reflects exhaustion or a "blue mood." Mrs B shrugs her shoulders and sighs, "I guess it is all part of getting old."

CHARACTERISTICS OF DEPRESSION IN OLDER PEOPLE

Unfortunately, society has perpetuated the myth that depression is a natural consequence of old age so much that older people often believe it themselves. Yet, the prevalence of a clinical diagnosis of Major Depressive Episode (as defined by *Diagnostic and Statistical Manual of Mental Disorders*, 3rd ed., revised [*DSM-III-R*], American Psychiatric Association, 1987), in community-dwelling adults over 65 is between 1% and 4%, which is lower than the extent of depression generally found in younger and middle-aged adults (Blazer, Hughes, & George, 1987). However, rates of clinical depression are higher for certain subgroups. For example, throughout adulthood and old age, unipolar depression is significantly more prevalent in women than in men (Nolen-Hoeksema, 1987). Also, medically ill or frail older adults (whether evaluated in an outpatient clinic setting or in inpatient hospital or nursing home facilities) are much more likely to be depressed than those in relatively good health (Rapp, Parisi, Walsh, & Wallace, 1988; Parmelee, Katz, & Lawton, 1992). These studies have reported prevalence rates in the range of 10% to 15%, for major depression in those patients. As pointed out by Futterman, Thompson, Gallagher-Thompson, and Ferris (1995), there is a linear increase in the extent of clinically significant depression when comparing community-dwelling, outpatient, and residential care samples.

In addition to the fact that rates of diagnosable depression vary considerably among older adults, it should be noted that an additional 9% to 30% of community-dwelling older adults report significant depressive *symptoms* that are a subset of the full clinical diagnosis of depression, as defined by existing standards (Baker, 1991; Blazer, 1993; Fitten, Morley, Gross, Petry, & Cole, 1989; Ruegg, Zisook, & Swerdlow, 1988; Thompson, Futterman, & Gallagher, 1988).

Thus, on the one hand, depression may be regarded as the common cold of geriatric mental health (because it is the most frequent psychiatric disorder found in older persons), yet on the other hand, some studies have reported that it tends to be underdiagnosed in older adults. For example, Rapp, Parisi, Walsh, and Wallace (1988) found that screening for depression among medically ill elders was poor to nonexistent, thus leading to failure to identify and treat this disorder, a failure that often complicates effective medical therapies. In our experience, this situation is further complicated by the fact that there is considerable conceptual difficulty in diagnosing depression in older persons. First, older adults themselves tend not to label or describe their negative feelings as "depressed" but often report symptoms that are metaphors for depression, such as cognitive complaints of worthlessness, demoralization, hopelessness, or despair (Blazer, 1993). Second, it is not always clear how to interpret behavioral and somatic symptoms of which older persons complain. For instance, behavioral symptoms (such as low energy, agitation or psychomotor retardation, and decreased pleasure in activities that were previously enjoyable), along with somatic complaints (such as difficulty sleeping, decreased appetite and weight loss, and loss of libido), may be due to undetected medical problems or to chronic illnesses for which the individual is undergoing treatment, including use of medications that can have these symptoms as their side effects (see National Institutes of Health Consensus Development Conference Consensus Statement, 1991, for a fuller discussion of this issue). Related to this is the fact that depressed older adults often present with increased health complaints and concern over their physical functioning, even in the absence of known medical problems. In fact, referrals to mental health professionals often follow a visit to the elder's primary care physician. Third, we and others have noted that, emotionally, older adults may present with a depressed tone that may be quite obvious to an interviewer but will often be denied by the patient, as in the case of Mrs. B. Unfortunately, the majority of older adults who are either clinically depressed or who have significant depressive symptoms (not accounted for by their physical health status) are not referred for treatment. This seems to reflect confusion about what constitutes an accurate diagnosis, as well as confusion of these symptoms with "normal aging."

In general, this diagnostic process is made even more difficult because most of the present standards for assessment and diagnosis of depressive disorders were developed without considering the specifics of late-life depression. In addition, not all health care professionals are trained to be sensitive to the issues of geriatric depression and some still maintain the bias that depression is a normal part of the aging process. This chapter will discuss these issues further and present our ideas about optimal assessment and treatment of depression in the older adult.

CASE IDENTIFICATION OF DEPRESSION
IN OLDER PEOPLE

The current, standard diagnostic criteria is the *Diagnostic and Statistical Manual of Mental Disorders* (*DSM-IV*; APA, 1994). Unfortunately, in our opinion and that of others in the field (e.g., Blazer, 1994), these criteria for diagnosing mood disorders are an imperfect fit to the characteristics of depression in older adults. This volume of the *DSM* has recently updated the *DSM-III-R* (APA, 1987), with an expansion of the description and the range of mood disorders but still with little attention to how these disorders present themselves in later life. Comments about differences seen by gender, age, and culture are cursory or virtually absent. For example, Dysthymic Disorder, which describes a chronic state of mild depression, does not include age-related issues at all, yet in clinical practice, this seems to be commonly present in older adults seeking treatment for mental health problems. Thus, there are presently no standardized means to capture the clusters of symptoms that are more typical of geriatric depression, as described earlier. A further discussion of this issue can be found in Pachana, Gallagher-Thompson, and Thompson (1994). Omission of the specifics of these disorders in late life most probably leads to underdiagnosis of geriatric depression, which in turn results in fewer patients being treated appropriately— despite the fact that a range of effective treatments does exist at the present time. This has led to a public health problem of considerable magnitude in that the most severe outcome of undiagnosed depression is suicide (Fitten et al., 1989; Salzman, 1994). Suicide rates are the highest among older, Caucasian men, particularly those with chronic or terminal health problems (Osgood, 1985). Undetected and untreated depression may exacerbate to such severe levels that suicidal ideation and plans develop. Yet few older people leave notes or recognizable clues of their intentions (Fitten et al., 1989). Older people also make few suicidal gestures or openly report their suicidal ideation. Mental health professionals serving older people should ask directly about suicide and be sensitive to the early detection of late-life depression. A very useful practitioner's guide to the assessment instruments available, as well as other methods for diagnosis of suicidal ideation and intent in the elderly, has been provided by Osgood (1985). In addition, Richman's (1993) volume on individual, group, and family therapy with suicidal elders provides a wealth of valuable treatment information for this most difficult of patients.

PSYCHOLOGICAL ASSESSMENT
OF DEPRESSION

Despite difficulties noted above in nomenclature, psychologists and other mental health practitioners engage daily in the process of assessment for late-life depression. The two popular formats used for this purpose are the self-report measure and the structured interview, with the former providing a quick screen and the latter used for actual diagnostic purposes. Among the most widely used self-report measures for late-life depression are the Beck Depression Inventory (BDI; Beck, Ward, Mendelson, Mock, & Erbaugh, 1961) and the Geriatric Depression Scale (Yesavage, Brink, & Rose, 1983). The Hamilton Rating Scale for Depression (HRSD; Hamilton, 1967) and the Schedule for Affective Disorders and Schizophrenia (SADS; Endicott & Spitzer, 1978) are two interview formats that require use of a trained clinician for best results. Due to space limitations, only these measures will be discussed here, but a comprehensive review of many additional measures used to assess late-life depression (including detailed validity and reliability of information) can be found in Pachana et al. (1994).

Mental Status Examination

The assessment of older people often begins with administration of a brief evaluation of mental status, such as the Mini-Mental Status Examination

(MMSE; Folstein, Folstein, & McHugh, 1975). This is a 20-item screening tool that offers general information about a patient's cognitive function. It is quick to administer as well as portable. Patients can score a maximum of 30 points across areas of orientation, attention and concentration, recall memory, ability to follow a three-step command, and other gross indices of cognitive function. Errors in any of these areas may indicate cognitive deficits, as well as point out the need for further neuropsychological testing. Often, depressed patients have memory complaints that may mimic some symptoms of dementia (discussed later in greater detail); thus the administration of the MMSE can help in making a differential diagnosis. Furthermore, a treatment plan can be better designed within the framework of an older person's cognitive capabilities. The MMSE is a reliable and valid screening tool to detect cognitive impairment in older people (Braekhus, Laake, & Engedal, 1992; Folstein, Folstein, & McHugh, 1975; Engedal, Haugen, Gilje, & Laake, 1988).

Interviewer-Administered Measures of Depression

Schedule for Affective Disorders and Schizophrenia (SADS)

This measure has been a widely used, structured interview that inquires about a full range of affective disorders, including various subtypes of depression and the spectrum of anxiety disorders. There are also sections on psychotic symptoms, bipolar events, and substance abuse, and the interview is arranged so that detailed inquiries can be made about both the patient's current status and his or her prior history with these disorders. The reliability and validity of this technique with the geriatric population is reported in Dessonville, Gallagher, Thompson, Finnell, and Lewinsohn (1982). More recently, other structured interviews have been developed to assess depression, including the Diagnostic Interview Schedule (DIS; Robins, Helzer, Croughan, & Ratcliff, 1981) and the Structured Clinical Interview for *DSM-III-R* (SCID; Spitzer, Williams, Gibbon, & First, 1992). These measures have been widely used with younger and middle-aged adults and have gradually replaced the SADS in many clinical and clinical research settings because they are shorter and can be given in a briefer period of time; however, their utility with older adults has yet to be demonstrated. Thus, we continue to recommend use of at least relevant sections of the SADS in clinical practice with older adults.

Hamilton Rating Scale for Depression

Psychiatry generally regards the Hamilton Rating Scale for Depression (HRSD) as one of the gold standards for assessing depression; unfortunately, its use is problematic with older adults for the following reasons. First, 9 of its 17 items are somatic in nature. High scores on these can reflect genuine physical changes that are common with aging and/or reflect health problems of the patient, rather than be indicative of depression. Examples of these questions include: What time have you been waking up in the morning for the last time, this past week?, or In the last week, how much have your thoughts been focused on your physical health or how your body is working? Thus, the HRSD may overdiagnose depression with an interviewer who is not knowledgeable about the problems of later life and who fails to inquire about actual health status and current medication usage (Thompson et al., 1988). Second, since no specific instructions are given in the original HRSD for how each question should be asked, individual interviewers may vary in their style of phrasing questions and probing for answers, thus leading to lack of standardization in administration of the measure (Pachana et al., 1994). To address some of these issues, the Structured Interview Guide for the HRSD (SIGH-D) was developed by Williams (1988). It provides specific wording for all questions, thus increasing the extent to which the measure is uniformly administered. Reliability was improved with these new guidelines (but not for all items) and unfortunately, no norms are yet available for this measure with older adults.

Self-Report Measures

Beck Depression Inventory

The Beck Depression Inventory (BDI) is a brief and portable self-report measure of depression containing 21 areas (short form has 13), each representing a common complaint of depression. Each area is represented by four statements of varying intensity (rated 0 to 3), and patients are asked to select which statement best reflects their belief about that area during the past week. For example, a question about a sad mood includes the following statements: (0) "I do not feel sad," (1) "I feel sad," (2) "I am sad all the time and I can't snap out of it," and (3) "I am so sad or unhappy I can't stand it." Advantages of the BDI include the ability to classify a person's score within varying ranges of the severity of depression, as well as the opportunity to track responses on each item to get a clearer picture of the issues involved. Second, the BDI directly asks about suicidal ideation to ensure an immediate intervention if necessary (Thompson et al., 1988).

One difficulty with the BDI for older patients is that they are asked to retain this four-point rating scale in order to respond properly to each question; this makes it very difficult to get accurate responses from elders who are cognitively impaired, extremely anxious, or otherwise suffering from a reduced attention span. It is also possible that older adults with chronic health problems may look depressed on this measure by simply endorsing items that may be more attributable to the management of their health. For example, items referring to worries over health, decrease in sleep, and decrease in appetite may inadvertently create a false-positive diagnosis. Yet a clinician can track each item with the older person to distinguish which endorsements are more distinctive of depressive symptoms. A review of the reliability and validity of the BDI with older adults is found in Gallagher (1986).

Geriatric Depression Scale

The Geriatric Depression Scale (GDS) was developed partially in response to the difficulties of using the BDI and other similar complex self-report measures with older people (Yesavage et al., 1983). Older adults can respond more easily to the GDS' yes/no format, which does not include any somatic items. This measure focuses on more of the cognitive and behavioral components of depression, including items such as: "Do you feel your life is empty?," "Have you dropped many of your activities and interests?," "Do you have trouble concentrating?," or "Do you enjoy getting up in the morning?" In addition, the GDS has been demonstrated to be more effective in distinguishing depressed older adults from nondepressed older adults than the HRSD and the Zung Depression Scale (Brink et al., 1982) or the BDI (Hyer & Bloust, 1984; Kiernan et al., 1986). It has also been effectively used to assess depression in persons with mild-to-moderate cognitive impairment, including individuals residing in nursing homes and other types of institutional placements (Parmelee et al., 1992).

In summary, an unsophisticated interviewer plus too general guidelines (as in the case of the HRSD) can under- or overestimate depression in older adults. Thus, these assessment measures must not be used as the sole source of information. Assessment of depression in older adults must be an interactive and interdisciplinary endeavor, including a thorough medical history and a complete list of medications to determine if any other physical conditions are contributing to depression. Additional assessments should include activities of daily living (to evaluate the patient's functional abilities) and eating habits (to ensure that vitamin deficiencies or malnutrition are not precipitants to depressive symptoms). It goes without saying that an individual's symptoms need to be understood within the context of that person's overall life situation. Thus, a detailed assessment of current and past stressors, methods of coping, available social supports (including relationships with family members and friends), living arrangements, and sociocultural or ethnic factors needs to be made in order to fully understand the older patient.

Specific Issues in Differential Diagnosis

One of the challenges in diagnosing geriatric depression is to be able to differentiate between conditions that often share symptoms of depression, including health complaints and problems, cognitive disturbances, bereavement and grief reactions, and medication side effects.

Many chronic health difficulties, such as heart disease, arthritis, stroke, thyroid disease, or cancer may produce weight and sleep changes, somatic concerns, or depressed mood that may be concurrent with the medical disorder or caused by a secondary depression (Fitten et al., 1989; Ruegg et al., 1988; Salzman, 1994). On the other hand, natural age-related changes in sleep patterns can mimic criteria for the sleep disorders found in depression. Older adults require less sleep and awaken earlier, but this behavior alone does not qualify as a symptom of depression, especially if the older person is not distressed over these changes. Recall that the HRSD asks specifically about sleep habits without considering the person's satisfaction or distress. Here, an endorsement for early morning awakening would add points toward a positive diagnosis of depression.

Differentiating between age-related physical changes and depressive symptoms is further complicated by the fact that older adults tend to focus their presentation on somatic complaints, often not attending to or masking any depressive symptoms (Ruegg et al., 1988). Many older adults are not socialized to discuss their difficulties in psychological terms: a phenomenon that may reflect their cohort's beliefs about the reputation of psychology and psychiatry when they were young adults. For example, when today's seniors were young adults, mental health care did not have the outpatient or client-centered focus that it does today. Older adults are more likely to be familiar with terms like "crazy," or "to be committed to a loony bin." These stereotypes may certainly contribute to older adults' lack of utilization of mental health services. Consider the case of Mrs. B, who initially presents with symptoms of pain and sleep disturbance to her primary physician. Even she does not consider the possibility of depression, even though her mood indicates a sad affect.

Symptoms of cognitive impairment (such as memory complaints) may also accompany depression, in the absence of a dementia. For example, it is often the case that a markedly depressed older adult's unresponsiveness and apathy during an assessment interview or a testing session will become labeled as cognitive decline when in fact that is not the case. It can be helpful to observe the patient's style of responding to questions to assist in evaluating the responses. Depressed older adults will often respond with "I don't know" or will not try to complete an item or answer a given question, while demented patients will try to respond, although their responses will be incorrect (Fitten et al., 1989; Wells, 1979). At other times, difficulties in concentration and memory may actually reflect a dementing process. Mental health practitioners must be careful to avoid allowing any biases to operate here and to not assume that mild cognitive confusion indicates a dementing disorder; rather, they must assess further (usually in collaboration with other health care providers) in order to either rule out or rule in the presence of serious cognitive impairment (Wells, 1979). Furthermore, information about the course of the disorder, as well as the duration and progression of symptoms, can be useful to tease apart the diagnosis of depression versus dementia. For example, most dementias are characterized by an insidious onset and a slow progressive deterioration, while depression often comes on more abruptly, with a distinct change from the individual's "typical self." It is also important to know whether symptoms of depression preceded or followed the symptoms of "dementia." On the one hand, depression is known to be common during the early stages of dementia—often as a reaction to the experience of cognitive changes—but on the other hand, it diminishes as the dementia progresses. Since assessment of both depression and dementia (when present simultaneously) requires considerable skill, the reader is referred to several review chapters which, taken together, should provide additional guidelines on this subject (Albert, 1994; Teri & Logsdon, 1994).

Recently bereaved individuals may also experience common symptoms of depression such as frequent, intense sadness, sleep and appetite disturbances, lack of interest in usual activities, and social and emotional withdrawal. Should these be considered indicative of a clinical level of depression that needs specialized treatment, or are they part and parcel of "normal grief," which would mean that they probably would resolve with the passage of time and adequate social support, in the absence of any specialized treatment for depression? This is also not a simple question to answer, and a full discussion is considerably beyond the scope of this chapter. The interested reader is referred to a comprehensive handbook on the top of bereavement that includes several chapters on late-life issues (Stroebe, Stroebe, & Hansson, 1993). For our purposes we will focus on two studies that do shed light on the issue. Breckenridge, Gallagher, Thompson, and Peterson (1986) found that certain symptoms distinguished between normal grief and depression in older adults (based on response to the BDI and measures of grief intensity): depressives were self-deprecating, generally guilty, and evidenced a strong negative image of themselves, whereas those who were simply experiencing grief did not endorse these particular symptoms. They more strongly endorsed feeling sad, having sleep and appetite difficulties, and being withdrawn from usual activities, but still basically having a positive self-image. Further research by this group found that when spousally bereaved older adults were followed for 30 months post-loss, their responses to similar measures indicated that symptoms of depression abated over time, whereas symptoms specific to grief (such as thinking about the deceased, searching for meaning in the death, and reviewing past memories of that person) were still very common at that time (Thompson, Gallagher-Thompson, Futterman, & Peterson, 1991). Thus, older adults who have had a recent significant loss (such as death of a spouse or close family relative) should be assessed for both grief and depression; if both are present, it seems clinically prudent to treat the depression first, and then to encourage the individual to continue in the normal grief process. However, if the diagnosis is that of a normal grief reaction, then the individual should be directed to self-help and other programs specifically designed to address those concerns (Worden, 1991).

The side effects of many medications may precipitate a secondary depression (Fitten et al., 1989; Kayalam & Shamoian, 1993; Wood, Harris, Morreale, & Rizos, 1988). According to these authors, medications that commonly cause depressive symptoms are histamine blockers, some antiparkinsonian drugs, some analgesics and anti-inflammatories, and some antihypertensives. In fact, Wood et al. (1988) found that some reserpine (an antihypertensive) induced depression became so severe that electroconvulsive therapy (ECT) was required. It is important to be aware that the sample sizes of these reports were quite small, and some in fact involved single case studies. Yet, that fact should not disregard the practice of inquiring about all of an older person's medications to investigate all possible contributors to the depression before diagnosis and treatment.

In summary, several factors need to be carefully evaluated in order to determine the nature and intensity of an individual's depression. Hopefully, increased availability of information about the aging population will result in fewer diagnostic errors. Let us return now to Mrs. B.

Medical Assessment of Mrs. B

Luckily, this physician does not believe that Mrs. B's sad mood is simply characteristic of her age rather than a possible depression. Yet Mrs. B continues to assert that she is more concerned about her increased leg pain and how it is interfering with her caregiving duties. The physician inquires about these caregiving tasks and discovers that many of them are physically challenging to Mrs. B, ultimately straining her joints. The physician inquires about whether Mrs. B has help; she explains that she would rather not call on her children for help, often pretending (to them) that she manages fine.

The physician gently explains that Mrs. B is experiencing both an exacerbation of her arthritis and some depression. She explains to Mrs. B that depressive symptoms are common for people who are managing a chronic health problem as well as a severe stressor, like caregiving, but not common for someone just because of increased age. She explains that the strain of caregiving is increasing her pain, which interferes with her sleep, which interferes with her stamina, her mood, and her interest for doing any activities besides caregiving. As Mrs. B eventually acknowledges that her increased leg pain and lack of interest in pleasant activities has made some contribution to her isolation from her friends, she becomes tearful. Mrs. B is referred to a psychologist.

Psychological Assessment of Mrs. B

The psychologist's assessment of Mrs. B's distress includes having her complete a Geriatric Depression Scale to indicate her self-reported level of depression. This scale was chosen because of the possibility that Mrs. B's chronic health difficulties would weigh the Beck Depression Inventory in a way that might confound her psychological symptoms. Mrs. B scores a 16, which indicates that she is on the high side of the moderately depressed range. Mrs. B admits that she has dropped many of her activities and interests, she feels hopeless and downhearted most of the time, she is lethargic, and she is having trouble making decisions even about everyday tasks. The therapist also interviews her with a Hamilton Rating Scale for Depression, where Mrs. B scores an 18, with a heavy loading of somatic items that are consistent with her arthritis. The therapist also gathers information about her health history and her current medication regimen.

During this comprehensive intake interview, Mrs. B reports that for the last year, she has had limited contact with her friends and no longer has been interested in spending the time on hobbies that she once enjoyed. She declares that she has a great difficulty concentrating on anything that is not part of caring for her husband. Mrs. B does not endorse any suicidal ideation or any dramatic changes in her weight in the past several months.

The psychologist determines that Mrs. B presents several depressive symptoms that have been present for longer than 2 months: (1) depressed mood, which was evaluated by the GDS, the HRSD, and the clinician's impressions, but not readily admitted to by Mrs. B, (2) decreased interest and pleasure in activities that she used to enjoy, (3) insomnia, and (4) diminished ability to concentrate. There are several points to consider in clarifying this diagnosis. First, there is a strong contribution of both a psychological stressor (caregiving) and physical stressors (arthritis and physically demanding caregiving tasks) to her depressive symptoms. Second, Mrs. B's current presentation does not fit a *full* clinical diagnosis of depression as outlined by the *DSM-IV*, but the magnitude of her complaints have certainly affected her physical, psychological, and social functioning. The psychologist explains her findings to Mrs. B while assuring her that her situation is not one that simply reflects "old age," but that it is a highly treatable psychological disorder.

The therapist offers Mrs. B a short-term therapy program based on the model of cognitive-behavioral psychotherapy. Mrs. B reports no previous history of significant depression and no therapy experience. She is asked to sign a release form to allow the therapist to speak with her physician and a consent for treatment.

HISTORY OF DEPRESSION
AND OLDER ADULTS

In order for clinicians to predict the prognosis or prescribe treatment for a depressed older person, information is needed regarding the history of the individual's disorder (Blazer, 1993). One important piece of information is whether the older person is experiencing his or her first depressive episode or whether this is the recurrence of previous episodes (after some remission). It has been reported that the duration of time between depressive episodes (symptom-free periods) decreases with increased age (Angst, 1980). Information about number of prior episodes in one's lifetime may relate to the prognosis for treatment: it will help the clinician to hypothesize whether the current depression must be managed as a chronic problem or whether more of a full recovery is possible. Blazer (1993) describes recovery in terms of the "rule of thirds": one-third recover and show no return of symptoms; one-third recover but experience chronic repeated episodes of depression; and one-third apparently never recover but remain more or less depressed throughout their lifetime.

Age of onset of the first depressive episode was once believed to distinguish different courses of depression, particularly for those who were experiencing their first episode later in life. Research has shown little evidence to support this belief (Greenwald & Kramer-Ginsberg, 1988). Age of onset is also not predictive of the course of a delusional depression (Nelson, Conwell, Kim, & Mazure, 1989) or of bipolar affective disorders (Carlson, Davenport, & Jenison, 1977).

Major depression alone is quite a challenge for someone of any age, but as mentioned earlier, additional physical or psychiatric diagnoses may accompany a depressive episode. In general, a poorer prognosis is indicated when depression is experienced along with anxiety (Paykel, 1972; Van Valkenburg, Akiskal, Puzantian, & Rosenthal, 1984), psychotic symptoms (Aronson, Shukla, Guyjavarty, Hoff, DiBuono, & Khan, 1988; Coryell, Keller, Lavori, & Endicott, 1990; Tsuang, Wollson, & Fleming, 1979), a severe medical illness (Keitner, Ryan, Miller, Kohn, & Epstein, 1991; Shulberg, McClelland, & Goding, 1987), or a personality disorder (Shea et al., 1990). Be aware, however, that this body of literature has not specifically investigated the comorbidity of these factors and depression in older adults. Future research should attend to these issues to clarify our understanding of the course and prognosis of depression in older adults.

PSYCHOLOGICAL TREATMENT
OF DEPRESSION

Psychotherapy

Older adult outpatients successfully respond to both individual therapy (Gallagher & Thompson, 1982; Gallagher-Thompson, Hanley-Peterson, & Thompson, 1990; Thompson, Gallagher, & Breckenridge, 1987) and group therapy (Arean et al., 1993; Beutler et al., 1987; Gallagher, 1981; Steuer et al., 1984). Not only do older adults respond very well to psychotherapy, but they respond equally well to various therapeutic modalities, particularly when conducted in a brief (16 to 20 session) format, including such modalities as cognitive, behavioral, and psychodynamic therapy (Gallagher, 1981; Gallagher & Thompson, 1982; Thompson et al., 1987). Brief psychotherapy has also been found to be more effective for treating major depression in older adults than no treatment at all (Thompson et al., 1987). Further, a recently completed clinical trial compared cognitive-behavioral therapy alone with desipramine alone (a tricyclic antidepressant with relatively few side effects in the elderly), versus the two in combination (Thompson, Gallagher-Thompson, Hanser, Gantz, & Steffen, 1991; Thompson & Gallagher-Thompson, 1991, 1993). Patients were 102 individuals over age 60 in a current major depressive episode who sought treatment; about half had features of a concurrent personality disorder as well. Results after 4 months of treatment indicated that those in the drug alone condition did most poorly, whereas the combined condition produced most improvement in their depression. Of great interest is the fact that patients who received cognitive-behavioral therapy alone also made significant gains across time: at the conclusion of treatment, their improvement was quite comparable to those who had received both forms of therapy, while most of those patients who had received the drug alone were still clinically depressed (despite the fact that this condition was administered by skilled geropsychiatrists who met regularly with patients and actively managed their negative side effects).

These findings are of particular interest given the current concerns with managed care. Mental health professionals will be required to provide the most effective care in the briefest time, and it is important to know that research has proven the utility of brief therapies with older people. A thorough review of the outcome literature on the effectiveness of psychosocial therapies with depressed older adults can be found in Niederehe (1994) and Teri, Curtis, Gallagher-Thompson, and Thompson (1994).

It is important to note that these conclusions are based on samples of community-dwelling older individuals (primarily) who were active and often in good general health. It is noteworthy that similar findings have been found when psychotherapy outcome research has included older adults with cardiovascular and respiratory disease (Godbole & Verinis, 1974), with severe visual defects (including blindness) (Evans, Werkhoven, & Fox, 1982), and depressed older adults with chronic physical disorders such as arthritis or hypertension (Steuer et al., 1984). Short-term cognitive-behavioral and psychodynamic psychotherapies are also effective interventions for distressed older people who are caring for a frail elder with cognitive impairment (Gallagher-Thompson & Steffen, 1994). Here it is noteworthy that a significant interaction was found between length of time as a caregiver and treatment modality: cognitive-behavioral therapy was more effective than psychodynamic therapy for long-term caregivers (those in the role longer than 40 months), while the reverse was true for shorter-term caregivers. This may reflect the fact that cognitive-behavioral therapy permitted caregivers to gain control of their mood, thoughts, and activities, which was particularly helpful as their relative deteriorated further and lost more and more functional ability.

Even though older adults respond to psychotherapy as well as young adults, psychotherapy with older adults does require some special considerations (Knight, 1986; Thompson, Davies, Gallagher, & Krantz, 1986). First, as mentioned earlier, older adults are not socialized to the process of psychotherapy and may view it similar to a visit to a physician who can offer a "cure" or "quick fix." Thus, the therapist has a responsibility to educate older clients about the therapy process reinforcing the client's responsibility to take an active role in the therapy, which may mean between-session homework assignments, setting goals with the therapist, or other activities. In addition, older adults may have specific beliefs or assumptions about their own depression that need to be discussed up front, as Mrs. B did when she thought that her depression was a normal consequence of aging.

At times, therapy must accommodate to some of the natural aging changes in sensory perception and cognitive slowing (Knight, 1986; Thompson et al., 1986). There are some basic techniques that can aid an older adult in the therapy process so these changes do not detract from the therapeutic issues at hand. For example, older adults can be assisted in remembering the therapy material by asking them to keep a notebook of the work as well as take an active role in frequently summarizing the work done in each session. Therapists must be prepared to cover less material with an older client to ensure that significant points of the therapy are retained. In addition, simple adjustments in the physical environment can be quite helpful. For example, selecting a therapy room with easy physical access (e.g., the ground floor or right by the elevator), adequate lighting, less susceptibility to outside noises) and moving the chairs closer together can help the older client concentrate better in session.

Some therapists (particularly those using the more "structured" therapies such as a cognitive-behavioral approach) may also need to find a comfortable way to interrupt tangential older adults in order to keep the session focused. This process reflects the need for therapists to consider their views about treating older adults. Specifically, does the therapist have strong beliefs about whether older adults can change? Is a young therapist comfortable working with an older client? Knight (1986) encourages younger therapists to consider that older adults bring to the session a set of moral values, religious beliefs, family values, and often increased somatization that reflect the cohort differences. Thus, a therapist must be willing to provide treatment within the context of the older adults' value system.

In our center, we have a clear preference for use of cognitive-behavioral therapy with depressed older adults for several reasons. First, as indicated earlier, there is a growing body of literature on the efficacy of this model of treatment compared to others that have been empirically studied with the elderly. Recently, a meta-analysis of psychotherapy outcome studies with the elderly, published by Scogin and McElreath (1994), found that effect sizes were comparable to those reported in other meta-analytic studies of psychotherapy with nonaged samples, with the median effect size being .78. They also found that various modes of treatment were effective, though individual therapy was more effective than group therapy, overall. Finally, the average effect size for cognitive therapy in these studies was .85 versus .41 for psychodynamic therapy. Although only 17 studies were available for the meta-analysis, these results are suggestive of the strength of cognitive therapy and its efficacy with older adults. Second, our own scholarly review of the literature on the results of various forms of psychotherapy led us to conclude that: "On balance, the cognitive and behavioral approaches have been shown to elicit the most consistent responses from distressed elders" (Gallagher-Thompson & Thompson, 1995, p. 374). Although many questions remain to be addressed, such as specifying the most effective match of patient to treatment method or modality, there seems to be a general acceptance of cognitive-behavioral approaches by older adults, particularly those who want more control over their lives and their distressing symptoms.

Finally, over the years we have developed several treatment protocols for implementing cognitive-behavioral therapy in both individual and group formats with depressed elders. The fact that we have been able to "manualize" this approach has aided us in teaching it to psychologists and psychiatrists in training and has provided a platform for our own outcome research. While we are not saying that this is a panacea for all psychological/psychiatric problems of later life, we do believe that cognitive-behavioral methods can be used flexibly with many types of problems with good results.

It is beyond the scope of this chapter to provide detailed information about the mechanics of doing cognitive-behavioral therapy with depressed older adults, as well as the utility of this approach with other common late-life problems. For these purposes, the reader is referred to publications such as DeVries and Gallagher-Thompson (1994) on crisis intervention; Dick and Gallagher-Thompson (1995) on treatment of more complex depression; Florsheim, Leavesley, Hanley-Peterson, and Gallagher-Thompson (1991) on incorporating more of an interpersonal focus into the approach; Gantz, Gallagher-Thompson, and

Rodman (1991) on facilitation of inhibited grief; Qualls (1988) on the use of cognitive-behavioral therapy with distressed older couples and families; Rodman, Gantz, Schneider, and Gallagher-Thompson (1991) on therapy issues when treatment involves medication as well as psychotherapy; and finally, Thompson et al. (1991), which presents more of the basic "nuts and bolts" of the approach for treatment of patients in individual therapy.

Space limitations also prevent us from discussing in detail the use of psychoeducational approaches with this population, but they will be mentioned, and the interested reader is encouraged to seek out the references provided for a fuller perspective. Psychoeducational approaches combine features of both group therapy and educational programs, in that usually specific content is taught (including certain cognitive-behavioral skills, such as methods for inducing relaxation and methods of challenging negative thoughts) along with discussion of one's individual experience in a supportive and sharing atmosphere. Psychoeducational groups have been widely used in a preventive manner (for example, with mildly depressed older individuals to forestall the development of a full-blown clinical depression; see Thompson, Gallagher, Nies, & Epstein, 1983, for an illustration) and also for treatment purposes for certain types of problems (see Gallagher-Thompson & DeVries, 1994; Lovett & Gallagher, 1988; Pinkston & Linsk, 1984, all of which describe their use with distressed family caregivers). A recent meta-analysis of interventions for family caregivers (which included several psychoeducational programs) was conducted by Knight, Lutzky, and Macofsky-Urban (1993). They found varying effect sizes for psychoeducational groups, depending on length and complexity of the program and type of outcome measure employed. Some studies (with clear content focus, using well-validated outcome measures) had high effect sizes (above .65), while others that included a great deal of content in a short time had much less impact. Thus, while it can be said that psychoeducational programs offer a promising alternative for treatment that is more cost effective than individual therapy or traditional open-ended group therapy, more research is needed about the type of patient most likely to benefit from these much less intensive therapeutic efforts, as well as what the most appropriate mix of content and process should be for best results.

MEDICAL TREATMENT OF DEPRESSION IN OLDER ADULTS

General Considerations for Prescribing Medications to Older Adults

Prescribing medications for older adults requires an understanding of the age-related sensitivities to side effects as well as older adults' use of medications. Medications are metabolized slowly in older adults, prolonging and enhancing side effects as well as potentially increasing toxicity due to drug interactions. Drug toxicity due to adverse interactions is further complicated by the fact that older people may take an average of 13 medications per year, prescribed by different physicians, who may not be aware of the total medication regimen

(Blazer, Federspiel, Ray, & Schaffner, 1983; Lamy, Salzman, & Nevis-Olsen, 1993; Salzman, 1990). Older people also take a high number of over-the-counter medications, which are not always reported to doctors. Finally, older people are the age group that shows the greatest misuse of medications, as they make frequent dosage errors, mix prescribed and over-the-counter medications, as well as share medications with others. Health care professionals must be proactive in educating, monitoring, and asking about all medications taken by the older adults they see. It is also necessary to obtain a detailed medical history to further rule out the possibility of drug interactions as well as identify those at risk for cardiac complications from antidepressants (Alexopoulos, 1993). Prescriptions must be simple and direct, and it is even recommended that geriatric physicians work with the older person's pharmacist to reduce usage errors (Blazer, 1993).

Pharmacological Treatment of Depression in Older Adults

Pharmacological treatment of depression can be quite effective for older adults, but the greatest challenge is selecting an antidepressant whose side effects are tolerable (Alexopoulos, 1993; Blazer, 1993; Salzman, 1994). It is believed that most antidepressants are equally effective, but the varying intensity of side effects make some less useful for older people. The most common side effects of traditional tricyclic antidepressants are anticholinergic side effects, orthostatic hypotension, sedation, and cardiac toxicity (Alexopoulos, 1993; Blazer, 1993; Salzman, 1994). Anticholinergic side effects include dry mouth, constipation, urinary retention, increased anxiety, confusion, and restlessness. Severe dry mouth can result in decreased food intake and malnutrition, or even the loss of some dental fillings. Mild constipation can be helped with a high-fiber diet, but severe constipation can result in paralysis of the bowel. The milder manifestation of urinary retention is difficulty with initiation, but a severe form is bladder infection. Orthostatic hypotension refers to a significant drop in blood pressure from a sitting or a lying position to standing. Thus, the older person will feel unsteady and dizzy, becoming at risk for falls, head injuries, and broken bones. For the sedating side effects, an older depressed person with insomnia may initially benefit from increased sleep, but as the depression lifts, the sedation may remain. If an older adult is already experiencing cardiac symptoms, it is recommended that consistent electrocardiographic (ECG) monitoring be done throughout the pharmacological trial.

Often these side effects can be so unpleasant that older adults request to stop the medication or will stop taking it on their own. Medication trials frequently end prematurely because of the assumption that the older person will not respond to antidepressants that ultimately foster hopelessness and despair about this otherwise treatable condition. It is recommended that physicians be patient with the "trial and error" approach necessary to match the older person with a medication that has the most tolerable side effects (Salzman, 1994). To minimize side effects, physicians should start with a very low dosage and slowly increase dosage by approximately 10-mg increments every few days while monitoring blood pressure and pulse rate (Alexopoulos, 1993; Blazer, 1993). In general, antidepressants can be quite effective for the older person, yet research within the past decade has demonstrated that the greatest gains are seen when older people participate in a combined treatment of medications and psychotherapy (Thompson et al., 1991, 1993).

Tricyclic Antidepressants

For years, tricyclic antidepressant medications have been the most widely used first-line treatment for depression at any age but particularly older adults (Alexopoulos, 1993; Blazer, 1993; Gershon, Plotkin, & Jarvik, 1988; Salzman, 1993). Differences in the intensity of the side effects divide this group into two domains. The first group, known as the tertiary amines, which include amytriptyline, imipramine, and doxepin, are less useful for older people because of the severity of anticholinergic side effects (Alexopoulos, 1993; Blazer, 1993). The second group, with milder side effects, known as the secondary amines, includes nortriptyline, protriptyline, desipramine, amoxapine, and maprotiline. Physicians must be careful about prescribing an antidepressant without knowing the complete medication regimen of the older adult. For example, if a tricyclic interacts with a barbituate, the effects of the antidepressant are reduced. If the antidepressant interacts with an anticholinergic, confusion or delirium will be enhanced.

Research has demonstrated that desipramine and nortriptyline are quite effective for treating geriatric depression and have the most tolerable side effect profile of the whole tricyclic group (Alexopoulos, 1993; Georgotas, Friedman, & McCarthy, 1983). Another distinct advantage for the choice of nortriptyline or desipramine is that plasma levels in the older adult can accurately guide dosage for these medications better than other antidepressants (Alexopoulos, 1993; Blazer, 1993).

Monoamine Oxidase Inhibitors

Monoamine oxidase inhibitors (MAOIs) are useful in treating older people because monoamine oxidase is believed to be responsible for metabolizing mood-regulating neurotransmitters such as serotonin and norepinephrine (Alexopoulos, 1993). One explanation of a biological determinant of depression claims that depressive symptoms more likely occur when norepinephrine and serotonin are depleted, thus inhibiting the depletion (from the MAOI) will counteract the depression (Alexopoulos, 1993; Robinson, Nies, Davis, & Bunney, 1972). The efficacy of MAOIs in treating geriatric depression has been well documented (Ashford & Ford, 1979; Georgotas et al., 1983; Jenike, 1984; Salzman, 1990), yet these medications have a complicated profile of side effects. First, MAOIs have a higher risk for drug interactions than other classes of medications. For example, the interaction of an MAOI and a tricyclic can increase the antidepressant effect to the point of a hypertensive crisis (Blazer, 1993). Second, the interaction of MAOIs and foods with tyramine can also send a patient into a hypertensive crisis. Consequently, patients must get nutritional education as well as be proactive in their food choices to ensure the safe use of this medication. Other side effects include weight gain and severe orthostatic hypotension. It is recommended that blood pressure baselines be obtained and consistently monitored throughout the treatment (Blazer, 1993). Older adults should be informed that they can manage the drop in blood pressure by rising from a sitting or resting place very slowly and using stable supports to steady their posture.

MAOIs are typically used with younger adults experiencing atypical depression (e.g., anxious depression). There are few empirical data about the efficacy of these drugs and atypical depressions in older adults. Clinical reports as well as studies with small samples claim that MAOIs, particularly phenelzine, can be effective for older adults experiencing anxious depression (Alexopoulos, 1993; Ashford & Ford, 1979; Blazer, 1993).

Selective Serotonin Reuptake Inhibitors

The selective serotonin reuptake inhibitors (SSRIs) are a new generation of antidepressants. This group includes trazodone, sertraline (Zoloft), fluoxetine (Prozac), and paroxetine (Paxil). These drugs show the mildest profile for anticholinergic side effects and cardiac toxicity but can cause difficulties with orthostatic hypotension and sedation (except for fluoxetine), particularly a drug hangover the next morning (Blazer, 1993). Empirical research has reported that trazodone and imipramine (a tricyclic) are comparable therapeutically, but trazodone had significantly more tolerable side effects (Gerner, Esterbrook, Steuer, & Jarvik, 1980).

Fluoxetine appears to be far more tolerable than any tricyclic, as it has significantly fewer anticholinergic side effects, minimal sedation, and fewer complications with detrimental cardiac effects or orthostatic hypotension. Yet fluoxetine still can cause difficulties with insomnia, nausea, nervousness, and weight loss, as well as having a somewhat long elimination half-life (Alexopoulos, 1993; Salzman, 1990). The efficacy of fluoxetine has not been adequately studied in older patients. Paroxetine is the newest of the SSRIs and is believed to have the fewest of all side effects, but to date it has had limited use with older adults and no empirical work has been reported. It does, however, have a very short half-life (24 hours), no active (potentially problematic) metabolites, and uses a simple once-per-day dosage schedule. Therefore, it is likely to be widely used with elders in the future.

Electroconvulsive Therapy

The safety and the efficacy of electroconvulsive therapy (ECT) for late-life depression has been well documented. Several reports indicate that the average proportion of patients who experience a full recovery is over 50%, with another 20% to 30% considered "much improved" (Alexopoulos, 1993; Benbow, 1987; Godber, Rosenvinge, Wilkinson, & Smithes, 1987; Karlinsky & Shulman, 1984;

Kramer, 1987). It has also been shown that among those who improve with ECT, young and older adults respond alike (Benbow, 1989; Blazer, 1993).

The older patient with the best prognosis is one with severe depression who has not responded to more conventional treatments, such as medication or psychotherapy. Such severe depression might also include high suicide risk, severe appetite and sleep difficulties, psychomotor disturbances, and even psychotic symptoms (Benbow, 1991; Salzman, 1982; Weiner, 1982). ECT may also be effective for depressed patients with concurrent medical illnesses (Coryell, Pohl, & Zimmerman, 1985; Jenike, 1985) or psychotic depression (Mulsant, Rosen, Thornton, & Zubenko, 1991). It may be less effective for older adults who have dementia (Zorumski, Rubin, & Burke, 1988).

Blazer (1993) reports three contraindications for use of ECT with older adults. The first is if the individual has a lesion in the central nervous system with accompanying intracranial pressure. The seizure that accompanies ECT could exacerbate this pressure and potentially herniate the brain stem. The second high-risk area is for patients with cardiovascular difficulties such as coronary artery disease or hypertensive cardiovascular disease. Finally, ECT does not interact well with many medications, such as anticonvulsants, antihypertensives, or antidepressants. In fact, it is recommended that the patient discontinue these medications until the ECT trial is complete and then resume them as part of maintenance and relapse prevention.

To maintain the safety of ECT, a comprehensive medical work-up is necessary. This work-up should rule out cardiovascular disease, previously undetected medical illnesses, neurological disease, presence of organic brain syndrome, or compression fractures of the spine or degenerative spinal disease (Blazer, 1993). Along with the medical work-up, it is recommended that psychiatrists carefully educate the patient and family about the procedure, which may include a tour of the facilities to further allay anxiety about the procedure (Blazer, 1993).

ECT is often an inpatient procedure that can be administered three times a week for several weeks. Prior to the procedure, patients are given a short-acting anesthetic and a mild muscle relaxant. Two electrodes placed unilaterally are preferred for older patients to minimize the temporary posttreatment confusion that may occur (Alexopoulos, 1993). A brief pulse current begins for an initial trial of a 25- to 30-second seizure. If this fails (i.e., there is no seizure) then a second trial is attempted after 30 to 60 seconds. It is common for older adults not to seize on the first try. Mild side effects include headache, nausea, and muscle pains. There are also reports of mild memory complaints and posttraumatic amnesia, but decreased memory performance consistent with complains has not been documented in the current research literature (Blazer, 1993).

COURSE OF TREATMENT

The following is an explanation of Mrs. B's course of treatment within a cognitive-behavioral framework. This model has been selected due to the authors' expertise in this area and the general consensus in the available literature as to the efficacy of this approach with older adults. In brief, the basis of cognitive-behavioral therapy is the interrelationship of thoughts, emotions, behavior, and health. This theory states that negative emotions are initiated by automatic dysfunctional beliefs, occurring so quickly that the patient is not even aware of their existence. These beliefs, in turn, affect one's future choice of behaviors or activities. For example, one of Mrs. B's beliefs that is causing her depressed mood is "I am the only person capable of helping my husband," which ultimately affects her choice not to spend time with her friends, which further depresses her mood and may even affect her level of pain.

Cognitive therapy includes (1) the active monitoring of these beliefs to recognize dysfunctional patterns, (2) challenging the evidence for these beliefs, and (3) replacing these beliefs with ones that result in more tolerable emotions (Beck, Rush, Shaw, & Emery, 1979). The behavioral component to this therapy is based on the correlation of high pleasant activity and high mood (Lewinsohn, Antonuccio, Steinmentz, & Teri, 1984; Lewinsohn, Munoz, Youngren, & Zeiss, 1986). Thus, actual behaviors to increase pleasant events, time for oneself, and even relaxation exercises are built into the therapy. Additional components of the therapy process include the strong collaboration of the therapist and client to establish clear and measurable goals for treatment. Let us now return to Mrs. B.

Mrs. B and the therapist identify two primary goals for therapy: (1) to replace her dysfunctional thoughts about caregiving with more helpful ones and (2) to increase pleasant events and time for herself. Mrs. B was initially doubtful of seeing any change in the second goal, but she was open to trying.

Cognitive Interventions. Mrs. B was taught to monitor, challenge, and replace her dysfunctional thought patterns with the use of a *Dysfunctional Thought Record* (*DTR*), a five-column form requiring the monitoring of the distressing event, the beliefs that are present, the emotions that are felt, the challenges to the dysfunctional thoughts, and the new emotional consequences (see Figure 9-1). In this example, Mrs. B was upset when she perceived that her daughter was not considerate of Mrs. B's caregiver distress. She employed such unhelpful thought patterns (see column 2) as *jumping to conclusions* regarding her perceptions of her daughter's unwillingness to help; *should statements* regarding her expectations of her daughter's behavior, and *catastrophizing* about her husband's reaction to a change in his schedule.

Several techniques were employed to change these dysfunctional thoughts. The therapist used cognitive challenges to Mrs. B's assumptions that good caregivers must be at home all day and that her children should recognize (on their own) that she could use some help without her asking. The therapist pointed out her thought patterns, remarking that she often jumped to conclusions about what other people thought about her as well as envisioning the most dramatic outcome to future situations. The therapist also invited Mrs. B to try role-play exercises where she practiced assertiveness skills and got the chance to understand other people's point of view. Eventually Mrs. B was able to independently challenge her dysfunctional thoughts to replace them with ones that initiated more positive emotions (see Figure 9-1, columns 4 and 5).

Behavioral Interventions. The initial stage of therapy also involved an evaluation of the types of activities that Mrs. B once enjoyed. This evaluation was done

Distressing Event	Negative Beliefs	Emotions	Helpful Beliefs	New Emotions
Daughter calls to cancel a visit and asks her mother to go out to lunch the next day. As a result, Mrs. B yells at her daughter, "You know I can't leave him!"	She never wants to help me. She should offer to help me. If I get someone else to stay with him it will ruin his day and make things worse for me. DYSFUNCTIONAL THOUGHT PATTERNS: Jumping to conclusions, should statements, and catastrophizing.	Anger Resentment Depression	She may not know that I need help because I always say that everything is OK. I should check this out! I also do not know how my husband would be with another caregiver- I have never tried -- I have no evidence for this.	Less resentful Hopeful

Figure 9-1. Mrs. B's Dysfunctional Thought Record.

using the Older Adult's Pleasant Events Scale (an interested reader should refer to Gallagher & Thompson, 1981, for an explanation of this measure). It was discovered that Mrs. B has enjoyed reading, visiting museums, lunching with friends, and walking in her neighborhood and the adjoining park. The therapist and Mrs. B developed a program to slowly incorporate these pleasant activities into her daily schedule. Mrs. B had several tasks within this program: (1) to do the actual pleasant activities, (2) to keep track of which activities she's done, and (3) to rate her mood on a daily basis on a scale from 0 (very depressed) to 9 (very happy). It was explained to Mrs. B that as she increased her daily, pleasant activities, her mood would increase as well.

Mrs. B generated the list of activities with ease but articulated a good deal of resistance in actually starting. She began to monitor her mood on a daily basis, but no change was seen, which is consistent with the fact that she showed no increase in her pleasant activities. To understand her resistance, it was necessary to implement cognitive strategies to identify and challenge her negative beliefs about taking time for herself. It was revealed that Mrs. B thought that her needs were not important, that she was the only person capable of helping her husband "the way it should be done."

At first Mrs. B agreed to spend ½ hour each morning reading a novel, which she was able to do 5 out of 7 days. Not only did her mood monitoring reveal a small elevation in mood on the days that she made time to read, but she reported that reading alone had a calming effect on her tension and mood. She also explained that on the days that she read she was more focused on her caregiving tasks. This time was soon expanded to 1 hour of reading each morning. Thus these positive outcomes reinforced Mrs. B's continued compliance with these techniques.

Eventually Mrs. B added daily walks to her list of pleasant events. This activity had multiple benefits for her. Not only did the activity and time for herself help her mood in general, but it was of additional benefit for her arthritis pain. Thus, as Mrs.

B managed her pain more independently, she had more energy to do both the caregiving tasks as well as activities for herself. Finding time for herself required Mrs. B to be more comfortable and to believe that she deserved a break as well as be assertive in asking others to help her. With all of these gains, Mrs. B's level of depression (as measured on the GDS) was at a 6 (nondepressed range) after 16 sessions of individual therapy. After termination, she returned for two "booster sessions," held at 4 weeks and 8 weeks after completing her treatment.

Follow-Up

During the first booster session, Mrs. B's GDS was a 4. She reported beginning each day with a relaxation exercise as well as setting aside time in the afternoon to focus her thoughts and reduce tension. She explained that her reduction in tension has made a noticeable difference in her pain level and in her ability to manage caregiving tasks. She also described her continued use of the DTR to quickly replace her negative thoughts regarding frustrating caregiving situations. Mrs. B also reported that she continued to do pleasant events each day such as walking in the neighborhood, reading, or taking care of her plants. She still supported breaks from her caregiving duties, but she was anxious about contacting her friends after such a long time. A DTR was completed during this session allowing Mrs. B to acknowledge that she was catastrophizing and jumping to conclusions about her friends' opinions of her. The therapist involved Mrs. B in a role-play to practice what she would say to her friends as she introduced new social interactions. She was given the homework to phone three friends as well as maintain her skills before the next booster session.

At the final booster session, Mrs. B's GDS was 2, and she demonstrated a maintenance of the skills that she learned in therapy stating, "It's becoming a comfortable style of my life." Mrs. B reported that she had called several friends to "catch-up," and she found that none of her catastrophized outcomes were realized. In fact, one friend joined her on several daily walks around the neighborhood and then stayed for lunch. Her friend told her that she knew of someone who was looking for a new job as a paid caregiver, and she thought Mrs. B could use the help. Mrs. B admitted that at first she rejected the idea, but after completing a DTR she realized that she wanted more continuous contact with her friends, and this help would give her the opportunity to leave her home for pleasant events. Mrs. B reported to the therapist that she had scheduled a meeting with the paid caregiver, and she was impressed with the woman's kind demeanor towards her husband. The therapist remarked that Mrs. B had made considerable gains in accepting help from others and making herself a priority. No further follow-up sessions were scheduled.

SUMMARY

In general, we have shown that the diagnosis of depression in older adults is quite a challenging task, requiring attention to multiple disciplines with minimal reliance on the current standards (*DSM-IV*; American Psychiatric Association, 1994). Without standardized diagnostic criteria, it is difficult to state incidence of depression in older adults with certainty. This debate is well documented in the literature with some explaining that incidence of depression in older adults is less than what is found in the younger population (Blazer, 1994), while others suggest that it is severely underdiagnosed (Rapp et al., 1988).

One issue of less debate is that both missed and the "falsely positive" diagnosed cases of depression place older adults in potentially dangerous situations. An undetected, (thus untreated) case of depression can leave an older person with increased despair, isolation, and an increased risk of suicide. On the other hand, those given a false-positive diagnosis may receive treatment that they neither want nor need, which can have negative consequences for their quality of life. To increase diagnostic accuracy, clinicians must be sensitive to distinguishing conditions whose symptoms overlap with symptoms of depression, such as bereavement, cognitive decline, medication side effects, and health complaints. A clinician must also be aware of how the normal aging process presents some of the same indicators of depression using the *DSM-IV* criteria, such as health concerns and reduction in sleep. Furthermore, older people are less likely to describe themselves as "depressed," instead using less intense descriptors such as "feeling blue" or "under the weather." It is for these reasons that clinicians should consider multiple sources of information, such as information from family members as well as the patients, along with a self-report and an interview to assess depression and related conditions.

It is important for the reader to appreciate that older adults respond quite well to both pharmacological and brief psychological treatments of depression. Individual therapy, group therapy, family therapy, and psychoeducational groups have all been used successfully with older persons and have been found efficacious when carefully studied in controlled research. Overall, it can be said that most forms of psychotherapy with older adults require no change to the basic therapeutic model being used, but is may require changes to the therapy process, such as adapting the session and the environment to account for cognitive changes as well as vision or hearing difficulties that are common in older adults.

Research on the efficacy of psychotherapy with older adults has largely attended to the depressed older person with few complicating additional diagnoses. Future research should address the kinds and duration of psychotherapy needed to treat depressed older adults with significant personality disorders or with other concomitant psychiatric diagnoses such as substance abuse, posttraumatic stress disorder, generalized anxiety disorder, and the like. Additional research is also needed to more clearly specify patient characteristics that would be most predictive of positive outcome for a given type of therapy. For example, depressed elders over age 80 (the "old-old") or those with mild cognitive impairment and significant health problems (the "frail elderly") may respond better to X or Y form of treatment; this won't be known until controlled studies have been done with patients having these characteristics.

Finally, practitioners need to be trained in the special issues of late life so that more trained clinicians are available in the next century to treat the ever-increasing proportion of elders in the U.S. population.

ACKNOWLEDGMENTS.   This project was supported in part by the National
Institute of Mental Health (Grants MH19104 and MH37196) to Larry W.
Thompson, Ph.D., Principal Investigator.

REFERENCES

Albert, M. S. (1994). Brief assessments of cognitive function in the elderly. In M. P. Lawton & J. Teresi
    (Eds.), *Annual review of gerontology and geriatrics* (Vol. 14, pp. 93–106). New York: Springer.
Alexopoulos, G. S. (1993). Treatment of depression. In C. Salzman (Ed.), *Clinical geriatric psycho-
    pharmacology* (pp. 137–176). Baltimore, MD: Williams & Wilkins.
American Psychiatric Association. (1987). *Diagnostic and statistical manual of mental disorder* (3rd
    ed., revised). Washington, DC: Author.
American Psychiatric Association. (1994). *Diagnostic and statistical manual of mental disorder* (4th
    ed.). Washington, DC: Author.
Angst, J. (1980). Course of unipolar depressive, bipolar manic-depressive, and schizoid affective
    disorders: Results of a longitudinal study. *Fortschritte Der Neurologie-Psyciatrie, 48,* 3–30.
Arean, P., Perri, M. G., Nezu, A., Schein, R., Christopher, F., & Joseph, T. (1993). Comparative
    effectiveness of social problem-solving therapy and reminiscence therapy as treatments for
    depression in older adults. *Journal of Consulting and Clinical Psychology, 61,* 1003–1010.
Aronson, P. A., Shukla, S., Gujavarty, K., Hoff, A., DiBuono, M., & Khan, E. (1988). Relapse and
    delusional depression: Retrospective study of the course of treatment. *Comprehensive Psychia-
    try, 29,* 12–21.
Ashford, W., & Ford, C. V. (1979). Use of monoamine oxidase inhibitors in elderly patients. *American
    Journal of Psychiatry, 136,* 1466–1467.
Baker, F. M. (1991). A contrast: Geriatric depression versus depression in younger age groups. *Journal
    of the American Medical Association, 83,* 340–344.
Beck, A. T., Rush, J., Shaw, B., & Emery, G. (1979). *Cognitive therapy of depression.* New York:
    Guilford.
Beck, A. T., Ward, C. H., Mendelson, M., Mock, J., & Erbaugh, J. (1961). An inventory for measuring
    depression. *Archives of General Psychiatry, 4,* 561–571.
Benbow, S. M. (1987). The use of electroconvulsive therapy in old-age psychiatry. *International
    Journal of Geriatric Psychiatry, 2,* 25–30.
Benbow, S. M. (1989). The role of electroconvulsive therapy in the treatment of depressive illness in
    old age. *British Journal of Psychiatry, 155,* 147–152.
Benbow, S. M. (1991). Old-age psychiatrists view of the use of ECT. *International Journal of Geriatric
    Psychiatry, 6,* 317–322.
Beutler, L. E., Scogin, F., Kirkish, D. S., Corbishley, A., Hamblin, D., Meredith, K., Potter, R., Bamford,
    C. R., & Levenson, A. I. (1987). Group cognitive therapy and alprazolam in the treatment of
    depression in older adults. *Journal of Consulting and Clinical Psychology, 55,* 550–556.
Blazer, D. G. (1993). *Depression in late life* (2nd ed.). St. Louis: C. V. Mosby.
Blazer, D. (1994). Epidemiology of late-life depression. In L. Schneider, C. F. Reynolds, B. Lebowitz, &
    A. Friedhoff (Eds.), *Diagnosis and treatment of depression in late life* (pp. 9–19). Washington,
    DC.: American Psychiatric Press.
Blazer, D. G., Federspiel, C. F., Ray, W. A., & Schaffner, W. (1983). The risk of anticholinergic toxicity
    in the elderly: A study of prescribing practices in two populations. *Journal of Gerontology, 38*(1),
    31–35.
Blazer, D. G., Hughes, D. C., & George, L. K. (1987). The epidemiology of depression in an elderly
    community population. *Gerontologist, 27,* 281–287.
Braekhus, A., Laake, K., & Engedal, K. (1992). The mini-mental state examination: Identifying the
    most efficient variables for detecting cognitive impairment in the elderly. *Journal of the Ameri-
    can Geriatrics Society, 40,* 1139–1145.
Breckenridge, J., Gallagher, D., Thompson, L. W., & Peterson, J. (1986). Characteristic depressive
    symptoms of elder bereaved. *Journal of Gerontology, 41,* 163–168.

Brink, T. L., Yesavage, J. A., Lum, O., Hersema, P. H., Adey, M., & Rose, T. L. (1982). Screening tests for geriatric depression. *Clinical Gerontologist, 1,* 37–43.

Carlson, G. A., Davenport, Y. B., & Jenison, K. (1977). A comparison of adolescence and late-onset bipolar manic-depressive illness. *American Journal of Psychiatry, 134,* 919–922.

Coryell, W., Keller, M., Lavori, P., & Endicott, J. (1990). Affective syndromes, psychotic features, in prognosis. I. Depression. *Archives of General Psychiatry, 47,* 651–657.

Coryell, W., Pohl, B., & Zimmerman, M. (1985). Outcome following electroconvulsive therapy: A comparison of primary and secondary depression. *Convulsive Therapy, 1,* 10–14.

Dessonville, C., Gallagher, D., Thompson, L. W., Finnell, K., & Lewinsohn, P. (1982). The relationship of age and health status to symptoms of depression in normal and depressed elderly. *Essence, 5*(2), 99–117.

DeVries, H., & Gallagher-Thompson, D. (1994). Crises with geriatric patients. In F. Dattilio & A. Freeman (Eds.), *Cognitive-behavior therapy and crisis intervention* (pp. 200–218). New York: Guilford Press.

Dick, L. P., & Gallagher-Thompson, D. (1995). Cognitive therapy with the core beliefs of a distressed, lonely caregiver. *Journal of Cognitive Psychotherapy: An International Quarterly, 9*(4), 215–227.

Endicott, J., & Spitzer, R. L. (1978). A diagnostic interview for affective disorders and schizophrenia. *Archives of General Psychiatry, 35,* 837–844.

Engedal, K., Haugen, P. K., Gilje, K., & Laake, P. (1988). Efficacy of short mental tests in the detection of mental impairment in old age. *Comprehensive Gerontology, 2,* 87–93.

Evans, R. L., Werkhoven, W., & Fox, H. R. (1982). Treatment of social isolation and loneliness in a sample of visually impaired elderly persons. *Psychological Reports, 51,* 103–108.

Fitten, L. J., Morley, J. E., Gross, P. L., Petry, S. D., & Cole, K. D. (1989). Depression: UCLA geriatric grand rounds. *Journal of the American Geriatrics Society, 37*(5), 459–472.

Florsheim, M., Leavesley, G., Hanley-Peterson, P., & Gallagher-Thompson, D. (1991). An expansion of the A-B-C approach to cognitive/behavioral therapy. *Clinical Gerontologist, 10*(4), 65–69.

Folstein, M. F., Folstein, S. E., & McHugh, P. R. (1975). "Mini-mental state": A practical method for grading the cognitive state of patients for the clinician. *Journal of Psychiatric Research, 12,* 189–198.

Futterman, A., Thompson, L. W., Gallagher-Thompson, D., & Ferris, R. (1995). Depression in later life: Epidemiology, assessment, etiology and treatment. In E. E. Beckham & W. R. Leber (Eds.), *Handbook of depression* (2nd ed., pp. 494–525). New York: Guilford Press.

Gallagher, D. (1981). Behavioral group therapy with elderly depressives: An experimental study. In D. Upper & S. M. Ross (Eds.), *Behavioral group therapy: An annual review* (pp. 187–224). Champaign, IL: Research Press.

Gallagher, D. (1986). The Beck Depression Inventory and older adults: Review of its development and utility. *Clinical Gerontologist, 5,* 149–163.

Gallagher, D., Nies, G., & Thompson, L. W. (1982). Reliability of the Beck Depression Inventory with older adults. *Journal of Consulting and Clinical Psychology, 50*(1), 152–153.

Gallagher-Thompson, D., & DeVries, H. (1994). "Coping with Frustration" classes: Development and preliminary outcomes with women who care for relatives with dementia. *The Gerontologist, 34,* 548–552.

Gallagher-Thompson, D., Hanley-Peterson, P., & Thompson, L. W. (1990). Maintenance of gains versus relapse following brief psychotherapy for depression. *Journal of Consulting and Clinical Psychology, 58,* 371–374.

Gallagher-Thompson, D., & Steffen, A. (1994). Comparative effectiveness of cognitive/behavioral and brief psychodynamic psychotherapies for the treatment of depression in family caregivers. *Journal of Consulting and Clinical Psychology, 62,* 543–549.

Gallagher-Thompson, D., & Thompson, L. W. (1995). Psychotherapy with older adults in theory and practice. In B. Bongar & L. Beutler (Eds.), *Comprehensive textbook of psychotherapy: Theory and practice* (pp. 359–379). London: Oxford University Press.

Gallagher, D., & Thompson, L. W. (1982). Treatment of major depressive disorders in older outpatients with brief psychotherapies. *Psychotherapy: Research and Practice, 19,* 482–490.

Gallagher, D., & Thompson, L. W. (1981). *Depression in the elderly: A behavioral treatment manual.* Los Angeles: University of Southern California Press.

Gantz, F., Gallagher-Thompson, D., & Rodman, J. (1991). Cognitive behavioral facilitation of inhibited grief. In A. Freeman & F. Dattilio (Eds.), *Comprehensive casebook of cognitive/behavior therapy* (pp. 201–207). New York: Plenum Press.

Georgotas, A., Friedman, E., & McCarthy, M. (1983). Resistant geriatric depression and therapeutic response to monoamine oxidase inhibitors. *Biological Psychiatry, 18,* 195–205.

Gerner, R., Esterbrook, W., Steuer, J., & Jarvik, L. (1980). Treatment of geriatric depression with trazadone, imipramine, and placebo; a double blind study. *Journal of Clinical Psychiatry, 41,* 216–221.

Gershon, S. C., Plotkin, D. A., & Jarvik, L. F. (1988). Antidepressant drug studies, 1964–1986: Empirical evidence for aging patients. *Journal of Clinical Psychopharmacology, 8,* 311–322.

Godber, C., Rosenvinge, H., Wilkinson, D., & Smithes, J. (1987). Depression in old age: Prognosis after ECT. *International Journal of Geriatric Psychiatry, 2,* 19–24.

Godbole, A., & Verinis, J. S. (1974). Brief psychotherapy in the treatment of emotional disorders in physically ill geriatric patients. *Gerontologist, 14,* 143–148.

Greenwald, B. S., & Kramer-Ginsberg, E. (1988). Age onset in geriatric depression: Relationship to clinical variables. *Journal of Affective Disorders, 15,* 61–68.

Hamilton, M. (1967). Development of a rating scale for primary depressive illness. *British Journal of Social and Clinical Psychology, 6,* 278–296.

Hyer, L., & Bloust, J. (1984). Concurrent and discriminant validities of the geriatric depression scale with older psychiatric inpatients. *Psychological Reports, 54,* 611–616.

Jenike, M. A. (1985). *Handbook of geriatric psychopharmacology.* Littleton, MA: PSG.

Jenike, M. A. (1984). Use of monoamine oxidase inhibitors in elderly depressed patients. *Journal of American Geriatric Society, 32,* 571–575.

Kalayam, B., & Shamoian, C. A. (1993). Treatment of depression: Diagnostic considerations. In C. Salzman (Ed.), *Clinical Geriatric Psychopharmacology* (pp. 115–136). Baltimore, MD: Williams & Wilkins.

Karlinsky, H., & Shulman, K. T. (1984). The clinical use of electroconvulsive therapy in old age. *Journal of the American Geriatric Society, 32,* 183–186.

Keitner, G. I., Ryan, C. E., Miller, I. W., Kohn, R., & Epstein, N. B. (1991). "Double depression": Two-year follow-up. *American Journal of Psychiatry, 148,* 345–350.

Kiernan, B. U., Wilson, D., Suter, N., Naqvi, A., Moltzen, J., & Silver, G. (1986). Comparison of the Geriatric Depression Scale and Beck Depression Inventory in a nursing home setting. *Clinical Gerontologist, 6,* 54–56.

Knight, B. G., Lutzky, S., & Macofsky-Urban, F. (1993). A meta-analytic review of interventions for caregiver distress: Recommendations for future research. *The Gerontologist, 33,* 240–248.

Knight, B. (1986). *Psychotherapy with older adults.* Beverly Hills, CA: Sage.

Kramer, B. A. (1987). Electroconvulsive therapy use in geriatric depression. *Journal of Nervous and Mental Diseases, 175,* 233–235.

Lamy, P., Salzman, C., & Nevis-Olsen, J. (1993). Drug prescribing patterns, risks, and compliance, guidelines. In C. Salzman (Ed.), *Clinical Geriatric Psychopharmacology* (pp. 15–38). Baltimore, MD: Williams & Wilkins.

Lewinsohn, P. M., Antonuccio, D. O., Steinmetz, J. S., & Teri, L. (1984). *The coping with depression course: A psychoeducational intervention for unipolar depression.* Eugene, OR: Castalia.

Lewinsohn, P. M., Munoz, R. F., Youngren, M. A., & Zeiss, A. M. (1986). *Control your depression.* New York: Prentice-Hall.

Lovett, S., & Gallagher, D. (1988). Psychoeducational interventions for family caregivers: Preliminary efficacy data. *Behavior Therapy, 19,* 321–330.

Mulsant, B. H., Rosen, J., Thornton, J. E., & Zubenko, G. S. (1991). A prospective naturalistic study of electroconvulsive therapy in late-life depression. *Journal of Geriatric Psychiatry and Neurology, 4,* 3–13.

National Institutes of Health Consensus Development Conference Consensus Statement (1991). Diagnosis and treatment of depression in late life, *9*(3), 1–27.

Nelson, J. C., Conwell, Y., Kim, K., & Mazure, C. (1989). Age of onset in late-life delusional depression. *American Journal of Psychiatry, 146,* 785–786.

Niederehe, G. (1994). Psychosocial therapies with depressed older adults. In L. S. Schneider, C. F.

Reynolds, B. D. Lebowitz, & A. J. Friedhoff (Eds.), *Diagnosis and treatment of depression in late life* (pp. 293–315). Washington, DC: American Psychiatric Press.

Nolen-Hoeksema, S. (1987). Sex differences in unipolar depression. *Psychological Bulletin, 101,* 259–282.

Osgood, N. (1985). *Suicide in the elderly: A practitioners guide to diagnosis and mental health intervention.* Rockville, MD: Aspen Systems Corp.

Pachana, N., Thompson, L. W., & Gallagher-Thompson, D. (1994). Measurement of depression. In M. P. Lawton & J. Teresi (Eds.), *Annual review of gerontology and geriatrics* (Vol. 14, pp. 234–256). New York: Springer.

Parmelee, P. A., Katz, I. R., & Lawton, M. P. (1992). Incidence of depression in long-term care settings. *Journals of Gerontology: Medical Science, 47,* M189–M196.

Paykel, E. S. (1972). Depressive topologies in response to emtripline. *British Journal of Psychiatry, 120,* 147–156.

Pinkston, E., & Linsk, N. (1984). *Care of the elderly: A family approach.* New York: Pergamon.

Qualls, S. H. (1988). Problems in families of older adults. In N. Epstein, S. S. Schlesinger, & W. Dryden (Eds.), *Cognitive-behavioral therapy with families* (pp. 215–253). New York: Brunner/Mazel.

Rapp, S., Parisi, S. A., Walsh, D. A., & Wallace, C. E. (1988). Detecting depression in elderly medical inpatients. *Journal of Consulting and Clinical Psychology, 56,* 509–513.

Richman, J. (1993). *Preventing elderly suicide: Overcoming personal despair, professional neglect, and social bias.* New York: Springer.

Robins, L. N., Helzer, J. E., Croughan, J., & Ratcliff, K. S. (1981). National Institute of Mental Health Diagnostic Interview Schedule: Its history, characteristics and validity. *Archives of General Psychiatry, 38,* 381–389.

Robinson, D. S., Nies, A., Davis, J. M., & Bunney, W. E. (1972). Aging, monoamines, and monoamine oxidase levels. *Lancet, 1,* 290–291.

Rodman, J., Gantz, F., Schneider, J., & Gallagher-Thompson, D. (1991). Short term treatment of endogenous depression using cognitive/behavioral therapy and pharmacotherapy. *Clinical Gerontologist, 10*(3), 81–84.

Ruegg, R. G., Zissok, S., & Swerdlow, N. R. (1988). Depression in the aged: An overview. *Psychiatry Clinics of North America, 11,* 83–99.

Salzman, C. (1982). Electroconvulsive therapy in the elderly patient. *Psychiatric Clinics of North America, 5,* 191–197.

Salzman, C. (1990). Practice considerations in the pharmacologic treatment of depression and anxiety in the elderly. *Journal of Clinical Psychiatry, 51*(1), 40–43.

Salzman, C. (1993). Pharmacologic treatment of depression in the elderly. *Journal of Clinical Psychiatry, 54*(2), 23–28.

Salzman, C. (1994). Pharmacological treatment of depression in elderly patients. In L. S. Schneider, C. F. Reynolds, B. D. Lebowitz, & A. J. Friedhoff (Eds.), *Diagnosis and treatment of depression in late life* (pp. 181–244). Washington, DC: American Psychiatric Press.

Scogin, F., & McElreath, L. (1994). Efficacy of psychosocial treatment for geriatric depression: A quantitative review. *Journal of Consulting and Clinical Psychology, 62*(1), 69–74.

Schulberg, H. C., McClelland, M., & Goding, W. (1987). Six-month outcomes for medical patients with major depressive disorders. *Journal of Internal Medicine, 2,* 312–317.

Shea, M. T., Pilkonis, P. A., Beckham, E., Collins, J. F., Elkin, I., Stotsky, S. M., & Docherty, J. P. (1990). Personality disorders and treatment outcomes in the NIMH treatment depression collaborative research program. *American Journal of Psychiatry, 148,* 1336–1340.

Spitzer, R. L., Williams, J., Gibbon, M., & First, M. B. (1992). The Structured Clinical Interview for DSM-III-R (SCID) I.: History, Rationale, and Description. *Archives of General Psychiatry, 49,* 624–629.

Steuer, J. L., Mintz, J., Hammen, C. L., Hill, M. A., Jarvik, L. F., McCarley, T., Motoike, P., & Rosen, R. (1984). Cognitive-behavioral and psychodynamic group psychotherapy in treatment of geriatric depression. *Journal of Consulting and Clinical Psychology, 52,* 180–189.

Stroebe, M. S., Stroebe, W., & Hansson, R. O. (Eds.) (1993). *Handbook of bereavement: Theory research and intervention.* New York: Cambridge University Press.

Teri, L., Curtis, J., Gallagher-Thompson, D., & Thompson, L. (1994). Cognitive-behavioral therapy with depressed older adults. In L. S. Schneider, C. F. Reynolds, B. D. Lebowitz, & A. J. Friedhoff

(Eds.), *Diagnosis and treatment of depression in late life: Results of the NIH consensus develop-ment conference* (pp. 279–291). Washington, DC: American Psychiatric Press.

Teri, L., & Logsdon, R. (1994). Assessment of behavioral disturbance in older adults. In M. P. Lawton & J. A. Teresi (Eds.), *Annual review of gerontology and geriatrics* (Vol. 14, pp. 107–124). New York: Springer.

Thompson, L. W., Davies, R., Gallagher, D., & Krantz, S. E. (1986). Cognitive therapy with older adults. *Clinical Gerontologist, 5*(3/4), 245–279.

Thompson, L. W., Futterman, A., & Gallagher, D. (1988). Assessment of late life depression. *Psycho-pharmacology Bulletin, 24*(4), 577–585.

Thompson, L. W., Gallagher, D., & Breckenridge, J. (1987). Comparative effectiveness of psycho-therapies for depressed elders. *Journal of Consulting and Clinical Psychology, 55*, 385–390.

Thompson, L. W., Gallagher, D., Nies, G., & Epstein, D. (1983). Evaluation of the effectiveness of professionals and nonprofessionals as instructors of "Coping with Depression" classes for elders. *The Gerontologist, 23*, 390–396.

Thompson, L. W., & Gallagher-Thompson, D. (1991, November). Comparison of desipramine and cognitive/behavioral therapy in the treatment of late-life depression: A progress report. Paper presented at the annual meeting of the Gerontological Society of America, San Francisco, CA.

Thompson, L. W., & Gallagher-Thompson, D. (1993, November). Comparison of desipramine and cognitive/behavioral therapy for the treatment of late-life depression: A progress report. Paper presented at the 27th annual meeting of the Association for the Advancement of Behavior Therapy, Atlanta, GA.

Thompson, L. W., Gallagher-Thompson, D., Futterman, A., & Peterson, J. (1991). The effects of late-life spousal bereavement over a thirty-month interval. *Psychology and Aging, 6*, 434–441.

Thompson, L. W., Gallagher-Thompson, D., Hanser, S., Gantz, F., & Steffen, A. (1991, August). Comparison of desipramine and cognitive/behavioral therapy for the treatment of depression in the elderly. Paper presented at the annual meeting of the American Psychological Association, San Francisco, CA.

Thompson, L. W., Gantz, F., Florsheim, M., DelMaestro, S., Rodman, J., Gallagher-Thompson, D., & Bryan, H. (1991). Cognitive/behavioral therapy for affective disorders in the elderly. In W. Myers (Ed.), *New techniques in the psychotherapy of older patients* (pp. 3–19). Washington, DC: American Psychiatric Press.

Tsuang, M. T., Wollson, R. G., & Fleming, J. A. (1979). Long-term outcome of major psychosis. I. Schizophrenia and affective disorders compared with psychiatrically symptoms-free surgical conditions. *Archives of General Psychiatry, 36*, 1295–1301.

Van Valkenburg, C., Akiskal, H. S., Puzantian, V., & Rosenthal, T. (1984). Anxious depressions: Clinical, family history, and naturalistic outcome-comparisons with panic and major depressive conditions. *Journal of Affective Disorders, 6*, 67–82.

Weiner, R. D. (1982). The role of electroconvulsive therapy in the treatment of depression in the elderly. *Journal of the American Geriatric Society, 30*, 710–712.

Wells, C. E. (1979). Pseudodementia. *American Journal of Psychiatry, 136*, 895–900.

Williams, J. B. W. (1988). A structured interview guide for the Hamilton Depression Rating Scale. *Archives of General Psychiatry, 45*, 742–747.

Wood, K. A., Harris, M. J., Morreale, A., & Rizos, A. L. (1988). Drug-induced psychosis and depression in the elderly. *Psychiatric Clinics of North America, 11*(1), 167–193.

Worden, J. W. (1991). *Grief counseling and grief therapy* (2nd ed.). New York: Springer.

Yesavage, J. A., Brink, T. L., & Rose, T. L. (1983). Development and validation of a geriatric depression scale: A preliminary report. *Journal of Psychiatric Residents, 17*, 37–49.

Zorumski, C. F., Rubin, E. H., & Burke, W. J. (1988). Electroconvulsive therapy for the elderly: A review. *Hospital and Community Psychiatry, 39*, 643–647.

CHAPTER 10

Depression in Alzheimer's Disease

LINDA TERI

DESCRIPTION OF THE DISORDER

Depression and dementia often coexist. Although estimates vary, approximately 30% of patients with Alzheimer's disease (AD) also meet criteria for the clinical syndrome of depression (Teri & Wagner, 1992; Wragg & Jeste, 1989). This syndrome is characterized by dysphoric mood, loss of interest or pleasure in previously enjoyable activities, and associated symptoms such as disturbances of sleep, appetite, fatigue; feelings of worthlessness, guilt, self-reproach; and suicidal ideation or attempts. In addition, an even higher percentage of patients

---

LINDA TERI • Department of Psychiatry and Behavioral Sciences, University of Washington School of Medicine, Seattle, Washington 98195.
Psychological Treatment of Older Adults: An Introductory Text, edited by Michel Hersen and Vincent B. Van Hasselt. Plenum Press, New York, 1996.

exhibits individual depression symptoms, although not of sufficient severity or duration to merit the diagnosis of depression.

Depression may add "excess disability" to the clinical picture of dementia patients. Kahn (1975) defined excess disability as disability that exists above and beyond the disability that can be explained by the primary disease process. Since depression is not necessarily characteristic of dementia, the depressive symptoms themselves may be an area of excess disability. Patients with coexistent depression and dementia have significantly more dysphoric mood, vegetative signs, social withdrawal, loss of interest, feelings of guilt and worthlessness, and suicidal ideation (Teri et al., 1991; Weiner, Steven, Edland, & Luszczynska, 1994). They are more likely to have delusions and hallucinations; experience greater levels of general behavior disturbance; have more problems with restlessness, falling, agitation, suspiciousness, and incontinence; and have increased functional disability (Logsdon & Teri, 1988; Pearson, Teri, Reifler, & Raskind, 1989; Rovner, Broadhead, Spencer, Carson, & Folstein, 1989). Thus, depression is associated with additional problems in patients with coexistent depression and dementia. These associated problems are particularly striking when one takes into account that depression symptoms appear most prevalent in patients with milder levels of cognitive impairment (Ballard, Cassidy, Bannister, & Movan, 1993; Burns, Larson, & Goldstrom, 1990; Fischer, Simamyi, & Danielezyk, 1990; Pearson et al., 1989).

Depression also affects the patients' care providers. Several have found positive associations between patient depression and caregiver stress, burden, and depression (Niederehe et al., 1983; Drinka, Smith, & Drinka, 1987; Greene, Smith, Gardiner, & Timbury, 1982; Barnes, Raskind, Scott, & Murphy, 1981; Haley, Brown, & Levine, 1987). These experienced difficulties may explain the often reported high rate of depression in caregivers of demented patients; as many as 55% of caregivers experience significant depression symptoms themselves (Drinka et al., 1987; Haley et al., 1987; Kiecolt-Glaser, Dura, Speicher, Trask, & Glaser, 1991; Pagel, Becker, & Coppel, 1985). Caregivers have also been found to have higher levels of clinically significant anger, anxiety, and guilt than age-matched noncaregivers (Gallagher, Nies, & Thompson, 1989). They have significantly more physical illness than noncaregivers (Kiecolt-Glaser et al., 1991). They have reported higher levels of negative reaction in response to patient depressive behaviors (such as tearfulness and comments about sadness) than they did to patient memory-related or disruptive behaviors (e.g., asking repetitive questions and agitation, respectively), even though the latter are more frequent. And finally, caregivers of depressed patients reported significantly higher levels of depression and burden than caregivers of patients without depression (Pearson, Teri, Wagner, Truax, & Logsdon, 1993; Teri, Truax, & Pearson, 1988).

In summary, depression is a prevalent characteristic for many patients with dementia and highly associated with other aspects of patient disturbance and caregiver distress. Effective depression treatment, therefore, may improve not only the patient's depression but also lead to a decrease in depression-associated problems for patients and caregivers. For a more detailed discussion of depression in dementia, the reader is referred to two reviews in this area (Teri & Wagner, 1992; Wragg & Jeste, 1989).

CASE IDENTIFICATION
AND PRESENTING COMPLAINTS

Mrs. H.[1] was a 74-year-old Caucasian woman referred to a geriatric clinic by her family. Mrs. H. lived by herself in her own home. She cooked her own meals and cleaned her own house. She had three children (two daughters and one son). Her closest daughter lived within 25 minutes of her home. Her family was quite concerned about her cognitive status. By their report, Mrs. H. often forgot things, misplaced objects, and was confused in new situations. They believed that these problems had been evident 3 to 4 years with "slow, but steady" progressive loss. Mrs. H. herself complained about an inability to remember things and difficulty with concentration, but she believed that these problems had developed only over the previous few months.

Mrs. H. was given a comprehensive geriatric evaluation, including an intake examination, neuropsychological evaluation, social work home environmental assessment, and physical examination with laboratory tests. (For a more detailed discussion of this evaluation, the reader is referred to Reifler, Larson, & Teri, 1987.) During the course of her evaluation she was cooperative but often tearful and self-deprecatory: "I'm an old lady, no good for anything anymore."

Mrs. H. evidenced definite cognitive impairment on neuropsychological testing and in the diagnostic interview. When given a mental status screening examination, she was oriented and was able to perform simple cognitive tasks (such as repeating phrases, writing a sentence, copying two geometric shapes, and carrying out a simple three-step command), but she had difficulty completing more complex tasks requiring sustained attention, cognitive flexibility, and abstract concept formation (e.g., she could not complete a symbol substitution task, had difficulty doing a serial subtraction task, and could not interpret proverbs). At intake, her Mini-Mental State Exam (Folstein, Folstein, & McHugh, 1975) score, an index of global cognitive function, was 21, placing her in the mildly to moderately impaired range of cognitive function. On more detailed neuropsychological evaluation, which included the Wechsler Adult Intelligence Scale (Wechsler, 1981), Wechsler Memory Scale (Wechsler, 1945; Russell, 1975) and the Dementia Rating Scale (Coblentz et al., 1973), she showed considerable memory difficulties and additional problems with complex tasks, especially those requiring new learning. This performance was significantly poorer than one would expect given her prior level of independent function and educational level. (For more detailed discussion of neuropsychological assessment of dementia, the reader is referred to Storandt & VandenBos, 1994.)

---

[1]This case presentation represents a composite of true cases but does not describe any one individual.

HISTORY

In addition to being demented, Mrs. H. was clinically depressed. She was often tearful and sad and complained of fatigue and feeling worthless and lonely. She had difficulty sleeping, had a poor appetite, and seemed very slow to move or speak. At intake, her Hamilton Depression Rating Scale (Hamilton, 1967) and Beck Depression Inventory (Beck, Ward, Mendelson, Mock, & Erbaugh, 1961) scores indicated moderately severe levels of depression, with scores of 22 and 24, respectively.

As a widow of 15 years, Mrs. H. reported that "her life ended" when her husband died. She said that although she was "close" to her family, they were "too busy with their own lives to spend time with an old burden like me." As already mentioned, during the intake interview, Mrs. H. was often tearful, apologetic, and self-deprecatory. She rarely engaged in eye contact and generally looked down at her hands. During the 1½ hour interview, she smiled only once, when she spoke about her past family experiences, when her husband was alive and her children were younger. She spoke quite calmly about wanting to die and was tearful when discussing her feelings of loneliness and worthlessness that she said were "always" with her. After recounting a tale of unhappiness and isolation, she observed, "Well, what can I expect, after all I'm an old lady. It's time for me to die."

Because cognitive impairments in older adults can be attributable to a variety of physical conditions and medications, Mrs. H. was given a comprehensive medical examination. Her physical exam failed to reveal any medical problems that could cause the level of cognitive impairment she was experiencing. Nor were any medical conditions or medications thought to be causing her depression. She was in generally good health with the exception of some arthritis that was helped by an over-the-counter medication. She wore glasses and had a cataract developing in one eye. She was somewhat hard of hearing but wore no hearing aid. As a result of these evaluations, Mrs. H. was given a diagnosis of dementia of the Alzheimer's type, with coexistent depression.

SELECTION OF
PSYCHOLOGICAL TREATMENT

Several treatment approaches were considered for Mrs. H., including supportive psychotherapy, support group involvement for her family, pharmacotherapy, and behavioral treatment. For a discussion of these other approaches, the reader is referred to Reynolds (1992) and Zarit, Orr, and Zarit (1985). Mrs. H. was considered to be a good candidate for behavioral treatment for a number of reasons, not the least of which was that her depression seemed to be maintained by four factors: infrequent engagement in pleasant events, considerable social isolation, negative cognition, and unwitting reinforcement by her family. After discussion with her and her family, a trial of behavioral treatment was implemented.

An overview of Mrs. H.'s treatment may be helpful here. (Portions of this description have been published elsewhere. See, for example, Teri, 1986; Teri & Uomoto, 1986; Teri, 1992.) Treatment consists of nine weekly sessions of approximately 1 hour duration. Patients and caregivers are (1) provided with education about AD and the rationale for behavioral intervention, (2) taught methods of behavior change, (3) given strategies for identifying and increasing patient-pleasant activities, (4) instructed in methods to help understand and maximize the patient's remaining cognitive and functional abilities, (5) taught effective problem-solving techniques for the day-to-day difficulties of patient care, especially those related to depression behaviors, (6) given aid with caregiving responsibilities, and (7) provided with plans for maintaining and generalizing treatment gains once treatment ends.

Treatment incorporates behavioral theory and treatment of depression with gerontological theory and clinical writings on AD. Behavioral theory suggests that decreased positive person–environment interactions (and increased aversive interactions) are related to increased depressed mood (Lewinsohn, Antonuccio, Steinmetz, & Teri, 1984). Depressed people do little that is pleasant and are often withdrawn and apathetic; the less they do, the more depressed they become, the more depressed, the less active, and so on. The same cycle can be seen with demented depressed patients. Due to cognitive impairment, demented patients eventually lose the ability to engage in many of the activities they once enjoyed. They no longer function as independently as they once could and often must rely on others to initiate and maintain activities. The less they do that they enjoy, the more depressed they feel; the more depressed they feel, the less they do, and so on. By identifying and increasing their involvement in activities that they still might enjoy, and by maximizing their level of independence consonant with their degree of cognitive and functional impairment, rates of positive and negative experiences may be altered and their depressive behaviors alleviated.

Caregivers of demented patients play an essential role throughout treatment. Because patients are often limited in their ability to learn new skills, remember treatment content, and understand explanations and techniques independently, caregivers are essential in helping to plan and implement treatment strategies (Teri, Logsdon, Wagner, & Uomoto, 1994). Each of the weekly sessions actively trains caregivers in systematic behavior management techniques designed to alleviate depression in patients. The patient also plays an important role in treatment. As much as possible, considering the patient's level of understanding and ability to participate, they are involved in all aspects of treatment design and decision making. Minimal caregiver involvement and more patient reliance may occur in the early stages of the disease, when the patient can still function relatively independently and understand and follow through on treatment goals. More severely demented patients will require more caregiver involvement as communication and memory deficits become more problematic. (Readers interested in more general discussion of caregiving strategies to aid in patient care are referred to Mace and Rabins [1981] and Powell and Courtice [1983] for excellent examples of caregiver-directed reading materials.)

CONCURRENT MEDICAL TREATMENT

In Mrs. H.'s case, there were no concurrent medical illnesses that needed attention. She was in remarkably good health, except for some minor arthritic pain that was adequately treated with an over-the-counter medication, visual impairment for which she wore glasses, and hearing loss for which she had a hearing aid she frequently failed to wear. Consequently, the main issues were to ensure she was not abusing her medication and that she was wearing her glasses and hearing aid. For all older adults, however, a thorough medical work-up is essential to rule out or identify specific medical conditions or medications that might be causing or contributing to the depressive behaviors and/or the cognitive impairments of the older person. A sensory assessment should always be included. Correction of vision or hearing problems may markedly improve a patient's functioning.

Depression is well recognized as a side effect of many medications commonly prescribed for older adults and for many medical illnesses, especially those with a chronic course, such as coronary artery disease, endocrine abnormalities, neurological disorders, metabolic disturbances, and cancer (Raskind, 1993).

Some of the conditions that may cause cognitive deterioration if left untreated include nutritional disorders, infections, endocrine disorders, cerebral disease, and toxic conditions (e.g., drug reactions). Inclusion of such laboratory tests as serum enzymes and electrolytes, blood cell counts, chest radiograph, a serological test for syphilis, tests of thyroid function, vitamin B_{12} and foliate levels, urinalysis, and an electrocardiogram will aid in ruling out most reversible causes of dementia. Additional tests when specifically indicated might include a spinal tap, an electroencephalogram, and a computed tomography (CT) scan of the brain.

Since coexistent disease is most likely the rule rather than the exception in older adults, the physical examination will enable the behavioral clinician to set realistic goals and avoid misinterpreting medical symptoms.

COURSE OF TREATMENT

Education and Rationale

Early in treatment, the therapist introduces the caregiver and patient to the scientific and clinical logic behind intervention. In easy-to-understand terms, the behaviors that constitute depression, their impact on and association with other problems, and the potential for treatment are discussed. Educational information about the progressive course of Alzheimer's disease, the importance of long-term planning, and other topics of interest to individual caregivers and patients is provided. Through discussion and examples from their own experiences patients and caregivers are educated about the disease process and realistic expectations for change are established.

For Mrs. H., the diagnoses of depression and dementia of the Alzheimer's type were discussed with her and her family at the end of the evaluation. Mrs. H. was assured that she need not be depressed "just because she was 74" and that she could learn to feel better. The therapist stressed that although little could be done for her memory, a good deal could be done for her depression. The therapist took time to explain the relationship between depression and memory loss and the association between pleasant events and depressed mood to Mrs. H. and family. Although Mrs. H. consistently made disparaging remarks about her inability to engage in activity, she acknowledged that the ideas made sense and that she could understand how "someone" could feel better if "they" did more. She could not, however, imagine herself doing more at the present time.

The possibility of medication was also discussed with Mrs. H., her family, and the clinic psychiatrist. On the basis of the behavioral assessment, all agreed that a behavioral approach seemed hopeful and would be tried first. Although not optimistic, Mrs. H. agreed to come to our clinic for 2 months to see if her mood would improve. Mrs. H.'s family was quite eager to pursue treatment, and Mrs. H.'s daughter, who lived in town, agreed to accompany the patient to each appointment and participate in treatment.

Fundamentals of Behavior Change

Using examples from their own experience, as well as the therapist's experience with other caregiver-patient dyads, Mrs. H. and her daughter were introduced to the importance of behavioral observation and analysis. They were asked to complete the Pleasant Events Schedule-AD (PES-AD) (Teri & Logsdon, 1991). The PES-AD is a 53-item list of potential pleasant activities that demented patients may enjoy. It was developed to help caregivers and therapists identify activities that the patient currently enjoys or has enjoyed in the past, determine how frequently she engages in these activities, and devise ways of increasing frequency of selected activities. The therapist works with the caregiver and patient to determine what pleasant activities are still realistic for the patient given the patient's level of cognitive impairment and helps the caregiver plan and carry out these activities throughout treatment.

Mrs. H. and her daughter were also asked to complete a daily behavioral diary of activity and a mood-rating scale. The diary was an open-ended report of how Mrs. H. spent her time. The mood-rating scale was a simple 0 to 10 scale, with zero representing the worst she had ever felt (very unhappy) and 10 representing the best she had ever felt (very happy). Examples of situations in which she felt "0" and "10" were discussed. Mrs. H. and her daughter decided that early evening was the best time to evaluate her mood. The activity diary supported information obtained in the intake interview. Mrs. H. spent most of her day alone, at home, sitting in a chair, inactive. Her daughter would visit her two or three times per week. During those times, as well as during visits with her other children, they often struggled with trying to "make her happy," but visits often ended sadly. She shopped for food only when her daughter took her or if a neighbor invited her to go. She initiated little activity and viewed herself as a burden to family and friends.

Mrs. H. and her daughter also monitored the sources of conflict between them and other family members. They were taught to identify individual behavior problems, observe antecedents and consequences, and consider how altering one or the other can change behavior. This process is named the A-B-C's of behavior change: A is the antecedent or triggering event that precedes the problem behavior; B is behavior; and C is the consequences of the behavior. (This strategy of problem identification and treatment is detailed in a video training program by the author, entitled "Managing and Understanding Behavior Problems in Alzheimer's Disease and Related Disorders [Teri, 1990]. It may be obtained by writing Northwest Geriatric Education Center, University of Washington, HL-23, Seattle, WA 98195.) Once the A-B-C's of the problem behavior have been outlined, an intervention strategy targeting either the antecedents or the consequences of the problem behavior can be developed later in treatment.

Increasing Pleasant Events

The depressive cycle (as described earlier) and the importance of identifying, planning, and increasing pleasant events were discussed with Mrs. H. and her daughter. From the PES-AD, four activities were identified that could provide Mrs. H. with pleasant experiences. One activity was a community-based program for older adults that was open from 11:30 a.m. to 2:30 p.m. and offered lunch, group activities, and special events. The program was located about two blocks from Mrs. H.'s home and was easily accessible, although she had never visited it. The second activity involved a friend with whom Mrs. H. had once enjoyed a close relationship, but whom she had not seen in the last year. According to her daughter, Mrs. H.'s friend had occasionally called and invited Mrs. H. to join her, but Mrs. H. had refused invitations and the friend had gradually stopped calling. Mrs. H. was sure her friend would not want to be "bothered" with her. The third activity involved hand needlework that Mrs. H. previously enjoyed but no longer did because of her poor vision.

The fourth activity involved family. Mrs. H. greatly enjoyed her family's attention, although she thought that the times she saw them or spoke with them by phone had become difficult. During the course of the interview, it became clear that her family spent most of their time trying to cheer her, and she spent most of the time complaining. Each of these activities was discussed with Mrs. H. and her daughter, and specific plans were made for scheduling the first three activities. The fourth was postponed for future discussion.

In each of the activities planned, Mrs. H. needed assistance. To attend the community association, she had to cope with her discomfort about going into new situations, meeting new people, and being out of her home. She and her daughter had to coordinate their schedules to arrange for her safe travel. By discussing the logistics of attending the community center, Mrs. H., her daughter, and the therapist were able to anticipate and problem-solve potential obstacles to attendance. All aspects of attendance were discussed. For example, a hierarchy of steps was developed for Mrs. H. that progressed from walking into the community center, introducing herself, initiating conversation, and arranging for continued involvement. Topics of "conversational chatter" were discussed and practiced. A similar approach was taken with the second activity. Mrs. H. rehearsed making a telephone call to her old friend and practiced what she would say. Her daughter planned how she would help Mrs. H. with that activity and involve the friend in advance. The third activity was more solitary. Rather than rehearsing interactions, Mrs. H., her daughter, and the therapist worked at identifying a type of handiwork she was still capable of performing. She was an avid quilter. She could see well enough to sew but threading the needles was almost impossible. Planning the quilting design and following a pattern was also too complex. After one or two visits to a quilting store in the area, Mrs. H.'s daughter found some preprinted material that Mrs. H. could quilt. She also had devised a way to thread multiple needles in advance so her mother always had needle and thread ready. This allowed Mrs. H. the joy of sewing without the frustration of threading the needle or needing to follow a pattern.

Maximizing Cognitive Functioning

The nature of dementia is to reduce the day-to-day abilities of the afflicted individual. These reductions have far-reaching effects and are directly associated with depression in two basic ways. First, cognitive impairments reduce the availability of enjoyable activities to the patient. Because so much of our enjoyment is related to what we can and cannot do, maximizing the patient's cognitive function is essential and integral to the behavioral treatment of depression. Second, cognitive impairments and their functional correlates increase the potential for conflict between the caregiver and patient. Disagreements about how and when to engage in certain activities, added chores for the caregiver, and decreased functional independence of the patient may all contribute to increased aversive interactions. Consequently, treatment seeks to identify individual patient's relative strengths and weaknesses and abilities and disabilities and to teach caregivers and patients how to maximize the former while minimizing the later. Common clinical strategies, such as putting labels on cabinets or providing one-step commands, are discussed and tailored to the needs of the particular patient.

Because Mrs. H. was not severely impaired, she required very few modifications of her home and environment. Those that were implemented mainly focused on her safety and maintaining her independence. Although not physically frail, as already stated, Mrs. H. was taking a number of over-the-counter medications, including pain medicine for her arthritis and laxatives as needed. Because of Mrs. H.'s memory problems, a medication monitoring system was established to ensure she did not overmedicate.

Problem-Solving Techniques

As treatment progresses, strategies are developed for identifying and confronting behavioral disturbances that either interfere with engaging in planned pleasant activities or cause conflict between the patient, caregiver, and others. Using the skills in behavior observation and analysis taught and reinforced throughout each session, caregivers follow the A-B-Cs to devise strategies for modifying problems. Problem behaviors that are addressed include depressive behaviors, such as crying and self-deprecatory statements, and other behaviors, such as wandering and agitation. The therapist introduces behavioral strategies for decreasing problem behaviors and increasing incompatible behaviors, as appropriate.

Mrs. H.'s daughter completed the Revised Memory and Behavior Problems Checklist (RBMPC) (Teri et al., 1992) that was designed to aid caregivers and therapists in identifying observable and potentially modifiable behaviors. This inventory of 24 items evaluates frequency of three domains of problems relevant to dementia: memory-related problems such as repeated questioning, depression problems such as crying, and disruption problems such as verbal aggression. The RBMPC also evaluates the caregiver's reaction to each behavior, providing a measure of the impact of different behaviors on the individual caregiver. Clinically, administration of the RBMPC is useful to highlight the constellation of problem behaviors of a specific AD patient and those behaviors most distressing to the caregiver. Psychometric data have been published, indicating the RBMPC is a reliable and valid assessment tool (Teri et al., 1992).

Recall that the fourth pleasant activity identified earlier involved Mrs. H.'s time with her family. Although she looked forward to hearing from them, they were beginning to dread these interactions because they were so difficult. The therapist began with Mrs. H.'s daughter, who was accompanying her mother to each session. The objective was that as she learned how to better help her mother, other family members could model her behavior. As antecedents and consequences to various depressive statements were discussed, Mrs. H.'s daughter became aware of how she was inadvertently encouraging inactivity and depression. She learned to decrease the attention she gave to depressive behaviors and increase her attention to incompatible (nondepressive) behaviors. For example, when Mrs. H.'s daughter was shown how to initiate and maintain conversations that would focus on nondepressive topics (such as what activities Mrs. H. enjoyed or positive reminiscences), she was also shown how to divert depressive topics and keep her responses to them to an absolute minimum. Over time, she and Mrs. H. reported they increasingly each enjoyed their time together.

Aid with Caregiving Responsibilities

Caregiver problems, such as depression, stress, anger, and burden, are addressed as they relate to treatment plans and patient care. Caregivers are encouraged to plan pleasant events for themselves as well as for the patient, and to develop and use a support system to help with the patient's care as well as maintain their own sense of well-being and physical health. Availability of respite services and other community assistance is also discussed.

Mrs. H.'s daughter worked full-time and, although a very caring person, was beginning to express anger and guilt about her perceived responsibilities to her mother. The commonality of these experiences was discussed with her, and she was encouraged to enlist other family members, friends, and community groups to provide certain aspects of care. For example, she had gradually taken over paying her mother's bills. Each month she dreaded paying the bills, which often began with an acrimonious argument with her mother about keeping them better organized. She was encouraged to talk with one of her brothers about this and enlist his help. Living a distance away, the brother rarely helped with day-to-day chores of caregiving. An active problem-solving approach was taken. Mrs. H.'s daughter and the therapist role-played how she would handle the request and her feelings about it. The brother was agreeable and suggested the bills be forwarded directly to him, thus saving them all a difficult interchange. Mrs. H.'s daughter was fearful of not being a "good daughter" but indeed was very involved in helping the patient. By discussing her own fears she learned to redefine "good daughter," to obtain assistance from others, and to encourage Mrs. H.'s independent activity when appropriate.

Planning for Maintenance and Generalization

Prior to termination, plans are developed for continuing pleasant events and implementing problem-solving strategies that have been learned. Generalization of the caregiver's behavioral skills to new or different patient problem behaviors in the future is also encouraged. The final session serves as a summary session, to review treatment, and as a planning session to develop strategies for ongoing care.

The progressive nature of AD and the possibility of depression symptoms recurring were discussed with Mrs. H. and her daughter. To ensure that progress made in treatment was maintained, they both agreed to talk with each other every day to be certain Mrs. H. was continuing her activities and to monitor her memory. They were saddened by the certainty that cognitive problems would continue but optimistic that the family would work together. Hrs. H.'s daughter believed that she would continue to monitor her mother's mood, although she doubted whether she would write down each activity because that was "such a big job."

FOLLOW-UP

Following treatment, Mrs. H. was seen 1, 3, 6, and 12 months after her last session. Mrs. H. continued to have cognitive difficulties, but her depression had not returned. Her family and friends continued to see her or call on a regular basis, and she remained involved with the community center.

OVERALL EVALUATION

For Mrs. H. and others like her, an association between pleasant activities and depressed mood was demonstrated and found to be influential in reducing depression and associated problems. Caregivers such as Mrs. H.'s daughter have been successful in improving both the patient's activity level and their depressed mood. The efficacy of this approach has been subjected to a controlled clinical outcome study. Patients were randomly assigned to either the behavioral treatment, as described for Mrs. H., or to control conditions, such as a wait-list control. Patients and caregivers were assessed on a battery of measures, including standardized depression, cognition, and burden measures, at pretest, posttest, and follow-up intervals. Preliminary results suggest that patients assigned to behavioral treatment improved significantly more than those assigned to wait-list and also improved significantly from pre- to posttest. Furthermore, caregivers also reported significant improvements in their own level of depression (Teri et al., 1994).

Behavioral treatment, as described herein, is very structured and involves a gradually increasing approach to reinvolving the patient in pleasant activities and altering the contingencies that maintain depression. Each strategy is integrated into a structured and well-thought-out intervention aimed at the particular complaint or constellation of complaints that seems most relevant for a given patient. Second, the caregiver, who is often a family member, is enlisted to assist with these efforts in a natural setting.

Although many activities previously enjoyed by patients are no longer available to them (due to a variety of factors, including their degree of cognitive impairment, physical limitations, and/or limited community access), therapists are able to assist the caregiver in identifying "new" and realistic enjoyable activities. Third, few contraindications exist. Behavioral intervention can be offered instead of, or in conjunction with, medical interventions. The main requirement is that caregivers and patients are willing and able to devote the time and effort necessary to successful intervention.

SUMMARY

As has been illustrated with the preceding case example, clinical strategies used with younger patients can be successfully adapted to older adults. The degree to which such adaptation is successful depends, in part, upon the therapists' ability to utilize the very skills they are teaching their patients: namely, to focus on progress, to keep steps small and realistic, to reinforce success, and to avoid setting unrealistic goals, attending to failure, or providing nonconstructive feedback. The more the therapist is successful in implementing and encouraging patients and caregivers to implement behavior change strategies, the more treatment will be successful.

ACKNOWLEDGMENTS.   Preparation of this chapter was supported in part by National Institute of Aging grants AG10845 and AG05136.

REFERENCES

Ballard, C. G., Cassidy, C., Bannister, C., & Mohan (1993). RNC, Prevalence, symptom profile, and aetiology of depression in dementia suffers. *Journal of Affective Disorders, 29*, 1–6.

Barnes, R. F., Raskind, M., Scott, M., & Murphy, C. (1981). Problems of families caring for Alzheimer's patients: Use of a support group. *Journal of the American Geriatrics Society, 29*, 80–85.

Beck, A. T., Ward, C., Mendelson, M., Mock, J., & Erbaugh, J. (1961). An inventory for measuring depression. *Archives of General Psychiatry, 4*, 561–571.

Burns, B. J., Larson, P. A., & Goldstrom, I. D. (1990). Psychiatric phenomena in Alzheimer's disease. 3. Disorders of mood. *British Journal of Psychiatry, 157*, 81–86.

Coblentz, J. M., Mattis, S., Zingesser, L. H., Kasoff, S. S., Wisniewski, H. M., & Katzman, R. (1993). Presenile dementia: Clinical evaluation of cerebrospinal fluid dynamics. *Archives of Neurology, 29*, 299–308.

Drinka, J. K., Smith, J. C., & Drinka, P. J. (1987). Correlates of depression and burden for informal caregivers of patients in a geriatrics referral clinic. *Journal of the American Geriatrics Society, 35*, 522–525.

Fischer, P., Simamyi, M., & Danielezyk, W. (1990). Depression in dementia of the Alzheimer's type and in multi-infarct dementia. *American Journal of Psychiatry, 147*, 1484–1487.

Folstein, M. F., Folstein, S. E., & McHugh, P. R. (1975). Mini-mental state: A practical method for grading the cognitive state of patients for the clinician. *Journal of Psychiatric Research, 12*, 189–198.

Gallagher, D., Nies, G., & Thompson, L. (1982). Reliability of the Beck Depression Inventory with older adults. *Journal of Consulting and Clinical Psychology, 50*, 152–153.

Greene, J. G., Smith, R., Gardiner, M., & Timbury, G. C. (1982). Measuring behavioral disturbance of elderly demented patients in the community and its effect on relatives: A factor analysis study. *Age and Aging, 11*, 121–126.

Haley, W. E., Brown, S. L., & Levine, E. G. (1987). Family caregiver appraisals of patients behavioral disturbance in senile dementia. *Aging & Human Development, 25*, 25–33.

Hamilton, M. (1967). Development of a rating scale for primary depressive illness. *British Journal of Social and Clinical Psychology, 6*, 278–296.

Kahn, R. L. (1975). The mental health system and the future aged. *Gerontologist, 15*, 24–31.

Kiecolt-Glaser, J. K., Dura, J. R., Speicher, C. E., Trask, J., & Glaser, R. (1991). Spousal caregivers of dementia victims: Longitudinal changes in immunity and health. *Psychosomatic Medicine, 53*, 345–362.

Lewinsohn, P. M., Antonuccio, D. O., Steinmetz, J., & Teri, L. (1984). *The coping with depression course.* Eugene, OR: Castalia.

Logsdon, R., & Teri, L. (1988). Neuropsychological and behavioral assessment in the identification and treatment of DAT. Paper presented at the meeting of the Association for Advancement of Behavior Therapy, New York.

Mace, N. L., & Rabins, P. V. (1981). *The 36-hour day.* Baltimore: Johns Hopkins University Press.

Niederehe, G., Furge, E., Woods, A. M., et al. (1983). Caregiver stress in dementia: Clinical outcomes and family considerations. Paper presented at the meeting of the Gerontological Society of America, San Francisco.

Pagel, M. D., Becker, J., & Coppel, D. B. (1985). Loss of control, self blame and depression: An investigation of spouse-caregivers of Alzheimer's disease patients. *Journal of Abnormal Psychology, 94*, 169–182.

Parmelee, P., & Lawton, M. P. (1990). The design of special environments for the aged. In E. Birren & K. W. Schaie (Eds.), *Handbook of the psychology and aging*, 3rd ed. San Diego, CA: Academic Press.

Pearson, J., Teri, L., Reifler, B., & Raskind, M. (1989). Functional status and cognitive impairment in Alzheimer's disease patients with and without depression. *Journal of the American Geriatrics Society, 37*, 1117–1121.

Pearson, J. L., Teri, L., Wagner, A., Truax, P., & Logsdon, R. G. (1993). The relationship of problem behaviors in dementia patients to depression and burden in caregiving spouses. *American Journal of Alzheimer's Care and Related Disorders, 8*, 15–22.

Powell, L. S., & Courtice, K. (1983). *Alzheimer's disease: A guide for families.* Reading, MA: Addison-Wesley.

Raskind, M. A. (1993). Geriatric psychopharmacology. *Psychiatric Clinics of North America, 16*, 815–827.

Reifler, B. V., Larson, E., & Teri, L. (1987). An outpatient geriatric psychiatry assessment and treatment service. *Clinics in Geriatric Medicine, 3*, 203–209.

Reynolds, C. F. (1992). Treatment of depression in special populations. *Clinical Psychiatry, 53*, 9, 45–53.

Rovner, B. W., Broadhead, J., Spencer, M., Carson, K., & Folstein, M. F. (1989). Depression and Alzheimer's disease. *American Journal of Psychiatry, 146*, 350–353.

Russell, E. W. (1975). A multiple scoring method for the assessment of complex memory functions. *Journal of Consulting and Clinical Psychology, 48*, 800–809.

Storandt, M., & VandenBos, G. R. (1994). Neuropsychological assessment of dementia and depression in older adults: A clinician's guide. Washington, DC: American Psychological Association.

Teri, L. (1986). Severe cognitive impairments in older adults. *The Behavior Therapist, 9*, 51–54.

Teri, L. (1990). *Managing and understanding behavior problems in Alzheimer's disease and related disorders* (training program with videotapes and written manual).

Teri, L. (1992). Non-pharmacological approaches to management of patient behavior: A focus on behavioral intervention for depression in dementia. In G. M. Gutman (Ed.), *Shelter and care of persons with dementia* (pp. 101–113). Vancouver, BC: The Gerontology Research Centre, Simon Fraser University.

Teri, L., Baer, L., & Reifler, B. (1991). Depression in Alzheimer's patients: Investigation of symptom patterns and frequency. *Clinical Gerontologist, 11*, 47–57.

Teri, L., Larson, E., & Reifler, B. V. (1988). Behavioral disturbance in dementia of the Alzheimer's type. *Journal of the American Geriatrics Society, 36*, 1–6.

Teri, L., & Logsdon, R. (1991). Identifying pleasant activities for individuals with Alzheimer's disease: The Pleasant Events Schedule-AD. *The Gerontologist, 31*, 124–127.

Teri, L., Logsdon, R., Wagner, A., & Uomoto, J. (1994). The caregiver role in behavioral treatment of depression in dementia patients. In E. Light, B. Lebowitz, & G. Niederehe (Eds.), *Stress effects on family caregivers of Alzheimer's patients* (pp. 185–204). New York: Springer.

Teri, L., Truax, P., Logsdon, R., Uomoto, J., Zarit, S., & Vitaliano, P. P. (1992). Assessment of behavioral problems in dementia: The Revised Memory and Behavior Problems Checklist. *Psychology and Aging, 4*, 622–631.

Teri, L., Truax, P., & Pearson, J. (1988, November). Caregiver depression and burden: What are the correlates? Paper presented at the Gerontological Society of America 41st Annual Meeting, San Francisco, CA.

Teri, L., & Uomoto, J. (1986). Treatment of depression in Alzheimer's disease: Helping caregivers to help themselves and their patients. Paper presented to Gerontology Society of America.

Teri, L., & Wagner, A. (1992). Alzheimer's disease and depression. *The Journal of Consulting and Clinical Psychology, 3*, 379–391.

Wechsler, D. (1945). A standardized memory scale for clinical use. *Journal of Psychology, 19*, 87–95.

Wechsler, D. (1981). WAIS-R Manual. New York: Psychological Corporation.

Weiner, M. F., Steven, D., Edland, M. S., & Luszczynska, H. (1994). Prevalence and incidence of major depression in Alzheimer's disease. *American Journal of Psychiatry, 7*, 1006–1009.

Wragg, R. E., & Jeste, D. V. (1989). Overview of depression and psychosis in Alzheimer's disease. *American Journal of Psychiatry, 146*, 577–587.

Zarit, S. H., Orr, N. K., & Zarit, J. (1985). *The hidden victims of Alzheimer's disease: Families under stress*. New York: New York University Press.

CHAPTER 11

Schizophrenia

SHIRLEY M. GLYNN, KIM T. MUESER, AND STEPHEN J. BARTELS

DESCRIPTION OF THE DISORDER

Schizophrenia is one of the most debilitating adult mental illnesses. More psychiatric hospital beds are occupied by persons with schizophrenia than any other psychiatric disorder, and the illness accounts for the majority of admissions to psychiatric hospitals. Over the past 40 years, significant gains have been

SHIRLEY M. GLYNN • West Los Angeles Veterans Affairs Medical Center and Department of Psychiatry, University of California at Los Angeles, Los Angeles, California 90073. KIM T. MUESER AND STEPHEN J. BARTELS • Departments of Psychiatry and Community and Family Medicine, Dartmouth Medical School, Concord, New Hampshire 03301.
Psychological Treatment of Older Adults: An Introductory Text, edited by Michel Hersen and Vincent B. Van Hasselt. Plenum Press, New York, 1996.

made in both the pharmacological and psychosocial treatment of schizophrenia. Despite these gains, the effects of the illness continue to be pervasive and chronic. The limited efficacy of currently available treatments for schizophrenia is illustrated by the high rate of relapse for outpatients living in the community and the poor social functioning of most patients.

In this chapter, we first present an overview of current knowledge about schizophrenia over the life-span, including attention to onset, course, gender differences, comorbidities, and etiological theories. We then outline a heuristic model for understanding the course of the disorder and implementing treatments. We follow this with an expanded discussion of empirically validated interventions for schizophrenia. We then discuss issues of special concern in treating the aging persons with schizophrenia and detail the unique case of late-onset schizophrenia. We conclude with recommendations for comprehensive assessment and treatment.

SCHIZOPHRENIA: AN OVERVIEW

Onset

The lifetime prevalence of schizophrenia in the general population is approximately 1%. The illness most often develops in late adolescence or early adulthood, between the ages of 16 and 30 years. Childhood onset of schizophrenia before the age of 10 is rare. Although it was previously believed that new cases of schizophrenia rarely developed during middle or late adulthood, recent epidemiological studies counter this view. For example, Castle and Murray (1993) reported that over one-quarter (28%) of the new cases of schizophrenia in the Camberwell (London) catchment area from 1965 to 1984 occurred after age 44, and 12% occurred after age 64.

Course

Schizophrenia usually develops over a period of several months to a few years, during which time *prodromal symptoms* appear, such as social withdrawal, decreased spontaneity and interests, and perceptual and cognitive aberrations. Frequently, even before the onset of prodromal symptoms, the pre-schizophrenic person has poorer premorbid social and sexual adjustment than others (Zigler & Glick, 1986).

The first to describe schizophrenia was Emil Kraepelin (1919/1971), a German professor of psychiatry. In 1889, he grouped several types of mental abnormalities under one heading, *dementia praecox*, the early term for schizophrenia. The term dementia praecox literally meant progressive mental deterioration in early life. He believed that changes in the brain were the primary cause of dementia praecox and that psychological factors were of secondary importance.

Kraepelin suggested the disorder started in early adolescence and was incurable because of the brain's deterioration.

This pessimistic view of schizophrenia is not warranted by recent data. Clinically, once a person has developed schizophrenia, the course of the illness is usually episodic, with some residual impairment evidenced between exacerbations. However, there is a trend for gradual improvement, and in some cases, total remission, later in life (Ciompi, 1980; Harding, Brooks, Askikage, Strauss, & Breier, 1987a,b). On a biological level, imaging studies do not generally find evidence of increasing deterioration in the brains of persons with schizophrenia assessed regularly for as long as 9 years (Degreef et al., 1991). Rather, any brain abnormality seems to be static once the disorder is evidenced. Cognitively, neuropsychological assessments of cohorts of schizophrenic patients in their third, fourth, fifth, sixth, and seventh decades of life do not suggest progressive dementia or deterioration (Goldberg, Hyde, Kleinman, & Weinberger, 1993).

Gender Differences

Data from a wide series of studies suggest that gender may have a critical influence on many aspects of schizophrenia. At a most basic level, the compelling evidence that schizophrenia tends to be a more benign disorder in females suggests that male gender, by itself, may represent a vulnerability factor (Goldstein, 1988; Seeman, 1986). While the etiology of this vulnerability is uncertain, possible sources include differences in neuroanatomy (Lewine, Gulley, Risch, Jewart, & Houpt, 1990) reflecting more compromised male brains, or differences in protective hormonal levels, such as estrogen, which may offer an advantage for females (Seeman & Lang, 1990).

While gender-based biological differences likely contribute to the more positive course of the disorder in women, other nonbiological influences on illness course also merit attention. In particular, higher levels of social skills found in women with schizophrenia (e.g., Mueser, Bellack, Morrison, & Wade, 1990) may serve as a protective factor. Similarly, women with schizophrenia are more likely to marry or cohabitate (Test & Berlin, 1981) and have contact with their children (e.g., Test, Burke, & Wallisch, 1990) than men, and thus may have access to stronger environmental protection in the form of a supportive community network. Consistent with findings in the general population, women with schizophrenia report significantly less substance and alcohol abuse than men (Drake, Osher, & Wallach, 1989; Mueser et al., 1990); thus, they may be less exposed to a significant illness-potentiating variable.

Causes

The causes of schizophrenia are unknown, but current theories suggest the illness is related to abnormalities in brain structure and/or functioning and that environmental stress contributes to the onset of symptoms and subsequent symptom relapses (Liberman & Mueser, 1989). There is evidence that the vulnerability of schizophrenia is influenced by genetic factors (Holtzman & Matthysse, 1990); however, most individuals who develop the illness have no afflicted family members.

Approaches to investigating the brain defects that may cause schizophrenia can be classified according to those that look at differences in brain *structure* and those that examine differences in brain *function*. Brain imaging of persons with schizophrenia has shown atrophy, or deterioration, of their frontal lobes (Andreasen et al., 1986), although failures to replicate this finding have also been reported (Andreasen et al., 1990). Researchers have hypothesized that factors present at or before birth may be responsible for the observed deterioration (Murray, 1994). Computed tomography (CT) and magnetic resonance imaging (MRI) scans give images of brain structure, while another procedure, dynamic brain imaging, permits researchers to study cerebral blood flow, oxygen use, and other brain functions. Results of positron emission tomography (PET) scan studies generally support the view that persons with schizophrenia have abnormally low activity in their frontal lobes, the "executive planning" center of the brain (Weinberger, Berman, Suddath, & Torrey, 1992).

Symptoms

Once schizophrenia has fully developed, there is a wide range of symptoms that may be present at varying levels of severity, including negative, positive, and affective symptoms. Negative symptoms are defined by the absence or paucity of behaviors, mood states, or cognitions ordinarily present in healthy individuals. Common negative symptoms include blunted (or flattened) affect, alogia (reduced amount of speech or poverty of content), emotional withdrawal, apathy, social withdrawal, attentional impairment, and motor and psychomotor retardation. Severe negative symptoms are strongly associated with poor social functioning and are weakly related to social skill deficits (Bellack, Morrison, Wixted, & Mueser, 1990). These symptoms are relatively stable over time (Lewine, 1990; Mueser, Sayers, Schooler, Mance, & Haas, 1994). Despite overlap between some negative symptoms and depression (e.g., decreased interests), prominent negative symptoms occur in schizophrenia independent of depression. While each of the negative symptoms can have a particularly pernicious effect on outcome, attentional impairments are especially insidious and may require systematic modifications of psychotherapeutic techniques. Patients who evidence severe deficits in attention and concentration often have difficulty with more abstract reasoning and thus may be especially poor candidates for cognitive or psychodynamic therapies, which rely more heavily on conceptualization and/or interpretation.

Positive symptoms, in contrast to negative symptoms, are defined as the presence of thoughts or behaviors that are ordinarily absent in healthy persons. The most common positive symptoms include hallucinations and delusions.

Examples of other positive symptoms are loose associations, word salad, stereotypic behaviors, mannerisms, and posturing. Positive symptoms are less stable than negative symptoms over time, and exacerbations of positive symptoms frequently require rehospitalizations for acute treatment. Because relapses of positive symptoms are associated with a marked worsening in social functioning and negative symptoms, lowering patients' vulnerability to relapses of positive symptoms is an important goal of pharmacological and psychotherapeutic interventions for schizophrenia.

In addition to negative and positive symptoms, affective symptoms, such as depression, anxiety, and anger, are common in schizophrenia. Most patients experience bouts of severe depression, which often presage relapses (Ventura, Nuechterlein, Lukoff, & Hardesty, 1989). Approximately 50% of persons with schizophrenia attempt suicide at some time during their lives, with a 10% rate of mortality (Roy, 1986). Affective symptoms in schizophrenia tend to be related to high levels of unremitting positive symptoms (Mueser, Douglas, Bellack, & Morrison, 1991) and lead patients to develop personal coping strategies to manage these distressful experiences (Falloon & Talbot, 1981).

The symptoms of schizophrenia vary widely among individuals; however, all patients experience problems initiating and maintaining meaningful interpersonal relationships, meeting socially defined roles (e.g., student, homemaker, wage-earner), and self-care skills (e.g., grooming and hygiene). Many people with schizophrenia experience a poor quality of life. Substandard housing or homelessness, limited access to medical care, poor nutrition, few friendships, and limited finances would be expected to take a heavy toll on any person; concurrent psychiatric difficulties only compound the situation. Quality of life, which might best be conceptualized as the individual's satisfaction with the life he or she is living, is an important but too often neglected aspect of the clinical care of persons with schizophrenia.

STRESS–VULNERABILITY–COPING SKILLS
MODEL OF SCHIZOPHRENIA

A variety of different stress–vulnerability models have been proposed to account for the episodic course of schizophrenia (Ciompi, 1987). These models share the basic assumptions that the presence and severity of schizophrenic symptoms are the result of the combined influences of psychobiological vulnerability and environmental stress. Biological vulnerability is believed to be determined early in life by genetic and other biological factors, although substance abuse may increase vulnerability to psychosis. Environmental stressors, such as life events (e.g., the death of a significant other), exposure to high levels of negative ambient emotion (i.e., "expressed emotion") (Kavanagh, 1992), and lack of meaningful structure impinge on vulnerability to increase risk of relapse and rehospitalization. Coping skills (e.g., social skills) reduce the noxiousness of stressors on the individual, thereby lowering vulnerability to stress-induced relapses (Liberman & Mueser, 1989).

There are several implications of the stress–vulnerability model for the treatment of schizophrenia. Generally, the model suggests that the outcome of the illness can be improved by reducing vulnerability, reducing environmental stress, or enhancing coping skills. Most currently available treatments for schizophrenia share one or more of these goals. Thus, biological vulnerability can be lessened by providing antipsychotic medications and decreasing substance abuse. Family interventions have been developed with the primary aim of reducing environmental stress (Mueser & Glynn, 1995). Individual treatment approaches, such as social skills training (Liberman, DeRisi, & Mueser, 1989), tend to focus mainly on improving patients' coping skills.

TREATMENT OF SCHIZOPHRENIA

Pharmacological Treatment for Biological Vulnerability

The discovery of antipsychotic medications almost 40 years ago revolutionized the treatment of schizophrenia, enabling the majority of patients to be treated as outpatients in the community. Numerous double-blind, controlled studies have been conducted that attest to the efficacy of antipsychotic medications for schizophrenic patients. Antipsychotics serve two primary purposes in the treatment of schizophrenia. First, they reduce acute symptoms that appear during an exacerbation, including both positive and negative symptoms (Kane & Marder, 1993). Second, the prophylactic administration of antipsychotics after a relapse lowers the probability of subsequent relapses by 30% to 60% (Kane, 1989). Recent research indicates that very low dosages of antipsychotic medication are effective at lowering risk of relapse (Van Putten & Marder, 1986), suggesting that patients' vulnerability to long-term side effects of these medications (e.g., tardive dyskinesia) can be reduced. Further, recent advances in the development of atypical antipsychotic medications (e.g., clozapine, risperidone) hold promise for improving the functioning of patients who are treatment-refractory to the standard antipsychotics (Meltzer, 1990). Nevertheless, the antipsychotics are not a cure for schizophrenia, and significant residual symptoms usually persist between episodes, resulting in severe impairments in social functioning. For these reasons, antipsychotic medications are a mainstay in all treatment programs for schizophrenia, yet there is still a great need for effective psychotherapeutic interventions that impact on the pervasive deficits of schizophrenia.

Family Therapy to Reduce Environmental Stress

In view of the limited data available substantiating the efficacy of individual psychotherapy (Mueser & Berenbaum, 1990), the preponderance of rigorously conducted studies demonstrating the benefits of family therapy for persons with schizophrenia is especially welcome. A confluence of critical historical and scientific factors no doubt contribute to the growing interest in this area. The prominence of the deinstitutionalization movement and the commitment to community care included the expectation that family members would shoulder more of the burden for caring for their mentally ill relatives. Caring for the mentally ill can be a challenging, onerous, and demanding task, however, and family members became quite vocal in their need for support and aid. In addition, the past 25 years have witnessed a revolution in the conceptualization of psychological interventions. While dynamically based treatments tend to be long term, intensive, less structured, and focused on the inner workings of the individual, more recently developed interventions are frequently shorter, more structured, and problem-focused and thus lend themselves easily to use in a family format.

Perhaps most importantly, a series of studies in the 1970s and 1980s demonstrated that family attitudes assessed at the time of a symptom exacerbation of a schizophrenic person predicted his or her relapse during the subsequent 9 months (Brown, Birley, & Wing, 1972; Kavanagh, 1992; Vaughn & Leff, 1976a; Vaughn, Snyder, Jones, Freeman, & Falloon, 1984). These family attitudes are assessed using the Camberwell Family Interview (CFI; Vaughn & Leff, 1976b), which is a 90-minute assessment conducted with the relative while the patient is absent. The CFI is a semistructured interview focused on obtaining a brief chronology of the patient's illness in addition to the specifics of his or her behavior, and the relative's response to it, in the 3 months prior to the index hospitalization. Interviews are scored for (1) number of critical comments, (2) number of positive comments, (3) hostile attitudes, (4) warmth, and (5) overinvolvement. Higher levels of critical comments, hostility, and overinvolvement (high "expressed emotion" or EE), which is likely normative among Anglos in the United States (Vaughn et al., 1984), appears to reflect the extraordinary toll that caring for a mentally ill relative exacts. High EE is associated with increased rates of relapse, although the directionality of this relation is controversial (Glynn et al., 1990). Nevertheless, studies demonstrating the importance of ambient stress, as indicated by EE, on prognosis in schizophrenia, quickly evolved into investigations of whether the more facilitative low EE family attitudes and behaviors could be taught.

In all, 10 published family studies meet at least minimal experimental design standards, including random assignment of rigorously diagnosed, recently exacerbated schizophrenic subjects to carefully developed and reliably conducted family treatment interventions compared to standard treatment (Falloon et al., 1982; Glick et al., 1985; Goldstein, Rodnick, Evans, May, & Steinberg, 1978; Hogarty et al., 1986; Kottgen, Sonnichsen, Mollenhauer, & Jurth, 1984; Leff, Kuipers, Berkowitz, Eberlein-Vries, & Sturgeon, 1982; Mingyuan et al., 1993; Randolph et al., 1994; Tarrier et al., 1988; Xiong et al., 1994). All study designs involved embedding the family intervention in a comprehensive treatment program, including psychiatric medication administration. Most, but not all, also utilized outcome assessors blind to treatment group assignment. Importantly, these studies differed on a variety of dimensions, including location of intervention (home, inpatient, or outpatient clinic), modality (single family treatment versus multiple family groups), intervention duration (6 weeks to 2 years), inclusion of the ill relative in sessions, and the degree of formal structure in the intervention. With the exception of the psychodynamically oriented treatment conducted by Kottgen et al. (1984), these studies have established that family-based interventions can have a significant, positive impact on many patients with schizophrenia and, frequently, on their relatives as well. The consistency of these positive findings is particularly striking in light of the variations in the treatments provided and the methodological difficulties in the investigations.

Social Learning Interventions to Increase Coping Skills

For decades, psychodynamic psychotherapy for schizophrenia was the dominant treatment approach, but recent evidence has questioned the efficacy of this intervention for schizophrenia (May, 1968, 1984; Mueser & Berenbaum, 1990). As the lack of efficacy of psychodynamic treatments for schizophrenia has become recognized, the role of social skills training as a viable alternative has grown. Since the publication of Ayllon and Azrin's (1968) seminal book on the token economy for chronic psychiatric patients, there has been a proliferation of social learning–based treatments for schizophrenia. Most early social learning interventions for schizophrenia were based on the token economy (see review by Glynn, 1990). However, by the 1970s, social skills training had become the focus of extensive research. The token economy appears to be the treatment of choice for chronic, treatment-refractory inpatients (Paul & Lentz, 1977). Nevertheless, most patients with schizophrenia require outpatient interventions that can be provided on a group or individual basis (e.g., social skills training).

A survey conducted by Taylor and Dowell (1986) indicated that over 50% of board-and-care homes for chronic mental patients provide social skills training to their clients. Unfortunately, this same survey also found that most board-and-care operators had a poor understanding of the principles of social skills training. It is likely that many treatment settings claiming to conduct social skills training fail to adhere to the core ingredients of treatment, including demonstration, behavior rehearsal, feedback, and homework. However, the body of research on social skills training has grown in recent years, and evidence suggests that this approach may be beneficial for schizophrenia.

The fundamental premise of social skills training is that the social impairments of schizophrenia can be rectified through systematically teaching the behavioral components of social skill (e.g., appropriate voice tone and loudness, gaze, verbal content). Teaching is conducted through a combination of therapist modeling (i.e., demonstration of the skill), patient behavioral rehearsal (i.e., role playing), positive and corrective feedback, and homework assignments to program generalization of the skill to the natural environment. Targeted social skills span a wide range of adaptive interpersonal and self-care behaviors, including the expression of feelings, conflict resolution skills, and medication management. While social skills training has been applied extensively to persons with schizophrenia, the social skills model makes no specific assumptions about the origins of skill deficits, and the approach has been used with a variety of different clinical populations (Liberman, DeRisi, & Mueser, 1989).

Six controlled studies have been conducted on social skills training for schizophrenic patients that have assessed the impact of treatment on social adjustment, symptomatology, and/or relapse. Bellack, Turner, Hersen, and Luber (1984) examined the efficacy of skills training in a group of schizophrenic patients who had recently received inpatient treatment for an acute symptom exacerbation. Results of the study indicated that, 6 months after the initiation of treatment, patients who received skills training had maintained their improvements in symptomatology that had occurred over the first 3 months of treatment, whereas the symptoms of patients who had not received skills training deteriorated from 3 to 6 months post hospital discharge.

Liberman, Mueser, and Wallace (1986; Wallace & Liberman, 1985) examined the effects of an intensive social skills training program compared to an equally intensive "Holistic Health Treatment" program (e.g., exercise, yoga) for inpatients with schizophrenia awaiting discharge into the community. The social skills training patients were more adjusted and less symptomatic at the 2-year follow-up. Hogarty and his colleagues have conducted the largest study of social skills training for schizophrenia, which compared skills training with family psychoeducation over 2 years (Hogarty, Anderson, & Reiss, 1987; Hogarty et al., 1986; Hogarty et al., 1991). Outpatients who had recently been treated for an acute symptom exacerbation were assigned to 2 years of social skills training, family psychoeducation, skills training and family psychoeducation, or standard treatment (medication, case management, day treatment). In contrast to the Bellack et al. (1984) and Liberman et al. (1986) studies, patients were treated individually with social skills training, rather than in groups. Overall, the pattern of results supported the efficacy of the family treatment over social skills training, which was better than the control treatment.

Dobson, McDougall, Busheikin, and Aldous (1995) examined the effects of a brief social skills training program (four sessions per week for 9 weeks) provided in a day hospital. Thirty-three patients with schizophrenia were randomly assigned to skills training or a social milieu group (supportive discussion, exercise, and activity groups) and were then followed up 3 months after the end of treatment. Throughout the course of treatment, symptom severity ended to lessen for patients in both groups. Patients who received social skills training had significantly fewer negative symptoms throughout and at the end of treatment than the social milieu patients, although this difference was no longer significant at the 3-month follow-up. There were no differences in positive symptoms between the groups.

Hayes, Halford, and Varghese (1995) compared social skills training to discussion groups for 63 outpatients with schizophrenia receiving treatment in a day hospital. Skills training consisted of 36 sessions over 18 weeks with nine additional booster sessions conducted over the following 6 months. Patients who received skills training improved more in social skills than discussion group patients; however, the groups did not differ in symptoms, relapses, social adjustment, or quality of life. A limitation of this study was the fairly high dropout rate (35%).

Finally, Marder and colleagues (1995) compared 2-year outcome of randomly assigned patients receiving either group social skills training (with an emphasis on medication management, symptom management, and social problem-solving) or supportive group therapy. All patients were prescribed a low dose of injectable fluphenazine. Concurrently, patients were also randomized to receive either a fluphenazine supplement or placebo when they experienced an increase in prodromal symptoms. Patients in the social skills training groups evidenced better social adjustment at 2 years.

Overall, the controlled studies on social skills training for schizophrenia provide some support for its efficacy, especially when treatment is provided over the long term (Mueser, Wallace, & Liberman, 1995). It is clear the skills training can improve social skills, and there is some evidence supporting its effect on social functioning. The impact of social skills training on the symptoms of schizophrenia is less clear, but it remains an important avenue for improving social functioning.

THE AGING INDIVIDUAL
WITH SCHIZOPHRENIA

Long-term studies of the natural history of schizophrenia suggest that the first 10 years of the illness are marked by exacerbations and remissions, but symptoms substantially remit in over half of the patients later in life. This improvement is likely a result of many factors. First, age-related decreases in dopamine and other changes in neurotransmitters and receptor sensitivity may result in symptom reductions. Second, with increasing illness experience, many patients develop a greater understanding into their disorder and its treatment. They may especially acquire illness management skills in the identification and avoidance of stressors that contribute to exacerbations, as well as to the benefits of medication that may result in increased compliance. Third, substance abuse tends to decline with age in both the general population and among patients (Chen & Kandel, 1995; Mueser, Yarnold, & Bellack, 1992). Substance abuse can worsen the course of schizophrenia (Drake, Mueser, Clark, & Wallach, 1996), and decreased use over time can improve patients' symptoms and level of functioning (Zisook et al., 1992).

In spite of these positive aspects, the aging person with schizophrenia faces many social and physical challenges. The deinstitutionalization movement has perhaps had the most profound influence on the lives of persons with schizophrenia, whether young adults or older. Compared to a person without a psychiatric disorder, persons with schizophrenia are less likely to marry, less likely to have children, and less likely to work. In the community, their social networks are often restricted to members of their families of origin and a few friends. Thus, they often have few self-perceived life accomplishments with which to buffer the effects of aging.

The literature on family burden of psychiatric illness is replete with reports of aging parents (usually mothers) caring for their middle-aged children with schizophrenia (e.g., Bulger, Wandersman, & Goldman, 1993; MacGregor, 1994;

Platt, 1985). Even if parent and child no longer reside together, the parent often plays a critical role in supervising the patient's treatment and life-style, as well as in supplementing any other financial resources available to him or her (Salo-kangas, Palo-oja, & Ojanen, 1991). When the parent becomes ill or dies, the child, then frequently in his or her 40s, must become accustomed to a dramatic reduction in financial and social support, which may also coincide with a loss of residence. Even if they feel an emotional bond with their ill relative, siblings are often reluctant to assume the burden the parent bore, contributing to the meager circumstances of many patients' lives. Many older adults who become frail or develop dementia reside with their children (especially their daughters), who become care providers. In contrast, many individuals with life-long schizo-phrenia who have grown older never had children, leaving them without this family care provider resource.

This situation is further complicated by the fact that mortality rates in per-sons with schizophrenia are higher than nonpsychiatric comparison groups (Tsuang, Woolsen, & Fleming, 1980). In addition to relatively high rates of sui-cide (Drake, Gates, Whittaker, & Cotton, 1985), the physical health of many persons with schizophrenia is more typical of those much older (Mulsant et al., 1993) and no doubt yields shortened life-spans. Factors that may contribute to this poor physical health include a high prevalence of health-damaging behav-iors, such as smoking (Hughes, Hatsukami, Mitchell, & Dahlgren, 1986) and substance abuse (Drake et al., 1989), limited access to good health care because of financial constraints, and a delay in seeking medical treatment as a result of the high pain threshold found in many persons with schizophrenia (Dworkin, 1994).

A final area of concern in the aging person with schizophrenia is neuroleptic treatment response. Antipsychotic-induced tardive dyskinesia is a neurological syndrome of persistent abnormal involuntary movements that is more prevalent in older patients. Age and duration of exposure to antipsychotic medications are extensively documented as primary risk factors for the development of tardive dyskinesia. Some researchers have also suggested that diagnosis is a risk factor. For example, increased risk of tardive dyskinesia may be associated with cogni-tive impairment or organic brain damage (Kane et al., 1992). However, there does not appear to be any difference in the risk of developing tardive dyskinesia in older adults with schizophrenia compared to older patients in other diagnostic groups. The annual incidence rate of tardive dyskinesia elderly with schizo-phrenia is 26% to 45%, depending on the criteria for tardive dyskinesia that are applied (Jeste, Lacro, Gilbert, Kline, & Kline, 1993). The more conservative estimate of 26% is nearly six times the rate reported for younger patients (Kane, Woerner, & Lieberman, 1988).

Age is associated with remission of symptoms in more than half of individ-uals with schizophrenia (Harding et al., 1987a,b), suggesting that some elderly individuals may be spared the risks of continued exposure to antipsychotic medications. Jeste and colleagues (1993) reviewed six double-blind studies of antipsychotic drug withdrawal that included older adults with schizophrenia followed for a mean of 6 months and found an average relapse rate of 40%, compared to a relapse rate of 11% for those who continued on medication.

Predictors of psychotic relapse following withdrawal included younger age, higher dose, longer duration of treatment, more severe symptoms, and recent psychiatric hospitalization. Adverse effects of withdrawal in addition to relapse include restlessness and social withdrawal. The authors concluded that stable, chronic outpatients without a history of antipsychotic discontinuation should be considered for a carefully monitored trial of antipsychotic withdrawal.

Controlled, prospective data on the efficacy and side effects of the newer atypical antipsychotic medications in late life schizophrenia are needed. The reduced extrapyramidal (parkinsonian) side effects and reported efficacy with respect to negative symptoms suggest that trials with agents such as clozapine and risperidone, are indicated. These agents have their own unique profile of side effects that will warrant special attention in the elderly patient.

LATE-ONSET SCHIZOPHRENIA

Late-life schizophrenia is a term used to describe older individuals with schizophrenia comprising two diagnostic groups. The first group consists of elderly individuals who had the onset of schizophrenia in young adulthood or "early-onset schizophrenia." The second group includes people who had their first episode in middle age or old age, or "late-onset schizophrenia." The diagnosis of late-onset schizophrenia has evolved from early descriptions of paraphrenia. Kraepelin (1919/1971) used the term *paraphrenia* to describe a group of patients, frequently older in age, with symptoms similar to dementia praecox but with fewer affective and volitional symptoms (e.g., apathy). Kay and Roth (1961) described late paraphrenia as a paranoid syndrome occurring in late life in the absence of dementia or confusional states. Late paraphrenia was characterized by onset after age 45 of a well-organized paranoid delusional system, with or without auditory hallucinations, and often occurring with preserved personality. Late paraphrenia was more common among women than men.

More recently, psychiatric diagnostic criteria including the *Diagnostic and Statistical Manual of Mental Disorders* (*DSM*) and the *International Classification of Diseases* (*ICD*) have been revised to reclassify most individuals formally diagnosed with late paraphrenia as schizophrenia. For example, the third edition of the *Diagnostic and Statistical Manual* (*DSM-III*; American Psychiatric Association, 1980) required onset of symptoms before the age of 45 for a diagnosis of schizophrenia. Recent revisions allow for a diagnosis of schizophrenia with the first onset of symptoms after age 45 (*DSM-III-R*, APA, 1987; *DSM-IV*, APA, 1994). However, the precise relationship of late-onset schizophrenia (LOS) to early onset schizophrenia (EOS) remains controversial.

A variety of views have been expressed on the validity of including LOS within the general diagnostic category of schizophrenia (Almeida, Howard, Levy, & David, 1995a,b). First, it has been argued that LOS is essentially the manifestation of schizophrenia in older age (Harris & Jeste, 1988; Pearlson et al., 1989; Rabins, Pauker, & Thomas, 1984). This view suggests that the chronological delay in age of onset is associated with some characteristic differences from EOS, but it is most accurately classified as a schizophrenic syndrome. A second view argues that LOS (or more accurately late paraphrenia) has different risk factors and characteristics supporting a different etiology and different pathogenic mechanisms that are distinct from schizophrenia (Almeida et al., 1995a; Almeida, Förstl, Howard, & David, 1993). A third view suggests that LOS may have a different pathogenic mechanism consistent with age-related organic brain damage or early manifestations of a progressive degenerative dementia (Castle & Murray, 1991, 1993; Holden, 1987; Hymas, Nauguib, & Levy, 1989; Murray, 1994). Finally, LOS has been described as a heterogeneous condition representing a variety of etiologies and disorders (Holden, 1987; Howard, Castle, Wessely, & Murray, 1993; Lesser et al., 1993; Post, 1966). This later view most accurately represents the practitioner's dilemma when assessing older adults with late-onset psychotic disorders in clinical settings who are not screened with research exclusionary criteria (Harris & Jeste, 1988).

Prevalence

In a review of eight studies reporting on the occurrence of late-onset schizophrenia, Harris and Jeste (1988) estimated that almost one-quarter (23%) of patients with schizophrenia have the onset of their disorder after age 40, including 13% between age 40 to 50, 7% ages 50 to 60, and 3% after age 60. These studies predominantly consider hospitalized patients, although similar findings are reported for community-residing individuals. In a 20-year study of first diagnosis of psychiatric disorders in the community in Camberwell catchment area of London, England, Castle, Wessely, Der, and Murray (1991) reported that 28% of patients with schizophrenia had onset of the illness after age 44, and 12% after age 64. The annual incidence rate for late-onset schizophrenia was 12.6/100,000, approximately half that for those age 16 to 25.

Gender and Family History

In a comprehensive review of the literature, Harris and Jeste (1988) found that virtually all studies report a greater proportion of women compared to men in late-onset schizophrenia. This finding is in contrast to hospital-based studies on young persons with EOS, where male gender is reported to be more prevalent. Community studies report an equivalent proportion of women to men with EOS (*DSM-IV*). In contrast, the reported ratio of women to men ranges from 1.9:1 to 54:2. This difference is not accounted for by disparities in life expectancy for women compared to men.

Several hypotheses for this difference have been proposed. One view suggests that EOS and LOS represent different forms of schizophrenia with distinct characteristics. An alternative view suggests that the onset of schizophrenia is differentially delayed in women due to a variety of biological factors. This latter hypothesis is supported by the consistent finding across many studies on EOS showing that the onset in women is approximately 5 years later than in men (Lewine, 1988). In LOS, this difference may be even more pronounced. In a community study that included EOS and LOS, Castle and Murray (1993) found a mean age of onset of 31.2 years for males and 41.1 years for females. By gender, 16% of males had the onset of schizophrenia after age 45, compared to 38% of females. Speculation about the difference in age of onset between men and women includes a possible protective antidopinergic effect of estrogens, precipitating effect of androgens, and neurodevelopmental differences (Castle & Murray, 1993).

Family studies suggest that there is a higher prevalence of schizophrenia in relatives of patients with late-onset schizophrenia compared to the general population, but lower compared to early-onset individuals with schizophrenia (Harris & Jeste, 1988). However, this finding is not reported in all studies of family history and remains controversial (Almeida et al., 1995b).

Symptoms and Phenomenology

Delusions and hallucinations are common symptoms in late-onset schizophrenia and occur at a rate comparable to those found in young adults with early-onset schizophrenia. Delusions tend to be paranoid and are often well systematized (Almeida et al., 1995a; Howard et al., 1993; Kay & Roth, 1961). Auditory hallucinations are substantially more common than visual or somatic hallucinations, similar to young adults with EOS (Almeida et al., 1995a). In contrast to EOS, LOS is significantly less likely to manifest formal thought disorder, negative symptoms, or inappropriate affect (Almeida et al., 1995a; Howard et al., 1993; Kay & Roth, 1961; Pearlson & Rabins, 1988; Pearlson et al., 1989). Compared to EOS, individuals with LOS are more likely to show better premorbid occupational adjustment (Post, 1966) and higher marriage rates. However, compared to normal comparison groups, individuals with LOS are frequently socially isolated and often have schizoid or paranoid premorbid personalities (Harris & Jeste, 1988; Kay & Roth, 1961).

Neuropsychological studies of elderly EOS and LOS patients do not support the presence of a progressive cognitive impairment in schizophrenia. Elderly with EOS and LOS both have global cognitive deficits when compared to normal controls, although these deficits are stable in most patients and have been described as a static encephalopathy following initial onset of the disorder (Goldberg et al., 1993; Heaton et al., 1994). The absence of a decline in cognitive functioning over age groups is consistent with many neuroimaging and neuropathological studies that have not found evidence for an active, age-related degenerative process (Goldberg et al., 1993). However, several studies suggest that a subset of individuals with LOS progress to states of dementia (Lesser et al., 1993). For example, Holden (1987) reported that 35% of individuals with late-onset paraphrenia developed a dementia within 3 years.

Differential diagnosis should include special consideration to ruling out psychiatric disorders secondary to medical causes (formerly organic mental disorders), major affective disorders, and delusional (paranoid) disorders (Harris

& Jeste, 1988). Delusional disorder has been differentiated from LOS in *DSM-IV* by the presence on prominent nonbizarre delusions and nonprominent (or absent) hallucinations. Nonbizarre delusions involve situations that may occur in real life such as being poisoned, followed, having a disease, or deceived by a spouse or lover. In contrast, bizarre delusions involve phenomena that are considered within one's culture as totally implausible (APA, 1994; Yassa & Suranyl-Cadotte, 1993).

Sensory Impairment

In a review of 27 articles that assess visual and hearing abilities in elderly with late-onset disorders, Prager and Jeste (1993) concluded that sensory deficits are overrepresented in elderly with late-onset psychotic disorders. An association between visual impairment and visual hallucinations is suggested by the literature, although a specific relationship between visual impairment and late-onset paranoid psychosis remains controversial. On the other hand, the majority of studies reviewed support a specific association between hearing deficits and late-onset paranoid psychosis. Moderate-to-severe hearing deficits have been reported in approximately 40% of those with late-onset paranoid psychoses (Herbert & Jacobson, 1967; Kay & Roth, 1961). Proposed mechanisms include sensory deprivation, social isolation, deficits in attending and perception, and central nervous system lesions (Prager & Jeste, 1993). Significant reductions in psychotic symptoms have been reported for some individuals who have late-onset paranoid disorders after fitting with a hearing aid, suggesting that deafness may precipitate or exacerbate symptoms (Almeida et al., 1993).

Clinically, the strong association between sensory impairments, psychotic symptoms, and LOS suggests that these patients may benefit from systematic instruction in coping strategies for the management of positive symptoms. In recent years, growing evidence has emerged that patients with schizophrenia employ a wide range of different strategies for coping with positive symptoms (Carr, 1988; Falloon & Talbot, 1981; Mueser & Gingerich, 1994). Methods for managing positive symptoms typically involve either disattention or relaxation, with coping efficacy strongly related to the number of coping methods employed by the patient. One investigation by Tarrier and his colleagues (1993) indicated that patients who were taught coping strategies experienced significant reductions in positive symptoms compared to patients who received training in social problem-solving. This encouraging study suggests that elderly persons with schizophrenia characterized by persistent psychotic symptoms might benefit from receiving similar training in coping skills.

Brain Lesions

The most commonly reported structural lesions in LOS are increases in ventricle-to-brain ratio (VBR), which have also been observed in a subset of individuals with EOS (Pearlson et al., 1987; Pearlson et al., 1993). These differences in brain structure are also reported for a subset of individuals with EOS and are complicated by age-related changes and methodological concerns. Functional brain imaging techniques that examine regional differences in brain-blood perfusion have shown reductions in frontal and temporal perfusion (Miller et al., 1992) on single photon emission computed tomography (SPECT) in late-onset psychosis. A subgroup of individuals with LOS have this deficit, though the majority have multiple areas of reduced blood flow with white matter abnormalities (Lesser et al., 1993). Finally, Corey-Bloom, Jernigan, Archibald, Harris, and Jeste (1995) found that LOS elderly had larger ventricular volumes compared to normal older controls, and larger thalamic volumes compared to older patients with EOS. The authors hypothesize that this finding may be relevant to prefrontal and dopamine abnormalities in schizophrenia and differences in age of onset.

PET scan study of dopamine receptor density suggests elevated numbers of dopamine receptors in LOS compared to normal controls, a finding also reported in EOS. Men start adult life with higher numbers of dopamine receptors but lose them at a greater rate with age compared to women, perhaps due to protective effects of estrogen. This difference may account for the overrepresentation of early-onset males and late-onset females in schizophrenia (Pearlson et al., 1993). Overall, imaging studies suggest that late-onset psychoses are heterogeneous, with at least one-third showing a variety of brain pathologies (Lesser et al., 1993).

Treatment

Little is known about the pharmacological treatment of elderly with schizophrenia (Jeste et al., 1993). In a review of the few available investigations, most report that antipsychotic medications result in reduced symptoms and earlier discharge from the hospital (Jeste et al., 1993). For example, in retrospective chart review studies, Post (1966) reported that 62% of patients with late-onset schizophrenia receiving adequate antipsychotic doses responded, and Rabins et al. (1984) found that 30 out of 35 improved. Age-related alterations in drug distribution and metabolism may result in higher plasma levels of antipsychotic medications in elderly compared to younger schizophrenic patients. In addition, age-related changes in receptors and neurotransmitters may cause elderly to be more sensitive to the effects of medications. These physiological changes contribute to increased risk of acute adverse side effects to antipsychotic medications in the elderly, as previously discussed. Overall, these findings support the principle that effective serum levels of medication are achieved with substantially lower doses of antipsychotic medication in elderly patients with schizophrenia.

Conclusions

In summary, late-onset schizophrenia tends to be similar to early-onset schizophrenia with several notable exceptions. Individuals with late onset are more likely to be women and to have better premorbid functioning, including better occupational history and a greater likelihood of having been married. The clinical presentation is more likely to include a predominance of positive symptoms such as paranoid delusions and auditory hallucinations and less likely to have negative symptoms. Formal thought disorder is rare in late-onset schizophrenia. Among those with onset after age 60, there is a greater incidence of hearing loss compared to the general population. Finally, the limited data on treatment suggest that response to antipsychotic medication is comparable to early-onset schizophrenia, however, lower doses are indicated and the risk of adverse side effects, such as tardive dyskinesia, substantially increases with age. Much remains unknown with respect to etiology, long-term course, and treatment outcome.

SUMMARY

The research literature on older persons with schizophrenia is quite limited (Belitsky & McGlashan, 1993), and thus few definitive conclusions can be reached at this time. Further, there is a paucity of research on treatments and services for older persons with severe and persistent mental illness, particularly in the area of psychosocial treatment (Light & Lebowitz, 1991). Recent interest in late-onset disorders has stimulated a series of studies on late-onset schizophrenia. In comparison, relatively little attention has focused on the individual with life-long early-onset schizophrenia who is now in late middle age or old age. Assessment of the needs and preferences of these individuals is sorely lacking. Specific attention to the service needs and residential supports for older persons with schizophrenia is needed. Considering the advances made over the past decade in psychosocial treatments for schizophrenia (Bellack & Mueser, 1993), the time is ripe for systematic investigation of how to tailor these interventions for the older population. Until more definitive research on the psychological treatment of older adults with schizophrenia has been conducted, clinicians will need to base their interventions on strategies found to be effective with younger patients, tempered by an understanding of the unique challenges faced by elder individuals.

REFERENCES

Almeida, O. P., Förstl, H., Howard, R., & David, A. S. (1993). Unilateral auditory hallucinations. *British Journal of Psychiatry, 162,* 262–264.
Almeida, O. P., Howard, R. J., Levy, R., & David, A. (1995a). Psychotic states arising in late life (late paraphrenia): The role of risk factors. *British Journal of Psychiatry, 166,* 215–228.
Almeida, O. P., Howard, R. J., Levy, R., & David, A. (1995b). Psychotic states arising in late life (late paraphrenia): Psychopathology and nosology. *British Journal of Psychiatry, 166,* 205–214.
American Psychiatric Association. (1980). *Diagnostic and statistical manual of mental disorders* (3rd ed.). Washington, DC: Author.
American Psychiatric Association. (1987). *Diagnostic and statistical manual of mental disorders* (3rd ed., revised). Washington, DC: Author.

American Psychiatric Association. (1994). *Diagnostic and statistical manual of mental disorders* (4th ed.). Washington, DC: Author.

Andreasen, N. C., Ehrhardt, J. C., Swayze, V. W., II, Alliger, R. J., Yuh, W. T., Cohen, G., & Ziebell, S. (1990). Magnetic resonance imaging of the brain in schizophrenia: The pathophysiologic significance of structural abnormalities. *Archives of General Psychiatry, 47,* 35–44.

Andreasen, N. C., Nashrallah, H. A., Dunn, V., Olson, S. C., Grove, W. M., Ehrhardt, J. C., Coffman, J. A., & Crossett, J. H. W. (1986). Structural abnormalities in the frontal system in schizophrenia. *Archives of General Psychiatry, 43,* 136–144.

Ayllon, T., & Azrin, N. H. (1968). *The token economy.* New York: Appleton-Century-Crofts.

Belitsky, R., & McGlashan, T. H. (1993). The manifestations of schizophrenia in late life: A dearth of data. *Schizophrenia Bulletin, 19,* 683–689.

Bellack, A. S., Morrison, R. L., Wixted, J. T., & Mueser, K. T. (1990). An analysis of social competence in schizophrenia. *British Journal of Psychiatry, 156,* 809–818.

Bellack, A. S., & Mueser, K. T. (1993). Psychosocial treatment of schizophrenia. *Schizophrenia Bulletin, 19,* 317–336.

Bellack, A. S., Turner, S. M., Hersen, M., & Luber, R. F. (1984). An examination of the efficacy of social skills training for chronic schizophrenic patients. *Hospital and Community Psychiatry, 35,* 1023–1028.

Brown, G. W., Birley, J. L. T., & Wing, J. K. (1972). Influence of family life on the course of schizophrenic disorders: A replication. *British Journal of Psychiatry, 121,* 241–258.

Bulger, M. W., Wandersman, A., & Goldman, C. R. (1993). Burdens and gratifications of caregiving: Appraisal of parental care of adults with schizophrenia. *American Journal of Orthopsychiatry, 63,* 255–265.

Carr, V. (1988). Patients' techniques for coping with schizophrenia: An exploratory study. *British Journal of Medical Psychology, 61,* 339–352.

Castle, D. J., & Murray, R. (1991). The neurodevelopmental basis of sex differences in schizophrenia. *Psychological Medicine, 21,* 565–575.

Castle, D. J., & Murray, R. M. (1993). The epidemiology of late-onset schizophrenia. *Schizophrenia Bulletin, 19,* 691–700.

Castle, D. J., Wessely, S., Der, G., & Murray, R. (1991). The incidence of operationally defined schizophrenia in Camberwell, 1965 to 1984. *British Journal of Psychiatry, 159,* 790–794.

Chen, K., & Kandel, D. B. (1995). The natural history of drug use from adolescence to the mid-thirties in a general population sample. *American Journal of Public Health, 85,* 41–47.

Ciompi, L. (1980). The natural history of schizophrenia in the long term. *British Journal of Psychiatry, 136,* 413–420.

Ciompi, L. (1987). Toward a coherence multidimensional understanding and therapy of schizophrenia: Converging new concepts. In J. S. Strauss, W. Boker, & H. D. Brenner (Eds.), *Psychosocial treatment of schizophrenia: Multidimensional concepts, psychological, family, and self-help perspectives* (pp. 48–62). Toronto: Hans Huber.

Corey-Bloom, J., Jernigan, T., Archibald, S., Harris, M., & Jeste, D. (1995). Quantitative magnetic resonance imaging of the brain in late-life schizophrenia. *American Journal of Psychiatry, 152,* 447–449.

Degreef, G., Ashtari, M., Wu, H., Borenstein, M., Geisler, S., & Lieberman, J. (1991). Follow-up MRI study in first episode schizophrenia. *Schizophrenia Research, 5,* 204–205.

Dobson, D. J. G., McDougall, G., Busheikin, J., & Aldous, J. (1995). Social skills training and symptomatology in schizophrenia. *Hospital and Community Psychiatry, 46,* 376–380.

Drake, R. E., Gates, C., Whitaker, A., & Cotton, P. G. (1985). Suicide among schizophrenics: A review. *Comprehensive Psychiatry, 26,* 90–100.

Drake, R. E., Mueser, K. T., Clark, R. E., & Wallach, M. A. (1996). Course, treatment, and outcome of substance disorder in persons with severe mental illness. *American Journal of Orthopsychiatry, 66,* 42–51.

Drake, R. E., Osher, F. C., & Wallach, M. A. (1989). Alcohol use and abuse in schizophrenia: A prospective community study. *Journal of Nervous and Mental Disease, 177,* 408–414.

Dworkin, R. H. (1994). Pain insensitivity in schizophrenia: A neglected phenomenon and some implications. *Schizophrenia Bulletin, 20,* 235–248.

Falloon, I., Boyd, J., McGill, C., Razani, J., Moss, H., & Gilderman, A. (1982). Family management in the prevention of exacerbations of schizophrenia. *New England Journal of Medicine, 306*, 1437–1440.

Falloon, I. R. H., & Talbot, R. E. (1981). Persistent auditory hallucinations: Coping mechanisms and implications for management. *Psychological Medicine, 11*, 329–339.

Glick, I., Clarkin, J., Spencer, J., Haas, G., Lewis, A., Peyser, J., DeMane, N., Good-Ellis, M., Harris, E., & Lestelle, V. (1985). A controlled evaluation of inpatient family intervention: I. Preliminary results of a 6-month follow-up. *Archives of General Psychiatry, 42*, 882–886.

Glynn, S. M. (1990). Token economy approaches for psychiatric patients: Progress and pitfalls over 25 years. *Behavior Modification, 14*, 383–407.

Glynn, S. M., Randolph, E., Eth, S., Paz, G., Shaner, A., & Strachan, A. (1990). Patient psychopathology and expressed emotion in schizophrenia. *British Journal of Psychiatry, 157*, 877–880.

Goldberg, T. E., Hyde, T. M., Kleinman, J. E., & Weinberger, D. R. (1993). Course of schizophrenia: Neuropsychological evidence for a static encephalopathy. *Schizophrenia Bulletin, 19*, 797–804.

Goldstein, J. M. (1988). Gender differences in the course of schizophrenia. *American Journal of Psychiatry, 145*, 684–689.

Goldstein, M., Rodnick, E., Evans, J., May, P., & Steinberg, M. (1978). Drug and family therapy in the aftercare of acute schizophrenics. *Archives of General Psychiatry, 35*, 1169–1177.

Harding, C. M., Brooks, G. W., Ashikaga, T., Strauss, J. S., & Breier, A. (1987a). The Vermont longitudinal study of persons with severe mental illness. I. Methodology, study sample, and overall status 32 years later. *American Journal of Psychiatry, 144*, 718–726.

Harding, C. M., Brooks, G. W., Ashikaga, T., Strauss, J. S, & Breier, A. (1987b). The Vermont longitudinal study of persons with severe mental illness. II. Long-term outcome of subjects who retrospectively met DSM-III criteria for schizophrenia. *American Journal of Psychiatry, 144*, 727–735.

Harris, M., & Jeste, D. (1988). Late-onset schizophrenia: An overview. *Schizophrenia Bulletin, 14*, 39–55.

Hayes, R. L., Halford, W. K., & Varghese, F. T. (1995). Social skills training with chronic schizophrenic patients: Effects on community functioning. *Behavior Therapy, 26*, 433–449.

Heaton, R., Paulsen, J. S., McAdams, L. A., Kuck, J., Zisook, S., Braff, D., Harris, M. J., & Jeste, D. V. (1994). Neuropsychological deficits in schizophrenics: Relationship to age, chronicity, and dementia. *Archives of General Psychiatry, 51*, 469–476.

Herbert, M., & Jacobson, S. (1967). Late paraphrenia. *British Journal of Psychiatry, 113*, 461–469.

Hogarty, G. E., Anderson, C. M., & Reiss, D. J. (1987). Family psychoeducation, social skills training, and medication in schizophrenia: The long and short of it. *Psychopharmacology Bulletin, 23*, 12–13.

Hogarty, G. E., Anderson, C. M., Reiss, D. J., Kornblith, S. J., Greenwald, D. P., Javna, C. D., & Madonia, M. J. (1986). Family psychoeducation, social skills training, and maintenance chemotherapy in the aftercare treatment of schizophrenia. I. One-year effects of a controlled study on relapse and expressed emotion. *Archives of General Psychiatry, 43*, 633–642.

Hogarty, G. E., Anderson, C. M., Reiss, D. J., Kornblith, S. J., Greenwald, D. P., Ulrich, R. F., & Carter, M. (1991). Family psychoeducation, social skills training, and maintenance chemotherapy in the aftercare treatment of schizophrenia. II. Two-year effects of a controlled study on relapse and adjustment. *Archives of General Psychiatry, 48*, 340–347.

Holden, N. L. (1987). Late paraphrenia or the paraphrenias? A descriptive study with a 10-year follow-up. *British Journal of Psychiatry, 150*, 635–639.

Holtzman, P. S., & Matthysse, S. (1990). The genetics of schizophrenia: A review. *Psychological Science, 1*, 279–286.

Howard, R., Castle, D., Wessely, S., & Murray, R. (1993). A comparative study of 470 cases of early- and late-onset schizophrenia. *British Journal of Psychiatry, 163*, 352–357.

Hughes, J. R., Hatsukami, D. K., Mitchell, J. E., & Dahlgren, L. A. (1986). Prevalence of smoking among psychiatric outpatients. *American Journal of Psychiatry, 143*, 993–997.

Hymas, N., Nauguib, M., & Levy, R. (1989). Late paraphrenia: A follow-up study. *International Journal of Geriatric Psychiatry, 4*, 23–29.

Jeste, D. V., Lacro, J. P., Gilbert, P. L., Kline, J., & Kline, N. (1993). Treatment of late-life schizophrenia with neuroleptics. *Schizophrenia Bulletin, 19*, 817–830.

Kane, J. M. (1989). Innovations in the psychopharmacologic treatment of schizophrenia. In A. S. Bellack (Ed.), *A clinical guide for the treatment of schizophrenia* (pp. 43–75). New York: Plenum Press.

Kane, J. M., Jeste, D., Barnes, T., Casey, D., Cole, J., Davis, J., Gualtieri, C., Schooler, N., Sprague, R., & Wattstein, R. (1992). *Tardive dyskinesia: A task force report of the American Psychiatric Association*. Washington, DC: American Psychiatric Association.

Kane, J. M., & Marder, S. R. (1993). Psychopharmacologic treatment of schizophrenia. *Schizophrenia Bulletin, 19*, 287–302.

Kane, J. M., Woerner, M., & Lieberman, J. (1988). Tardive dyskinesia: Prevalence, incidence, and risk factors. *Journal of Clinical Psychopharmacology, 8*, 52–56.

Kavanagh, D. J. (1992). Recent developments in Expressed Emotion and schizophrenia. *British Journal of Psychiatry, 160*, 601–620.

Kay, D., & Roth, M. (1961). Environmental and hereditary factors in the schizophrenias of old age ("late paraphrenia") and their bearing on the general problem of causation in schizophrenia. *Journal of Mental Science, 107*, 649–686.

Kottgen, C., Sonnichsen, I., Mollenhauer, K., & Jurth, R. (1984). Group therapy with families of schizophrenic patients: Results of the Hamburg Camberwell-Family-Interview Study III. *International Journal of Family Psychiatry, 5*, 83–94.

Kraepelin, E. (1971). *Dementia Praecox and Paraphrenia* (R. M. Barclay, Trans.). Huntington, NY: Robert E. Kreiger. (Original work published in 1919)

Leff, J., Kuipers, L., Berkowitz, R., Eberlein-Vries, R., & Sturgeon, D. (1982). A controlled trial of social intervention in the families of schizophrenic patients. *British Journal of Psychiatry, 141*, 121–134.

Lesser, I., Miller, B., Swartz, R., Boone, K., Mehringer, C., & Mena, I. (1993). Brain imaging in late-life schizophrenia and related psychoses. *Schizophrenia Bulletin, 19*, 773–782.

Lewine, R. R. J. (1988). Gender in schizophrenia. In H. A. Nasrallah (Ed.), *Handbook of schizophrenia* (Vol. 3, pp. 379–397). Amsterdam: Elsevier.

Lewine, R. R. J. (1990). A discriminant validity study of negative symptoms with a special focus on depression and antipsychotic medication. *American Journal of Psychiatry, 147*, 1463–1466.

Lewine, R. R. J., Gulley, L. R., Risch, S. C., Jewart, R., & Houpt, J. L. (1990). Sexual dimorphism, brain morphology, and schizophrenia. *Schizophrenia Bulletin, 16*, 195–203.

Liberman, R. P., DeRisi, W. D., & Mueser, K. T. (1989). *Social skills training for psychiatric patients*. Needham Heights, MA: Allyn & Bacon.

Liberman, R. P., & Mueser, K. T. (1989). Schizophrenia: Psychosocial treatment. In H. I. Kaplan & B. J. Sadock (Eds.), *Comprehensive textbook of psychiatry* (Vol. V, pp. 792–806). Baltimore: Williams and Wilkins.

Liberman, R. P., Mueser, K. T., & Wallace, C. J. (1986). Social skills training for schizophrenic individuals at risk for relapse. *American Journal of Psychiatry, 143*, 523–526.

Light, E., & Lebowitz, B. D. (1991). *The elderly with chronic mental illness*. New York: Springer.

MacGregor, P. (1994). Grief: The unrecognized parental response to mental illness in a child. *Social Work, 39*, 160–166.

Marder, S. R., Liberman, R. P., Wirshing, W. C., Mintz, J., Eckman, T. A., & Johnston-Cronk, K. (1995). Management of risk relapse in schizophrenia. Manuscript under review.

May, P. R. A. (1968). *Treatment of schizophrenia: A comparative study of five treatment methods*. New York: Science House.

May, P. R. A. (1984). A step forward in research on psychotherapy of schizophrenia. *Schizophrenia Bulletin, 10*, 604–607.

Meltzer, H. Y. (1990). Clozapine: Mechanism of action in relation to its clinical advantages. In A. Kales, C. N. Stefanis, & J. Talbott (Eds.), *Recent advances in schizophrenia* (pp. 237–256). New York: Springer-Verlag.

Miller, B., Lesser, I., Mena, I., Villanueva-Meyer, J., Hill-Gutierrez, E., Boone, K., & Mehringer, C. (1992). Regional cerebral blood flow in late-life-onset psychosis. *Journal of Neuropsychiatry, Neuropsychology, and Behavioral Neurology, 5*, 132–137.

Mingyuan, Z., Heqin, Y., Chengde, Y., Jianlin, Y., Qingfeng, Y., Peijun, C., Lianfang, G., Jizhong, Y., Guangya, Q., Zhen, W., Jianhua, C., Mingua, S., Junshan, H., Longlin, W., Yi, Z., Buoying, Z., Orley, J., & Gittelman, M. (1993). Effectiveness of psychoeducation of relatives of schizophrenic patients: A prospective cohort study in five cities of China. *International Journal of Mental Health, 22,* 47–59.

Mueser, K. T., Bellack, A. S., Morrison, R. L., & Wade, J. H. (1990). Gender, social competence, and symptomatology in schizophrenia: A longitudinal analysis. *Journal of Abnormal Psychology, 99,* 138–147.

Mueser, K. T., & Berenbaum, H. (1990). Psychodynamic treatment of schizophrenia: Is there a future? [Editorial]. *Psychological Medicine, 20,* 253–262.

Mueser, K. T., Douglas, M. S., Bellack, A. S., & Morrison, R. L. (1991). Assessment of enduring deficit and negative symptom subtypes in schizophrenia. *Schizophrenia Bulletin, 17,* 565–582.

Mueser, K. T., & Gingerich, S. (1994). *Coping with schizophrenia: A guide for families.* Oakland, CA: New Harbinger.

Mueser, K. T., & Glynn, S. M. (1995). *Behavioral family therapy for psychiatric disorders.* Needham Heights, MA: Allyn & Bacon.

Mueser, K. T., Sayers, S. L., Schooler, N. R., Mance, R. M., & Haas, G. L. (1994). A multi-site investigation of the reliability of the Scale for the Assessment of Negative Symptoms. *American Journal of Psychiatry, 151,* 1453–1462.

Mueser, K. T., Wallace, C. J., & Liberman, R. P. (1995). New developments in social skills training. *Behavior Change, 12,* 31–40.

Mueser, K. T., Yarnold, P. R., & Bellack, A. S. (1992). Diagnostic and demographic correlates of substance abuse in schizophrenia and major affective disorder. *Acta Psychiatrica Scandinavica, 85,* 48–55.

Mueser, K. T., Yarnold, P. R., Levinson, D. F., Singh, H., Bellack, A. S., Kee, K., Morrison, R. L., & Yadalam, K. G. (1990). Prevalence of substance abuse in schizophrenia: Demographic and clinical correlates. *Schizophrenia Bulletin, 16,* 31–56.

Mulsant, B. H., Stergiou, A., Keshavan, M. S., Sweet, R. A., Rifai, A. H., Pasternak, R., & Zubenko, G. S. (1993). Schizophrenia in late life: Elderly patients admitted to an acute care psychiatric hospital. *Schizophrenia Bulletin, 19,* 709–721.

Murray, R. M. (1994). Neurodevelopmental schizophrenia: The rediscovery of dementia praecox. *British Journal of Psychiatry, 165,* 6–12.

Paul, G. L., & Lentz, R. J. (1977). *Psychosocial treatment of chronic mental patients: Milieu versus social-learning programs.* Cambridge, MA: Harvard University Press.

Pearlson, G. D., Garbacz, D., Tompkin, R. H., Ahn, H. S., & Rabins, P. V. (1987). Lateral cerebral ventricular size in late onset schizophrenia. In N. E. Miller & G. D. Cohen (Eds.), *Schizophrenia, paranoia, and schizophreniform disorders in later life* (pp. 246–248). Bethesda, MD: National Institute of Mental Health Center on Aging.

Pearlson, G. D., Kreger, L., Rabins, P. V., Chase, G. A., Cohen, B., Wirth, J. B., Schlaepfer, T. B., & Tune, L. E. (1989). A chart review study of late onset and early-onset schizophrenia. *American Journal of Psychiatry, 146,* 1568–1574.

Pearlson, G. D., & Rabins, P. V. (1988). The late onset psychoses—Possible risk factors. *Psychiatric Clinics of North America, Psychosis and Depression in the Elderly, 11,* 15–33.

Pearlson, G. D., Tune, L., Wong, D., Aylward, E., Barta, P., Powers, R., Tien, A., Chase, C. A., Harris, G., & Rabins, P. (1993). Quantitative D2 dopamine receptor PET and structural MRI changes in late-onset schizophrenia. *Schizophrenia Bulletin, 19,* 783–795.

Platt, S. (1985). Measuring the burden of psychiatric illness on the family: An evaluation of some rating scales. *Psychological Medicine, 15,* 383–393.

Post, F. (1966). *Persistent persecutory states of the elderly.* London: Pergamon Press.

Prager, S., & Jeste, D. V. (1993). Sensory impairment in late-life schizophrenia. *Schizophrenia Bulletin, 19,* 755–772.

Rabins, P. V., Pauker, S., & Thomas, J. (1984). Can schizophrenia begin after age 44? *Comprehensive Psychiatry, 25,* 290–293.

Randolph, E. T., Eth, S., Glynn, S. M., Paz, G. G., Leong, G. B., Shaner, A. L., Strachan, A., Van Vort, W., Escobar, J. l., & Liberman, R. P. (1994). Behavioural family management in schizophrenia: Outcome of a clinic-based intervention. *British Journal of Psychiatry, 164,* 501–506.

Roy, A., (1986). Suicide in schizophrenia. In A. Roy (Ed.), *Suicide* (pp. 97–112). Baltimore: Williams & Wilkins.

Salokangas, R. K. R., Palo-Oja, T., & Ojanen, M. (1991). The need for social support among outpatients suffering from functional psychosis. *Psychological Medicine, 21,* 209–217.

Seeman, M. V. (1986). Current outcome in schizophrenia: Women vs. men. *Acta Psychiatrica Scandinavica, 73,* 609–617.

Seeman, M. V., & Lang, M. (1990). The role of estrogens in schizophrenia gender differences. *Schizophrenia Bulletin, 16,* 185–194.

Tarrier, N., Barrowclough, C., Vaughn, C., Bamrah, J., Porceddu, K., Watts, S., & Freeman, H. (1988). The community management of schizophrenia: A controlled trial of a behavioral intervention with families to reduce relapse. *British Journal of Psychiatry, 153,* 532–542.

Tarrier, N., Beckett, R., Harwood, S., Baker, A., Yusupoff, L., & Ugarteburu, I. (1993). A trial of two cognitive behavioral methods of treating drug-resistant residual psychotic symptoms in schizophrenic patients: I. Outcome. *British Journal of Psychiatry, 162,* 524–532.

Taylor, A., & Dowell, D. A. (1986). Social skills training in board and care homes. *Psychosocial Rehabilitation Bulletin, 10,* 55–69.

Test, M. A., & Berlin, S. B. (1981). Issues of special concern to chronically mentally ill women. *Professional Psychology, 12,* 136–145.

Test, M. A., Burke, S. S., & Wallisch, L. S. (1990). Gender differences of young adults with schizophrenic disorders in community care. *Schizophrenia Bulletin, 16,* 331–344.

Tsuang, M. T., Woolson, R. F., & Fleming, J. A. (1980). Premature deaths in schizophrenia and affective disorders. *Archives of General Psychiatry, 37,* 979–983.

Van Putten, T., & Marder, S. R. (1986). Low-dose treatment strategies. *Journal of Clinical Psychiatry, 47* (Suppl. 5), 12–16.

Vaughn, C., & Leff, J. (1976a). The influence of family and social factors on the course of psychiatric illness. *American Journal of Psychiatry, 129,* 125–137.

Vaughn, C., & Leff, J. (1976b). The measurement of expressed emotion in the families of psychiatric patients. *British Journal of Psychiatry, 15,* 156–165.

Vaughn, C., Snyder, K., Jones, S., Freeman, W., & Falloon, I. (1984). Family factors in schizophrenia relapse. *Archives of General Psychiatry, 41,* 1169–1177.

Ventura, J., Nuechterlein, K. H., Lukoff, D., & Hardesty, J. P. (1989). A prospective study of stressful life events and schizophrenic relapse. *Journal of Abnormal Psychology, 98,* 407–411.

Wallace, C. J., & Liberman, R. P. (1985). Social skills training for patients with schizophrenia: A controlled clinical trial. *Psychiatry Research, 15,* 239–247.

Weinberger, D. R., Berman, K. F., Suddath, R., & Torrey, E. F. (1992). Evidence of dysfunction of a prefrontal-limbic network in schizophrenia: A magnetic resonance imaging and regional cerebral blood flow study of discordant monozygotic twins. *American Journal of Psychiatry, 148,* 890–897.

Xiong, W., Phillips, M. R., Hu, X., Ruiwen, W., Dai, Q., Kleinman, J., & Kleinman, A. (1994). Family-based intervention for schizophrenic patients in China: A randomized controlled trial. *British Journal of Psychiatry, 165,* 239–247.

Yassa, R., & Suranyl-Cadotte, B. (1993). Clinical characteristics of late-onset schizophrenia and delusional disorder. *Schizophrenia Bulletin, 19,* 701–707.

Zigler, E., & Glick, M. (1986). *A developmental approach to adult psychopathology.* New York: Wiley.

Zisook, S., Heaton, R., Moranville, J., Kuck, J., Jernigan, T., & Braff, D. (1992). Past substance abuse and clinical course of schizophrenia. *American Journal of Psychiatry, 149,* 552–553.

CHAPTER 12

Mental Retardation

JOHNNY L. MATSON AND LINDA A. LeBLANC

CHAPTER OUTLINE

Description of the Problem
  Aging Persons with Mental Retardation
  Dual Diagnosis
Case Identification and Presenting
  Complaints
History
Selection of Psychological Treatment
  Psychotherapy
  Cognitive-Behavioral and Behavioral
  Techniques

Depression
Sleep Problems
Concurrent Medical Treatment
Course of Treatment
Follow-Up
Overall Evaluation
Summary
References

DESCRIPTION OF THE PROBLEM

Mental retardation is a condition characterized by impaired or below average cognitive functioning, concurrent deficits in adaptive abilities and manifested before the age of 18 (American Psychiatric Association, 1994). The diagnosis is usually based on the results of an individually administered test of cognitive abilities (IQ test) and an assessment of adaptive behavior. Within the condition of mental retardation, four levels of severity have been described (APA, 1994). Each of these categories is noted below.

The term *mild* mental retardation is used for persons whose IQ ranges from 50 to 55 to approximately 70 and who demonstrate comparable deficits in adaptive behavior. This group constitutes 85% of all individuals with mental retardation (Payne & Mercer, 1975). People with mild mental retardation often do

---

JOHNNY L. MATSON AND LINDA A. LeBLANC • Department of Psychology, Louisiana State University, Baton Rouge, Louisiana 70803.
Psychological Treatment of Older Adults: An Introductory Text, edited by Michel Hersen and Vincent B. Van Hasselt. Plenum Press, New York, 1996.

not demonstrate deficits until school age, when it may become evident that cognitive deficits or delays are present. Difficulties in other areas of functioning (e.g., social adjustment) may arise due to academic difficulties; these difficulties may be alleviated as soon as the person is no longer in the academic setting. Thus the term *6-hour retardate* came into being to describe children who only demonstrated deficits at school age (Dietz & Repp, 1989).

Moderate mental retardation is diagnosed in persons whose IQ falls in the range of 35 to 40 to 50 to 55. Approximately 10% of people with mental retardation fall into this category. Three to 4% of persons with mental retardation have *severe* mental retardation and have an IQ in the range of 20 to 25 to 35 to 40. The remaining and smallest category is *profound* mental retardation. Approximately 1% to 2% of people with mental retardation are at this level, which is characterized by IQ below 20 to 25. Most people at this level have an identified organic (neurological) condition that accounts for their extreme skills deficits in most areas of functioning (Mercer & Payne, 1975).

The American Psychiatric Association has retained these categories, as has the newest—4th—edition of the *Diagnostic and Statistical Manual of Mental Disorders (DSM-IV)* (APA, 1994). *DSM-IV*, in addition to retaining these categories, has accepted part of the new American Association on Mental Retardation definition (AAMR, 1992). AAMR has dropped the mild, moderate, severe, and profound levels and substituted 10 adaptive behavior areas. These include communication, self-care, home living, social skills, community use, self-direction, health and safety, functional academics, leisure, and work. If the person has an IQ below 75 (versus 70 adopted by the APA) and deficits in 2 of the 10 adaptive skill areas, the person qualifies as mentally retarded. At present, there is no scale that measures all 10 areas, and there are no cutoff scores established to determine what constitutes a deficiency in an area. AAMR is hopeful that the proposed definition will help redefine the condition as a transient versus a fixed condition.

Incidence refers to the number of people who might be classified as mentally retarded at any time in their lives. Prevalence refers to the proportion of people classified at any given time period. Thus, incidence is higher than prevalence. Since mental retardation is currently considered a lifelong problem, one might expect that incidence and prevalence would be the same. However, the large number of mildly retarded persons who are only diagnosed during school-age years, and the relatively poor reliability of standardized instruments for evaluating the lower end of the continuum, skew the figures. For these reasons, the incidence is slightly greater than the prevalence of mental retardation (Payne & Mercer, 1975). Additionally, there has never been a national register of handicapped persons in this country. As a result, precise numbers are hard to determine. Finally, changing definitions of mental retardation will affect the prevalence and particularly the incidence rate if this new AAMR definition is followed.

Statistical models based on the normal distribution suggest that just over 2% of the population should be classified as having mental retardation. Using this same model, the new AAMR definition would increase the expected incidence to approximately 8% of the population. However, organic and genetic etiologies of mental retardation elevate the numbers. Prevalence estimates range from 1% to 9%, with incidence rates somewhat higher but difficult to ascertain (McGrath & Kelly, 1987). These prevalence estimates use the existing definition; no data for the new AAMR definition are available.

Etiology of mental retardation is usually unknown (Matson & Mulick, 1991). In cases of known etiology, genetic or organic factors, environmental factors, or a combination of these contribute to the condition of mental retardation. In some cases of biological etiology, such as phenylketonuria (PKU), mental retardation is reversible or treatable if detected soon after birth. Most other forms of mental retardation are not reversible or curable (Dietz & Repp, 1989).

Aging Persons with Mental Retardation

In the past, mental retardation usually indicated a shorter life expectancy. However, the growing number of elderly adults with developmental disabilities now parallels the "aging" of America's population. Biomedical advances and drastic improvements in service provision have increased the life expectancy of the majority of people with developmental disabilities. Prevalence estimates of developmentally disabled people aged 60 or older range from 200,000 to 500,000, signifying a substantial population needing special services (Janicki, 1990). If this burgeoning trend continues, it is predicted that the population of older mentally retarded adults will double in the next 30 years (Janicki, 1990; O'Brien, Tate, & Zaharia, 1991). With this increase in age come accompanying problems that will place a greater and somewhat different burden on health providers. These problems will be unique for persons working in the area of developmental disabilities, given the general lack of experience with this age group in the past.

Residential or day placement may become a concern for many developmentally disabled persons who have lived at home for their entire lives. As elderly parents become unable to care for their developmentally disabled child, they must find new resources and possible community or institutional placements. Drastic changes in the living environment can create enormous stress for the developmentally disabled person and his or her family. In addition, preexisting physical and cognitive impairments are often exacerbated by the aging process. Both the physical and cognitive aging processes may begin earlier and advance at an accelerated pace for people with developmental disabilities, particularly those with Down's syndrome (Zigman, Schupf, Lubin, & Silverman, 1987).

Preexisting memory impairments may be exacerbated by the natural decline in memory functioning seen in any elderly person. An elderly person of normal intellectual functioning may maintain other cognitive abilities that can assist memory (e.g., reasoning abilities, habit of writing things down). An elderly person with mental retardation may never have developed those skills and may have fewer executive functioning skills to rely upon in lieu of memory. Confusion and fear may result from memory loss because the person with mental retardation probably will not understand or expect the natural changes in memory processing associated with aging (Haxby, 1989).

Physical decline may also be a concern for the elderly developmentally disabled person. For a person who has limited verbal and cognitive skills, decline in visual acuity, gradual loss of hearing, or changes in balance may go unnoticed. If the person does notice the changes, he or she may not be able to communicate the problem effectively, as when an increased number of falls is due to visual problems instead of physical fragility or loss of agility. Thus, vigilance must be maintained for all physical abilities as a developmentally disabled person ages.

Many aging persons with developmental disabilities also experience increased frequency of seizures (a common problem among people with developmental disabilities). Increase in seizures frequency is actually a hallmark of the course of dementia of the Alzheimer's type in persons with Down's syndrome. More seizures result in more medication, which can have sedating effects. In addition, the seizures themselves can cause confusion, increased falls, and raised anxiety levels.

Dual Diagnosis

Mental retardation not only defines a disorder but also a group of people who can suffer from the entire spectrum of behavioral and mental health problems. People with mental retardation can have a variety of behavioral and mental health problems that accompany developmental disability. The past belief that psychopathology required a level of cognitive development not possessed by developmentally disabled persons has been challenged repeatedly (MacLean, 1993; Sovner & Hurley, 1983). Most prevalence studies have found rates of emotional disorders in persons with developmental disabilities to be higher than rates for the general population (Borthwick-Duffy, 1994). Elderly developmentally disabled people may experience many of the same mental health problems prevalent in nondevelopmentally disabled elderly populations, such as dementia, depression, and anxiety (Foelker & Luke, 1989; Menolascino & Potter, 1989).

An examination of life events in many elderly developmentally disabled individuals provides ample reason for depression or anxiety. For example, elderly persons with mental retardation may face decline in health and mobility, an increased number of falls, loss of significant others (e.g., parents), and possible institutionalization. In addition, developmentally disabled persons may lack the emotional sophistication necessary to cope with difficult life events or the verbal skills needed to communicate unhappiness or fear.

As opposed to the condition of mental retardation, coexisting mental health, adjustment, and/or behavior problems should be targeted for treatment. Many treatments that have proven effective with nondevelopmentally disabled persons can be used or modified for use with developmentally disabled persons. Behavior modification, social skills training, psychotherapy, and pharmacotherapy have all proven to be effective treatments for the developmentally disabled and should be considered in treatment planning.

CASE IDENTIFICATION
AND PRESENTING COMPLAINTS

Roger is a 63-year-old man with mild-to-moderate mental retardation. Etiology is unknown. He resides in an institutionally based residential facility for the elderly. Staff report that Roger has been withdrawn since his arrival 6 months ago. Efforts of staff and other residents to interact socially with Roger have been consistently rebuffed. Roger reports feeling "sad" and tired most of the time. He has lost 20 pounds in the last 6 months, though he has not been on a weight loss diet and he has not exercised regularly. Roger states that "nothing tastes good anymore" and that he is hardly ever hungry.

Roger has recently developed a disturbed sleep pattern. He has trouble falling asleep at night and wakes up several times each night. As a result, he is suffering from excessive daytime sleepiness. He naps frequently during the day and refuses to participate in group activities or outings because he is tired.

Other problems reported by staff at the facility include emotional outbursts and urinary incontinence. Roger has episodes of crying several times a week during which he states that he is no good because he is unable to work anymore and can no longer live with his family. He also states that he misses his mother and wishes she could come back to him so that things would get better again. Roger has been incontinent (urinary) one or two times a day since moving to the present setting. All incontinence has occurred during the day.

HISTORY

Until the age of 60, Roger resided in a small town with his mother. He lived at the same residence and worked at the same grocery store for 40 years. Roger rode his bicycle to work every day and rode around town in the evenings or walked with his mother for exercise. He had two friends from work with whom he enjoyed seeing movies and other activities. He traveled with his mother to visit relatives several times a year.

Upon the sudden death of his mother (cardiac failure) 3 years ago, Roger moved to a large city in a different state to live with his younger sister, her husband, and their teenage daughter. Roger lived with his sister's family for 2½ years. During this time he did not work or participate in any community activities. His sister states that Roger had difficulty adjusting to the city and seldom went out alone or with family members. After a year and a half, Roger began to have frequent emotional outbursts, and incontinence; he refused to leave the house for any reason, and his adaptive skills, such as self-help and domestic skills, decreased. Roger's sister and her husband decided to place Roger in a residential facility when the demands of caring for Roger began to overburden their family.

SELECTION OF
PSYCHOLOGICAL TREATMENT

Two basic approaches to treating depression in persons with mental retardation have been pharmacological and behavioral interventions. However, past research indicates that psychotherapy may also prove successful (Matson, 1984). Cognitive-behavioral interventions and psychotherapy have been employed with both young developmentally disabled populations and elderly general populations. Although there have been no empirical investigations of the efficacy of these techniques for elderly persons with mental retardation, the clinician may find these techniques useful.

Psychotherapy

Counseling and psychotherapy may have value with developmentally disabled persons functioning in the high moderate-to-mild range of mental retardation (Matson, 1984). Some indicators of the appropriateness of psychotherapy for a client are (1) verbal skills beyond simple labeling; (2) ability to label simple emotional states, such as "happy," "sad," "afraid"; (3) ability to distinguish between thoughts and feelings (this skill may need to be taught); and (4) absence of extreme social anxiety. In addition, willingness of the client to participate in counseling should be considered. Often persons with mental retardation are referred to therapy by relatives or staff. The client may be afraid of what will happen in counseling or mistakenly think that because he is in therapy he must be "crazy."

Client fears or concerns should be addressed immediately in therapy through techniques designed to establish rapport and explain the psychotherapy process. The therapist may wish to participate in some daily activities with the client in the natural setting (Prout & Cale, 1994). This approach should help establish the therapist as a "regular" person who can be a friend or someone to talk with about problems. In addition, the therapist should explain to the client in simple terms what will happen in sessions. It is recommended that the therapist use nonthreatening statements, such as I am interested in hearing about some of the things which make you sad, or When you some to see me, we can talk about the things that worry you and together we will try to figure out ways to make those things better.

Once rapport is established, a conversational approach can be utilized to determine psychosocial causes or factors associated with depression. Several psychosocial stressors may be implicated in Roger's depression. The death of his mother precipitated not only grief, but also loss of security and stability, a complete change in living environment, and loss of the opportunity to participate in a variety of enjoyable activities (e.g., visiting friends and relatives, working). Roger may never have had the opportunity or skills to express his grief and anger at these rapid major life changes or the fear they may have elicited. Roger may also feel (correctly so) that he has no control over his life or activities.

Once relevant psychosocial stressors have been identified, the therapist should use an instructional and problem-solving approach to assist the client in overcoming or coping with them. Treatment should focus on teaching the client how to express emotions, such as grief, fear, and anger, in appropriate ways. These techniques include talking to family or staff, focusing on pleasant memories of his mother instead of negative emotions, and developing new interests and activities in the present setting.

Cognitive-Behavioral and Behavioral Techniques

Depression

Cognitive-behavior therapy techniques focus on monitoring emotions and negative self-statements and improving problem-solving skills. Persons with mental retardation may never have learned to recognize their own emotions until the emotions become uncontrollable. Identification of sadness or fear when the emotional state is beginning to become uncomfortable is the first step in learning to control emotional outbursts. Instruction about the physiological responses that accompany heightened emotional reactions may be necessary to teach a person with mental retardation to identify and label their emotional responses.

Role-playing and feedback may be useful in teaching the client to express emotions appropriately before the emotions become overwhelming. Clients may need to practice making statements regarding their own emotions while calm. Role-playing or describing situations and thoughts that usually provoke strong emotional reactions can be used to allow the client to generate and practice appropriate emotional reactions. In addition to making statements about their emotional state, clients could also learn to cry in a private place when they become overwhelmed, and/or ask someone to spend time with them when they are lonely or upset. Another tactic might involve learning to focus on previously identified pleasant memories as soon as the "sad" mood begins. Again, role-playing, practice, and feedback are essential to teach clients this skill.

Problem-solving skills training constitutes another important component of the successful treatment of depression in elderly adults with mental retardation. Having relied or depended on another person for problem-solving and decision making for years, many elderly persons with mental retardation may have lost or never acquired problem-solving skills. These skills determine a person's ability to identify enjoyable retirement activities, access entertainment sources independently, and reestablish independent functioning in the event of declining skills and strength.

The therapist can help the client brainstorm and evaluate options for enjoyable daily and weekly activities. Many elderly persons with mental retardation may not participate in group activities because they do not enjoy the particular event, but cannot or do not suggest alternatives. The skills necessary to explore resources and possible activities can be taught through problem-solving skills training. In addition, the therapist can address the issue of safe methods of exercise for elderly persons who have become frail.

Behavioral techniques have proven effective in treating many mental health and behavioral problems in persons with developmental disabilities (Whitman, Hantula, & Spence, 1990). Matson, Dettling, and Senatore (1981) and Matson (1982) reduced condemning self-statements in depressed developmentally disabled persons using the behavioral techniques of modeling, performance feedback, and token reinforcement. In therapy sessions, clients were asked questions that could elicit positive or negative self-statements. The following are examples of such questions: Do you like yourself?, What do other people think of you?, and Do you like your home? Patients were reinforced for positive statements with tokens and social praise. If a negative answer was given, the therapist identified the statement as negative and modeled an appropriate positive answer (e.g., There are some things I like about myself). Thus, the client could practice using the positive self-statements in session.

Positive reinforcement is an essential component of any treatment for depression in an elderly person with a developmental disability, particularly for those in residential settings. Decreased levels of activity and social support often create a situation of diminished opportunities for reinforcement. Along with other techniques previously mentioned, any intervention should incorporate a dense schedule of reinforcement for increased activity, group participation, positive affect, and positive statements.

In summary, the psychological treatment of depression in an elderly person with mental retardation creates several roles for the therapist. First, the therapist must establish rapport that implies the role of a friend or confidante. Second, the therapist must become a teacher. Skills training and role-playing require the use of extensive instructional skills. Third, the therapist must play an active role in changing the environment to provide additional opportunities for activity and positive reinforcement.

Incontinence

Urinary incontinence is a common problem among the elderly that has been responsive to behavioral interventions. Burgio, Burgio, McCormick, Hawkins, and Scheve (1988) decreased urinary incontinence on an inpatient unit using frequent and regular prompts to use the toilet (every 2 to 3 hours) plus contingent praise or corrective feedback. Prompts were eventually faded to 3- to 4-hour intervals. Treatment of urinary incontinence generally consists of a regular schedule of frequent prompts and toileting opportunities. Although this protocol has not been evaluated for effectiveness with elderly persons with mental retardation, the techniques involved are commonly used with that population.

In addition to decreasing urinary incontinence, this treatment may result in more opportunities for positive interactions with staff.

Sleep Problems

In the past decade, behavioral interventions have also been applied to sleep problems in elderly persons. There is no reason to believe that the same techniques would not work with mentally retarded persons as well. Morin and Rapp (1987) recommend several behavioral strategies for insomnia, most of which emphasize modification of the individual's schedule and living environment. Also, education about differences in sleep patterns with age may alter unrealistic expectations of both staff and the elderly person.

Several changes in normal sleep patterns accompany the aging process. Studies indicate that over 35% of people over age 65 have some sleep problem (NIH, 1990). Problems of initiating and maintaining sleep are common. In addition, nighttime sleep disturbances frequently result in excessive daytime sleepiness, napping, and confusion. One theory is that sleep disturbances result from a natural redistribution of sleep across a 24-hour day as a result of changes in circadian rhythms. However, the effects of other factors that may affect sleep cannot be discounted. Decreased activity, boredom, loneliness, depression, and increased medication use may also affect sleep patterns (Hoch, Buysse, Monk, & Reynolds, 1992).

Explanation of these natural changes in sleep patterns may be helpful in reducing anxiety over a sleep disturbance. If individuals revise their expectations of their ability to sleep and realize the possible causes of the disturbance, they may be able to accept environmental modifications more readily. Altering environmental factors, such as light, temperature, and noise, to increase comfort may decrease interference with sleep. Similarly, alterations in life-style (i.e., increased activity, exercise, decreased evening caffeine intake) may diminish sleep disturbances. Explanations must be kept in simple terms when the client has mental retardation, with greater emphasis on environmental modification and positive reinforcement of increased activity.

CONCURRENT MEDICAL TREATMENT

Pharmacotherapy is a primary treatment for depression in the mentally retarded. In a study of psychoactive drugs used with 369 elderly developmentally disabled adults, Pary (1993) found that 10% of the subjects in the 55 and older age group were prescribed antidepressants. Tricyclic antidepressants have been frequently prescribed for treatment of depression in persons with mental retardation. Further, new antidepressants, such as fluoxetine, a serotonergic drug, have also been used successfully for treating depressed developmentally disabled adults (Howland, 1992). However, potential side effects of anticholinergic drugs may make other avenues of intervention more attractive.

Pharmacotherapy is also a common treatment for sleep problems. The pharmacological treatments of choice are sedative/hypnotics and tricyclic antidepressants. Each may offer temporary relief of transient insomnia. However, when used on a long-term basis, they can cause various problems, including habituation, tolerance, apnea, slowed psychomotor functioning, and rebound insomnia (Prinz, Vitiello, Rasknid, & Thorpy, 1990). Sedative hypnotics may be contraindicated for elderly persons with mental retardation because of the possible negative effects on memory and cognitive functioning, which may already be impaired. The negative effects on memory are particularly troublesome due to the dangers of overdosing if a person forgets that they have already taken a dose of medication.

Pharmacotherapy with elderly adults with mental retardation can be problematic for several reasons. First, changes in the distribution and metabolization of psychotropic drugs can result in increased toxicity, need for larger doses, prolonged elimination, and extended half-life of certain drugs. Second, deteriorating organ function, particularly liver function, may be exacerbated by the extended use of several drugs. Finally, the synergistic effects of multiple medications may result in an increase in side effects or a decrease in the positive effects of one drug due to the other (Rinck & Calkins, 1989).

COURSE OF TREATMENT

For those elderly persons whose health will not be compromised by the potential side effects of pharmacotherapy, a combination of drug therapy, behavior therapy, and planned adjustments to the living environment should be the minimal treatment for depression. Access to appropriate reinforcers and leisure activities is vital to improving quality of life in elderly persons with mental retardation. Although no empirical investigations have examined the use of cognitive behavioral procedures, psychotherapy, or art therapy with elderly persons with mental retardation, the success shown with the other related populations indicates that such treatments could be promising.

In the present case illustration, Roger's treatment incorporates several of the above mentioned psychological and pharmacological techniques. The first component would be evaluation of physical status to determine risks associated with antidepressants and to ascertain whether there is any biological reason for incontinence (e.g., infection, kidney problems). The medication of choice would likely be a tricyclic antidepressant because of the therapeutic effects on both depression and sleep problems.

A second component of treatment for Roger involves the establishment of a psychotherapeutic relationship with someone Roger believes cares about his problems. Psychotherapy should focus first on an explanation of death, loss, and the natural process of grief and recovery in simple terms. A second focus of psychotherapy would be acquisition and use of appropriate expression of anger, grief, and fear. A third emphasis of psychotherapy would be on the acceptance of the present living situation, followed by problem-solving to determine how to make the living situation more pleasant and acceptable.

Behavior modification techniques were considered an essential third component of treatment for Roger. Reinforcement for more positive self-statements, increased participation in activities, and independent toileting play an integral role in increasing positive affect. Role-playing and skills training may foster independence and increase opportunities for positive reinforcement.

The final component of Roger's treatment would be modifications to his living environment to provide additional appropriate sources of entertainment, comfort, and autonomy. Staff in residential facilities may unknowingly "enable" elderly persons to be more dependent than they need to be. Staff may be so overtaxed in meeting the physical needs of clients that they may neglect to provide for their social and emotional needs. In addition, staff should help Roger begin to regulate his sleep and toileting by providing the necessary cues and prompts and altering the sleep environment as recommended by Morin and Rapp (1987).

FOLLOW-UP

After 10 weeks of treatment, Roger showed marked improvement. As a result, his medication was reduced and eventually discontinued. Booster treatment sessions of psychotherapy and behavior modification were conducted once every other week for 2 months. Gains were maintained and thus sessions were faded to monthly for 3 more months. Roger's problems at that point appeared to have been resolved. In addition, Roger was able to reestablish a more positive relationship with his sister and her family. As a result, all treatment was discontinued at that point.

OVERALL EVALUATION

Roger was a client who presented with a broad range of depressive symptoms, most of which could also be identified in persons of normal intelligence. Treatment consisted of a multimethod approach, based on the best empirical evidence available concerning potentially efficacious procedures. Roger responded well to these interventions; consequently, individual components were terminated and the total treatment package was faded out. Decreases in therapeutic support were based on data indicating his degree of responsiveness to treatment.

SUMMARY

The clinician must keep three factors in mind when assessing and making treatment decisions for elderly developmentally disabled clients. These considerations are important whether the client is depressed, has an anxiety disorder, dementia, or other condition. The first issue concerns assessment. The clinician should be sensitive to the wide range of mental health problems associated with aging in the developmentally disabled (e.g., dementia, depression, anxiety).

Second, in making treatment decisions, the clinician should be aware of the potential problems with pharmaceutical and behavioral interventions. Other intervention options, such as psychotherapy, group therapy, and art therapy, should be fully explored. Treatment should also be evaluated regularly to determine effectiveness and to assist in modifying the approach when necessary.

Finally, the treatment of choice should be the most acceptable efficacious treatment available, and should serve the needs of the client rather than simply making the client more manageable. In a study evaluating the acceptability of behavioral treatment and pharmacotherapy, elderly adults of normal intelligence preferred positively oriented behavioral interventions to drug treatment (Burgio & Sinnott, 1990; Lundervold, Lewin, & Bourland, 1990). While administration of medication may be less time consuming than psychotherapy or behavior modification, it may be less acceptable to the client. The client's ability and need to make some of their own decisions regarding treatment should be of primary concern. However, the client's level of cognitive skills should guide the service provider's decisions about the client's level of involvement in decision-making.

REFERENCES

American Psychiatric Association. (1994). *Diagnostic and statistical manual of mental disorders* (4th ed.). Washington, DC: Author.

Borthwick-Duffy, S. A. (1994). Epidemiology and prevalence of psychopathology in people with mental retardation. *Journal of the Consulting and Clinical Psychology, 62,* 17–27.

Burgio, L. D., & Sinnott, J. (1990). Behavioral treatments and pharmacotherapy: Acceptability ratings by elderly individuals in residential settings. *Gerontologist, 30,* 811–816.

Burgio, L. D., Burgio, K. L., McCormick, K., Hawkins, A., & Scheve, A. (1988). Behavioral treatment for urinary incontinence in elderly inpatients: Initial attempts to modify prompting and toileting procedures. *Behavior Therapy, 19,* 345–357.

Dietz, D. E., & Repp, A. C. (1989). Mental retardation. In T. H. Ollendick & M. Hersen (Eds.), *Handbook of child psychopathology* (2nd ed., pp. 75–92). New York: Plenum Press.

Foelker, G. A., & Luke, E. A. (1989). Mental health issues for the aging mentally retarded population. *Journal of Applied Gerontology, 8,* 242–250.

Haxby, J. V. (1989). Neuropsychological evaluation of adults with Down's syndrome: Patterns of selective impairment in developmentally disabled old adults. *Journal of Mental Deficiency Research, 33,* 193–210.

Hoch, C. C., Buysse, D. J., Monk, T. H., & Reynolds, C. F. (1992). Sleep disorders and aging. In J. E. Birren, B. Sloane, & G. D. Cohen (Eds.), *Handbook of mental health and aging.* San Diego: Academic Press.

Howland, R. H. (1992). Fluoxetine treatment of depression in mentally retarded adults. *The Journal of Nervous and Mental Disease, 180,* 202–205.

Janicki, M. P. (1990). Growing old with dignity: On quality of life for older persons with a lifelong disability. In R. L. Schalock (Ed.), *Quality of life: Perspectives and issues.* Washington, DC: American Association on Mental Retardation.

Lundervold, D., Lewin, M., & Bourland, G. (1990). Older adults' acceptability of treatments for behavior problems. *Clinical Gerontologist, 10,* 17–28.

MacLean, W. E., Jr. (1993). Overview. In J. L. Matson & R. P. Barrett (Eds.), *Psychopathology in the Mentally Retarded* (2nd ed., pp. 1–16). Needham, MA: Allyn & Bacon.

Matson, J. L. (1982). The treatment of behavioral characteristics of depression in the mentally retarded. *Behavior Therapy, 13,* 209–218.

Matson, J. L. (1984). Psychotherapy with persons who are mentally retarded. *Mental Retardation*, *22*, 170–175.

Matson, J. L., & Mulick, J. L. (Eds.) (1991). *Handbook of mental retardation* (2nd ed.). New York: Pergamon.

Matson, J. L., Dettling, J., & Senatore, V. (1981). Treating depression of a mentally retarded adult. *British Journal of Mental Subnormality*, *16*, 86–88.

McGrath, M. L., & Kelly, J. A. (1987). Mental retardation. In C. L. Frame & J. L. Matson (Eds.), *Handbook of assessment in childhood psychopathology: Applied issues in differential diagnosis and treatment evaluation* (pp. 511–530). New York: Plenum Press.

Menolascino, F. J., & Potter, J. F. (1989). Mental illness in the elderly mentally retarded. *The Journal of Applied Gerontology*, *8*, 192–202.

Mercer, A., & Payne, J. S. (1975). Biological and environmental causes. In J. M. Kauffman & J. S. Payne (Eds.), *Mental retardation: Introduction and personal perspectives* (pp. 50–75). Ohio: Charles E. Merrill.

Morin, C. M., & Rapp, S. R. (1987). Behavioral management of geriatric insomnia. *Clinical Gerontologist*, *6*, 15–23.

National Institutes of Health. (1990). *The treatment of sleep disorders of older people*. Washington, DC: U.S. Government Printing Office.

O'Brien, K. F., Tate, K., & Zaharia, E. S. (1991). Mortality in a large southeastern facility for persons with mental retardation. *American Journal on Mental Retardation*, *95*, 397–403.

Pary, R. (1993). Psychoactive drugs used with adults and elderly adults who have mental retardation. *American Journal on Mental Retardation*, *98*, 121–127.

Payne, J. S., & Mercer, A. (1975). Definition and prevalence. In J. M. Kauffman & J. S. Payne (Eds.), *Mental retardation: Introduction and personal perspectives* (pp. 22–49). Ohio: Charles E. Merrill.

Prinz, P. N., Vitiello, M. V., Rasknid, M. A., & Thorpy, M. J. (1990). Geriatrics: Sleep disorders and aging. *The New England Journal of Medicine*, *323*, 520–525.

Prout, H. T., & Cale, R. L. (1994). Individual counseling approaches. In D. C. Strohmer & H. T. Cale (Eds.), *Counseling and psychotherapy with persons with mental retardation and borderline intelligence* (pp. 103–142). Brandon, VT: Clinical Psychology.

Rinck, C., & Calkins, C. F. (1989). Patterns of psychotropic medication use among older persons with developmental disabilities. *The Journal of Applied Gerontology*, *8*, 216–277.

Sovner, R. S., & Hurley, A. D. (1983). Do the mentally retarded suffer from affective illness? *Archives of General Psychiatry*, *40*, 61–67.

Whitman, T. L., Hantula, D. A., & Spence, B. H. (1990). Current issues in behavior modification with mentally retarded persons. In J. L. Matson (Ed.), *Handbook of behavior modification with the mentally retarded* (2nd ed., pp. 9–50). New York: Plenum Press.

Zigman, W. B., Schupf, N., Lubin, R. A., & Silverman, W. P. (1987). Premature regression of adults with Down's syndrome. *American Journal of Mental Deficiency*, *92*, 161–168.

CHAPTER 13

Organic Disorders

ROGER L. PATTERSON

DESCRIPTION OF THE DISORDERS

Obviously, older people may suffer from all of the same types of organic diseases as younger people. However, there are a limited number of these disorders that appear with increased frequency in elderly groups and that are considered particularly problematic. These generally fall within the categories of Dementia and Delirium as categorized in the fourth edition of the *Diagnostic and Statistical Manual of Mental Disorders* (*DSM-IV*; American Psychiatric Association, 1994). These will be described below. Some consideration also will be given to aspects of depression and grieving, because these conditions may be mistaken for dementia or may serve as coexistent complicating conditions with organic dysfunction.

The primary presenting problem in the case of delirium and various kinds of

---

ROGER L. PATTERSON • Mental Hygiene Clinic, Veterans Affairs Outpatient Clinic, Daytona Beach, Florida 32117.

Psychological Treatment of Older Adults: An Introductory Text, edited by Michel Hersen and Vincent B. Van Hasselt. Plenum Press, New York, 1996.

dementia is loss of cognitive function. The victims of these conditions are deficient in significant areas of knowledge about their lives regarding location, time, or personal identity. They may also be deficient in ordinary self-care functions such as dressing, bathing, or eating. Because of such similarities, these conditions may be confused when insufficient examination is made. Tragically, treatment opportunities may be missed in this way.

A full description and categories of the organic disorders may be found in *DSM-IV*, a brief summary of which appears below.

Delirium

Three specifiable categories of delirium are included: Delirium as caused by (1) a general medical condition, (2) substances, and (3) multiple etiologies. There is also a fourth category: Not otherwise specified.

A diagnosis of delirium, regardless of category of etiology, requires that three general criteria be met:

1. Disturbance of consciousness (i.e., reduced clarity of awareness of the environment) with reduced ability to focus, sustain, or shift attention.
2. Change in cognition (e.g., memory deficit, disorientation, language disturbance, perceptual disturbance) that is not better accounted for by a preexisting, established, or evolving dementia.
3. The disturbance develops over a short period of time (usually hours to days) and tends to fluctuate during the course of the day.

The diagnosis of a specific category of delirium depends on a fourth criterion, which requires evidence relating the condition to one or more specific etiologies, including general medical and substance-induced conditions. More specific information regarding these etiologies, such as the particular nature of the relevant medical condition(s) or the substance, should be included insofar as such information is available.

Dementias

As with delirium, *DSM-IV* includes criteria common to all categories of dementia:

I. The development of multiple cognitive deficits manifested by both:
   (1) memory impairment (inability to learn new information and to recall previously learned information), and
   (2) at least one of the following cognitive disturbances:
       a. Aphasia (language disturbance)
       b. Apraxia (inability to carry out motor activities despite intact motor function)
       c. Agnosia (failure to recognize or identify objects despite intact sensory function)

   d. disturbance to executive functioning (i.e., planning, organizing, sequencing, abstracting)
II. The cognitive deficits cause significant impairment in social or occupational functioning, and represent a significant decline from a previous level of functioning. (APA, 1994, p. F:3)

Conditions that are diagnosed as dementia are subdivided into four subcategories based on additional criteria.

A very important criterion for Dementia of the Alzheimer's type (DAT) is that the course of the illness is characterized by gradual onset and continuing cognitive decline. This generally is noticed over periods of months and years as contrasted with delirium, which develops in minutes, hours, days, or a few weeks.

To diagnose DAT, it is necessary to exclude dementia due to other conditions. These include Vascular Dementia (DVT), Dementia Due to Other General Medical Conditions (DMC), and Substance-Induced Persisting Dementia (DSI).

In addition to the general criteria for dementia, a diagnosis of DVT requires that there be "local neurological signs and symptoms (e.g., exaggerated deep tendon reflexes, extensor plantar response, pseudo-bulbar palsy, gait abnormalities, weakness of an extremity)" (APA, 1994, p. F:5), or laboratory evidence such as brain images that indicate cerebrovascular disease. It also must be determined that the disturbances occur not only during the course of delirium.

A diagnosis of DMD requires evidence from medical examination of the presence of one or more specified medical conditions known to be etiologically related to dementia. These include (1) human immunodeficiency virus (HIV); (2) head trauma or Parkinson's disease; (3) Huntington's disease; (4) Pick's disease; (5) Creutzfeldt-Jakob disease; and (6) DMC, a variety of other general medical conditions including hyperthyroidism, vitamin B_{12} or folic acid deficiencies, niacin deficiencies, hypercalcemia, normal pressure hydrocephalus, hyperthyroidism, brain tumor, and others. The latter or specific general medical conditions mentioned in *DSM-IV* may produce dementia, but this list is certainly not exhaustive.

A diagnosis of Substance-Abuse Persisting Dementia (DSA) requires historical, physical, or laboratory-based findings of the abuse of substances judged to be etiologically related to dementia. These may include drugs of abuse, medications, and toxins. Since such substances often produce brief delirium, it is necessary to exclude this relatively short-term state to make a DSA diagnosis.

A final category included in *DSM-IV* is Dementia Due to Multiple Etiologies which emphasizes the important point that a demented elder may present with evidence of several conditions that may relate to his or her condition. Unfortunately for all, such an occurrence is not infrequent.

CASE IDENTIFICATION
AND PRESENTING COMPLAINTS

According to Horvath, Siever, Mohs, and Davis (1989), the organic disorder with the highest incidence is delirium. It is said to affect 40% of hospitalized geriatric patients some time during their hospital stay for a particular illness. Probably the second largest group of organically disordered is those with DAT. In 1989, Horvath et al. estimated that the number of DAT cases in the United States exceeded one million. Due to the rapid aging of the general population of this country and many others, the absolute number (though not the relative percentage) is growing quite rapidly. The population age 85 and older is the fastest growing segment, and approximately 15% of this group are severely demented. Counting those with lower degrees of DAT, Horvath et al. (1989) estimated that more than 50% of those with dementia suffer from Alzheimer's disease.

The second largest cause of dementia is vascular (DVT). Horvath et al. (1989) estimate that 10% of dementia cases are of this type. These authors rank alcoholism as the third largest cause of dementia, noting that about 10% of alcoholics show signs of dementia.

Most patients with delirium will likely be seen in general hospitals and general practitioners' offices. A few of these continue to live in their primary residences (which may be a nursing home) while receiving treatment. Most of the dementia cases can be found in the same places, although the greatest concentration of dementia cases of all types within a confined population is to be found in nursing homes. German, Rovner, Burton, Brant, and Clark (1992), in a careful prospective study of new admissions to eight nursing homes (n = 454) for 1 year, found that 80% of these residents had some form of mental illness, 60% of them having dementia. In addition, about one-half of the demented residents had other, complicating mental illnesses.

Presenting complaints for cases of true dementia and delirium usually come from family members and institutional staff, as well as consultations with physicians. The affected elder may be unaware of his or her condition, and/or unable to communicate it adequately. In dementia, early complaints are of getting lost and/or forgetting to perform or complete well-learned tasks, such as activities of daily living (ADL). Self-reports of poor memory are more likely related to depression. In cases of more advanced dementia, problems usually focus on disruptive or aggressive behavior or fears of caregivers leaving the person alone. The elder may likewise be afraid of being alone. Incontinence also is often a problem.

With conditions of more acute onset, such as stroke or delirium, complaints often have to do with anxiety and depression in both the affected elder and the caregivers. Neuropsychological assessment to define specific behavioral losses related to residual organically based conditions may be of considerable help for developing care and rehabilitation plans. Specific deficits in ADL and social skills are complaints that the psychologist may address, either by working with caregivers or as a member of the treatment team.

HISTORY

Declines in mental functioning associated with aging have been noted since ancient times (Crook, 1987). Torack (1983) found references to such declines in the Grecian Laws of Solon in 500 B.C. The term dementia is later in origin and was used by the Roman physicians Galen and Celsus, who first clinically de-scribed some of the cognitive and behavioral dysfunctions now attributed to this term. Celsus also used the term delirium in somewhat the way we do today (Alexander & Sellesick, 1966).

In the 19th century, Philippe Pinel and his student Jean Esquirol described senile dementia. In the early 20th century, Paul Eugen Bleuler made use of physiological research by Broca, Wernicke, Korsakoff, and others, combined with clinical observations, to originate the concept of chronic organic psycho-syndromes (Crook, 1987).

The officially sanctioned diagnosis of Organic Brain Syndrome (OBS), which is found in the second edition of the *Diagnostic and Statistical Manual of Mental Disorders* (*DSM-II*; APA, 1968) has greatly affected the thinking and functioning of the current generation of practitioners (Horvath et al., 1989). In *DSM-II*, OBS was further categorized as acute or chronic and psychotic or nonpsychotic. This categorization has since been officially abandoned, primar-ily because it is overly simplistic. Also, it ignores known disease processes that produce many cognitive and behavioral changes in the elderly.

One of the more widely recognized of these diseases is Alzheimer's disease, also called Senile Dementia of the Alzheimer's Type (DAT). In the early 20th century, Alois Alzheimer was concerned with the cause of dementia symptoms in patients in their 40s or 50s who were considered to have presenile dementia (Crook, 1987). He was able to identify specific neuronal changes in the brains of such patients that seemed to be related to the relevant cognitive and behavioral declines. In 1970, Tomlinson, Blessed, and Roth reported that the same histo-pathological changes were found in younger and older patients with dementia, giving rise to the modern concept of DAT. These same researchers identified Multi-Infarct Dementia as a frequently occurring problem. This condition is caused by a series of strokes and also produces dementia.

In general, progress in differentiating causes of dementia has continued, as reflected by the relatively large number of officially recognized diagnoses (see *DSM-IV*; APA, 1994).

PSYCHOLOGICAL TREATMENTS

Teri and Logsdon (1992) have discussed the history of psychotherapy with older adults. They note that, as early as 1919, Abraham argued that psycho-therapy could be helpful to people of advanced age. Freud (1905/1953) disputed this notion by asserting that psychoanalysis was not appropriate for this target group. Subsequent developments in the field of psychological study and treat-ments, especially in the last half of this century, have clearly demonstrated that psychological treatments are both necessary and useful. The result has been greatly accelerated professional attention to such disorders. The American Psy-chological Association established a Division on Aging in 1945, which was devoted to addressing issues related to older adults. This division has continued to grow and by 1992 had 1,405 members (Teri & Logsdon, 1992). Several other organizations also have developed groups devoted to psychological study and treatment of the elderly (e.g., Association for Advancement of Behavior Therapy). Today, there is probably no major school of psychological thought that does not advocate its application in some form to older adults. Silver (1994), in an editorial discussing current priorities and trends in psychotherapy, targeted the elderly as an important group for future practice and development.

Psychodynamic Therapies

As discussed by Turner (1992), psychodynamic therapists have slowly but increasingly turned their attention to the elderly. One of the more useful approaches has been that of Kahana (1979). This author described a system of three categories of elderly with appropriate psychotherapeutic approaches for each. The *aging group* consists of the relatively healthy elders who have no significant cognitive deficit or disabling chronic illness. Obviously, these would not be among the organically impaired. Her second category is the *debilitated aged*, which includes the frail and demented. In *DSM-IV* terms, this group would contain those suffering from dementia. Kahana recommended providing basic support, both to elders and caregivers. Other suggested therapeutic efforts for this group should include appropriate prosthetic environments, family therapy, and educational approaches. The goal of therapy is partial recovery of function. Kahana's third category is called *intermediate*. This group consists of those in crisis situations, which would include people suffering from delirium or acute grief. Appropriate therapy in these cases would utilize crisis intervention techniques and grief therapy if appropriate.

In contrast, psychoanalysis is said to be the proper treatment for those who have intact selves and specific psychological problems and are capable of self-observation. The psychoanalytic care is said to come from the intensive transference experience.

Turner (1992) points out that issues in transference and countertransference differ in elderly and younger clients. Many differences are attributable to the fact that the client may be in an older generation than the therapist. Therefore, clients may transfer or project issues relating to problems with their own children and younger people in general onto the therapists. Similarly, therapists may find themselves involved with feelings related to their own parents, as well as aging in general.

Regardless of the particular theoretical orientation of the therapist, he or she needs to be aware of his or her own beliefs and feelings about older people, as well as issues of death and dying. Likewise, the therapist should be aware of the possibility of intergenerational differences affecting the beliefs and feelings of the older client. Existential problems may influence the perception and feelings of both the client and the therapist and should be treated in therapy as they occur.

A major development in psychotherapy of the elderly has been promoted by the recognition of life-span development. Developmental psychology once dealt only with the maturation of the child to the adult stage of life (e.g., Freudian psychoanalysis). In 1963, Erickson published a theory that life may be divided into eight stages. The successful development of the person was said to depend on completing tasks that are required during each stage. Sherman (1981) developed an approach to counseling the elderly that incorporates this theory. Erickson's stages seven and eight are the two that concern us primarily in later life. Stage seven is said to occupy middle adulthood (35 to 60), and is called generativity versus stagnation. Generativity requires interest and involvement in establishing and guiding the next generation. Stagnation signifies a general lack of involvement in the creative process, a failure of generative involvement, and a lack of purpose.

Stage eight is called integration versus despair. Integration refers to the process of looking at one's life, past and present, and seeing it as a whole, a complete picture—as if one is saying, given the circumstances that existed and continue to exist, one's life is the way it had to be, and that is as it should be. Despair is the bitterness, frustration, and depression generated by the refusal to accept reality as it was and is. The person ends his or her life protesting all that was undesirable, as if to say, It should not have been that way, or, It can't really have happened that way.

Sherman (1981) advocates the use of several techniques in helping an elder achieve satisfactory resolution of developmental issues. An important component is called life review (Butler, 1963), in which the subject comes to view his life as an integrated whole by recounting it and understanding it better. Cognitive techniques are also used to help the elder to relabel or reframe various experiences to be seen more positively. Case-work, counseling, and other methods are also advocated.

An octogenarian known by the author illustrated integration in this way: In the early years of the Great Depression, he was a young man who had acquired a desirable piece of land in the Midwest and planted it with corn. He planned to become a prosperous farmer. The "dust bowl" occurred and destroyed his hopes of being a successful farmer. He reacted by riding his horse West with his few belongings and spent some time camping in the mountains. He rode on to Sacramento and started his life over as a tradesman. He never did as well as a successful farmer. At the age of 80+, he would have exhibited despair if he had remained bitter about the loss of his dream. Instead, he enjoyed telling tales of his travels and jobs in the West, seeing his whole adult life as somewhat of an adventure. He was also enjoyable to be around and had many friends. This integration of his life remained after he had lost his wife and began to show obvious symptoms of dementia. Undoubtedly, his ability to integrate the positive and negative aspects of his life into a desirable whole experience helped him to cope with these devastating problems.

Specific Milieu Therapies

One of the more influential and better known approaches to psychosocial milieu treatment of dementia victims living in special residences is Reality Orientation (RO; Folsom, 1968). In its fullest extent, RO required the posting of clocks, calendars, and "reality boards" containing information about meal time, weather, time of day, season, year, and other matters. It also required regular classrooms conducted by ward staff in which residents spent time discussing current information such as that found on the reality board.

A third component was a special phase of attitude therapy in which *all* staff were to insist kindly but firmly that the residents respond to self-care tasks and conversation in a realistic, useful way insofar as they could. RO has spread across the United States, Canada, and England, so that one may encounter reality boards in a vast number of facilities.

Patterson (1985) reviewed RO as used specifically with dementia residents (many studies do not specify the type of subjects used). He found mixed results in these studies, partly because of variations in the populations and the specific RO components used (e.g., classroom versus milieu). Baines, Saxby, and Ehlert (1987) reported that RO followed by Reminiscence Therapy was effective in improving behavior and memory, but not when used singly or in the opposite order.

A number of studies have shown that enriched environments may stimulate desirable social skills in populations of cognitively impaired elderly. As examples, Langer and Rodin (1976) demonstrated that giving such people plants to take care of had positive effects. Similarly, Kongable, Buckwalter, and Stolley (1989) showed that DAT institutional residents responded with increased appropriate behavior in the presence of a pet dog. Many other examples exist.

The Behavior Therapies

In the last 25 years, there has been a rapidly increasing application of various forms of behavior therapy (BT) to many problems of the elderly, especially those problems that characterize depression, anxiety, and organic brain disease (Patterson, 1992; Patterson & Jackson, 1980). Increased theoretical development and experience with practical application have made it useful to divide BT into three categories:

1. Cognitive behavior therapies seek to change the way that people perceive or think about events in their lives. By learning to be more realistic about troublesome events, they can influence their emotional reaction to be less extreme or devastating.
2. Behavior therapy has acquired connotations that associate it with conditioning techniques, such as desensitization or various forms of exposure to disturbing stimuli, while replacing the undesirable emotional reaction with others (e.g., relaxation).
3. Applied behavior analysis (ABA) changes problematic responses by a careful analysis of events preceding and following the response. The behavior is changed by altering either or both of the antecedents and consequences of the undesired behavior.

Psychologists will recognize the tripartite division as inaccurate and greatly oversimplified. However, these divisions are useful for explanatory responses and are found frequently in the literature.

Cognitive Behavior Therapies

Cognitive behavior therapies (CBT) with elderly people have received a considerable amount of attention; information regarding the application of these techniques to elders is readily available (e.g., Rybarczyk, Gallagher-Thompson, Rodman, Zeiss, Gantz, & Yeasavage, 1992; Hibbard, Grober, Gordon, Aletta, & Freeman, 1990). Most of the applications have been directed to depression and anxiety. Use of these techniques specifically to alleviate these conditions is often appropriate for treating those with organic disorder, because depression and anxiety often coexist with organic problems. Anxiety and depression are more common in the initial stages of dementia as opposed to later stages. These conditions may be much more common with stroke patients and acute conditions. Alleviation of these problems can result in considerable benefit to both the elder and the caregiver, since these conditions exacerbate many other problems. It may seem contradictory to use cognitive therapy with cognitively impaired people; however, such therapy may be useful with those elders who are mildly or moderately impaired. Even more frequently, it may be of use with caregivers. When the latter are depressed or anxious, it affects not only themselves, but also the quality of care provided.

Special guidelines for using CBT in treating the chronically ill elderly have been provided by Rybarczyk et al. (1992). First, there are practical barriers to be overcome when using CBT. Specifically mentioned were transportation and remembering to do therapy assignments. Whatever the problems may be, Rybarczyk et al. (1992) recommend starting the therapeutic process by using the problem-solving strategy described by D'Zurilla (1988). The latter served both to achieve solutions and to introduce the elder to the CBT process. Essential items in this procedure include (1) defining the problem; (2) brainstorming in order to list as many solutions as possible; (3) selecting the best solution based on consideration of the advantages and disadvantages of each; and (4) implementing the selected solution. This process may be repeated as needed. The example given was a Parkinson's patient who kept forgetting to do assignments. It was decided that the elder could remind himself with notes taped to his watch.

A second obstacle to be overcome is the problem of elders not recognizing the psychiatric problem (e.g., depression). Rather, all symptoms tend to be treated as side effects of physical illnesses. Unfortunately, their view may be reinforced by caregivers and even medical personnel. Psychiatric diagnoses are also perceived as stigmatizing by these people. Steps to overcome these obstacles included educating the elder and the caregivers about the nature of symptoms of anxiety and depression and how they may relate or not relate to relevant diseases. It is also said to be useful to encourage the elder to at least entertain a hypothesis that psychological courses of treatment may be relevant so that they may try CBT.

The issue of excess disabilities was related to CBT by Rybarczyk et al. (1992) in the following way: Several cognitive distortions may operate to magnify existing physical problems. Included are "all or none" ideas. For example, some may think: Since I can't do things as much or as well as I used to, I might as well do nothing. Developing and implementing realistic goals may help to correct this belief. Another relevant cognitive distortion is negative forecasting or cata-strophic thinking. This would occur when a person imagines much worse outcomes than are probable. "I can't" statements are also problematic. Having the person think through realistic probable outcomes helps with this belief. The person needs to phrase this more positively by admitting that he or she can substitute activities and/or modify the way things are done rather than abandoning them.

A different behavioral approach to modifying negative affect is to work with the person to develop a schedule of activities that are, or might be, pleasant to him or her and to plan to try these out on a regular basis. It is important that the person acknowledge that these activities do indeed improve feelings at the time they are performed. *The Older Person's Pleasant Events Schedule* (Gallagher & Thompson, 1982) is useful for helping an elder select appropriate activities.

Another important issue involves treatments for overcoming loss of self-esteem caused by actual material or social losses. As part of their behavioral treatment program, Patterson et al. (1982) included a group therapy approach in which elders learned to publicly state things about themselves and their lives about which they could feel positive. Social reinforcement and token rewards followed desirable statements. Rybarczyk et al. (1992) suggest identifying things that they actually can do for themselves in spite of disabilities. The perception of being a "burden" may be attacked by realistic discussion and planning with caregivers. The focus would be on what the elder may contribute to his or her self-care and to others (e.g., providing emotional support or advice). The care-giver should *not* handle this issue by refusing to admit to the elder that it does require some effort to provide care; this is obviously untrue.

Behavior Therapy

The successful use of behavior therapy for eliminating problematic emo-tional reactions has been demonstrated by Hussian (1981) and by Haley (1983). The former investigator was able to use a combination of education, relaxation, and training in utilizing coping statements to overcome fears of riding an eleva-tor in four elderly women residents of a long-term care facility. Haley (1983) used combinations of positive reinforcement, extinction, stimulus control, and relax-ation to eliminate problem behavior of three demented elderly people living in their communities. For example, one demented woman would cry out as if in fear anytime she was left alone, even for brief periods. Relaxation training, placing a clock and reassuring messages in her view, and positive reinforcement (ice cream) were used to teach her to remain alone in her room without causing disturbance for increasing periods of time. Similarly, obsessive-compulsive checking behavior by an elderly woman was eliminated by Juninger and Ditto (1984), who used behavioral practice and response prevention accompanied by medication with imipramine. There is even some indication that the reduction of anxiety by behavioral techniques may actually result in improved cognitive functioning (Yeasavage, 1985), although this needs clinical demonstration.

Applied Behavior Analysis

Applied behavior analysis (ABA) has been found to be especially useful with the problematic behavior of elders with more advanced cognitive loss. The particular utility of ABA stems in part from the fact that little or no verbal instruction or discussion is required of the therapist, and no ability to use verbally mediated cognitive processes by the elder is necessarily assumed. Also, minimal memory is required. The reason for these advantages is that ABA relies strictly on analyses of the interaction of the elder with his or her immediate environment as it exists. The process starts by defining particular problem behaviors (e.g., yelling, searching, throwing things, accusing others). The therapist accomplishes this task by encouraging and prompting the caregiver to discuss and verbally describe problem behaviors. Further observation will reveal when the behavior occurs, what events in the environment precede it, and other events in the environment that usually follow it. Through such careful observation, it will be possible to note a repeating pattern of events in which the occurrence of the problem behavior may be reliably triggered by external factors and/or followed by certain consequent events. The problem of changing the behavior then becomes one of altering the antecedent and/or the consequent events. Changing one or both of these will very often result in the gradual elimination of the problem behavior over a period of time.

Pinkston and Linsk (1984) have provided detailed instructions of how behavior therapists may work with caregivers in the home setting to accomplish these tasks. These authors also offer a selection of data gathering and other instruments to assist this process. Further, they present a number of examples of how ABA has been successfully applied. One example was that of a 73-year-old man with severe DAT. The problems were verbal statements made by the man to his wife, which a social worker described as paranoid and verbally abusive. He also had significant memory problems. Observation revealed that problem verbalizations were preceded 93% of the time by the wife's withdrawal of her attention or presence (e.g., talking on the telephone, cooking). Careful observation revealed that the DAT patient also made some positive statements, and it was found that these were usually followed by praise or attention from his wife. The intervention was to instruct the wife to ignore all the problematic statements and to praise or attend to all positive statements. The result was that occurrence of undesirable statements dropped to about 15% of that prior to treatment. His desirable positive statements more than doubled after intervention. This greatly reduced the burden on the wife, as measured by the Zarit Family Scale (Zarit, Reever, & Bach-Peterson, 1981).

Success with modifying several problem behaviors of a 61-year-old man with mild dementia related to the diagnosis of Parkinson's disease and arteriosclerosis was also reported by Pinkston and Linsk (1984). The client also had numerous other medical problems, including diabetes. Some of the targeted problem behaviors included improved compliance with self-dressing and self-hygiene, reduced messy saliva output, improved toileting to reduce urinary accidents, better eating behavior, and reduced hallucinations. Although this man was only mildly demented, the maladaptive responses created a serious burden on his wife so that placement in an institution was strongly considered. In this case, approaching multiple target behaviors was accomplished by means of a daily checklist, which spelled out the target behaviors with spaces to indicate how the task was performed by the elder (i.e., not at all, with help, when asked, independently) and how his wife had responded to the performance (i.e., didn't notice, ignored, asked to do something, praised). This list provided a means of monitoring the performance of both the elder and his wife. That is, the wife was made aware of how she responded to the various behaviors and whether or not her response was therapeutic.

A behavioral contract with the elder was also useful in this case. Although mildly demented, he was a retired businessman who maintained the ability to keep track of his own task assignments in the areas of daily exercise, self-dressing, and self-hygiene. Using the contract as a device for prompting, both wife and elder were reminded of appropriate behavior. The elder could self-reinforce by noting his fulfillment of the contract, and his wife could determine which behavior to praise and which to ignore or to respond in other ways deemed appropriate. The outcome was that the elder and his wife were able to maintain more comfortable and successful community living for many months.

An example of behavioral group treatment of dementia clients was offered by McEvoy and Patterson (1989) as part of a large-scale rehabilitation-focused behavioral treatment program for the elderly (Patterson et al., 1982). These investigators compared the responsiveness of 15 dementia residents with 15 residents with other psychiatric diagnoses, matched on age, sex, and chronicity to structured group and individual training in five areas. Included were (1) personal information (orientation to time, place and person); (2) spatial orientation (e.g., ability to locate the cafeteria, one's bedroom); (3) communications (ability to express pleasure and displeasure to another in socially appropriate ways); and (4) ADL at two levels: ADL-I was concerned with activities such as self-feeding and self-grooming, and ADL-II concerned laundry, meal selection, elementary money management.

As expected, demented patients were lower initially in all skills areas. After 1 month of training (some components of which occurred every day), the demented subjects acquired a level equal to the nondemented in ADL-I, improved location skills (almost to the level of the other group), and acquired appropriate assertiveness in simple situations at a level similar to the other groups. In contrast, the demented group failed to improve in the more complex and cognitively demanding tasks required for ADL-II.

Tappen (1994) also reported clinically and statistically significant success in teaching targeted, basic ADL skills to demented nursing home residents. Daily training sessions involved operant conditioning methods and techniques. The practical significance of such skills training was illustrated by McEvoy and Patterson (1987), who found that 80% of their demented residents were discharged, either to boarding homes or private residences with family members.

Teri (1994) has described ways in which principles of behavior analysis can be modified for use with those in acute states such as delirium. Initial attention must be directed to antecedents of behavior, particularly when speaking to a victim. The following steps were recommended: (1) speak slowly and softly; (2) make one demand at a time; (3) wait until a response is complete before proceeding; (4) avoid fatigue, which will come very early; and (5) maintain good eye contact.

Teri (1994) also gave specific recommendations concerning how to respond therapeutically, contingent upon the elder's response: (1) soothe and empathize; (2) determine any stimuli that may be disturbing to the elder and remove them from the situation whenever possible (this includes both antecedent and consequent stimuli); (3) avoid any confrontation by distracting and redirecting attention away from whatever may be bothering the elder at a given time; (4) always avoid violence, get help whenever any violence is indicated, which in some cases may encourage violence in the short run, but there is no choice except to respond as safely as possible; and (5) give attention when the elder is behaving appropriately; however, some response with minimal attention is usually required for undesirable behavior.

CONCURRENT MEDICAL TREATMENT

It is essential to give any elderly person showing cognitive decline a thorough medical examination, including adequate laboratory testing. The reason for this is evident from the variety of conditions that can cause cognitive losses, many of which are medically treatable and at least partially reversible. The above statements hold true not only for new cases of cognitive decline, but also for exacerbation of previously existing cognitive losses or behavioral disturbances (e.g., a person with DAT).

This point is emphasized by a study of 116 patients 65 and older who were admitted to a psychiatric facility. Of these, 61.2% had treatable medical problems that were directly related to behavioral problems (Parker et al., 1976). Included among medical causes of dementialike symptoms are (1) medicine and drugs, including side effects and drug interactions; (2) metabolic disturbances such as uremia, dehydration, hyponatremia; and (3) other diseases and treatments for diseases. Hidden bacterial and viral infections, glandular dysfunction, vitamin deficiencies, and malfunctions of the liver, lungs, and heart were also found. Recovery from anesthesia and surgical procedures was also a frequent cause of delirium.

One may conclude from the above that it is necessary to rule out all possible reversible causes of cognitive decline (properly diagnosed as delirium) before treating a particular case as being exclusively due to an irreversible dementia of any type.

As described elsewhere in this text, it is also necessary to rule out complications due to depression and anxiety, which may exacerbate or even mimic dementia and delirium. For example, Patterson (1985) describes a case that apparently began as depression due to psychological losses and medical problems, and was further complicated by a severe toxic condition (snake bite).

Unfortunately, treatment of the medical illness and the lengthy recovery period following treatment was accompanied by greater psychosocial losses, including loss of income, status, friends, and independence. In this case, the person had received extensive medical diagnostic work-ups and treatment, which concluded with a diagnosis of DAT and a recommendation for institutional care. However, when subjected to a comprehensive behavioral treatment program (Patterson et al., 1982), this person improved dramatically; it became apparent that the operative condition at the time of intervention was major depression related to severe psychosocial losses. The correct diagnosis was discovered by the elder's response to behavioral treatment. Antidepressant medication was then prescribed but later discontinued with no return of major depression.

It is apparent from the above discussion that medical treatment concurrent with psychological treatment for organic disorders of elderly people may include the entire field of geriatric medicine. Fortunately, there are also some highly specialized medical treatments that are of particular use with organically disordered elderly.

Only recently has a drug treatment for DAT become available. This medicine is tacrine hydrochloride, which functions as a centrally active acetylcholinesterase inhibitor. A study by Knapp and colleagues (1994) found that patients treated with tacrine hydrochloride had significant, dose-related improvements on three different measures of function. A drawback to the use of this medicine was a very large drop-out rate. This was attributed to altered liver function (liver transaminase elevations) and gastrointestinal complaints. Of 653 Alzheimer's patients, 384 (59%) withdrew from the 30-week study, largely for these reasons.

A second study (Watkins, Zimmerman, Knapp, Gracon, & Lewis, 1994), of almost 2,500 Alzheimer's patients, found that the liver alterations produced no fatalities and that such changes appeared primarily during the first 12 weeks of treatment and subsequently diminished. Thus the drug, when properly used, is considered partially effective and reasonably safe for Alzheimer's patients.

Psychotropic medications have proven useful for controlling many symptoms associated with organic brain disease. Conditions that have improved due to pharmacotherapy have included anxiety, depression, agitation, and various psychotic symptoms, including behavioral disturbances. These improvements have often resulted in significant benefits to the elder and to the caregiver by permitting less restrictive and more comfortable living conditions. In spite of such benefits, such treatments should be used only with great expertise and care. Unfortunately, all classes of psychotropics, including anxiolytics, antidepressants, and antipsychotics, may also have deleterious effects. These and other drugs, either singly or (especially) in combination, may exacerbate present symptoms and/or create additional symptoms because of side effects. Ayd (1994) has reported that benzodiazepenes (widely prescribed anxiolytics) may cause amnesia, confusion, depression, and oversedation, which may be misdiagnosed as dementia. Similarly, withdrawal of these medications may cause mental disturbances. The antipsychotic drug haloperidol is often prescribed to control a variety of more severe symptoms related to organic brain disease. In one study, Devenand, Sackheim, Brown, and Mayeux (1989) found that this medication reduced many such behaviors, including hallucinations, physical aggression, and agitation. Unfortunately, some patients also suffered severe extrapyramidal side effects (e.g., movement disorders). Most notably, the medication also decreased cognitive functioning simultaneously with improvement in targeted symptoms. Many antidepressants strongly affect the anticholinergic system, which may cause various sources of distress. (This may not be true of the newer ones such as fluoxetine.)

Even when psychotropic medications are successful in controlling symptoms, there is an additional caveat to be noted. Especially in the case of delirium, the effective control of symptoms may complicate diagnosis and thus interfere with effective treatment (Wragg & Jeste, 1988). Because many elders suspected of having an organic brain disease may come to treatment having taken many medications, many clinicians may advocate the medically supervised withdrawal of drugs as a first step in treatment.

Considering the possible benefits and risks associated with such use of psychotropic medications, Wragg and Jeste (1988) offered some useful guidelines for appropriate use of medications employed for symptom control in organically impaired elders:

1. Start by targeting specific symptoms for treatment that have been found to be altered by such treatment. (Behavioral psychologists may also have expertise in this endeavor.)
2. Focus treatment and establish time limits. The smallest dose practical should be used, and this should be reduced or eliminated as the symptom improves.
3. Systematically monitor side effects and possible drug interactions. Medication to control side effects should *not* be routinely prescribed but prescribed only when there is demonstrated need.
4. Inform the patient (insofar as possible) and concerned family members and/or caregivers of the risk-benefit ratio and the rationale for treatment.

COURSE OF TREATMENT

The course of treatment for the organic disorders varies tremendously, depending on the nature of the disorder and the adequacy of treatment. Accordingly, the progress of any type of condition must be viewed against the background of the usual course of a particular syndrome or disorder.

The various kinds of delirium can be expected to be the most responsive. However, some recent studies have indicated that processes and outcomes related to delirium may be more complex than previously thought. Murray et al. (1993) found that the usual assumption that delirium is strictly a transient cognitive syndrome may not be true. They observed a sample of hospital and nursing home residents at 3- and 6-month periods after treatment for delirium. Results showed that these people continued to show significant functional decline (in ADLs) after the initial treatment was completed. They suggest that the definition of dementia be changed from that of an acute, reversible condition to that of a condition with acute onset with long-term sequelae.

The course of DVT is obviously related to success in treating the relevant cardiovascular disease. One of the more typical patterns has been called Multi-Infarct Dementia (MID) (Tomlinson et al., 1970). In MID, the progression of the disease is said to proceed in a stepwise fashion. That is, the elder may suffer from a series of small strokes, each followed by immediate decrease in functioning, accompanied by partial recovery. Overall, there is progressive deterioration over time.

DAT is characterized by much more steady decline overall. However, such decline is far from uniform, and the nature of the decline probably depends on the various ways that the disease may attack different parts of the brain. In spite of this variability, some very general characterization of the nature of decline is possible. While acknowledging the variable course of the disease, Carnes (1985) has written some general characteristics of expected changes over time. She reports that DAT can have very rapid progression but that it often develops slowly over 10 to 15 years, with plateaus occurring at any time before decreases are again observed.

Berger (1980) has reported that dementias in general can be thought of as occurring in a series of stages. In the earliest phase, the victim continues to function safely in any surrounding, but the ability to perform ADLS begins to slip. A second stage is characterized by ability of the elder to function only in familiar surroundings. He or she becomes lost or disoriented in other settings. This stage may be accompanied by confusion primarily occurring at night, sometimes referred to as "sundowning." A further period of development happens when the elder can still perform many functions but only when given cues by others. This stage may also be characterized by sleep and appetite disturbances. Increasing deterioration results in a loss of responsiveness to verbal cuing, and physical assistance is required. In the final stages the elder loses ability to ambulate, to communicate meaningfully, and is confined to a bed or wheelchair.

Treatment personnel of all disciplines should be optimistic about relatively short-term results but realistic about long-term outcomes. The relatively short-term results are well justified by the savings in treatment costs when the costs of long-term hospitalization and institutionalization are considered. Also, the humanitarian results of easing burdens and improving quality of life for both elders and caregivers are very rewarding and worthwhile.

FOLLOW-UP

All treatment of organic disorders requires long-term follow-up. As noted above, even medically treatable deliria are often followed by functional decline after identifiable causative conditions have been well treated (Murray et al., 1993). Areas that may be targeted as profitable for long-term follow-up, particularly for psychological interventions, include maintaining simple vocal skills, orientation to environment, and the simpler ADL skills (McEvoy & Patterson, 1989).

Challenges for the application of applied behavior analysis to problem behavior continue throughout the course of all organic disorders, regardless of the stage of development. Such behaviors as yelling, searching, incontinence, and wandering continue to require psychological as well as possible pharmacological interventions.

Anxiety and depression may vary in caregivers and elders throughout the course of the various disorders. Relevant psychological and medical interventions must continue to be made available as needed.

OVERALL EVALUATION

One cannot approach the evaluation of organic brain disease the way one approaches a diagnostic category such as depression. As was seen from the discussion of *DSM-IV*, a great number of very different etiologies may cause brain and behavioral disturbances in the elderly. In the past, this was poorly understood. Consequently, many studies have included diagnostically heterogeneous populations. Despite this limitation, it is evident from the above information that many options are available for improving the lives of organically impaired elders and those who care for them. Increased medical knowledge regarding the diagnosis of many conditions that may produce or exacerbate cognitive impairment along with improved treatment possibilities has become increasingly available. Similarly, psychological knowledge and methods have been increasingly applied to this group, often with considerable success. All practitioners concerned with the elderly or their families should become knowledgeable about these possibilities.

Cognitive-behavioral therapies have proven useful primarily with depression; they should always be considered when organic brain disorders are accompanied by depression and when the elder's cognitive skills are sufficiently intact (Gallagher & Thompson, 1982). It is important to note, however, that the potential effectiveness of these techniques should not be restricted to this or any other diagnosis. CBT is a potentially useful method for many target behaviors for which a person is capable of using verbally mediated self-direction.

The behavioral strategies of exposure along with appropriate instruction also have shown their usefulness and may be effective in eliminating fears, as well as other distressing emotions. These approaches may be applied in ways that require little if any verbal interaction. An example would be pairing a favorite food such as ice cream with some previously disturbing stimulus (Haley, 1983; Hussian & Davis, 1985).

Applied behavior analysis has no dependence upon verbal ability. Observing antecedents and consequences of particular behaviors need not be difficult, although time is required. Behavioral psychologists can function well in the role of consultants or trainers to either professional or family caregivers (e.g., Pinkston & Linsk, 1984).

Skills training approaches may incorporate many techniques and address disparate target behaviors. For example, Patterson et al. (1982) incorporated three levels of ADL training matched to three levels of competence. Their approach also included two levels of social skills training, self-esteem training, personal orientation, and a variety of leisure skills. All elements of the program included the behavioral techniques of shaping utilizing social and token reinforcement. Training also used verbal instruction, physical prompts, and modeling appropriate to the type and level of the activity as well as the functional level of the individual. This multicomponent approach served to address the needs of those with moderate cognitive impairment as well as those with a variety of other diagnoses and problems (McEvoy & Patterson, 1987).

Psychoanalysts remind us that generational differences may color the way we interact with elders (and vice versa) in ways we may not intend. I became aware early on that working with elders brought up thoughts and feelings regarding my own parents and of my own mortality. The therapies based on adult development (Erickson, 1963; Sherman, 1991) point out that there may be larger issues affecting the way we respond to aging, and we should take these into consideration.

The complexity of the subject of this chapter has not impeded a great deal of treatment progress. Thus far, significant gains have come from a parallel process of treating disease entities when they are known, while also addressing specific self-reported and observed problems by using psychological and symptomatic medical treatments in judicious ways.

SUMMARY

Through a long process of research and clinical work, several types of organic brain disorders have been defined that are more likely to occur among those of advanced age. All of these have in common a loss of cognitive and behavioral functioning. Major categories of these include delirium and dementia. Conditions of delirium are of relatively rapid onset and are usually at least partially treatable by medical means. The various kinds of dementia are much more insidious and less treatable. Delirium is generally caused by the ingestion of a substance or a general medical condition or a combination of these. Dementia results from lasting changes in brain structure. Types of dementia include Alzheimer's disease (DAT), Vascular Dementia (DVT), Dementia Due to Other Medical Conditions (DMC), and Substance-Induced Persisting Dementia (DSI). These may exist in mixed form. Dementia with delirium present as an overlay may also occur. Psychiatric conditions of anxiety and/or depression may also be complicating factors.

Delirium is the most common of these disorders, affecting 40% of geriatric patients at some point during a hospital stay. The number of cases of dementia in this country exceed one million and are increasing dramatically due to the aging of the population. The most common dementia is DAT, followed by DVT and DSI.

Most cases of organic disorder are first seen in outpatient medical facilities and general hospitals. Losses of memory and self-care ability are frequent early complaints. Medical diagnosis followed by appropriate treatment of all treatable conditions is required. Much research has been devoted to developing a direct medical intervention for DAT. Only recently has a medication (tacrine hydrochloride) become available for this purpose. Tacrine has been shown to slow the progress of this disease in people who can tolerate it.

Several forms of psychological treatment may be highly beneficial, both to the elder and the caregiver. Anxiety and depression need to be minimized. Crisis intervention counseling, reducing environmental stress, and behavior therapy may be useful for these purposes. Medications may also be useful but may cause complications of their own. Psychological interventions that reduce disruptive behaviors and improve self-care ability, spatial orientation, and social skills have been demonstrated to be successful and may make critical differences in the quality of life of the victim and the caregiver. Psychotropic medications have been used successfully to manage behaviors, but undesirable side effects are a distinct possibility and must be carefully monitored. Such medications may also exacerbate confusion and suppress desirable behaviors.

REFERENCES

Alexander, F., & Sellesick (1966). *The history of psychiatry.* New York: Harper & Row.

American Psychiatric Association. (1968). *Diagnostic and statistical manual of mental disorders* (2nd ed.). Washington, DC: Author.

American Psychiatric Association. (1994). *Diagnostic and statistical manual of mental disorders* (4th ed.). Washington, DC: Author.

Ayd, F. J., Jr. (1994). Prescribing anxiolytics and hypnotics for the elderly. *Psychiatric Annals, 24,* 91–94.

Baines, S., Saxby, P., & Ehlert, K. (1987). Reality orientation and reminiscence therapy. A controlled cross-over study of elderly confined people. *British Journal of Psychiatry, 151,* 222–231.

Berger, E. Y. (1980). A system for rating the severity of senility. *Journal of the American Geriatric Society, 28,* 234–237.

Butler, R. N. (1963). The life review: An interpretation of reminiscence in the aged. *Psychiatry, 26,* 65–75.

Carnes, M. (1985). Diagnosis and dementia in the elderly. *Physical to Occupational Therapy in Geriatrics, 3,* 11–23.

Crook, T. (1987). Dementia. In L. Carstensen & B. Edelstein (Eds.), *Handbook of clinical gerontology.* New York: Pergamon.

Devenand, D. P., Sackhesm, H. A., Brown, R. P., & Mayeux, R. (1989). A pilot study of haloperidol treatment of psychosis and behavioral disturbance in Alzheimer's disease. *Archives of Neurology, 46,* 854–857.

D'Zurilla, T. J., & Nazu, A. (1982). Social problem solving in adults. In P. Kendall & S. Hollon (Eds.), *Advances in cognitive-behavioral research and therapy* (Vol. 1, pp. 109–143). New York: Academic Press.

Erickson, E. (1963). *Childhood and society* (2nd ed.). New York: Norton.

Folsom, J. C. (1968). Reality, orientation for the elderly mental patient. *Journal of Geriatric Psychiatry, 1,* 291–306.

Freud, S. (1953). On psychotherapy. In J. Strachey (Ed. and Trans.), *The standard edition of the complete psychological works of Sigmund Freud* (Vol. 7, pp. 257–270). London: Hogarth Press. (Original work published 1905)

Gallagher, D. E., & Thompson, L. W. (1982). Differential effectiveness of psychotherapies for the treatment of major depressive disorders in older adult patients. *Psychotherapy, Theory, Research and Practice, 19,* 482–490.

German, P., Rovner, B., Burton, L. C., Brant, L. J., & Clark, R. (1992). The role of mental morbidity in the nursing home experience. *Gerontologist, 32,* 152–158.

Haley, W. E. (1983). A family-behavioral approach of the cognitively impaired elderly. *The Gerontologist, 23,* 18–20.

Hibbard, R., Grober, S. E., Gordon, W. A., Aletta, E. G., & Freeman, A. (1990). Cognitive therapy and the treatment of post stroke depression. *Topics in Geriatric Rehabilitation, 5,* 43–55.

Horvath, T. B., Siever, L. J., Mohs, R., & Davis, K. (1989). Organic mental syndromes and disorders. In H. I. Kaplan & B. J. Sadock (Eds.), *Comprehensive textbook of psychiatry* (Vol. IV, pp. 599–641). Baltimore: Williams & Wilkins.

Hussian, R. A. (1981). *Geriatric psychology: A behavioral perspective.* New York: Van Nostrand Reinhold.

Hussian, R. A., & Davis, R. L. (1985). *Responsive care: Behavioral interventions with elderly persons.* Champaign, IL: Research Press.

Juninger, J., & Ditto, B. (1984). Multitreatment of obsessive compulsive checking in a geriatric patient. *Behavior Modification, 8,* 379–390.

Kahana, R. (1979). Strategies of dynamic psychotherapy with the wide range of older individuals. *Journal of Geriatric Psychiatry, 12,* 71–100.

Knapp, M. J., Knopman, D. S., Solomon, E. R., Pendlebury, W. W., Davis, C. S., & Gracon, S. T. (1994). A 30-week randomized control trial of high-dose tacrine in patients with Alzheimer's disease. *Journal of the American Medical Association, 271,* 985–991.

Kongable, Buckwalter, & Stolley. (1989). The effects of pet therapy on the social behavior of institutionalized clients. *Archives of Psychiatric Nursing, 3,* 191–198.

Langer, E. J., & Rodin, J. (1976). The effects of choice and enhanced personal responsibility for the aged: A field experiment in an institutional setting. *Journal of Personality and Social Psychology, 34,* 191–198.

McEvoy, C. L., & Patterson, R. L. (1989). Behavioral treatment of deficit skills in dementia patients. *The Gerontologist, 26,* 475–478.

Murray, A. M., Levkoff, S. E., Wetle, T. T., Becket, L., Cleary, P. D., Schor, J. D., Lipsitz, L. A., Rowe, J. W., & Evans, D. A. (1993). Acute delirium and functional decline in the hospitalized elderly patient. *Journal of Gerontology, 48,* 181–186.

Parker, B., Diebler, S., Feldshuh, B., Frosch, W., Laureana, E., & Sillen, J. (1976). Finding medical reason for psychiatric behavior. *Geriatrics, 31,* 87–91.

Patterson, R. L. (1985). Dementias arising in the senium and presenium. In R. Daitzman (Ed.), *Diagnosis and intervention in behavior therapy and behavioral medicine* (Vol. 4, pp. 88–149). New York: Springer.

Patterson, R. L. (1992). Psychogeriatric rehabilitation. In R. P. Liberman (Ed.), *Handbook of psychiatric rehabilitation.* New York: Macmillan.

Patterson, R. L., Dupree, L. W., Eberly, D. A., Jackson, G. W., O'Sullivan, M. J., Penner, L. A., & Dee-Kelly, C. (1982). *Overcoming deficit of aging: A behavioral approach.* New York: Plenum Press.

Patterson, R. L., & Jackson, G. M. (1980). Behavior and modification with the elderly. In H. Hersen, R. M. Eisler, & P. M. Miller (Eds.), *Progress in behavior modification* (Vol. 9, pp. 206–239). New York: Academic Press.

Pinkston, E. M., & Linsk, N. L. (1984). *Care of the elderly: A family approach.* New York: Pergamon.

Rybarczyk, B., Gallagher-Thompson, D., Rodman, J., Zeiss, A., Gantz, F., & Yeasavage, J. (1992). Applying cognitive-behavioral psychotherapy to the chronically ill elderly: Treatment issues and case illustration. *International Psychogeriatrics, 4,* 127–140.

Sherman, E. (1981). *Counseling the aging: An integrative approach.* New York: Free Press.

Silver, W. H. (1994). Major trends in psychotherapy. *Psychotherapy, 31,* 227–229.

Tappen, R. M. (1994). The effect of skill training on functional abilities of nursing home residents with dementia. *Research in Nursing and Health, 17,* 159–165.

Teri, L. (1994, August 3). *Managing and understanding behavior problems in patients with Alz-*

heimer's disease. Paper presented in the satellite video conference sponsored by the Department of Veteran's Affairs.

Teri, L., & Logsdon, R. G. (1992). The future of psychotherapy with older adults. *Psychotherapy, 29,* 81–87.

Tomlinson, B. E., Blessed, G., & Roth, M. (1970). Observations on the brains of demented old people. *Journal of Neurological Science, 11,* 205–242.

Torack, R. M. (1983). The early history of senile dementia. In B. Reisberg (Ed.), *Alzheimer's disease: The standard reference* (pp. 23–28). New York: Free Press.

Turner, M. S. (1992). Individual psychodynamic psychotherapy with older adults: Perspective from a nurse psychotherapist. *Archives of Psychiatric Nursing, 5,* 266–274.

Watkins, P. B., Zimmerman, Knapp, M., Gracon, & Lewis (1994). Hepatutoxic effects of tacrine administration in patients with Alzheimer's disease. *Journal of the American Medical Association, 271,* 992–998.

Wragg, R. E., & Jeste, D. V. (1988). Neuroleptics and alternative treatments. *Psychiatric Clinics of North America, 11,* 194–213.

Yeasavage, J. E. (1985). Nonpharmacologic treatments for memory losses with normal aging. *American Journal of Psychiatry, 142,* 600–605.

Zarit, S., Reever, K. E., & Bach-Peterson, J. (1981). Relatives of the impaired elderly: Correlates of feelings of burden. *The Gerontologist, 21,* 158–164.

CHAPTER 14

Substance Abuse

LARRY W. DUPREE AND LAWRENCE SCHONFELD

CHAPTER OUTLINE

Prevalence of Substance Abuse Disorders
Alcohol Abuse
  Coping Skills
  Treatment
Medication Abuse and Misuse
  Treatment
Self-Management Approaches
  Drink Refusal Training
  Assertion Training

Management of Tension and Anxiety
Cues
Urges
Relapse Training
Case Examples
  Case 1: Alcohol Abuse
  Case 2: Medication Abuse
Conclusions
References

PREVALENCE OF SUBSTANCE
ABUSE DISORDERS

Substance abuse among older adults has been a problem of increasing concern over the past 25 years, with varying estimates of alcohol and drug abuse. Congress reports that 2.5 million older Americans have alcohol-related problems, and that 21% of people age 60 and older ("60+") hospitalized for medical problems have a diagnosis of alcoholism, with related hospital costs of $60 billion per year (HR Rep. No. 852, 1992). Others estimate that 5% to 60% of older medical inpatients abuse alcohol (Atkinson, 1984; Curtis, Geller, Stokes, Levine, & Moore, 1989).

In mental health settings, estimates of alcohol abuse among older patients also vary. For example, Atkinson (1984) suggests that alcohol abuse ranges from

LARRY W. DUPREE AND LAWRENCE SCHONFELD • Department of Aging and Mental Health, Florida Mental Health Institute, University of South Florida, Tampa, Florida 33612.
Psychological Treatment of Older Adults: An Introductory Text, edited by Michel Hersen and Vincent B. Van Hasselt. Plenum Press, New York, 1996.

3% to 17% in older psychiatric clinic patients and 23% to 44% in older patients in psychiatric screening wards. Reifler, Raskind, and Kethly (1982) report that alcohol problems among people referred for outpatient mental health evaluation as 21% of those ages 60 to 69 and 13% of those ages 70 to 79.

Illicit drug use is rare among older community residents or homeless people, with the exception of aging criminals and long-term heroin addicts (Atkinson, Ganzini, & Bernstein, 1992). The National Institute on Drug Abuse (NIDA) Household Survey on Drug Abuse (1992) revealed that less than 1% of people age 35+ (no other age group categories were used) reported using marijuana or cocaine. Less than 2% of all methadone maintenance clients in New York City in 1985 were age 60+ (Pascarelli, 1974).

In comparison to their percentage of the general population, relatively few older adults are found in treatment programs. In a 1989 national survey of 7,759 treatment programs, only 4% of clients were age 55+ (NIDA & National Institute on Alcohol Abuse and Alcoholism, 1990). In a national survey on drug-related emergency room visits, of the few (2.6%) admitted patients who were age 55+, most had alcohol and prescription medication problems (NIDA, 1990). Older men appear to be at greater risk for alcohol dependence than older women, who are at greater risk for prescription drug dependence. Treatment of and research on substance abuse among older adults therefore focuses mostly on use of legal substances (i.e., alcohol and medications), rather than illicit drugs. With the aging of America, there is increasing concern over these two forms of chemical addition. This chapter focuses on assessment and treatment of these two very different problems.

ALCOHOL ABUSE

Two major categories of older alcohol abusers have been identified (Atkinson, Turner, Kofoed, & Tolson, 1985; Janik & Dunham, 1983; Schonfeld & Dupree, 1991). Early-onset older alcohol abusers are those having alcohol-related problems over several decades, estimated as high as two-thirds of older alcohol abusers. Late-onset alcohol abusers are those whose alcohol problems began in their 50s or 60s, with estimates varying from 4% in a skid row sample to 88% in a hospital setting (Atkinson, 1984). Recent stressful events, including illness or death of a spouse, divorce, loss of employment, or disability, often precede late-onset alcohol abuse (Jennison, 1992; Rosin & Glatt, 1971; Wells-Parker, Miles, & Spencer, 1983). Research suggests that both categories of older alcohol abusers, in comparison to younger alcohol abusers, are more likely to drink in response to depression, loneliness, or grief (Schonfeld & Dupree, 1991; Schonfeld, Dupree, & Rohrer, 1995).

Older adults may be more sensitive to the effects of alcohol than their younger counterparts. Research suggests that with aging there is a decrease in lean body mass, volume of body water, blood flow, and distribution of ethanol, all of which lead to increased blood alcohol concentrations and sensitivity to alcohol (Bienenfeld, 1987; Hartford & Samorajski, 1982; Vestal et al., 1977).

Drinking in response to current stressors, plus an increased sensitivity to alcohol, places at risk those older adults who are drinking to cope.

Coping Skills

Within social learning theory, alcohol use is conceptualized as a general coping mechanism invoked in situations where other more appropriate coping behaviors are unavailable or unused. Lazarus and Folkman (1984) classified coping strategies as problem focused and emotion focused, with the former more often being associated with drinking problems. Moos, Brennan, Fondacaro, and Moos (1990) report that older problem drinkers, as compared to nonproblem drinkers, were more likely to use cognitive and behavioral avoidance responses to manage life stressors and that older drinkers who relied more on avoidance (emotional) coping tended to have more drinking problems and to report more depression and physical symptoms and less self-confidence. Also, Folkman, Bernstein, and Lazarus (1987) found that elderly drug misusers experienced their daily "hassles" (stresses) as more intense and experienced more threat emotions and more dissatisfaction with their coping abilities than did people who did not misuse.

Based upon coping research findings, it would seem that certain factors are related to levels of alcohol consumption: (1) personal appraisal of the stressfulness of the external event or circumstance (stressor); (2) the amount of perceived control the person experiences; (3) availability and use of adequate nondrinking coping responses (more likely problem focused rather than emotion focused); (4) perceived outcome of the coping response (which relates to items 2 and 3); and (5) expectations as to the benefits of alcohol as a fairly immediate coping resource.

Treatment

There is little research-based information regarding effective forms of treatment for older alcohol abusers, with many experts offering treatment recommendations without providing supportive evidence. Treatment approaches used with younger people are often recommended for older adults simply because of clinician's expertise with addictions or with a specific approach, but not necessarily expertise with older people or older abusers or treatment based upon outcome research. Only a few studies on older adults in alcohol treatment have reported outcome evaluation data (Dupree, Broskowski, & Schonfeld, 1984; Wiens, Menustik, Miller, & Schmitz, 1982–1983; Carstensen, Rychtarik, & Prue, 1985; Kofoed, Tolson, Atkinson, Toth, & Turner, 1987). Those few studies suggest positive treatment outcomes for older adults that are at least as promising as, if not better than, those for younger adults in treatment.

Only one study has used a control group outcome approach with random assignment of subjects to treatment conditions (Kashner, Rodell, Ogden, Guggenheim, & Karson, 1992), and only two studies have attempted to investigate the need for age-specific treatment programs by comparing treatment outcomes for older adults with younger adults (Janik & Dunham, 1983; Kofoed et al., 1987). Studies employing behavioral interventions show promise, as indicated by high rates of success after 1 or more years of follow-up (Schonfeld & Dupree, 1995).

Aversion therapy using counterconditioning with emetine-induced nausea has been found to be effective (Wiens et al., 1982–1983) but presents medical risks such as hypotension for the older adult, which could lead to injuries from falling. On the other hand, cognitive-behavioral and self-management approaches have shown low rates of relapse during follow-up without producing medical risks (Carstensen et al., 1985; Dupree et al., 1984).

MEDICATION ABUSE AND MISUSE

In contrast to alcohol abuse, older adults are more likely to use prescribed and over-the-counter (OTC) medications with therapeutic intent. For example, Finlayson (1984) reported that coping with pain was the most frequently reported reason for prescription drug dependence. Other reasons included insomnia, marital and family problems, retirement, death of a spouse, work stress, and depression. Also, while most medications are legitimately prescribed by one or more physicians, some older adults may be unable to manage the schedule and number of medications. They are also more susceptible to adverse reactions. Thus, medication problems are often considered unintentional misuse rather than abuse or recreational use (Glantz, 1981; Schwartz, Wang, Zeitz, & Gross, 1962).

Research indicates that almost 40% of physician visits and 44% of "drug mentions" are for people age 55+ (Burke, Jolson, Goetsch, & Ahronheim, 1992; IMS America, 1990) and that they use 30% to 40% of nonprescription or OTC medications (Coons, Hendricks, & Sheahan, 1988). With increased usage, there are increased risks. For example, older patients are far less likely to ask questions of their physician or pharmacist or receive written information about their prescriptions in comparison to younger adults (Olins, 1985). Also, noncompliance, or the failure to follow instructions for taking medications, varies from 2% to 95% (Landress & Morck, 1984; Simonson, 1984).

Additionally affecting medication use are age-related altered pharmacokinetics (how the body absorbs, distributes, metabolizes, and eliminates a drug), such as increased fat to lean body mass ratio, baroreceptor sensitivity, and decreased liver and renal function resulting in poor elimination of wastes. There are also altered pharmacodynamics (how the drug affects the individual), including changes in the density or integrity of neural receptors (affecting responses to certain concentrations of drugs), with an increased probability of adverse side effects (Atkinson et al., 1992; Kelly & O'Malley, 1992; Klein, German, & Levine, 1981; Lamy, 1982). Burke et al. (1992) found that older adults age 65+ account for the highest rates of adverse drug events (ADEs), with antidepressants ranked highest. Based on older patients' responses to a medical symptom inventory, Wasson et al. (1992) found that prednisone, antidepressants, certain antihypertensives, and diuretics were the medications most frequently suspected of causing adverse drug reactions of patients.

Physician-related variables contributing to medication problems include prescribing age-inappropriate medications, failure to identify adverse effects, and lack of training in geriatric medicine. For example, using a list of "age-inappropriate" medications determined by a panel of U.S. and Canadian experts (see Beers et al., 1991), Wilcox, Himmelstein, and Woolhandler (1994) surveyed 6,171 community-dwelling adults age 65+. Based on their survey, they projected that 32% of older Americans receive at least one inappropriate medication.

Treatment

Three levels of intervention may be considered in dealing with medication-related problems of older adults. The first is education of the patient. Education may involve use of written instructions in large print, monitoring and review sessions with the physician or pharmacist to identify errors or adverse reactions, and education of caregivers in assisting older adults having difficulty in managing the medication schedule.

The second level is the "education" of the physician. This has two aspects. The first is informing the physician about medication problems, adverse reactions, or noncompliance. This must be accomplished tactfully by the client or caregiver, respecting the physician's medical and prescribing judgment. The second aspect is the need for continuing eduction of health care professionals in identification of adverse reactions, assessment of the patient's ability to manage medications, knowledge of age-inappropriate medications, improved communication with older patients, and reduction of the complexity of medication regimen if feasible. The last step involves detailed assessment of the patient and the number and type of drugs prescribed. In one study, when physicians used a symptom inventory to identify patients at risk for adverse reactions, the physicians changed medications for 25% of the patients as compared to changing medications for 12% of those not at risk (Wasson et al., 1992).

A third level of intervention may be necessary for the older patient who abuses medications and may be psychologically and/or chemically dependent on them. Self-management approaches that provide coping skills as alternatives to improper use of medication are helpful.

SELF-MANAGEMENT APPROACHES

The therapeutic aim of a self-management approach is one of providing the older person with control over his or her drinking patterns and life in general. The older person assumes primary responsibility for his or her behavior. This is in contrast to treatment programs that alter the client's behavior through direct action by the therapist or treatment. Self-control or self-management in this context is not will power but knowledge of what causes personal abusive drinking, what specifically to do about it, and then implement the program. Because most abusive drinking patterns have multiple antecedents and may change over time, training of clients in the analysis of drinking chains and self-management skills makes them better prepared for future and evolving high-risk situations. They are prepared to analyze, understand, problem-solve, and respond to the factors affecting substance use. Also, self-monitoring and self-management responses decrease the likelihood of abusive drinking and are not merely alternatives to drinking. More is required than just abstinence.

Dupree et al. (1984) included three stages in teaching self-management skills to older substance abusers. The first step involved the functional analysis of the older abuser's drinking behavior using a structured interview incorporating an A-B-C (antecedents → behavior → consequences) paradigm. In this A-B-C approach, the therapist and client identify, often for the first time, the contingencies related to abusive drinking behavior, i.e., the "drinking behavior chain" (Miller, 1976). The antecedents are the "high risk situation(s)" for abuse and potential determinants of relapse after treatment.

The second stage involved teaching the client to recognize and understand the conditions that prompted excessive use of alcohol. This stage also required that each client be able to explain the relationship between the components of the chain and how that relationship defined his or her high risk situation(s) for abuse. Client construction (and diagraming) of personal drinking behavior chains provides both insight and preparation for instruction in ways to rearrange or control one's personal antecedents of abuse.

The third stage consisted of teaching more effective coping skills specific to the identified antecedents for abuse. Newly learned, self-directed behaviors have the capacity to disrupt, terminate, or preclude an individual's drinking chain. Within the self-management model, the therapist does not socially reinforce or punish drinking behavior per se but instead reinforces the older abuser's efforts to control his or her drinking behavior by using the techniques they have learned.

Incorporating the three-stage process, Dupree et al. (1984) taught older adults the behaviors necessary to manage a minimum of certain, high-frequency, high-risk situations: social pressure to drink, anger/frustration, tension/anxiety, presence of drinking cues, urges to drink, and "inoculation" for potential relapse situations. Description of antecedents or high-risk situations relevant to many older abusers, as well as to the case examples to be subsequently discussed, are noted below.

Drink Refusal Training

Social pressures to have a drink are common and difficult for problem drinkers. For the older person, rather than peer pressure, the high-risk situation may incorporate fears of not being liked, of losing a friend if the offer of a drink isn't accepted, or of feeling left out when the few friends they have are enjoying themselves. Thus, older persons need to develop the skills necessary to saying no, with the objective of controlling their behavior without losing the few friends they might have.

Assertion Training

Anger and frustration are feeling states that commonly present difficulties to problem drinkers and are often responded to with, I'll have a drink. For example, the predrinking chain may include Anger/frustration → Cues → Urge(s) → Self-statement (I'll feel better if I have a drink). Remaining passive or becoming aggressive sustains the interpersonal conditions for reexperiencing anger/frustration and contributes to problem drinking, especially if certain cues are present (e.g., a bottle of liquor on the counter, beer in the refrigerator, or passing by a favorite bar on the way home). Older adults can be taught how to learn not to drink by having another way of handling anger/frustration situations (e.g., by learning more assertive behavior).

Management of Tension and Anxiety

Older adults often refer to anxiety as "worry," "tension," "nervousness." As an antecedent to drinking, the drinking chain sequence may include Anxiety → Cues → Urge(s) → Self-statement (Have a drink, you'll relax and feel better). The chain needs to be broken at the situation–feeling link or the feeling–urge link. This is often done by avoiding anxiety-producing situations and/or by learning anxiety and tension-reducing skills.

Cues

Cues are concrete stimuli in a situation or reminders to drink. These include alcohol itself, certain places (bars, lounges, restaurants), and hearing others talk about drinking. However, cues are not always directly related to alcohol and may refer to activities one does while drinking (e.g., watching football on television, sitting in a particular chair while drinking, reading, gambling, certain times of the day, special events, or holidays). Thus, the older problem drinker needs to be aware of the cues that elicit drinking for him or her and acquire skills necessary to control those cues.

Urges

The urge to drink is the end of the antecedent part of the drinking behavior chain. It is a strong desire for alcohol, lasts different amounts of time, and has a beginning and an end even if one does not drink. It is important for the older abuser to believe that an urge can be waited out successfully, becomes weaker each time it is resisted, will not last as long next time, and will be easier to resist the more often it is resisted.

The self-management approach emphasizes control through the knowledge that one can successfully wait out an urge and that what is needed is *time*, placing one's thoughts on something else, and support from others. An urge is not physical craving but is instead a self-statement giving one permission, or a good reason, for drinking (e.g., This has really been a rough day. A drink will help me unwind). The urge is also based upon what the person expects from alcohol use (his or her personal or cultural expectations). Older adults more likely to develop alcohol problems, as well as relapse, are those who expect specific, immediate (short-term), positive outcomes from alcohol use.

Relapse Training

The self-management model discounts the self-fulfilling prophecy of "one drink—drunk." Dupree et al. (1984) emphasize and reinforce self-control with older abusers by teaching that they can stop by refraining from negative (condemning) self-statements and using self-management skills they have acquired. Also they are encouraged to call for help. To know when to call in order to avoid unpleasant consequences is another example of self-management, as defined earlier. Thus, relapse prevention includes behavioral assessment and self-monitoring, acquisition of relevant coping skills, and increased self-efficacy. It is an inherent, rather than a post discharge, concern. Relapse prevention begins from the moment of analysis of drinking behavior, right through training specific to individual antecedents. The absence of *relevant* coping skills in high-risk situations, in the presence of self-defeating cognitions or misperceptions, often leads to sustained alcohol use or abuse.

CASE EXAMPLES

Using the above assessment and intervention model two case examples will be presented. The first involves an older alcohol abuser (Dupree & Schonfeld, 1989) and the second involves prescription medication misuse/abuse (Schonfeld, 1992).

Case 1: Alcohol Abuse

The client was a 62-year-old, third-grade-educated, white woman who had been married twice, both of long duration, with the death of her second husband occurring less than 1 year prior to referral. An accounting of her alcohol history revealed that she had her first alcoholic beverage at age 16; had been a light social drinker (two to four beers on weekends) until her early 50s; that she first felt she had a drinking problem at age 55, when she began to drink steadily; and was first told she had a drinking problem (by her children) at age 61. Self-report and report by family members indicated that she consumed a minimum of 8 ounces of vodka, or five to six beers, or 28 ounces of wine per day within a 2-hour period. Also, based on collateral comments, she was argumentative, disoriented, and intoxicated daily. Assessment data (including the drinking behavior chain) were generated via the Gerontology Alcohol Project Drinking Profile (GAP-DP; Dupree et al., 1984), a modified version of Marlatt's (1976) Drinking Profile.

Drinking Behavior Chain

By moving to Florida at her children's insistence, she was separated from her friends, her homestead, and much of her personal property. Also, her children spent very little time with her, even though they lived in the same home. She was lonely, angry, depressed, and grieving the loss of loved ones. She responded to these feelings and losses with excessive alcohol consumption. In her failing attempts to convince others of her need for their attention, she became more isolated, angrier, more depressed, and more a consumer. Also, on the few occasions she had her neighbors over to her house, she became tense and anxious. Thus, she served alcoholic beverages and drank to excess. Her failing attempts to reduce isolation increased such; and, again, alcohol abuse was sustained. These antecedents in combination with her particular urges (her particular self-statements) resulted in abusive drinking. As shown in Figure 14-1, this older woman's high-risk situations included being home alone, thinking about her interpersonal losses and current circumstances (resulting in anger, anxiety, tension, loneliness, and dysphoric mood), and monotonous daily life. These situations, thoughts, and feelings, in the presence of alcohol cues and readily available alcohol, resulted in urges to drink.

The GAP-DP determined that the short-term consequences of her drinking were both positive (happy, relaxed, friendly, outgoing, calm, not lonely) and negative (children's dissatisfaction, becomes argumentative, disoriented), but that the long-term consequences were solely negative (uncontrolled hypertension, excessive weight gain, cost of drinking, alienation of family). Part of the intervention for this client was the carrying of a Consequences Card that listed the specific negative consequences for her of alcohol abuse. At the point of an urge, or at any point of the drinking behavior chain, the client was instructed to read the card as a reminder of the negative impact of alcohol use in her life. Also, the client was asked to remember a positive consequence of not drinking.

Intervention

Subsequent to the GAP-DP interview process, the client entered a behavior analysis group in which she was taught, first through simple examples and later with her own drinking behavior, to understand how to break down behavior into the antecedents-behavior-consequences chain and to diagram it. She was quizzed on knowledge of her drinking chain until she could demonstrate accuracy by

Antecedents →				Behavior →	Consequences
Situations/ + Thoughts	Feelings +	Cues +	Urges →	Drinking →	Positive (+) or negative (−)
Home, alone, thinking about:					Immediate/ Short term
Loss of her husband, loss of friends, loss of personal items	Depressed, lonely, angry	Having alcohol in the house	"A drink would make me feel better"	Has wine, beer, or a cocktail	Feels happier, less lonely, relaxed (+) Feels friendly and outgoing (+)
Going out Having visitors over	Anxious, tense	Serving alcohol to visitors			Argues with son or daughter, becomes disoriented (−)
Doing housework, nothing interesting to do	Depressed, bored, lonely	Watching TV plus alcohol in the house			Long term
					Increased blood pressure (−) Excessive weight gain (−) Alienates son and daughter (−)

Figure 14-1. Drinking behavior chain for Case 1.

recall, as well as explain the relationship between the components of the chain and how that relationship defined her high-risk situation(s). Subsequently, the client entered into self-management groups pertinent to her identified antecedents for drinking.

Group approaches used both behavior rehearsal and didactic techniques. Behavior rehearsal (role-play) consisted of sample problem situations that asked the client to rehearse what she would say and do in the presence of another individual who may be a key for change. Self-control behavior was assessed with rating scales, and she reached a criterion of proficiency before being asked to try the newer behaviors in the home or external environment. In summary, intervention was through the three-stage behavioral/self-management process mentioned earlier: (1) behavior analysis by staff with client participation, (2) teaching the older client behavior analysis and how to log and monitor behaviors, and (3) teaching self-management skills specific to the antecedent (high-risk) conditions defined for that individual in stages 1 and 2.

For this older woman, treatment focused on coping responses that were either not being expressed or were deficient. She was taught skills necessary for developing a social network; on how to manage depression; on how to manage tension and anxiety; assertion training to deal with anger and frustration; on how to handle environmental drinking cues; on how to handle her particular urges and self-statements; drink refusal training to deal with peer pressure; and what to do in the event of a slip or a relapse.

Outcome

The client's success in the Social Support Network Development module (a group using standardized, replicable assessment procedures and content) yielded new skills, as well as knowledge of community resources necessary to her creating and self-managing her own social network. She expanded her social network from three people of limited contact and quality to being involved with 10 people at discharge, 25 people 3 months postdischarge, 32 at 6 months, and a more manageable 16 at 12 months. Thus, not only did the client acquire the skills and knowledge necessary to expand her social network while in treatment, those skills generalized and were still being used months after discharge. She went from a drunken, argumentative recluse to a sober, pleasant, and effective interpersonal being. She became a social director in an apartment complex, and even outside of that setting her social activities markedly increased.

As she acquired self-management skills and became reengaged with the world, there were positive reductions in alienated-depressed scores (Personal Adjustment and Roles Skills Scales; Ellsworth, 1979) and anxiety scale scores (STAI-C2; Patterson, O'Sullivan, & Spielberger, 1980). Not only did she acquire skills necessary to regulate anxiety and depression, but those skills also apparently generalized. Both areas were reassessed 1, 3, 6, and 12 months after discharge. There was a continuing decline in anxiety scores and a very low end of the scale plateau for depression. Most importantly, acquisition of self-management skills resulted in controlled drinking. For a 12-month period post treatment, this client monitored her own drinking behavior by using "logs." Also, for the same period, those interacting with her completed assessments of her general behavior, as well as alcohol consumption. Data from both sources agreed, indicated excellent self-management, and described her as a positive (nonaversive) person to be around.

Reestablishing the social network and enhanced personal efficacy appeared to alter the abusive use of alcohol. At admission the client negotiated a drinking goal of "light social drinker." Prior to discharge from treatment she redefined her goal to be one of abstinence. The client was followed up for 12 months, and results indicated that at 30 days post discharge she had consumed one beer; at 3 months she had consumed one more beer; and by the 12-month follow-up she was consuming about two beers per month. Although she did not maintain abstinence, she was never intoxicated after discharge from treatment, and her social support network increased substantially. At 1-year follow-up both she and her family continued to be pleased with the treatment outcome.

Use of the structured GAP-DP gave the therapist, the client, and the family a picture of the client's drinking behavior chain. From this, an effective and efficient treatment plan was developed. The client was asked to change only that part of her life defined as needing change, and she was given hope for success by taking the mystery out of her alcoholic behavior. Thus, motivation to remain in treatment was enhanced, and perception of the potential for personal control of one's life was immediately augmented. Also, a concrete plan to gain actual control was understandable to this older abuser.

Case 2: Medication Abuse

The technology of the three-stage self-management approach illustrated in the alcohol case example was used effectively in treating a medication abuser (Schonfeld, 1992). This case involved a 55-year-old woman admitted to our day treatment, mental health program. In addition to depression and loneliness, her major complaint was back pain, diagnosed by her physician as osteoarthritis. Her records indicated a long history of medication abuse, and five previous hospitalizations over a 30-year span, for treatment of alcohol abuse, depression, or medication overdoses.

Medication Behavior Chain

In response to "flare-ups" of pain, on a typical day she reported consuming eight 100-mg Mellaril tablets (the prescribed dose was 250 mg), eight Darvocet-N 100 tablets (her prescription was to take one tablet as needed, with a prescription of only 20 tablets every 2 weeks), "several" tablets of Tylenol with codeine, eight 150-mg Elavil tablets, two ibuprofens, and six aspirins. She was frequently requesting prescription refills prior to the appropriate date. In response to lack of progress in the day treatment program, she began meeting with the senior author for 1 hour each weekday. Using a structured interview developed for this case, but closely paralleling the GAP Drinking Profile, the medication use chain was identified. As shown in Figure 14-2, this behavior analysis revealed that antecedents to pain flare-ups usually involved unpleasant interactions with her daughter or youngest son. She reported feeling depressed and lonely after such interactions, followed by onset of pain in her back and shoulders. She would cope with the pain by literally taking handfuls of medications, followed by the expectation that the pills would relieve pain (within an hour) or help her overcome the tension-producing situation. Unfortunately, the long-term consequences included several hospitalizations for medication overdoses and alienation from her oldest (and most concerned) son and his family, who were trying to help her.

Intervention

Four aspects of intervention were involved. First the client was taught to use a covert assertion procedure (Rimm & Masters, 1974). This involved learning to identify antecedent conditions leading to pain flare-ups (i.e., unpleasant family interactions), use of thought-stopping techniques to interrupt the associated negative self-statements, replacement with positive self-statements, and use of muscle relaxation techniques. Second, the woman was taught to monitor her medication intake using written, daily logs. These logs were reviewed regularly with the author. Third, using behavioral contracting with the author, the client set a goal of asking her physician and psychiatrist to reduce the number of prescriptions and/or dosage of medication. Fourth, the family and treatment program staff were coached to reinforce positive social interactions with the client.

	Antecedents →			Behavior →	Consequences
Situations/ + Thoughts	Feelings +	Cues +	Urges →	Medication → Use	Positive (+) or negative (−)
Home, alone:					Immediate/ Short term
Daughter takes advantage of her - asks her to babysit, borrow money, etc. Youngest son is in trouble with law and takes advantage by staying at her apartment; borrowing money	Angry, depressed, and tense	Pain in back and shoulders Pill bottles next to telephone	"The pills will make the pain go away" "I need to feel better"	Consumes several. Darvocets Takes handful of pills	Expects relief from pain (+) (Takes up to an hour for relief)
					Long term
					Medication overdose (−) Hospitalized (−) Alienates oldest son and his family

Figure 14-2. Medication use behavior chain for Case 2.

Outcome

There were several indicators of success at discharge and over a 1-year follow-up. The psychiatrist was able to decrease Mellaril intake to 150 mg/day, and at the 6-month follow- up all pain medications were discontinued. The number of pain events and severity of such events decreased significantly as did medication overdoses and errors. The client also lost 48 pounds (previously weighing 248). In addition, her improvement was demonstrated using psycho-social assessments. For example, anxiety scale scores (STAI-C2), which ranged from 18 to 54 (low to high anxiety), at admission, discharge, and 12-month follow-up, were 32, 20, and 22, respectively. The Beck Depression Inventory (Beck, 1972) scores were 16, 3, and 3, indicating a decrease from a clinically depressed level to little or no depression. Thus, anxiety and depression decreased after treatment and the lower levels were maintained throughout the follow-up. In addition there was some improvement in social support over the 1-year follow-up.

Improvement was apparently maintained until 3 years post discharge, when she was taken to the local emergency room for a medication overdose. At that time, her physician had moved out of state and a new physician, unaware of her substance abuse history, prescribed Darvocet, Ativan, and Pamelor. She was soon readmitted to our program for 2 months and appeared to resume the proper course of medication compliance thereafter.

This case example illustrates use of numerous patient-oriented and physician-oriented techniques to reduce medication misuse. Patient-oriented techniques involved behavioral, cognitive-behavioral, and self-management approaches.

Behavior analysis allowed the therapist to identify high-risk situations for drug use. The cognitive-behavioral appraoches allowed the client to identify and cope with private events (thoughts, feelings), as well as observable events (family interactions), and focus on cognitive restructuring. Self-management techniques allowed self-monitoring of behavior outside of the therapeutic environment and behavioral contracting with the therapist and physicians to reduce medications.

Working with the physician and psychiatrist necessitates a tactful approach by a therapist. The therapist must inform the physician and/or psychiatrist about a client's substance abuse history and work in partnership to reduce prescriptions when feasible or minimize medication errors. Presenting data from the client's self-report of pain flare-ups was sufficient evidence and incentive for the physicians to collaborate in obtaining a long-term goal of reducing medications.

CONCLUSIONS

There are several benefits of self-management approaches with older adults. First, treatment planning is individualized in that each person's antecedents and consequences of substance use are identified, and each is taught specific skills for addressing his or her high-risk situations for alcohol abuse. This avoids preconceived and incorrect notions about their behavior simply because they are "elderly" or "alcoholic." Second, the person is taught effective skills for use outside of the therapeutic setting and in the absence of the therapist, maximizing likelihood of generalization of treatment. Third, the intervention can be evaluated and modified as needed, selectively altering the client's life-style only to the degree necessary. This also provides a criterion for when to terminate treatment: successful acquisition of antecedent-specific skills. Fourth, should a "slip" occur while in treatment or follow-up, the therapist and client can use it as a learning experience (i.e., something to be discussed and learned from rather than hidden from staff and colleagues in treatment). Finally, instead of confrontation and medical interventions, self-management approaches rely on positive, supportive, and skill-building techniques, which are likely to be beneficial in treating depressed, lonely, or grieving older adults.

Relative to illicit drug use, the assessment and use of drinking behavior or medication use chains could be altered to identify and target drug-seeking behavior rather than "use" itself. The therapist would focus on coping skills to prevent the older person from feeling anxious, nervous, or depressed, which typically leads to drug expectancies, urges, and attempts to obtain the drugs. Use of self-management techniques might then preclude drug-seeking behaviors rather than drug use within the situation. For example, one injection of heroin usually has a more intense and immediate effect than one sip of alcohol. Thus, for the heroin addict, it would be preferable to break the chain earlier at the point of drug-seeking. Schonfeld, Peters, and Dolente (1993) found this alteration of the behavior chain useful for treating people likely to abuse multiple substances, including illicit drugs.

The value of the self-management approach to older adults is that it increases the probability of successful life in the community during periods of transition and threatened losses. The approach recommended in this chapter places greater emphasis on client analysis and self-intervention so as to have sustained positive outcome as the older person's environment continues to change. Newer problems need not have a "mysterious" basis, and, through enhanced feelings of self-efficacy, self-management and community stability are likely to be augmented. Self-management enhances generalization immediately and over time.

Schonfeld and Dupree (1995) identify six recommendations for treatment of the older alcohol abuser that have some empirical support. These should also be applicable to the older medication misuser. These recommendations include (1) placing an emphasis on age-specific, group treatment with supportive approaches and avoiding confrontation; (2) focusing on negative emotional states, such as depression, loneliness, overcoming losses (e.g., changes in health, altered self-esteem, death of a loved one, retirement); (3) teaching skills to rebuild the social support network; (4) employing staff interested and experienced in working with older persons; (5) developing linkages with aging and medical services for both referral into treatment and referral out, as well as "case management"; and (6) developing the pace and content of treatment appropriate for the older person.

REFERENCES

Atkinson, R. M. (1984). Substance use and abuse in late life. In R. M. Atkinson (Ed.), *Alcohol and drug abuse in old age* (pp. 1–21). Washington, DC: American Psychiatric Press Monograph Series.

Atkinson, R. M., Ganzini, L., & Bernstein, M. J. (1992). Alcohol and substance-use disorders in the elderly. In J. E. Birren, R. B. Sloan, & G. D. Cohen (Eds.), *Handbook of mental health and aging* (pp. 515–555). San Diego: Academic Press.

Atkinson, R. M., Turner, J. A., Kofoed, L. L., & Tolson, R. L. (1985). Early versus late onset alcoholism in older persons: Preliminary findings. *Alcoholism, 9,* 513–515.

Beck, A. (1972). *Depression: Causes and treatment.* Philadelphia: University of Pennsylvania Press.

Beers, M. H., Ouslander, J. G., Rollinger, I., Brooks, J., Ruben, D., & Beck, J. C. (1991). Explicit criteria for determining inappropriate medication use in nursing homes. *Archives of Internal Medicine, 151,* 1825–1832.

Bienenfeld, D. (1987). Alcoholism in the elderly. *American Family Physician, 36,* 163–198.

Burke, L. A., Jolson, H. M., Goetsch, R. A., and Ahronheim, J. C. (1992). Geriatric drug use and adverse drug event reporting in 1990: A descriptive analysis of two national data bases. In J. W. Rowe & J. C. Ahronheim (Eds.), *Annual review of gerontology and geriatrics: Focus on medications and the elderly,* (pp. 1–28). New York: Springer.

Carstensen, L. L., Rychtarik, R. G., & Prue, D. M. (1985). Behavioral treatment of the geriatric alcohol abuser: A long term follow-up study. *Addictive Behaviors, 10,* 307–311.

Coons, S. J., Hendricks, J., & Sheahan, S. L. (1988). Self-medication with nonprescription drugs. *Generations, 12,* 22–26.

Curtis, J. R., Geller, G., Stokes, E. J., Levine, D. M., & Moore, R. D. (1989). Characteristics, diagnosis, and treatment of alcoholism in elderly patients. *Journal of the American Geriatrics Society, 37,* 310–317.

Dupree, L. W., Broskowski, H., & Schonfeld, L. (1984). The Gerontology Alcohol Project: A behavioral treatment program for elderly alcohol abusers. *The Gerontologist, 24,* 510–516.

Dupree, L. W., & Schonfeld, L. (1989). Treating late-life onset alcohol abuses: Demonstration through a case study. *Clinical Gerontologist, 9,* 65–67.

Ellsworth, R. B. (1979). Personal Adjustment and Roles Skills (PARS) Scales. Roanoke, VA: Institute for Program Evaluation.

Finlayson, R. E. (1984). Prescription drug abuse in older persons. In R. M. Atkinson (Ed.), *Alcohol and drug abuse in old age* (pp. 61–70). Washington, DC: American Psychiatric Press.

Folkman, S., Bernstein, L., & Lazarus, R. S. (1987). Stress processes and the misuse of drugs in older adults. *Psychology and Aging, 2*, 366–374.

Glantz, M. (1981). Predictions of elderly drug abuse. *Journal of Psychoactive Drugs, 13*, 117–126.

Hartford, J. T., & Samorajski, T. (1982). Alcoholism in the geriatric population. *Journal of the American Geriatric Society, 30*, 18–24.

H.R. Report No. 852, 102nd Congress, 2nd session. (1992). Alcohol abuse and misuse among the elderly.

IMS America. (1990). *National disease and therapeutic index.* Plymouth Meeting, PA: Author.

Janik, S. W., & Dunham, R. G. (1983). A nationwide examination of the need for specific alcoholism treatment programs for the elderly. *Journal of Studies on Alcohol, 44*, 307–317.

Jennison, K. M. (1992). The impact of stressful life events and social support on drinking among older adults: A general population survey. *International Journal of Aging and Human Development, 35*, 99–123.

Kashner, T. M., Rodell, D. E., Ogden, S. R., Guggenheim, F. G., & Karson, C. N. (1992). Outcomes and costs of two VA inpatient programs for older alcoholics. *Hospital and Community Psychiatry, 43*, 985–989.

Kelly, J. G., & O'Malley, K. (1992). Principles of altered drug handling in the elderly. *Reviews in Clinical Gerontology, 2*, 11–19.

Klein, L. E., German, P. S., & Levine, D. M. (1981). Adverse drug reactions among the elderly: A reassessment. *Journal of the American Geriatrics Society, 24*, 525–530.

Kofoed, L., Tolson, R., Atkinson, R. M., Toth, R., & Turner, J. (1987). Treatment compliance of older alcoholics: An elder-specific approach is superior to "mainstreaming." *Journal of Studies on Alcohol, 48*, 47–51.

Lamy, P. (1982). Comparative pharmacokinetic changes and drug therapy in an older population. *American Geriatrics Society* (Suppl. 30), s11–s119.

Landress, H. J., & Morck, M. A. (1984). Prevalence and risk of medication mismanagement by the elderly. *Journal of the Florida Medical Association, 71*, 261–266.

Lazarus, R. S., & Folkman, S. (1984). *Stress, appraisal, and coping.* New York: McGraw-Hill.

Marlatt, G. A. (1976). The drinking profile: A questionnaire for the behavioral assessment of alcoholism. In E. J. Mash & L. G. Terdal (Eds.), *Behavior therapy assessment: Diagnosis, design, and evaluation.* New York: Springer.

Miller, P. M. (1976). *Behavioral treatment of alcoholism.* New York: Pergamon Press.

Moos, R. H., Brennan, P. L., Fondacaro, M. R., & Moos, B. S. (1990). Approach and avoidance coping responses among older problem and nonproblem drinkers. *Psychology and Aging, 5*, 31–40.

National Institute on Drug Abuse. (1990). *Data from the Drug Abuse Warning Network (DAWN), Series 1, No. 9* (DHHS Publication No. ADM 90-1717). Rockville, MD: U.S. Government Printing Office.

National Institute on Drug Abuse. (1992). *Socioeconomic and demographic correlates of drug and alcohol use: Findings from the 1988 and 1990 National Household Surveys on Drug Abuse* (DHHS Publication No. ADM 92-1906). Rockville, MD: U.S. Government Printing Office.

National Institute on Drug Abuse and National Institute on Alcohol Abuse and Alcoholism. (1990). *National drug and alcoholism treatment unit survey (NDATUS). 1989 Main findings report* (DHHS Publication No. ADM 91-1729). Rockville, MD: U.S. Government Printing Office.

Olins, N. J. (1985). Pharmacy interventions. In S. R. Moore & T. W. Teal (Eds.), *Geriatric drug use: Clinical and social perspectives* (pp. 22–33). New York: Pergamon Press.

Pascarelli, E. (1974). Drug dependence: An age-old problem compounded by old age. *Geriatrics, 29*, 209–225.

Patterson, R. L., O'Sullivan, M. J., & Spielberger, C. D. (1980). Measurement of state and trait anxiety in elderly mental health clients. *Journal of Behavioral Assessment, 2*, 89–97.

Reifler, B. V., Raskind, M., and Kethly, A. (1982). Psychiatric diagnoses among geriatric patients seen in an outreach program. *American Journal of Psychiatry, 1*, 220–223.

Rimm, D., & Masters, J. (1974). *Behavior therapy: Techniques and empirical findings.* New York: Academic Press.

Rosin, A. J., & Glatt, M. M. (1971). Alcohol excess in the elderly. *Quarterly Journal of Studies on Alcohol, 32,* 53–59.

Schonfeld, L. (1992). Covert assertion as method for coping with pain and pain related behaviors. *Clinical Gerontologist, 12,* 17–29.

Schonfeld, L., and Dupree, L. W. (1991). Antecedents of drinking for early- and late-onset elderly alcohol abusers. *Journal of Studies on Alcohol, 52,* 587–591.

Schonfeld, L., & Dupree, L. W. (1995). Treatment approaches for older problem drinkers. *International Journal of the Addictions, 30,* 1819–1842.

Schonfeld, L., Dupree, L. W., & Rohrer, G. E. (1995). Age-related differences between younger and older alcohol abusers. *Journal of Clinical Geropsychology, 1,* 219–227.

Schonfeld, L., Peters, R., & Dolente, A. (1993). *Substance Abuse Relapse Assessment (SARA). Professional manual.* Odessa, FL: Psychological Assessment Resources.

Schwartz, D., Wang, M., Zeitz, L., & Gross, M. E. W. (1962). Medication errors made by elderly chronically ill patients. *American Journal of Public Health, 52,* 2018–2029.

Simonson, W. (1984). *Medications and the elderly.* Rockville, MD: Aspen.

Vestal, R. E., McGuire, E. A., Tobin, J. D., Andres, R., Norris, A. H., & Mezey, E. (1977). Aging and ethanol metabolism. *Clinical Pharmacology and Therapeutics, 21,* 343–354.

Wasson, J., Nierenberg, D., Landgraf, J., Whaley, F., Malenka, D., Johnson, D., Keller, A., & the Dartmouth Primary Care Coop. (1992). The effect of a patient questionnaire on drug-related symptoms in elderly outpatients. In J. W. Rowe & J. C. Ahronheim (Eds.), *Annual review of gerontology and geriatrics: Focus on medications and the elderly* (Vol. 10, pp. 109–125). New York: Springer.

Wells-Parker, E., Miles, S., & Spencer, B. (1983). Stress experiences and drinking histories of elderly drunken-driving offenders. *Journal of Studies on Alcohol, 4,* 429–437.

Wiens, A. N., Menustik, C. E., Miller, S. I., and Schmitz, R. E. (1982–1983). Medical-behavioral treatment of the older alcoholic patient. *American Journal of Drug and Alcohol Abuse, 9,* 461–475.

Wilcox, S. M., Himmelstein, D. U., & Woolhandler, S. (1994). Inappropriate drug prescribing for the community-dwelling elderly. *Journal of the American Medical Association, 272,* 292–296.

CHAPTER 15

Sexual Dysfunction

WILLIAM T. O'DONOHUE AND BENJAMIN GRABER

CHAPTER OUTLINE

Description of the Disorders	Evaluation
Age-Related Changes	Diagnoses of Clinical Syndromes
Increased Probability of Disease	The Aging Male
Cohort Effects	The Aging Female
Opportunities for Sexual Behavior	Illness
Stereotypes and Myths Regarding	Treatment
Geriatric Sexuality	**Summary**
Concurrent Medical Evaluation and	**References**
Treatment	

DESCRIPTION OF THE DISORDERS

Sexual behavior is a complicated and important part of human functioning. Sexual behavior is important for several reasons: (1) it can create life (desired or undesired) with its attendant parenting duties and joys; (2) it can bring a tremendous amount of pleasure to oneself and others; (3) it can bring to us special kinds of relationships with other human beings; (4) it can significantly affect how we see ourselves and how others see us (e.g., whether we are "heterosexual," "homosexual," or "impotent"); and (5) it can have a tremendous downside or cost. If carried out "improperly," our sexual behavior can lead to harm to others (unwanted pregnancies, rape), as well as to ourselves. These kinds of problems include disease, death (HIV), or even incarceration (child molestation).

WILLIAM T. O'DONOHUE • Department of Psychology, University of Nevada Reno, Reno, Nevada 89557. BENJAMIN GRABER • Graber Psychiatric Associates, 12711 Davenport Plaza, Omaha, Nebraska 68154.
Psychological Treatment of Older Adults: An Introductory Text, edited by Michel Hersen and Vincent B. Van Hasselt. Plenum Press, New York, 1996.

Sexual behavior is also quite complicated. It usually involves complex interactions and negotiations with another person. These negotiations may be complicated because there is evidence to suggest that men and women view sex quite differently (Symons, 1987). It is also a heavily value-ladened activity. There is no other area of human functioning that contains as many concerns about what is permissible and not permissible (Geer & O'Donohue, 1987). Because of this, we need to come to decisions as to what is proper sexual behavior and perhaps be ready to defend ourselves and experience consequences from others who do not agree with our decisions (e.g., on the permissibility or non-permissibility of premarital sex). Finally, sex is complicated because it requires the proper interplay between values, opportunity, learning, and physiology.

The American Psychiatric Association (1994) has suggested that there are three broad kinds of sexual problems. One set of problems is known as the Paraphilias (meaning, literally, liking something outside the norm, e.g., sexual attraction to children). Another set of problems involves the Gender Identity Disorders. Individuals with these problems behave in ways that are inconsistent with their anatomical gender. For example, a male may feel that he is "really" a female trapped in a male's body. In this chapter we will focus on the third broad type of sexual problem: the Sexual Dysfunctions.

There are several subtypes of Sexual Dysfunctions. There are two general principles of categorization: gender (e.g., *Female* Orgasmic Disorder and *Male* Orgasmic Disorder) and what is known as the sexual response cycle. The sexual response cycle is a series of psychophysiological changes that are thought to describe the typical sequence of behaviors in normal sexual experience. These are:

1. *Desire*: This phase consists of fantasies about sexual activity and the desire to have sexual activity.
2. *Excitement*: This phase consists of a subjective sense of sexual pleasure and accompanying physiological changes. The major changes in the male consist of penile tumescence and erection. The major changes in the female consist of vasocongestion in the pelvis, vaginal lubrication and expansion, and the swelling of the external genitalia.
3. *Orgasm*: This phase consists of a peaking of sexual pleasure, with release of sexual tension and rhythmic contraction of the perineal muscles and reproductive organs. In the male there is the sensation of ejaculatory inevitability, which is followed by ejaculation of semen. In the female, there are contractions of the wall of the outer third of the vagina. In both genders, the anal sphincter rhythmically contracts.
4. *Resolution*: This phase consists of a sense of muscular relaxation and general well-being. During this phase, males are physiologically refractory to further erection and orgasm for a variable period of time. In contrast, females may be able to respond to additional stimulation almost immediately (APA, 1994, pp. 493–494).

Males and females can have problems in one or more of these phases. The specific diagnoses are included in Table 15-1. Any individual sufficiently physi-

Table 15-1. The Major Sexual Dysfunctions in the *DSM-IV*

Hypoactive Sexual Desire Disorder

Persistently or recurrently deficient (or absent) sexual fantasies and desire for sexual activity. The judgment of deficiency or absence is made by the clinician, taking into account factors that affect sexual functioning, such as age and the context of the person's life.

Sexual Aversion Disorder

Persistent or recurrent extreme aversion to, and avoidance of, all (or almost all) genital sexual contact with a sexual partner.

Female Sexual Arousal Disorder

Persistent or recurrent inability to attain, or to maintain until completion of the sexual activity, an adequate lubrication-swelling response of sexual excitement.

Male Erectile Disorder

Persistent or recurrent inability to attain, or to maintain until completion of the sexual activity, an adequate erection.

Female Orgasmic Disorder

Persistent or recurrent delay in, or absence of, orgasm following a normal sexual excitement phase. Women exhibit wide variability in the type or intensity of stimulation that triggers orgasm. The diagnosis of Female Orgasmic Disorder should be based on the clinician's judgment that the woman's orgasmic capacity is less than would be reasonable for her age, sexual experience, and the adequacy of sexual stimulation she receives.

Male Orgasmic Disorder

Persistent or recurrent delay in, or absence of, orgasm following a normal sexual excitement phase during sexual activity that the clinician, taking into account the person's age, judges to be adequate in focus, intensity, and duration.

Premature Ejaculation

Persistent or recurrent ejaculation with minimal sexual stimulation before, on, or shortly after penetration and before the person wishes it. The clinician must take into account factors that affect duration of the excitement phase, such as age, novelty of the sexual partner or situation, and recent frequency of sexual activity.

Dyspareunia

Recurrent or persistent genital pain associated with sexual intercourse in either a male or a female.

Vaginismus

Recurrent or persistent involuntary spasm of the musculature of the outer third of the vagina that interferes with sexual intercourse.

Substance-Induced Sexual Dysfunction

Clinically significant sexual dysfunction that results in marked distress or interpersonal difficulty predominates in the clinical picture.

Sexual Dysfunction Due to a General Medical Condition

Clinically significant sexual dysfunction that results in marked distress or interpersonal difficulty predominates in the clinical picture. There is evidence from the history, physical examination, or laboratory findings that the sexual dysfunction is fully explained by the direct physiologial effects of a general medical condition.

ologically mature to be capable of sexual behavior can experience problems in sexual functioning. Professionals must be careful to ensure that they do not too quickly attribute problems in an elderly individual's sexual functioning to the fact that they are elderly. Age may have little or nothing to do with the elderly person's sexual problem. The elderly can experience sexual problems for the same reasons as the nonelderly (e.g., performance anxiety). Advanced age may be a completely irrelevant factor.

Having said this, there are, however, several factors that may differentially impact upon the elderly to create a special susceptibility to sexual problems. These are (1) age-related physiological changes; (2) cohort effects; (3) increased probability of health problems; (4) stereotypes and stigma related to the elderly's sexual functioning; and (5) changes in opportunity.

Age-Related Changes

As people age, two broad sets of changes occur. First, their bodies change. Here we want to emphasize that age-related changes are not, in themselves, disease states. That is, decreased skin pliability, graying and thinning of hair, some muscular atrophy, decreased cardiac output, decreased lung capacity, decreased bladder capacity, as well as other physiological changes, inevitably occur as individuals age (Zarit & Zarit, 1987). There is little reason to believe that these developments should be regarded as pathological just because they represent a change from when the individual was younger. This is not to say, however, that the elderly do not experience a significant increase in their susceptibility to certain diseases. They do, and we will discuss some of the impact of these disease states (and the impact of the treatment of such diseases) on the elderly's sexual behavior in the next section. Here we simply make the point that certain physiological changes occur as a function of age and these can be considered part of "normal aging."

There are also certain psychological changes that occur as part of normal aging. The sensitivity of all five senses declines with age. This affects both sensation and perception. There are also changes in information processing, and some attitudes change in certain predictable directions (Fisher, Zeiss, & Carstensen, 1992).

How do these physiological and psychological changes that are part of normal aging affect the sexual behavior of the elderly? Currently we must say that we do not know because the studies that can best answer this question have not been carried out. Longitudinal research, which follows a representative sample of people over many years (say from late childhood to death) and accurately measures sexual behavior, would give the most informative data. However, this kind of study is very difficult to implement and has not yet been conducted.

At present, the best we can do is speculate. In general, we would expect some of these changes associated with normal aging to have a negative impact on sexual behavior. For example, there is evidence (Symons, 1987) to suggest that evolutionary pressures have selected males to be optimally aroused to age-related clues that signal maximal female fertility. The period of increased female fertility occurs in the early 20s. Thus there may be evolutionary or biological factors that influenced both other-perceived and self-perceived sexual attraction.

Increased Probability of Disease

In the previous section we have argued that certain physiological diseases occur as a function of age and that these should be regarded as part of normal aging and not pathological in and of themselves. However, the other side of the coin is that as people age they become more vulnerable to physiological disorders. This may be due to the cumulative harmful effects of living (e.g., long-term effects of poor health habits or additive effects of prolonged overexposure to sunlight) or to a part of a genetically encoded aging process. For example, Walford, Weindrich, Gottesman, and Tam (1981) have proposed that aging is caused by genetically programmed deterioration of the immune system.

Diseases can directly or indirectly lead to problems in sexual functioning. In fact, the *DSM-IV* (1994) contains a category of sexual disorders known as Sexual Dysfunction Due to a General Medical Condition (in light of the high frequency of this kind of problem). It is obvious that impaired cardiac functioning secondary to a heart attack can adversely affect sexual behavior. It is also obvious that increased age is associated with an increased risk of a heart attack. Thus, the elderly may have more physical problems that can affect their sexual functioning. What is less obvious is that sometimes it is not the physical problems themselves but the treatment of these problems that cause problems in sexual dysfunction. For example, many antihypertensives given to males who have high blood pressure cause, as an unintended side effect, erectile difficulties.

Fortunately, some evidence suggests that as one ages one is less susceptible to experiencing most mental health problems (Fisher, Zeiss, & Carstensen, 1992). Rates of depression, anxiety, and substance abuse are somewhat higher in the younger age ranges. Thus, on average, one should not expect sexual functioning of the elderly to be negatively impacted by psychological problems. However, there are some important exceptions. The most notable is that anxiety or irrational expectations associated with physiological problems may affect sexual functioning. For example, after a heart attack an individual may be anxious about sexual activity because he thinks that this may trigger yet another heart attack. We will discuss other examples of the repercussions of the elderly's increased probability health problems on sexual functioning throughout the chapter.

Cohort Effects

Cohort effects may be defined as the effects of unique historical events on the development of a generation. For example, the present-day generation of elderly individuals experienced, and were no doubt influenced by, the Great Depression and World War II. When present-day 20-year-olds are elderly, these two histori-cal events will have had much less influence on their development. Instead, other events will have influenced them.

Cohort effects are not confined to large historical events such as major wars. The present-day elderly were also affected by other historical forces, such as the more conservative sexual mores found in society between 1900 and 1960. It is important to distinguish between cohort effects and the effects of aging. Thus, considering the increased conservatism of the present elderly (as compared to people in their 20s), two explanatory hypotheses arise: (1) This is a cohort effect in that the development of this generation of elderly was influenced by the more conservative climate of this historical period, or (2) This is an age effect, i.e., as individuals become elderly they grow more sexually conservative.

Which of these hypotheses is true? Note that these are not mutually exclu-sive and therefore both could be true. That is, today's elderly could have been influenced by the particulars of the sexual conservatism in their environment *and* it can also be true that as individuals become elderly they grow more sexually conservative. Longitudinal designs are again needed to better under-stand the individual contributions of these two factors.

However, it is fair to say that today's elderly developed and were influenced by a sexually more conservative culture. Premarital sex, sexually explicit mate-rials, and homosexuality were less accepted from the 1930s to the 1950s than they are today. Moreover, sex therapy, open discussions of sex between partners, contraception, and sex education were also much less accepted. Moreover, it is important to note that present-day elderly did not have nearly the same access to effective contraception, thus sex and reproduction were more closely tied to one another for that generation. Therefore, the state of medical technology is also a factor influencing cohort effects. These factors may possibly impact the sexual dysfunction of today's elderly, in that they increase the probability of misinformation, increased anxiety about sex, and increased unwillingness to seek help for sexual problems. However, the point to remember is that if these are largely cohort effects, the next generation of elderly might not be affected in a similar fashion.

Opportunities for Sexual Behavior

The degree and kinds of opportunities to engage in sex affects one's sexual behavior. If a woman is locked inside a convent with no contact with males, it is not surprising if that individual experiences no heterosexual intercourse (a measure taken in the Middle Ages to protect female virginity). As another example, if an individual experiences no privacy, the individual experiences a difficult choice: either refrain from having sex or have sex in public. The follow-ing anecdote about two elderly residents of a nursing home illustrates this phenomenon in the elderly:

They visited an understanding physician and requested that he oversee, from his professional viewpoint, their lovemaking. He was to determine whether they were indulging in sexual intercourse properly. He agreed. After they completed the act, he told them it was perfect, and then charged them $10 for the office visit. They returned weekly for 8 weeks, and each time they paid $10 for the office visit. Finally, the doctor told them the continuation of their visits was senseless because he repeatedly confirmed that their sex life was perfect. The couple then confided that they were residents of the Shady Nook Nursing Home and that they could find no privacy for themselves. They could not go to their children's homes, and they could not afford $20 for a motel room. On the other hand, the doctor visits cost $10, and they received $8 refunds from Medicare. (Kassel, 1983, p. 179)

There are two major ways in which the elderly experience decreased opportunities to engage in sex. First, the elderly can experience decreased opportunities through the lack of privacy afforded to them, particularly in nursing homes. Nursing homes are often designed to maximize the efficiency of nursing care and to minimize cost. Thus, the elderly often have same-sex roommates, and there is little accommodation made for the elderly to have the privacy most people desire for sexual interactions. Second, due to earlier mortality of males, female heterosexual elderly can experience significant decreases in the number of available partners. This has led one author to suggest that elderly females consider becoming lesbian in later life (Caven, 1973). However, the practicality of this proposal is a serious problem. (We could never imagine seriously suggesting this to our grandmothers!)

Stereotypes and Myths Regarding Geriatric Sexuality

Several authors claim that there are a number of widely held false beliefs concerning the sexuality of the elderly. These general myths can be important because they can influence expectations the elderly have concerning their own sexual behavior as well as standards that others judge the elderly's behavior.

Kuhn (1976), for example, has suggested that there are five major myths concerning the sexual behavior of the elderly:

Myth 1: "Sex doesn't matter in old age. The later years of life are supposed to be (and usually are) sexless" (p. 118).
Myth 2: "Interest in sex is abnormal for old people" (p. 120).
Myth 3: "Remarriage after loss of spouse should be discouraged" (p. 121).
Myth 4: "It is all right for old men to seek younger women as sex partners, but it is ridiculous for old women to be sexually involved with younger men" (p. 122).
Myth 5: "Old people should be separated by sex in institutions to avoid problems for the staff and criticism by families and the community" (p. 123).

Hotvedt (1983), on the other hand, has suggested that there are three major myths:

Myth I: In the later years, individuals are not sexually desirable.
Myth II: In the later years, individuals are not sexually desirous.
Myth III: In the later years, individuals are not sexually capable.

O'Donohue (1987) has reviewed evidence that these are propositions that are believed by both the elderly and the nonelderly, but that these are *false* beliefs. However, clinicians need to determine if these are held by their elderly clients or significant others (e.g., nursing home staff and other caretakers) and whether changing these beliefs might have a beneficial effect.

In this chapter we will discuss both medical and psychological factors and treatments related to sexual dysfunction, as it is our view that good sexual functioning and problematic sexual functioning are caused by multiple factors, including physiological and psychological variables. Sexual dysfunction is a psychophysiological problem consisting of an interplay of physiological factors and psychological/social factors.

CONCURRENT MEDICAL EVALUATION
AND TREATMENT

Evaluation

A medical evaluation of sexual dysfunction in older adults should not differ from that in any other age group. A complete sexual history, psychiatric history, medical history, and physical examination are still the foundation of any evaluation. Laboratory tests are a follow-up to findings on history or examination. There are a number of specialized examination details. Graber (1993) reviews these for males.

Diagnoses of Clinical Syndromes

A study at Johns Hopkins Sexual Behavior Consultation Unit (Meyer, Schmidt, & Wise, 1983) showed that older adults present with the entire spectrum of sexual disorders. Older adults presented with premature ejaculation, impotence, arousal disorders, and general sexual withdrawal. In this study elderly males with erectile failure did not have a clearly increased incidence of organic dysfunction when compared to younger males. Also, in this particular study none of the elderly women were found to have sexual dysfunction secondary to menopausal estrogen loss. Older adults were clearly a small percentage of those who present for evaluation of sexual difficulties in this study. Of men presenting with erectile difficulties, those aged 60 to 69 were only 12% of the sample, and men aged 70 or over, only 1%. Of women who sought help for arousal disorders or anorgasmia, only 3% were 60 years of age or older and only 3% of the couples presenting with psychosexual difficulties were 60 or over, and no one was over 70 years of age. It is still not commonly understood that the aging process is part of the normal developmental cycle of life and not a disease state. The aging population has been steadily increasing and, as we all are painfully aware, the so-called "baby boomer" population wave eventually will take that trend to new heights. It is true that many older individuals have illnesses that limit their sexual functioning. A significant segment of over 65-year-olds is in good health and limited only to the degree that the normal aging process affects sexual functioning. Davidson (1985a) reported that, in a study of 80 men and women over 80 years of age, 52% of the men and 27% of the women reported sexual intercourse at least several times a year. Davidson also noted, however, there certainly is a sexual decline with the normal aging process and that it has a biological basis. Nonetheless, sexual dysfunction does occur in this age cohort. In this section we will look specifically at the physical and medical components involved in the sexual dysfunction of older adults.

The Aging Male

Kinsey, Pomeroy, Martin, and Gebhard (1953) reported that after a peak in adolescence there is a steady decline in sexual activity as measured by orgasmic activity over the life-span. However, these investigators did not find a significant increase in impotency until the seventh decade of life. Other studies have confirmed this gradual decline in male sexual activity associated with age (Pfeiffer, Verwoerdt, & Wang, 1968; Verwoerdt, Pfeiffer, & Wang, 1969); however, the conclusions from these studies have been questioned due to the nature of the questions, lack of validation from sexual partners, and lack of physiological measures (Schiavi, Schreiner-Engel, Mandell, Schanzer, & Cohen, 1990). As with many aspects of sexual biology, there have been considerably more studies in animals, especially rats, than in humans. One difference seems to be that while in rats the sexual decline that occurs with aging is equally divided between a largely androgen-mediated effect on erectile potency and a nonhormonally mediated effect of sexual motivation, in the older human male the age-related decline has a greater impact on potency than libido (Davidson, 1985b; Verwoerdt et al., 1969). Davidson (1985b) remarks that this phenomenon can create a "libido-potency gap," which causes suffering in many older male adults.

While aging affects both erectile function and ejaculation/orgasm, erectile changes are more likely to present clinically (Schiavi et al., 1990). In a laboratory study using electronic monitoring of changes in penile dimensions, Solnick and Birren (1977) reported that men aged 48 to 65 had a six times slower rate of erection in response to erotic films than males aged 19 to 30 years. Quantitative decreases in nocturnal penile tumescence (Hursch, Karacan, & Williams, 1972; Schiavi & Schreiner-Engel, 1988) are another measure of an age-related progressive decline in erectile capacity. With age there is a reduction of the frequency and degree of sleep erections as measured by nocturnal penile tumescence. A recent study (Schiavi et al., 1990) again demonstrated these decreases, and they were correlated significantly to decreased sexual desire, arousal, coital frequency, and prevalence of erectile problems in older adult males. The time to achieve full erection is also increased with age and preejaculatory fluid emission is decreased or absent (Kinsey et al., 1953).

Masters and Johnson (1966) described decreased strength and frequency in the contraction of the pelvic striated muscles involved in ejaculation. It is believed that these contractions have some correlation with what Davidson (1980) refers to as the orgasmic altered state of consciousness and as such may be a factor in a subjective decreased intensity in the experience of orgasm in many older adult men. The postejaculatory refractory period in males increases from minutes in adolescence to days or longer in older males, and latency to orgasm is prolonged presumably due to decreased sensitivity of the ejaculatory mechanism (Masters & Johnson, 1966). This has been considered a benefit; while other sexual dysfunctions do increase with age, premature ejaculation does not (Davidson, 1985a). There is in fact a specific decrease in penile sensitivity as tested by increased threshold to vibrotactile stimulation of the penis (Edwards & Husted, 1976; Newman, 1970).

Declining blood levels of testosterone in older adult males appears to be one factor in decreased sexual function with aging. The first sign of alteration in endocrine function in males is an elevation of pituitary-stimulating hormones, which is a sign that the testes are beginning to produce less testosterone. Testosterone levels fall to such a great extent that by age 80 they may be only a sixth of levels in younger males (Kinsey et al., 1953). When a large sample of men aged 41 to 93 had data collected on their sexual behavior simultaneously with blood sampling for hormone levels, circulating testosterone level and free testosterone decreased significantly as a function of age (Davidson et al., 1983). A statistical analysis, however, showed this to be only a part of the variance; in some patients with no testosterone decline there still were sexual behavior decreases with age. In hypotheses explaining the remainder of the physiological dysfunction, other neurotransmitter and neuropeptides have been suggested to be involved in age-related changes in the androgen sensitivity of the relevant target cells. A decline in the number, sensitivity, function or other aspects of androgen receptors or mechanisms may be relevant (Davidson, 1985a; Davidson et al., 1983). Recent cross-sectional studies have demonstrated that poor health status, vascular and hormonal conditions, and stress are major factors in the decline of sexual function and presence of erectile failure in older adult males (Kaiser et al., 1988; Mulligan & Katz, 1989; Mulligan & Katz, 1988).

The Aging Female

Women have been documented to undergo significant decreases of their sexual function in their 50s and beyond (Davidson, 1985a; Pfeiffer et al., 1968; Verwoerdt et al., 1969), although women are more likely to identify external factors (as opposed to biological factors) than similarly aged males (Davidson, 1985a). Menopause has been studied (Hallstrom & Samuelsson, 1990) and is believed to be significant in the sexual decline occurring in the fifth and sixth decades of older adult women. In women 46 to 54 years of age, results suggested that the declines were due to menopause itself, not aging. Others, however (Kinsey et al., 1953), point to enhancements in a woman's sexuality from menopause, with speculation suggesting the removal of fear of pregnancy being a factor. The anatomical effects of postmenopausal steroid deprivation are well known and include atrophic vaginitis, with thinning of the vaginal walls, atrophic changes in the labia, decreased vaginal lubrication during sexual activity from atrophy of the Bartholin glands, and a decrease in the amount and maturation of vaginal mucosal cells causing a change in the quantity and quality of vaginal secretions (Kinsey et al., 1953). These changes go beyond the effect of decreasing lubrication and can lead to vaginal infections, such as monilial, trichomonal, or others that through inflammatory reactions can lead to dyspareunia (i.e., painful intercourse). In fact, dyspareunia is the most common sexual complaint of older women who present to gynecologists (Kinsey et al., 1953). There is also decreased tumescence of the glans clitoris. The uterus elevates less during arousal, and the os cervix is less dilated (Masters & Johnson, 1966). The labia majora lose fullness, and there is a loss of pubic hair (Kinsey et al., 1953). There are changes in the sex response cycle, in that it takes longer for older women to become aroused and lubricated, and there is less engorgement. But orgasmic response is reported to not be not significantly altered, although there is a decrease in the number and intensity of "orgasmic and rectal contractions" (Kinsey et al., 1953). Reduced estrogen levels appear to be related to declining frequency of intercourse, and serum estradiol levels below 35 mg/ml are associated with reduced coital activity (Kinsey et al., 1953). Quantitative laboratory data in older adult postmenopausal women revealed a lowered volume of secretions, a lowered electrical potential difference across the vaginal mucosa, and an elevated pH (Semmens & Wagner, 1982). A study of photoplethysmographic assessment of vaginal blood in response to erotic films and fantasy showed a significantly lower response in older postmenopausal women than in younger women who were still cycling. Of those older adult women who were still cycling the responsiveness was much higher, implicating menopause in lowered responses. To confound the issue of normal and abnormal, disease, and sexual health, subjects in the photoplethysmographic study that demonstrated a significant diminished sexual response under laboratory conditions were not sexually dysfunctional. Indeed, their subjective response to the erotic stimuli did not differ from younger female adults.

Illness

Almost any illness associated with aging can impact sexual functioning, ranging from general malaise and pain to specific illness. Procedures frequently associated with erectile failure include prostate surgery, sympathectomy, cystectomy, proctectomy, abdominal colon resection, and aortoiliac vascular reconstruction. Pelvic radiation can also be a cause of erectile failure. Many medications can cause either erectile or ejaculatory problems, with commonly prescribed antihypertensives and other cardiac medications among the leading offenders. Other diseases that are common causes of sexual dysfunction include diabetes mellitus, neuropathies, thyroid disease, renal failure, multiple sclerosis, hepatic failure, alcoholic neuropathy, pelvic fracture, spinal cord injury, temporal lobe lesions, pituitary tumors, and cancer of virtually any organ.

Treatment

For a treatment to be regarded as therapeutic (or effective) evidence needs to be collected that compares the status of individuals given that treatment to the status of comparable groups of individuals given no treatment (to rule out the possibility that spontaneous remission accounts for the effects) and those given a placebo treatment (to rule out expectancy effects). Moreover, such research requires randomly assigned subjects to these groups, sound diagnostic procedures, psychometrically sound outcome measures, and a double-blind design to control for subject and experimenter biases. Also required are checks for treatment fidelity and follow-ups to determine the durability of treatment effects. These steps are necessary not only to determine how effective treatment is but also how dangerous it might be. One must always remember that interventions can have negative effects, despite the therapist's best intentions.

To date, there are only a few outcome studies of therapy for sexual dysfunctions of the elderly. Kaas and Rosseau (1983) reported a case study of a 65-year-old impotent male using psychological treatments. Rowland and Haynes (1978) also report a study of a sexual enhancement program designed to improve communication among the elderly. However, these studies obviously lack the necessary design features to conclude that currently psychological treatments are effective (or even safe) for the sexual dysfunction problems of the elderly. Considerably more research is needed with this neglected population.

Women

Given the confusion as to the relationship of hormones and aging, menopause and sexual function, and hormone replacement in general, it is not surprising that hormone replacement is not a clear panacea for the older adult female experiencing sexual dysfunction with clear menopausal changes. One study (Davidson, 1985a) demonstrated that while estrogen decreased vaginal dryness, no improvement was found in frequency of coitus, masturbation, orgasm, or sexual satisfaction. However, synthetic estrogen but not synthetic progesterone improved sexual desire, enjoyment, and orgasmic frequency in women who had their ovaries removed along with a hysterectomy.

It has been suggested that androgen (Schon & Sutherland, 1960; Waxenberg, Drellich, & Sutherland, 1959) is the important hormone in maintaining female sexual function. The success of estrogen-androgen combinations for sexual dysfunction in older adult females still requires further study, although some success has been reported (Davidson, 1985a). A simple treatment that should not be overlooked is the use of lubricants. Other common sense treatments should not be overlooked, for example, nonsteroidal analgesics to reduce joint pain in arthritic or simply aging joints. A recommendation of continued sexual activity as a treatment may seem strange at first. However, a fascinating confirmation of the "use it or lose it" theory was seen in a study in which gynecologists followed women's sexual activity. These investigators collected an index of vaginal atrophy assessing six genital dimensions, including hormonal blood samples, and found that sexually active older adult women displayed significantly less vaginal atrophy. Masturbation also was helpful in retarding atrophic changes in the genitals (Kinsey et al., 1953).

Men

There is no clear rationale for the use of androgen in males except for clearly hypogonadal men, in whom injections of 220 to 400 mg of testosterone enanthate at 3-week intervals have been found to be beneficial (Sparrow, Bosse, & Rowe, 1980). There are many new treatments for erectile disorders, covered in more depth by Graber (1993). Included are arterial reconstruction, implants and prostheses, yohibime, bromocriptine, and nitroglycerine paste. The most widespread, however, are the intracavernous injection therapies. The most common regimen involves papaverine or papaverine and phentolamine (usually a mixture of 25 mg/ml of papaverine with 0.83 mg/ml of phentolamine). The most popular technique is the pharmcoinjection program (PIP), in which the patient is instructed in the use of an ultrafine needle to inject in the side of the penis in a procedure that can be implemented at home. Finally, some of the same common sense ideas suggested for women apply to men as well. One of the simplest recommended, in addition to the analgesics noted above, is a hot bath before sexual activity to reduce pain and stiffness (Kinsey et al., 1953).

SUMMARY

The view that the elderly are not sexually desirable, desirous, or capable is a myth. It is a potentially dangerous myth, because if it is believed by the elderly or others it can seriously interfere with an important aspect of this functioning. Butler and Lewis (1978) have suggested that for the elderly sex may serve as a means of expressing passion, affection, admiration, and loyalty; affirming one's body and its functioning; asserting oneself; defying erroneously held stereotypes of the elderly; creating a sense of romance; affirming life; and experiencing pleasure through touch. Sexual activity, no doubt, is important for adults of all ages.

REFERENCES

American Psychiatric Association. (1994). *Diagnostic and statistical manual of mental disorders* (4th ed.). Washington, DC: Author.
Butler, R. N., & Lewis, M. I. (1978). The second language of sex. In R. Solnick (Ed.), *Sexuality and aging* (pp. 176–183). Los Angeles: University of Southern California Press.

Caven, R. S. (1973). Speculation on innovations to conventional marriage in old age. *Gerontology, 13*, 408–411.

Davidson, J. M. (1985a). The psychobiology of sexual experience. In J. M. Davidson & L. J. Davidson (Eds.), *The psychobiology of consciousness* (pp. 271–332). New York: Plenum Press.

Davidson, J. M. (1985b). Sexuality and aging. In R. Andres, E. L. Bierman, & W. R. Hazzard (Eds.), *Principles of geriatric medicine* (pp. 154–161). New York: McGraw-Hill.

Davidson, J. M., Chen, J. J., Crapo, L., Gray, G. D., Greenleaf, W. J., & Catania, J. A. (1983). Hormonal changes and sexual function in aging men. *Journal of Clinical Endocrinology and Metabolism, 57,* 71–77.

Edwards, A. E., & Husted, J. R. (1976). Penile sensitivity, age and sexual behavior. *Journal of Clinical Psychology, 32,* 697–700.

Fisher, J. E., Zeiss, A., & Carstensen, L. L. (1992). Psychopathology in the aged. In P. Sutker & H. Adams (Eds.), *Comprehensive handbook of psychopathology.* New York: Plenum Press.

Geer, J. H., & O'Donohue, W. T. (1987). Introduction and overview. In J. Geer & W. O'Donohue (Eds.), *Theories of human sexuality* (pp. 1–20). New York: Plenum Press.

Graber, B. (1993). Medical aspects of sexual arousal disorder. In W. T. O'Donohue & J. H. Geer (Eds.), *Handbook of sexual dysfunctions: Assessment and treatment* (pp. 103–157). Boston: Allyn & Bacon.

Hallstrom, T., & Samuelsson, S. (1990). Changes in women's sexual desire in middle life: The longitudinal study of women in Gothenburg. *Archives of Sexual Behavior, 19*(3), 259–268.

Hotvedt, M. (1983). The cross cultural and historical context. In R. B. Weg (Ed.), *Sexuality in the later years.* New York: Academic Press.

Hursch, C. J., Karacan, I., & Williams, R. L. (1972). Some characteristics of nocturnal penile tumescence in early middle-aged males. *Comprehensive Psychiatry, 13*(6), 539–548.

Kaas, M., & Rousseau, G. K. (1983). Geriatric sexual conformity: Assessment and intervention. *Clinical Gerontologist, 2,* 31–34.

Kaiser, F. E., Viosca, S. P., Morley, J. E., Mooradioa, A. D., Davis, S. S., & Korenman, S. G. (1988). Impotence and aging: Clinical and hormonal factors. *Journal of the American Geriatric Society, 36,* 511–519.

Kassel, V. (1983). Long term care institutions. In R. Weg (Ed.), *Sexuality in the later years* (pp. 167–184). New York: Academic Press.

Kuhn, M. E. (1976). Sexual myths surrounding the aged. In W. W. Oaks, G. Melchoide, & I. Ficher (Eds.), *Sex and the life cycle.* New York: Grune & Stratton.

Kinsey, A. C., Pomeroy, W. B., Martin, C. E., & Gebhard, P. H. (1953). *Sexual behavior in the human female.* Philadelphia: W. B. Saunders.

Masters, W. H., & Johnson, V. E. (1966). *Human sexual response.* Boston: Little, Brown.

Meyer, J. K., Schmidt, C. W., & Wise, T. N. (1983). *Clinical management of sexual disorders* (2nd ed.). Baltimore: Williams & Wilkins.

Midgley, A. R., Jr., Gay, V. L., Keys, P. L., & Hunter, J. S. (1973). Human reproductive endocrinology. In E. S. E. Hafez & T. N. Evans (Eds.), *Principles of geriatric medicine* (pp. 201–236). New York: McGraw-Hill.

Mulligan, T., & Katz, P. G. (1988). Erectile failure in the aged: Evaluation and treatment. *Journal of the American Geriatric Society, 36,* 54–62.

Mulligan, T., & Katz, P. G. (1989). Why aged men become impotent. *Archives of Internal Medicine, 149,* 1365–1366.

Newman, H. F. (1970). Vibratory sensitivity of the penis. *Fertility and Sterility, 21*(11), 791–793.

O'Donohue, W. (1987). The sexual behavior and problems of the elderly. In L. Carstensen & B. Edelstein (Eds.), *Handbook of clinical gerontology* (pp. 66–75). Elmsford, NY: Pergamon Press.

Pfeiffer, E., Verwoerdt, A., & Wang, H. S. (1968). Sexual behavior in aged men and women. *Archives of General Psychiatry, 19,* 753–758.

Rowland, K. F., & Haynes, S. N. (1978). A sexual enhancement program for elderly couples. *Journal of Sex and Marital Therapy, 4,* 91–113.

Sallsel, V. (1983). Long term care institutions. In R. Weg (Ed.), *Sexuality in the later years* (pp. 167–184). New York: Academic Press.

Schiavi, R. C., & Schreiner-Engel, P. (1988). Nocturnal penile tumescence in healthy aging men. *Journal of Gerontology: Medical Sciences, 43*(5), M146–M150.

Schiavi, R. C., Schreiner-Engel, P., Mandell, J., Schanzer, H., & Cohen, E. (1990). Healthy aging and male sexual function. *American Journal of Psychiatry, 147*, 766–771.

Schon, M., & Sutherland, A. M. (1960). The role of hormones in human behavior. III. Changes in female sexuality after hypophysectomy. *Journal of Gerontology, 20*, 833–841.

Semmens, J. P., & Wagner, G. (1982). Estrogen deprivation and vaginal function in postmenopausal women. *Journal of the American Medical Association, 248*, 445–448.

Solnick, R. L., & Birren, J. E. (1977). Age and male erectile responsiveness. *Archives of Sexual Behavior, 6*, 1–9.

Sparrow, D., Bosse, R., & Rowe, J. W. (1980). The influences of age, alcohol consumption, and body build on gonadal function in men. *Journal of Clinical Endocrinology and Metabolism, 51*, 508–512.

Symons, D. (1987). An evolutionary approach: Can Darwin's view of life shed light on human sexuality? In W. O'Donohue & J. Geer (Eds.), *Theories of human sexuality* (pp. 91–126). New York: Plenum Press.

Verwoerdt, A., Pfeiffer, E., & Wang, H. S. (1969). Sexual behavior in senescence. *Geriatrics, 24*, 137–154.

Walford, R., Weindrich, R., Gottesman, S., & Tam, C. F. (1981). The immunopathology of aging. In C. Eisdorfer, B. Starr, & V. J. Cristofalo (Eds.), *Annual review of gerontology and geriatrics* (Vol. 2). New York: Springer.

Waxenberg, S. E., Drellich, M. G., & Sutherland, A. M. (1959). The role of hormones in human behavior. I. Changes in female sexuality after adrenalectomy. *Journal of Clinical Endocrinology, 19*, 193–202.

Zarit, J. M., & Zarit, S. H. (1987). The physiology and psychology of normal aging. In L. L. Carstensen & B. A. Edelstein (Eds.), *Handbook of clinical gerontology* (pp. 18–32). New York: Pergamon Press.

CHAPTER 16

Marital Discord

GARY R. BIRCHLER AND WILLIAM FALS-STEWART

DESCRIPTION OF THE PROBLEM

Despite the fact that older people are reluctant to seek mental health services and tend to seek help from primary care physicians, even when their problems are psychological, there is little doubt that mental health practitioners will be called upon to treat a burgeoning number of elderly people as the graying of America continues. By the year 2000, it is estimated that approximately 20% of the population in the United States will be over age 65. The U.S. Bureau of the Census reported that in 1987, 75% of the men and 40% of the women over age 65

GARY R. BIRCHLER • Psychology Service, Veterans Affairs Medical Center, and Department of Psychiatry, University of California, San Diego, California 92161.   WILLIAM FALS-STEWART • Harvard Families and Addiction Program, Harvard Medical School, and Department of Psychiatry, Veterans Affairs Medical Center, Brockton, Massachusetts 02401.
Psychological Treatment of Older Adults: An Introductory Text, edited by Michel Hersen and Vincent B. Van Hasselt. Plenum Press, New York, 1996.

were married. Although most marriages of older people end because of the death of a spouse rather than through divorce, several studies of marital happiness in old age conclude that many older couples are emotionally disengaged, have poor communication skills, and are unhappy. As longevity impacts couples with major social, financial, and health-related stressors, there is increased concern that the divorce rate among elderly couples will rise (Peterson, 1980).

Marriage, an important and fascinating institution at any age, is particularly interesting in the latter stages of the life cycle. However, the study of long-term marriages (Levenson, Carstensen, & Gottman, 1993) and the development of marital therapies for older couples (e.g., Stone, 1987; Wolinsky, 1990) is only recently becoming the focus of clinical investigators. Such a mismatch between treatment implementation and evaluation is typical for a clinical population of emerging interest. However, this lag obfuscates our ability to draw definitive conclusions about the effectiveness of many interventions (Smyer, Zaut, & Qualls, 1990).

On the one hand, many therapeutic approaches designed for older persons do not differ significantly from those used with younger clients (Gatz, Popin, Pino, & VandenBos, 1985). In fact, most studies suggest that a majority of older persons respond well to traditional treatments (Gatz, 1988; Pinkston & Linsk, 1984). On the other hand, we need to gain a better understanding of the unique developmental problems experienced in the relationships of older adults to be sure that there are not special needs and opportunities for the enhancement of therapeutic engagement (Gafner, 1987; Neidhardt & Allen, 1993) and therapeutic efficacy (Wolinsky, 1986).

Marriage and Older Adults

There are four basic types of marriages among the elderly: (1) long-term marriages blessed with intimate companionship over many years, (2) long-term marriages characterized by chronic dissatisfaction, (3) short-term (second or third) marriages that bring a measure of pleasure and companionship to partners in their later years, and (4) short-term marriages that are not satisfying. As one might expect, the happy couples in both long- and short-term marriages tend to be financially secure and in reasonably good health. In contrast, the unhappy couples in short- or long-term relationships are more likely to be challenged by financial and/or serious health problems or by conflict with extended family members.

The Benefits and Challenges for Older Marriages

On the whole, marriage benefits older adults (Gubrium, 1974; Patrick & Moore, 1986). Compared with their single counterparts, married senior citizens tend to have a longer life expectancy, are physically more healthy, are more affluent, less vulnerable to mental illness, and less likely to be institutionalized (i.e., hospitalized or placed in nursing homes).

Role Reductions

On the other hand, married older adults have significant life stage challenges that are qualitatively different from those faced by the younger population. Typically, several major role reductions and gender role reversals affect older marriages. We call this the "postparental" stage of marriage (Birchler, 1992). Retirement marks a reduction in the vocational activities and financial resources of most couples. Loss of self-esteem, domestic power struggles, and other retirement-related adjustments can cause significant conflict both within and between partners. Formerly active parental roles shift back to a focus on the marriage. Accordingly, if the marriage has been neglected or maintained for "negative reasons" (e.g., for the sake of the children or because of financial concerns), the potential for marital discord and dissolution increases.

Inevitably, partners in mature marriages begin to experience multiple losses and life-style changes. The children leave home, physical and mental declines set in, jobs are lost or end in retirement, the couple or old friends may relocate, friends and family begin to pass away, and a variety of other life-style options are reduced or lost. These multiple losses are known to be important challenges to marital satisfaction and stability.

Role Reversals

Two types of gender role reversal are noteworthy. First, older men (especially those who have retired) tend to become more affiliative. If performance in the working world is no longer primary or possible, men often reorient toward the family. They may be at home more and solicit family interactions that they had been missing or avoiding for years. In contrast, the wives and mothers, usually freed up from certain parenting and husband-supporting roles, now tend to spread their wings. They may seek employment or avocational occupation that takes them outside the home. Older wives may become more assertive and even aggressive and egocentric. Of course, these changes are not necessarily disruptive to the marriage, but they are cause for marital adjustment and some couples definitely have problems making these transitions.

Similarly, a second area of role reversal may develop in the couple's sexual relationship. Again, the man is probably slowing down. His energy level and performance capacity in sexual activities often experience notable declines. However, his wife, free of the responsibilities of parenting, free of supporting work-day stresses, free of birth control concerns, and with a renewed energy for life, may become more comfortable and interested in an active sex life. Whereas complaints about sexual functioning are rarely primary in older couples who present for marital therapy, concerns about sexual interaction and function frequently emerge as an area needing therapeutic attention.

Health Concerns

Besides gender role and various personality changes that may occur in the mature-stage marriage, usually there is a mutual concern about health and its inevitable decline. In fact, unsuccessful attempts to cope with physical and/or mental health problems frequently are correlated with marital discord when older couples seek marital therapy (Gafner, 1987). As a consequence of increased longevity, people are unfortunately required to cope with acute and chronic forms of illness. Although marriage provides obvious benefit for the ill partner, the burden on the caregiving spouse may prove to be overwhelming. In such instances, the relationship will likely change from one of mutual exchange and support to one in which unidirectional caregiving becomes the dominant, over-riding issue (Barusch, 1988). Many couples become impoverished financially and emotionally as they expend life savings for medical care and nursing homes (Neidhardt & Allen, 1993). Moreover, although the phenomenon varies signifi-cantly from individual to individual, and naturally increases with age, a pre-occupation with and fear of death certainly accompanies these difficult efforts to manage debilitating illnesses.

The Seven C's of Marriage

Finally, although we have noted some unique reasons for marital discord among the elderly, these couples are not immune to the fundamental problems that threaten marital harmony for all couples. In our country, for any given couple, the status of marital accord or discord is determined by the functional quality of certain universal dimensions of marriage that we have called the "Seven C's": *Character features, Contract, Cultural and ethnic issues, Commitment, Caring, Communication*, and *Conflict resolution* (Birchler & Fals-Stewart, 1994). Distressed marriages undoubtedly have significant problems in one or more of these areas.[1] The complex and unpredictable effects of aging and the numerous challenges that confront a mature-stage marriage can produce ex-tremely diverse impacts on the respective partners; consequently, their experi-ences of and remaining goals for life and the marriage may no longer be compat-ible (Wolinsky, 1990).

CASE IDENTIFICATION
AND PRESENTING COMPLAINTS

Martin is a 69-year-old married, white man being seen in the Mood Disor-ders Clinic at the local Veterans Administration Medical Center. He is receiving

[1]Although the meaning of most of the Seven C's is obvious, "Character features" refers to the level of psychopathology that each partner may demonstrate in marital interaction. "Contract" refers to how well each partners' experience in the relationship matches their explicit or implicit expectations of the relationship. For example, as the marriage matures, partners' expectations and patterns of spousal interaction that may have been successful for years may now fail to achieve satisfactory results.

antidepressant medication for treatment of a major depression, which was exacerbated after his retirement 4 years previously. In the course of his visits to his psychiatrist for medication, he described increased marital discord with his wife, noting that she was threatening separation. The physician made the appropriate referral to the Family Mental Health Program. The couple agreed to come for an initial evaluation for marital therapy. Martin's wife Vera, aged 67, is a white woman who retired from a part-time job 2 years previously. The couple has been married for 43 years, and they have three children, including two married daughters, aged 39 and 35, and one divorced son, aged 41. They also have five grandchildren.

The Intake Session

The objectives of the first evaluation session were to (1) determine if marital therapy is indicated for their problems, (2) establish rapport with the couple, (3) understand their presenting complaints, and (4) if appropriate, gain a commitment from the couple to participate in additional evaluation sessions. In this section we will discuss their presenting complaints.

Following the typical introductions, the couple was asked the classic question: "What brings you to our clinic?" Martin peered at his wife with a gaze of inquiry and mild confusion. She promptly took this cue and told the therapists that Martin's increased irritability and verbal abuse of her (including unpredictable, intermittent temper outbursts) were becoming very upsetting, adding, "I can't take it anymore." She also complained that Martin would withdraw into one of his "blue" moods and spend hours on the couch reading or watching television. She reported that it was nearly impossible to get him to participate in any outside social, recreational, or home maintenance activities. Yet, on occasion, when she would want to go out with one of her daughters or a friend, he would complain about her leaving him home alone. Finally, she expressed resentment at the way Martin treated people who visited them. Whether it was their children, the neighbors, or her friends, his behavior of either rudely ignoring them or insulting them was "driving them all away."

After listening at some length to Vera's complaints, the therapists asked Martin what were his concerns about the marriage. He responded defensively, explaining how he had stopped arguing and brawling with people soon after he left the Marines; he had stopped heavy drinking about 10 years ago; and he had stopped smoking about 2 years ago. In his view, he had made some very important personal changes in his life, "and that's about all anyone can expect." When asked again what apprehensions he might have about the *marriage*, he said that the main problem was Vera's impatience with him. He admitted to being quite moody and sometimes "crabby," noting, "but that's why I see a psychiatrist." Vera's own "crabbiness" and her persistent demands that he engage in activities he did not want to do were his main complaints.

While the presenting problems were being aired, it was remarkable that the partners were able to display a significant measure of humor. Clearly, after several decades together, these partners cared for each other and retained the requisite attitudes to experience some pleasure in each other's company. At the end of this initial meeting, the therapists concluded by suggesting that they continue the evaluation process to further define aspects of their relationship that were providing satisfaction and those that were causing disharmony. The couple readily agreed to continue the assessment process.

HISTORY

In our behavioral-systems approach, history-taking in preparation for marital therapy takes two forms: a second conjoint session in which the developmental history of the marriage is solicited and then individual sessions with each partner to learn the history of their personal development and family of origin. The individual meetings also provide the partners an opportunity to disclose any issues that they might find uncomfortable discussing in the presence of their mates (for example, the limits of Vera's commitment to the marriage or the extent to which Martin's depression is caused by relationship factors).

It is important to note that older adults not only have more history to report, but also seem more invested in having the therapist listen to it than is the case for younger people. Whether listening to accounts of their positive accomplishments or their negative experiences, therapists treating older couples are well advised to use history-taking as a way to validate their clients' lives. Being interested and attentive to their life stores allows therapists to join with them in a way that increases the probability that older clients will enter and benefit from therapy (Butler, 1969, 1974).

Premarital Histories

Martin grew up in Oklahoma on a small farm. He was the fourth of six children, and his family was poor. He had enough to eat but reported few privileges. His father was an alcoholic who, during Martin's early adolescence, would disappear for several days at a time. His mother seemed to hold the family together, but everyone had to help on the farm. Martin was kept home from school frequently to do chores. When Martin reached 15 years of age, his father became physically violent toward Martin's older brothers and sometimes toward his mother. Two older brothers left home following family fights.

Martin graduated from high school as "a below average student" and entered the Marines after 1 year of holding odd jobs. His military career was unremarkable (i.e., no significant combat experiences, no medals, no significant problems) except that he did "much drinking and fighting" (apparently within bounds acceptable to the military). During this time he dated several women, most of whom he met in bars; however, he described these liaisons as "nothing serious." After 7 years in the service he elected to leave and was discharged near San Diego, where he obtained employment in a local shipyard as a welder. A consistent pattern of fairly heavy drinking continued. Within a year he met Vera and they were married after only a few months of dating.

Vera grew up with one younger sister in Washington state. Her father was an engineer with Boeing Company and her mother was a nursery school teacher. Her development through high school was unremarkable. She was a "B" student, socially popular with schoolmates, and dated frequently in her senior year. She completed 2 years of junior college and then moved to northern California for her first job as a law firm stenographer. Here she had a steady boyfriend for about 2 years and then he moved to San Diego. She decided to follow him, but the relationship terminated after several months. She was working as a secretary when she met Martin.

Marital History

Soon after the marriage, Vera realized that Martin had an alcohol problem. About once a month he would go out drinking "with the boys" after work and return home intoxicated; usually he was obnoxious and sometimes insulting. These episodes caused significant conflict in the early years but improved when their first child was born. Nevertheless, the pattern was set that Vera seemed to want more emotional support from her husband than he was able or willing to provide. His employment was fairly steady, but at times he would be furloughed from work for several weeks at a time.

Raising three kids was a source of pleasure and frustration for Martin and Vera. When he was in high school, their son became involved with drinking and drugs and was suspended from school briefly. One of their daughters also presented problems, as she was frequently depressed and experienced a moderate eating disorder. These concerns, along with Martin's persistent drinking, resulted in a stressful family life. Nevertheless, the three children graduated from high school, and the third daughter entered and graduated from college. All three children are now doing well, although their son recently went through a divorce. Contacts with their children were appropriate, except for the tendency for Martin to be irritable or withdrawn during family functions.

The couple describes the course of their marriage with a mixture of frustration, regret, and some relief. They are aware that the family as a unit showed considerable resilience to the various difficulties encountered. Martin was reluctant to become involved in the family conflicts and tended to withdraw from parent-child discussions. Vera resented his abandonment in this area but persevered in managing the family problems, including those problems involving her frequently disengaged and alcohol-abusing husband. About 10 years ago, when Martin was diagnosed with arteriosclerotic disease, he stopped drinking on his own. This was a welcome event because with abstinence, his temper outbursts virtually disappeared. However, Vera claims that other aspects of Martin's personality also changed. His general demeanor was marked by a low-grade irritability and a more subtle withdrawal from social activities. Martin acknowledged significant emotional adjustments when he stopped drinking alcohol and he described a similar challenge when he stopped smoking cigarettes 2 years ago. However, he was quite proud of himself as he related his success in stopping these habits.

Both partners agreed that the persistent marital discord began after Martin retired from the shipyard 4 years ago. Since then, he has seemed to lack purpose and direction. His explanation is that he cannot find anything worthwhile with which to occupy his time. He cannot seem to develop friendships or find part-time employment; further, he seems only to disappoint his wife. His discouragement reached such depths about 1 year ago that he sought assistance at the Mental Health Clinic and was prescribed antidepressant medication. A significant reduction in seriously depressed mood states was soon achieved, but the mood-enhancing effects of the medication have been inconsistent and his psychiatrist has had to modify the dosage frequently. Meanwhile, Vera is anxious "to do something with her life." She anticipated many enjoyable leisure activities with Martin after his retirement, but so far she has been sadly disappointed.

SELECTION OF PSYCHOLOGICAL TREATMENT

We emphasize at the outset of a discussion of the treatment of marital discord in older couples that in our experience this population has significantly more diverse needs than a younger or middle-aged population of maritally distressed couples. That is, to date, there is no empirically validated relationship treatment program designed specifically for older couples. Older couples are as likely to need (or to tolerate) one or two sessions to discuss an emergent problem as they are to require and to remain in support-oriented marital therapy for many months. In this chapter, we present a typical case, including discussion of some particular interventions that seemed to enhance therapeutic engagement and outcome for this couple. However, at this stage in the development of the field, our approach represents one way to understand and treat older couples; it is not presented as *the* approach for older couples.

In our program, when couples commit to the extended evaluation process at the end of the initial session, we give them a package of self-report instruments to complete and return at the second meeting. We administer an extensive battery of marital assessment instruments (see Birchler, 1983), including the *Dyadic Adjustment Scale* (*DAS*; Spanier, 1976), the *Areas of Change Questionnaire* (*ACQ*; Weiss & Birchler, 1975), the *Marital Status Inventory* (*MSI*; Weiss & Cerreto, 1980), and the *Response to Conflict Scale* (*RTC*; Birchler & Fals-Stewart, 1994). Usually we also administer the *Minnesota Multiphasic Personality Inventory* (*MMPI*; Hathaway & McKinley, 1943) and the *Beck Depression Inventory* (*BDI*; Beck, Ward, Mendelsohn, Mock, & Erbaugh, 1961). Measures of individual function, especially screens for depression and anxiety, are particularly important for older clients because they are so vulnerable to these disorders. Because some elderly couples find this 2- to 3-hour questionnaire task somewhat daunting, we take extra time to explain the benefits of a careful evaluation and we promise to provide complete feedback concerning the strengths and immediate concerns of the marriage.

For Martin and Vera, both the *BDI* and the *MMPI* proved the need for antidepressant medication for Martin. Moreover, a review of Martin's medical record indicated that many symptoms of depression had been reported during the past year. In addition, Vera's *MMPI* results suggested a low-grade depression. However, we believe that her depression was probably secondary to the marital discord and would likely improve with marital therapy.

The Communication Sample

In addition to the comprehensive marital battery and standard information gathered during the clinical interviews (Birchler & Schwartz, 1994), during the second conjoint session we also observe and record on videotape a 10-minute *communication sample* of the couple's marital conflict resolution skills. Briefly, this involves the partners discussing an identified problem area in their relationship; the therapists observe this interaction in silence. (For a more detailed explanation of conducting a communication sample, see Birchler and Schwartz, 1994.) In the behavioral approach to martial therapy, direct observation of a couple's ability to communicate and problem-solve has become an indispensable method of assessment. Only by direct observation can the therapist ascertain a couple's actual level of communication skill and assess the all-important affective variables that accompany this process (Gottman, 1979). All combined, data gathered from individual and conjoint interviews, the self-report questionnaires, and the communication sample provide ample information from which to plan psychological interventions to address marital discord (Birchler & Schwartz, 1994).

The Seven C's

There was little doubt that Martin and Vera were candidates for marital therapy. Feedback was given to the couple in the framework of the Seven C's. *Character features* were significant variables to account for in the treatment plan—mainly Martin's depression and dependency on Vera and Vera's low-grade depression. The marital *contract* was a potential target for intervention because much of Vera's frustration had to do with her expectation that Martin would be an active and enthusiastic retirement partner. The failure of her experience to match her expectations was cause for frustration and contributed to marital discord. In this case, we did not identify any significant *cultural or ethnic factors* requiring therapeutic attention.

Despite Vera's implied threat to leave Martin because "she couldn't take it anymore," this possibility was all but dismissed because of information learned during the individual meeting with Vera. Therefore, their level of *commitment* to the relationship was considered stable. Also, basic *caring* for one another was still intact, although the frustration accompanying their frequent discord was beginning to erode this relationship asset.

Similarly, *communication* between Martin and Vera had deteriorated over the past few years because these spouses were unable to meet each other's needs. Finally, *conflict resolution* skills also were deficient, as evidenced by persistent "demand-withdraw" and "conflict-avoidant" interaction patterns (see Notarius & Markman, 1993). Once operational, these particular types of marital interaction become resistant to change without therapeutic intervention.

In summary, conjoint marital therapy was the treatment of choice to address the following process goals: (1) resolving or coping with both partners' depression to the extent it affected the marriage, (2) clarifying and perhaps renegotiating the marital contract for the postparental stage of their lives, (3) affirming commitment and enhancing the support and caring aspects of their relationship, and (4) reducing the intensity and frequency of marital discord through improved communication and problem-solving training.

CONCURRENT MEDICAL TREATMENT

Because in so many settings seniors do not get comprehensive health care, it is particularly important to take a case manager's perspective when assessing the biopsychosocial needs of older adults (and couples). We encourage our patients to obtain complete physicals if they have not had one within the last year. We review their medical records for past and present major medical problems and recent follow-up.

Medical problems and functional limitations, especially chronic and debilitating ones, often preoccupy the daily lives of older couples and, for the sake of an effective marital treatment, must receive appropriate attention. Attempts to limit or ignore discussion of these health issues will interfere with the development of a strong rapport with these clients, which is necessary to engage dyads in relationship therapy. It is important in treating older couples to incorporate a recognition of physical concerns into the relationship assessment and treatment process.

Martin had several medical problems, the most serious being arteriosclerotic disease. In addition, he experienced mild to moderate arthritis in his hips and knees, which occasionally limited his ambulatory activity. Finally, a mild hearing loss in one ear had been documented; however, Vera humorously suggested that he had "selective" hearing because "he hears only what he wants." All of these conditions were monitored by the appropriate clinics, the vascular disease most regularly. Vera was healthy for her age, with the normal aches and pains. She had borderline high blood pressure, which was known to increase under stress. She was self-monitoring this condition and consulted her physician when levels became elevated. To some extent, the medical problems that Martin and Vera were experiencing could be exacerbated by frustrating or stressful marital discord. Therefore, in listening to this feedback, there was some extra incentive for them to reduce the level and frequency of marital conflict. Throughout therapy, we monitor and examine the impact of their health problems on the relationship.

COURSE OF TREATMENT

Facilitating Engagement in Therapy

The emerging literature on the psychological treatment of older couples (e.g., Stone, 1987; Wolinsky, 1990) suggests that there are many ways to enhance the likelihood and durability of therapeutic engagement. To be considered on a case-by-case basis, there are possible modifications of standard treatment formats and procedures, which are listed below.

1. *Compensate for reduction in memory and other deficits* by increasing the volume and slowing the rate of speech, using appropriate lighting, reducing any hectic or high-stimulus aspects of the practice setting, and writing down instructions and homework assignments.
2. *Adopt flexible session length and frequency of visits.* If transportation is readily available, two half-hour visits per week might be better than one hour-long visit. If travel is burdensome, instituting short breaks within longer sessions could be helpful.
3. *Be flexible with regard to session location*; this may be important in engaging some couples. Office visits should be closest to home or in locations where transportation is convenient and direct; even home visits may be necessary.
4. *Use time-limited treatment contracts*; these are best because older people are very concerned with time. They respond better to problem-oriented, highly structured, and goal-specific activities.
5. *Attend to social and physical limitations.* The full social context in which the couple is operating may be important to understand (e.g., access to extended family and other support services or options for low-cost, slower-paced social activities). As mentioned above, the incorporation of physical health discussions into treatment is usually necessary.
6. *Emphasize the interpersonal context of the problems* because personal relationships tend to be more salient for older persons. The number of family and social contacts can be greatly reduced as age increases. The remaining relationships, conflicted or not, become quite important.
7. *Be an active rather than a passive therapist.* Again, among older people there may be less patience for ambiguity and extended therapeutic activities. Structure, clarity, coaching, active mediation, and directed problem-solving are the most effective approaches.
8. *Be aware of drug effects.* Many older people are taking medications; some take multiple, highly interactive prescriptions. Unfortunately, these patients may not be followed up frequently or well enough by

their physicians to avoid untoward reactions. The marital therapist would do well to monitor the effects of drugs, especially as they impact interpersonal activities. In this regard, obtaining releases to speak to the partners' primary care physicians is recommended.

9. *Assess the interaction of physical and psychological factors.* In older people, the relative roles that psychological and medical or physical factors play in the etiology and maintenance of various presenting complaints can be confusing. These factors are highly reciprocal and must be assessed carefully.

10. *Beware of "ageism" in the therapist.* Our society discourages old age, tends to deny aging and death, and subtle biases therefore creep into even the most well-intended therapies. Although realistic physical and mental declines should be assessed and acknowledged, they should not be assumed, taken for granted, or discounted as normal and unimportant. For example, older couples may give up on an active and healthy sex life, although often such resignation is not necessary. For a given couple, pleasurable sexual activity may be possible far longer than is acknowledged by the couple or the therapist.

Also, therapists would do well to appreciate and adopt the older patients' world views and language rather than require the patients to learn the therapist's orientation and language. For example, traditional (and sometimes gender inequitable) sex role values, reticence to talk frankly about sex, and the use of dated phrases such as "down in the dumps" or "blue" instead of "sad" and "depressed" might be better accepted than modified by the therapist.

Mostly, these suggestions are simple modifications of typical psychological treatments. However, they can pay significant dividends in terms of engaging the older couple in treatment and should not be discounted. For Vera and Martin, several of the above procedural modifications proved to be helpful. These will be noted briefly. Because our clinic waiting area shares space with the check-in area for the Psychiatric Emergency Clinic (admissions), the area can become quite chaotic. Martin tended to become upset waiting for his marital therapy sessions to start. To avoid this frustration, the couple was asked to check in and go directly to the open therapy room, even if they arrived early or the therapists were delayed.

Once the session started, we found it very helpful to work for about 25 minutes, take a 5 to 10 minute break, and then meet for another 20 minutes. For this couple, the short rest period was far more beneficial than distracting. The format also forced the therapists to be more structured and organized in order to complete the agenda for the meeting. At the end of each session, all homework assignments were orally reviewed with the couple and written down. Initially, the treatment contract was designed for 6 weeks. After this period, everyone agreed to meet weekly for an additional month.

We made a special effort to assign male and female cotherapists to this case. Vera appreciated having another woman in the room. Both therapists paid particular attention to talking more loudly and clearly than usual because of

Martin's hearing loss. The more articulate they were, the more attentively he participated in the process. A cotherapy team also afforded the opportunity to model effective dyadic communication and problem-solving skills for the couple. They clearly benefitted from the opportunity to observe the target skills in action and be coached by their own same-gender therapist.

Martin was taking several medications, and he tended to give detailed descriptions of his physical symptoms, which appeared at times to be a way of avoiding or rationalizing the problems in the relationship. Although the therapists were sensitive to possible drug effects and the potential for drug interactions, Martin was politely validated and referred to his physician to address these "side effects." Moreover, the therapists modeled for Vera how to express appropriate and limited concern, without taking responsibility for Martin's symptoms or nagging him to take his medications or talk to his physician, etc.

In addition, apparently Martin suffered from a mild chronic pain syndrome with respect to his arthritis. Indeed, many activities that Vera wanted Martin to do required extensive walking or legwork (e.g., shopping at the mall, driving for an hour or more to visit relatives, yard work). Unfortunately, the couple had long stalemated on this issue. Vera attributed Martin's behavior to a lack of caring and motivation (instead of physical disability or discomfort). Martin felt "constantly criticized" for not doing these things with Vera, and often he would refuse to cooperate. This discussion should make it clear that the interrelationships between physical problems and interpersonal conflicts can be salient topics of treatment with older couples.

General Goals of Treatment

Besides the couple engagement procedures, recall that the general treatment goals included (1) helping Martin to adjust to retirement by initiating activities to enhance his self-worth and interest in life, to lessen his dependency on Vera, and to work toward meeting Vera's vision of enjoying a life of leisure together; (2) if needed, addressing Martin's mood disorder, specifically its impact on the relationship (i.e., his temper outbursts toward Vera and rudeness toward family and her friends); and (3) improving the skills and dysfunctional patterns of communication and problem-solving currently available to the couple, so they can better identify, understand, and resolve conflicts leading to marital discord.

Commitment and Caring

Initial objectives of the first few treatment sessions involved strengthening the couple's *commitment* to and *caring* for each other. To this end we employed two interventions. First, we helped Martin and Vera to acknowledge, *in relationship terms*, the positive and negative aspects of their marriage (i.e., develop a systemic perspective and a collaborative set). We explored and validated their personal positions regarding their respective presenting complaints and helped them to understand the interactional, developmental history of these problems. We encouraged them to affirm and to celebrate their strengths as the necessary foundation for their faith and ability to improve the marriage.

Second, we employed the "Caring Behaviors" exercise (Birchler, 1983; Stuart, 1980), designed to help couples identify and enhance their exchange of low-cost, low-conflict, highly pleasing, and relationship-affirmative behaviors on a daily basis. This intervention elicited several positive interactional behaviors, some of which were incompatible with their typical negative exchanges. Also, the results of this ongoing 2- to 4-week homework assignment were diagnostic of both the appropriate focus and pace of future therapeutic interventions. Interestingly, repeated descriptions of their demand-withdraw (or pursuer-distancer) and the conflict avoidant patterns of interaction seemed accurate to Vera and Martin. They mutually agreed to try to stop these ineffective patterns until we could teach them an alternate process. This 2- to 3-week moratorium, combined with the active caring behaviors assignment, made a significant difference in their attitudes about one another and their willingness to engage in the *communication* and *conflict resolution* phases of therapy.

Communication Training

Early in treatment, we decided to focus on Martin's retirement adjustment issues. The topic was used as content material for their basic skills communication training. We learned that Vera had a genuine concern about Martin's well-being, but that the way she tried to "push" Martin had a paradoxical effect on his behavior. The more she "encouraged" him to get out of the house, the more he resisted doing anything. Because the demand-withdraw dynamic of this classic communication style became the focus of their discord (see Christensen, Jacobson, & Babcock, 1995), the retirement adjustment issue was not addressed successfully. The communication training phase of treatment (cf. Birchler, 1983; Gottman, Notarius, Gonso, & Markman, 1976; Jacobson & Margolin, 1979) allowed each partner to learn about the pervasive good intentions that they each had and to develop a more collaborative (versus adversarial) approach to their problems.

Homework Assignments

Accordingly, over several weeks, the following homework assignments eventually were quite successful, although follow-through on Martin's part required considerable support from Vera and the therapists. Accomplishments included (1) joining a weekly self-help socialization group at the clinic (designed to help clients meet others in similar circumstances and to discuss their problems informally, without professional leadership); (2) hiring, supervising, and physically helping (only when he felt like it) a neighborhood boy to do some previously resisted yardwork and household maintenance projects; and (3) volunteering 2 hours 2 days per week at a local high school in the wood and metal shops. As one might expect, there was some initial resistance from Martin and we did some in-session work coaching Vera to remain in a supportive (versus nagging) role. However, once Martin got involved, he came to enjoy these activities, and we believe they helped him to improve his self-esteem and depressive symptoms and to reduce his general irritability and dependence on Vera.

Relationship Problems and Conflict Resolution

Research on the general population of married couples, and more recently among distressed marriages (e.g., Birchler & Schafer, 1990; Birchler & Fals-Stewart, 1994; Gilford & Bengston, 1979; Keith, 1987; Keith & Schafer, 1986; Levenson et al., 1993), has shown that, compared to younger couples, older couples (1) engage in less intense and less frequent overt marital discord, (2) are more likely to be depressed because of self-esteem and health-related issues than because of conflicts within the marriage or stressors from outside the home, and (3) are likely to be more cohesive as a couple, less dissatisfied with the relationship itself, and experience less conflict around gender equity issues.

Accordingly, as reflected in the case of Martin and Vera, the clinical problems encountered in older marriages often reflect life cycle "adjustment" issues (Birchler, 1992; Stone, 1987; Suitor & Pillemer, 1987): Adjusting to retirement and the postparental stage, adapting to gender role changes, coping with physical and mental declines and disorders, dealing with financial security and life-style changes, and eventually, confronting death and dying of self and spouse.

Martin and Vera are typical in the sense that they need assistance with both recognizing and resolving marital life cycle transitions. In this context, their demand-withdraw and conflict-avoidant styles of interacting needed to be modified toward a mutually focused and assertive approach to problem-solving. Accordingly, following a few weeks of basic communication training and the enhancement of caring activities as a solid foundation, the couple was trained to employ the universal problem-solving model (Gottman et al., 1976; Jacobson & Margolin, 1979; Notarius & Markman, 1993). Assertiveness training is incorporated into this five-step model as each partner learns to express his or her rights and responsibilities to improve the relationship. The five steps are agenda building, mutual definition of the problem, brainstorming solutions to the problem, implementing the solution, and evaluating the ongoing process and outcome of the solution.

Martin and Vera became adept at the use of this problem-solving approach. Issues addressed in session and at home during the latter part of treatment included (1) techniques to support rather than inhibit each partner's development and enjoyment of independent social and avocational activities, (2) advance planning to help Martin participate in or courteously avoid certain social encounters with neighbors, Vera's friends, or family, (3) specific ways for Vera to check with Martin when he appeared to be depressed, irritable, or in pain, so that she could discriminate the need to give him support or allow him to work out his own problems independently, (4) strategies for them to disengage from disagreements that had been escalating into arguments and/or a "cold war" and to return to a discussion of the issue when things had cooled down, and finally, (5) techniques to negotiate assertively, in a "win-win" fashion (i.e., so both partners gain from solutions to a given problem), and (6) when and how to increase the number and types of companionship activities.

Treatment Outcome

The main course of therapy was terminated after 5 evaluation sessions and 10 treatment sessions. Posttherapy assessment information, gathered from interviews and self-report measures, showed significant improvement in all of their presenting problems. Also, certain patterns of interaction, which had been contributing to both partners' depression and their experience of marital discord, were modified substantially.

It should be noted that although quite successful, the course of treatment was not without some typical difficulties. For example, Martin did not easily relinquish the secondary gains he had enjoyed because of his depression and chronic pain (i.e., attention from Vera and physicians, excuses for not interacting with Vera, friends, and family, justification for getting out of household chores). Vera also found it difficult to give up her role as caretaker and (unwelcomed) advocate of how Martin should be conducting his life. The therapists worked diligently, session-by-session, to shape and reinforce the development of personal and couple boundaries and responsibilities. Fortunately, an alternate communication pattern was learned in lieu of their previously relied upon demand-withdraw and conflict-avoidant styles of conflict resolution. Of course, for this long-married couple, there was not a complete elimination of all these problems and patterns. However, it was clear that significant gains had been made as a direct function of their participation in marital therapy.

FOLLOW-UP

Fifteen total sessions of marital therapy would be considered "brief" by most standards. However, without follow-up, it is known that the effects of such brief treatment are susceptible to decline and, sometimes, complete relapse, as couples return to their dysfunctional patterns of relating (Jacobson & Addis, 1993). In an attempt to maintain Martin and Vera's treatment gains, during the last several sessions the therapists progressively gave the responsibility of homework planning to the couple. In addition, after their last regular session, we asked Martin and Vera to return for a follow-up visit in 1 month. Like most couples, they were quite willing to schedule this meeting. They sensed the need to maintain contact with the therapist as they moved away from the security of weekly meetings.

At the 1-month "booster" session, Martin and Vera were maintaining most treatment gains. Martin was continuing his socialization group at the clinic and his volunteer work at the high school. However, he had stopped the yard work project because many tasks had been accomplished and winter was approaching. Overall, the couple had continued to participate in joint social and travel activities, but Vera was still meeting resistance from Martin in planning trips for more than a day or two. Relative improvements had been maintained in the frequency of arguments, in Martin's symptoms of irritability and depression, and in his pain complaints. Vera had gone on many short outings with friends and family, and if she "prepared" Martin by discussing her plans in advance, these separations seemed to go very well.

As part of the agenda for the 1-month follow-up session, we helped the couple to anticipate and recognize any signs of relapse, so that they could take preventive steps on their own. Also, we offered to see the couple 2 months hence for another booster session. Martin and Vera declined this offer, but they appreciated our alternate suggestion to contact them by telephone. We believe that a plan for continued contact helps older couples, in particular, to feel appreciated and in turn to focus on the goal of maintaining treatment gains.

We reached Vera on the telephone about 2 months later. Interestingly, when we call people for follow-up, the reception that we receive on the phone is very telling of the status of the relationship. If people seem hesitant to talk, apologetic about what they have been doing, or launch into a criticism of their partners, we know significant slippage has occurred. On the other hand, with Vera, compared to her subjective dissatisfaction at intake, we encountered a more optimistic and satisfied person. We learned that occasionally they still found themselves vulnerable to the dynamics inherent in their former patterns of interaction. Nevertheless, even these transactions were described by Vera in collaborative terms and in a humorous, more accepting perspective.

OVERALL EVALUATION

The couple was seen 16 times over the course of 5½ months. Overall, we believe that substantial gains were made by Martin in adjusting to retirement, to the impact of age-related gender role reversals, and to limitations associated with his depression and physical limitations. Vera, for the most part, learned that her ability to demand or push Martin into becoming the postparental mate whom she had envisioned, was limited. Indeed, the more she demanded, the more he withdrew. However, by better understanding and anticipating his needs, his aches and pains, and his moods and by first eliciting and reinforcing his "good intentions," she was far more able to shape Martin into the companion both wanted him to be.

The secondary gains that Martin had enjoyed over several years were not given up easily. However, we believe that through communication and problem-solving training, these relatively committed and caring partners learned how to express and to listen to one another in a more honest, open, focused, and effective manner. In addition, the structured homework assignments, mostly emphasizing Martin's adjustment to retirement and health problems, combined with Vera's strategy to approach Martin in a collaborative versus adversarial manner, contributed to a positive treatment outcome. As Martin experienced more pleasure than pain in his personal life and in his relationship, his attitude, mood, and sense of self-worth improved. In deliberative consultation with Martin's psychiatrist, one of our treatment recommendations following the 3-month follow-up phone contact was that Martin be given a trial period off the antidepressant medication. We believed that he could maintain the recent adjustments made in his life. If so, he would be better off attributing these gains to self-efficacy, rather than to the continuing effects of the drug.

SUMMARY

As the population in the United States grows older, as more and more couples reach their multidecade anniversaries, and as many of these people must cope with chronic and debilitating physical, mental, social support, and financial concerns, there will be an increasing need for psychotherapeutic support services to meet this need. We have described a typical case of an older couple seeking treatment for marital discord. Although most of the standard assessment procedures and treatment interventions for younger couples are appropriate for older couples, some accommodation usually needs to be made to facilitate their comfort and engagement in the treatment process. Compared to younger couples, marital discord among older couples is more likely due to age-related, life-cycle transitions or to problems concerning health, financial security, or the extended family. This case illustrates how positive outcomes can be achieved when treating older couples.

REFERENCES

Barusch, A. S. (1988). Problems and coping strategies for elderly spouse caregivers. The Gerontologist, 28, 677–685.
Beck, A. T., Ward, C. H., Mendelsohn, M., Mock, J., & Erbaugh, J. (1961). An inventory for measuring depression. Archives of General Psychiatry, 4, 561–571.
Birchler, G. R. (1983). Marital dysfunction. In M. Hersen (Ed.), Outpatient behavioral therapy: A clinical guide (pp. 229–269). New York: Grune & Stratton.
Birchler, G. R. (1992). Marriage. In V. B. Van Hasselt & M. Hersen (Eds.), Handbook of social development: A lifespan perspective (pp. 397–419). New York: Plenum Press.
Birchler, G. R., & Fals-Stewart, W. (1994). Marital dysfunction. In V. S. Ramachandran (Ed.), Encyclopedia of human behavior (Vol. 3, pp. 103–113). Orlando, FL: Academic Press.
Birchler, G. R., & Fals-Stewart, W. (1994). The response to conflict scale: Psychometric properties. Assessment, 1, 335–344.
Birchler, G. R., & Schafer, J. (August, 1990). Assessment of older couples entering marital therapy. Paper presented at the American Psychological Association Convention, Boston.
Birchler, G. R., & Schwartz, L. (1994). Marital dyads. In M. Hersen & S. M. Turner (Eds.), Diagnostic interviewing (2nd ed., pp. 277–304). New York: Plenum Press.
Butler, R. N. (1969). Age-ism: Another form of bigotry. The Gerontologist, 9, 243.
Butler, R. N. (1974). Successful aging and the role of the life review. Journal of the American Geriatric Society, 22, 529–535.

Christensen, A., Jacobson, N. S., & Babcock, J. C. (1995). Integrative behavioral couple therapy. In N. S. Jacobson & A. S. Gurman (Eds.), *Clinical handbook of marital therapy* (2nd ed., pp. 31–64). New York: Guilford Press.

Gafner, G. (1987). Engaging the elderly couple in marital therapy. *American Journal of Family Therapy, 15*, 305–315.

Gatz, M. (August, 1988). *Clinical psychology and aging*. Paper delivered at the annual convention of the American Psychological Association, Atlanta, GA.

Gatz, M., Popin, S. J., Pino, C. O., & VandenBos, G. R. (1985). Psychological interventions with older adults. In J. E. Birren & K. W. Schaie (Eds.), *Handbook of psychology and aging* (3rd ed., pp. 404–425). San Diego, CA: Academic Press.

Gilford, R., & Bengston, V. (1979). Measuring marital satisfaction in three generations: Positive and negative dimensions. *Journal of Marriage and the Family, 37*, 387–398.

Gottman, J. M. (1979). *Marital interaction: Experimental investigations*. New York: Academic Press.

Gottman, J. M., Notarius, C., Gonso, J., & Markman, H. (1976). *A couple's guide to communication*. Champaign, IL: Research Press.

Gubrium, J. E. (1974). Marital desolation and the evaluation of everyday life in old age. *Journal of Marriage and the Family, 32*, 107–113.

Hathaway, S. R., & McKinley, J. C. (1943). *The Minnesota Multiphasic Personality Inventory* (rev. ed.). Minneapolis: University of Minnesota Press.

Jacobson, N. S., & Addis, M. E. (1993). Research on couples and couples therapy: What do we know? Where are we going? *Journal of Consulting and Clinical Psychology, 61*, 85–93.

Jacobson, N. S., & Margolin, G. (1979). *Marital therapy: Strategies based on social learning and behavior-exchange principles*. New York: Brunner/Mazel.

Keith, P. M. (1987). Depressive symptoms among younger and older couples. *The Gerontologist, 27*, 605–610.

Keith, P. M., & Schafer, R. B. (1986). Housework, disagreement, and depression among younger and older couples. *American Behavioral Scientist, 29*, 405–422.

Levenson, R. W., Carstensen, L. L., & Gottman, J. M. (1993). Long-term marriage: Age, gender, and satisfaction. *Psychology and Aging, 8*, 301–313.

Neidhardt, E. R., & Allen, J. A. (1993). *Family therapy with the elderly*. Newbury Park, CA: Sage.

Notarius, C. I., & Markman, H. (1993). *We can work it out: Making sense of marital conflict*. New York: Putnam's Sons.

Patrick, L. F., & Moore, J. S. (1986). Life event types and attributional styles as predictors of depression in elderly women. *Journal of the Geriatric Psychiatry, 19*, 241–262.

Peterson, J. A. (1980). Marital and family therapy involving the aged. In G. Landreth & R. Berg (Eds.), *Counseling the elderly* (pp. 440–444). Springfield, IL: Charles C Thomas.

Pinkston, E. M., & Linsk, N. L. (1984). Behavioral family interventions with impaired elderly. *The Gerontologist, 24*, 576–583.

Smyer, M. A., Zaut, S. H., & Qualls, S. H. (1990). Psychological intervention with the aging individual. In J. E. Birren & K. W. Schaie (Eds.), *Handbook of the psychology of aging* (3rd ed., pp. 375–403). San Diego, CA: Academic Press.

Spanier, G. R. (1976). Measuring dyadic adjustment: New measures for assessing the quality of marriage and similar dyads. *Journal of Marriage and the Family, 38*, 15–28.

Stone, J. D. (1987). Marital and sexual counseling of elderly couples. In G. R. Weeks & L. Hoff (Eds.), *Integrating sex and marital therapy: A clinical guide*. New York: Brunner/Mazel.

Stuart, R. B. (1980). *Helping couples change*. New York: Guilford Press.

Suitor, J. J., & Pillemer, K. (1987). The presence of adult children: A source of stress for elderly couples' marriages? *Journal of Marriage and the Family, 49*, 712–717.

Weiss, R. L., & Birchler, G. R. (1975). *Areas of change questionnaire*. Unpublished manuscript, University of Oregon, Eugene.

Weiss, R. L., & Cerreto, M. (1980). The marital status inventory: Development of a measure of dissolution potential. *American Journal of Family Therapy, 8*, 80–86.

Wolinsky, M. A. (1986). Marital therapy with older couples. *Social Casework, 67*, 475–483.

Wolinsky, M. A. (1990). *A heart of wisdom: Marital counseling with older and elderly couples*. New York: Brunner/Mazel.

About the Editors

MICHEL HERSEN received his Ph.D. from the State University of New York at Buffalo in 1966, and has published over 300 articles and chapters and 100 books in a variety of areas in clinical psychology, including most recently *Advanced Abnormal Psychology* (1994) with Vincent B. Van Hasselt and *Introduction to Clinical Psychology* (1995) with Lynda A. Heiden. Dr. Hersen previously was Professor of Psychiatry and Psychology at the University of Pittsburgh, where he was Director of Post-Doctoral Training in Clinical Research at the Western Psychiatric Institute and Clinic. He also was the 14th President of the Association for Advancement of Behavior Therapy. Dr. Hersen is co-editor-in-chief of the following journals: *Journal of Clinical Geropsychology, Behavior Modification, Clinical Psychology Review, Journal of Anxiety Disorders, Journal of Family Violence, Aggression and Violent Behavior: A Review Journal,* and *Journal of Developmental and Physical Disabilities.* He is also associate editor of *Addictive Behaviors* and is editor of *Progress in Behavior Modification.* Dr. Hersen is a Diplomate of the American Board of Professional Psychology, Diplomate of the American Board of Medical Psychotherapists, and Distinguished Practitioner in Psychology, National Academies of Practice. He has been the recipient of federal grants totaling several million dollars from the National Institute of Mental Health, the U.S. Department of Education, and the National Institute on Disabilities and Rehabilitation Research. His current research interests involve the behavioral assessment and treatment of older adults.

VINCENT B. VAN HASSELT, Ph.D., is Professor of Psychology and Director of the Interpersonal Violence Program at Nova Southeastern University in Fort Lauderdale, Florida. Dr. Van Hasselt received his M.S. and Ph.D. from the University of Pittsburgh and completed an internship in Clinical Psychology at the Western Psychiatric Institute and Clinic of the University of Pittsburgh School of Medicine. He is coeditor of the *Journal of Child and Adolescent Substance Abuse, Handbook of Family Violence, Behavior Therapy for Children and Adolescents: A Clinical Approach,* and the soon-to-be-published *Handbook of Psychological Approaches with Violent Offenders: Contemporary Strategies and Issues* (Plenum Press). He has published over 150 journal articles, books, and book chapters, including several on the assessment and treatment of family violence and adolescent substance abuse. Dr. Van Hasselt also is a certified police officer working with the City of Plantation Police Department in Plantation, Florida. Further, he is a Lecturer at the Broward County Police Academy on the topics of domestic violence, suicide prevention, and mental illness, and recently gave a presentation on the "Psychology of Stress" at the FBI Academy in Quantico, Virginia. In addition, he has served as a consultant to several police departments on the utilization of psychological procedures to facilitate homicide investigations. Over the past year, Dr. Van Hasselt has collaborated with the Town of Davie Police Department on two new innovative programs. First, the Adolescent Drug Abuse Prevention and Treatment (ADAPT) program will provide intervention services for substance-abusing children and youth apprehended by the Davie Police for first offenses. Second, his "Strategies for Training of Police in Domestic Violence" (Project STOP) will provide a broad-spectrum, behaviorally oriented training program designed to assist law enforcement personnel in dealing with domestic violence disturbances. Funding for this project from the U.S. Department of Justice is anticipated this October.

Author Index

Subject Index